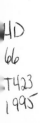

A Publication Sponsored by
the Society for Industrial and Organizational Psychology, Inc.,
A Division of the American Psychological Association

Other books sponsored by the Society include:

Career Development in Organizations
Douglas T. Hall and Associates

Productivity in Organizations
John P. Campbell, Richard J.Campbell, and Associates

Training and Development in Organizations
Irwin L. Goldstein and Associates

Organizational Climate and Culture
Benjamin Schneider, Editor

Work, Families, and Organizations
Sheldon Zedeck, Editor

Personnel Selection in Organizations
Neal Schmitt, Walter C. Borman, and Associates

TEAM EFFECTIVENESS AND DECISION MAKING IN ORGANIZATIONS

TEAM EFFECTIVENESS AND DECISION MAKING IN ORGANIZATIONS

Richard A. Guzzo
Eduardo Salas
and Associates

Foreword by Irwin L. Goldstein

 Jossey-Bass Publishers
San Francisco

Substantial discounts on bulk quantities of Jossey-Bass books are available to corporations, professional associations, and other organizations. For details and discount information, contact the special sales department at Jossey-Bass Inc., Publishers. (415) 433-1740; Fax (415) 433-0499.

For sales outside the United States, please contact your local Paramount Publishing International office.

TCF Manufactured in the United States of America on Lyons Falls Pathfinder Tradebook. This paper is acid-free and 100 percent totally chlorine-free.

Library of Congress Cataloging-in-Publication Data

Team effectiveness and decision making in organizations / Richard A. Guzzo, Eduardo Salas and Associates ; foreword by Irwin L. Goldstein.
— 1st ed.
    p.   cm. — (The Jossey-Bass management series) (The Jossey-Bass social and behavioral science series)
    Includes bibliographical references and index.
    ISBN 1-55542-641-7
    1. Work groups.   2. Decision-making, Group.   I. Guzzo, Richard A.
II. Salas, Eduardo.   III. Series.   IV. Series: The Jossey-Bass social and behavioral science series.
HD66.T423   1995
658.4'02—dc20   94-41296
                                                                      CIP

FIRST EDITION
HB Printing   10 9 8 7 6 5 4 3 2 1   *Code 9503*

A joint publication in
The Jossey-Bass Management Series
and
The Jossey-Bass
Social and Behavioral Science Series

Frontiers of Industrial and Organizational Psychology

SERIES EDITOR

Irwin L. Goldstein
University of Maryland, College Park

EDITORIAL BOARD

Walter C. Borman
University of South Florida

Ann Howard
Leadership Research Institute

Allen Kraut
Baruch University

Daniel Ilgen
Michigan State University

Benjamin Schneider
University of Maryland, College Park

Sheldon Zedeck
University of California, Berkeley

CONTENTS

FOREWORD

One of the principal objectives of the Society for Industrial and Organizational Psychology is, according to its bylaws, to "advance the scientific status of the field." In 1982, Richard J. Campbell, then president of the society, asked Raymond A. Katzell to assume the chair of the Committee on Scientific Affairs, with the express charge of intensifying the society's pursuit of that objective.

One result of those efforts was a plan to publish a series of volumes, each dealing with a single topic considered to be of major contemporary significance in industrial and organizational psychology. Each volume would present cutting-edge theory, research, and practice in chapters contributed by individuals doing pioneering work on that topic.

The society wisely chose Katzell to serve as the first series editor. Under his guidance, the editorial board specified a number of objectives. First, the volumes were to be aimed at members of the Society for Industrial and Organizational Psychology, in the hope and expectation that scholars, professionals, and advanced students would all find them of value. Second, each volume was to be prepared by an editor who was also a leading contributor to the topic the volume covered, and who would take responsibility for the development of the volume. Third, the choice of topics and editors was to be made by the editorial board in consultation with the volume editor of each book. The chairperson of the editorial board would serve as series editor and would also coordinate the relationships and responsibilities of the volume editors, the editorial board, the series publisher, and the executive committee of the society. Fourth, the volumes would be issued whenever they were timely, rather than on a fixed schedule, but at a projected rate of approximately one per year.

With Katzell's leadership, three significant volumes were developed and published: the first in the series: *Career Development in Organizations,* edited by Douglas T. Hall (1986); *Productivity in Organizations,* edited by John P. Campbell and Richard J. Campbell (1988); and *Training and Development in Organizations,* edited by Irwin L. Goldstein (1989). I know that the editors and authors of these three volumes consider their success to be directly related to Katzell's thoughtfulness and energy throughout the six years he served as series editor.

With the completion of the third volume, I was chosen as series editor, and with the continuing help of the editorial board and executive committee of the society, we looked forward to further success for the series. Since I became series editor, four other volumes have been published: *Organizational Climate and Culture,* edited by Benjamin Schneider (1990); *Work, Families, and Organizations,* edited by Sheldon Zedeck (1992); *Personnel Selection in Organizations,* edited by Neal Schmitt and Walter C. Borman (1992); and the present volume, *Team Effectiveness and Decision Making in Organizations,* edited by Richard A. Guzzo and Eduardo Salas. That the first six volumes have continued to achieve our objectives is evidenced by the number of sales, laudatory book reviews, and requests for translation rights. Over twenty thousand copies of these six volumes have been purchased.

Like the topics covered by the earlier volumes in this series, the topic of the present volume was chosen because of its theoretical and empirical significance. We were again fortunate that two leading scholars, Richard A. Guzzo and Eduardo Salas, were willing to serve as coeditors. The society owes them a deep debt of gratitude, as we do also to the authors who contributed their thoughts to this volume. As Rick, Eduardo, and the authors clearly show, there have been significant theoretical and empirical developments in our ways of approaching many of the issues that have to do with teams in organizations. The very conception of how work is performed in organizations is related to how people work on teams and to how they interact and make decisions. Simply consider the implications of what executives at a Mazda plant in Michigan expect of the work force:

> They want their new employees to be able to work
> in teams, to rotate through various jobs, to under
> stand how their tasks fit into the entire process, to
> spot problems in production, to trouble shoot, artic
> ulate the problems to others, suggest improvements
> and write detailed charts and memos that serve as
> a road map in the assembly of the car [Vobejda,
> 1987, p. A14].

Some of the chapters in the present volume that address these issues also include information on such topics as the dynamics of diversity, the effects of stress and crisis situations, how team competence is defined, and the relationship between individual and team-level decisions. All these issues have a significant impact on how we think about and perform research on teams. Thus this volume explores a dynamically changing area of research, and we hope it will be an important stimulus to greater theoretical and empirical interest.

Readers can expect the publication of additional significant volumes in the series in the future. The eighth volume will explore issues concerning the changing nature of work. Again, we are delighted that a leading scholar, Ann Howard, has agreed to serve as volume editor.

With the present volume, I complete my term as series

editor, an undertaking that has required the cooperation and effort of many dedicated people. I want especially to thank the volume editors, the authors, and the members of the editorial board. They have all contributed their wisdom and efforts to make this series a success. Much is also owed to the many members of the Society for Industrial and Organizational Psychology who have contributed to the volumes and supported the series by purchasing copies. I also want to thank William Hicks, Cedric Crocker, and their colleagues at Jossey-Bass, who worked with us to make the goals of this series a reality. Finally, I want to express my appreciation to Ray Katzell for the high standard he set as the first series editor, a standard that I hope my editorship has met.

In closing, I am delighted to announce that the next series editor, beginning with the eighth volume, will be Sheldon Zedeck. I know that the objectives of the series are in good hands with Shelly. I also know that he will look forward to the continued cooperation of editors, authors, and readers, which has made this opportunity so enjoyable for me.

January 1995   Irwin L. Goldstein
                                         University of Maryland
                                              Series Editor

Reference

Vobejda, B. (1987, April 14). The new cutting edge in factories. *Washington Post*, p. A14.

PREFACE

The possibility of creating a book on groups for this series existed for some time before the event got under way. There was an idea, left undeveloped, until the force of a confluence of different currents of interest was felt. These included an interest in having the Committee on Scientific Affairs of the Society of Industrial and Organizational Psychology sponsor a conference to promote the advancement of scientific research on groups and teams. A few key actors also became involved in the conduct and sponsorship of exciting new programs of research. The Naval Air Warfare Center Training Systems Division (formerly the Naval Training Systems Center), in Orlando, became especially active, partly in response to what were seen as recent critical failures of teams. The business eye, too, turned toward the power and usefulness of groups in organizations. Team-based management practices were seen as the way to restore America's productivity while creating a work environment that would better fit the nature of the new worker. Top stories in several editions of such magazines as *Fortune* and *Business Week* in recent years have attested to this interest in teams. This array of forces, some within industrial and organizational psychology and some outside, catalyzed the work that went into this book.

Interest in groups and teams has never been absent from industrial and organizational psychology. The power of groups was discovered in the Hawthorne studies, which began nearly two-thirds of a century ago. Since then, the importance of research and practice with teams in organizations has manifested itself in many ways. Groups were at the center of attention in the 1950s as researchers tried to figure out the sources of employees' attitudes toward and reactions to work and management practices. Work groups were at the heart of the sociotechnical approach to understanding and designing organizations. The *socio* in *sociotechnical* very much meant *group* as the theoretical framework emerged over the decades since the late 1940s. When organizational development emerged in the 1960s as a social technology for improving organizational effectiveness, groups were again a focus of attention, this time as agents of organizational change (or as impediments to it). From time to time, interest in teams at work did wane, as in the 1970s, although we find in the literature of that era the roots of organizational redesign, which stresses the importance of the work group to the business enterprise. By the early 1980s, interest in teams had spread like wildfire. In fact, it was during this time that organizational practice overtook research. Organizational psychologists and their intellectual kin were caught napping as organizations rushed to implement quality circles, project teams, autonomous work groups, and other forms of team-based work arrangements.

Now we are in the 1990s, and research is catching up. The amount of research on groups and teams that has appeared in recent years is both amazing and wonderful. As this volume confirms, this recently renewed vigor in research is being directed toward a fresh look at old issues, as well as toward completely new topics and methods of inquiry. Much of this zest comes from the interdisciplinary nature of current group research. We hope that this book captures that renewed vitality.

In keeping with the mission of this series, the present volume contains data, theory, and methods that are at the forefront of the field. Not all the current group research is documented here, of course. The emphasis here is on groups and teams in organizations, and so we have had to exclude a considerable amount of the valuable research on groups that goes on in social psychology and certain other disciplines. Moreover, the research frontier is always changing. For example, very little of this book will be relevant to teams at the top of an organization, such as CEO-led teams, but, as the team concept pushes its way up the organizational hierarchy, the interest of researchers will follow. How do we select executives for their potential to contribute to teams at the top of an organization? How can we design executive compensation systems that foster effective teamwork at the top? These are topics that will attract significant research interest in the not-so-distant future. Cultural influences in and on teams will also become an increasingly popular topic as organizations continue to become more global. Whatever the future frontier of organizationally relevant group research may be, it will have perceptible connections to the thinking and research presented in this volume. We believe that research on groups has both a long history and a promising future, and we hope that this book productively connects that past and future.

Audience

The primary audience for this book includes researchers engaged in the study of groups and teams, teachers, and graduate students engaged in the advanced study of teams and organizations. Members of this audience may make their homes in any of several disciplines (industrial and organizational psychology, of course, but also organizational behavior, social psychology, and management) and settings (psychology departments, business schools, the military, business organizations, and research institutes). This volume does emphasize research and theory, but it is also relevant to practitioners with an interest in improving the performance of groups and teams at work. Research, theory, and practice are never detached from one another in industrial and organizational psychology.

Acknowledgments

Many people deserve thanks for their direct and indirect contributions to the creation of this book. The single event that most catalyzed that process was a small conference, held at the University of Maryland, on groups and teams in organizations. Many of the chapters in this book owe their origins to the work of that conference, especially to the way of thinking that emerged from small discussion groups. We are thankful for the support of the University of Maryland and of the Society for Industrial and Organizational Psychology, in particular its Committee on Scientific Affairs, which made the conference possible. The editorial board of this series also deserves our gratitude. The faith and patience of its members, especially Irv Goldstein, are deeply appreciated. It has been said that managing the contributors to an edited volume such as this one is like herding cats. But that has not been true in this case, and we are indebted to our contributors for their goodwill and hard work. The Jossey-Bass staff, especially Cedric Crocker, showed great flexibility and thorough commitment to this project over a considerable length of time, a feat that deserves considerable praise. We thank all those who have contributed to the production of this volume, most of whom are dispersed throughout a multitude of institutions and locales, and who may never receive the full personal expression of our thanks that they deserve.

January 1995   RICHARD A. GUZZO
                                            College Park, Maryland

                                            EDUARDO SALAS
                                            Orlando, Florida

THE AUTHORS

Clint A. Bowers is assistant professor of psychology at the University of Central Florida. He received his Ph.D. degree (1987) in clinical and community psychology from the University of South Florida. His research interests include team performance, communication analysis, and the reduction of stress effects on performance.

Janis A. Cannon-Bowers is senior research psychologist in the Human Systems Integration Division of the Naval Air Warfare Center. She received her Ph.D. degree (1988) in industrial and organizational psychology from the University of South Florida. Her research interests include team training and performance, crew coordination training, training effectiveness, and tactical decision making. At present, she is principal investigator for the Tactical Decision Making Under Stress (TADMUS) project, conducting research concerned with improving individual and team decision making in the tactical environment of the Navy.

Michael D. Coovert is associate professor of psychology at the University of South Florida, where he is also founding director of the Institute for Human Performance, Decision Making, and Cybernetics. He received his Ph.D. degree (1985) in industrial and organizational psychology from Ohio State University. His research interests include quantitative methods, statistical models of human performance, the impact of technologies on organizations, and human–computer interaction.

J. Philip Craiger is assistant professor of psychology at the University of Nebraska, Omaha. He received his Ph.D. degree (1992) in industrial and organizational psychology from the University of South Florida. His research interests include information technology and decision-support systems, quantitative methods, computer simulation and modeling, and the use of artificial intelligence in the study of human behavior.

Richard A. Guzzo is professor of psychology and management at the University of Maryland. He received his Ph.D. degree (1979) in administrative sciences from Yale University and has served on the faculties of McGill University and New York University. His research concerns the productivity and effectiveness of individuals and teams at work.

John R. Hollenbeck is professor of management at the Eli Broad Graduate School of Business Administration, Michigan State University. He received his Ph.D. degree (1984) in management and organizational behavior from New York University. He has served on the editorial boards of the *Journal of Applied Psychology,* the *Academy of Management Journal, Organizational Behavior and Human Decision Processes, Personnel Psychology,* and the *Journal of Management.* He was also the first recipient, in 1992, of the Ernest J. McCormick Award for early contributions to the field of industrial and organizational psychology. His research focuses on self-regulation theories of work motivation, employee separation and acquisition processes, and team decision making and performance.

Andrea B. Hollingshead is assistant professor of speech communication and psychology at the University of Illinois, Urbana–Champaign. She received her Ph.D. degree (1993) in social psychology from the University of Illinois, Urbana–Champaign. Her current research investigates the cognitive and social processes that lead to effective decision making in groups.

Daniel R. Ilgen is the John A. Hannah distinguished professor in the Departments of Psychology and Management at Michigan State University. He received his Ph.D. degree (1969) in industrial and organizational psychology from the University of Illinois. His current research examines decision making in hierarchical teams composed of persons with differing expertise and often functioning under workload stress. He is presently associate editor of *Organizational Behavior and Human Decision Processes* and a member of four editorial boards.

Susan E. Jackson is professor of psychology at New York University. She was previously on the psychology faculty at the University of Maryland and the management faculty at the University of Michigan. She received her Ph.D. degree (1982) in industrial and organizational psychology from the University of California, Berkeley. She currently serves as editor of the *Academy of Management Review*. Her work on diversity emphasizes the importance of linking this issue to the business imperatives of organizations, a perspective reflected in her book, *Diversity in the Workplace: Human Resources Initiatives* (1992), published as a volume in the Society for Industrial and Organizational Psychology's Professional Practice Series.

Robert G. Jones is assistant professor of psychology at Southwest Missouri State University. He received his Ph.D. degree (1992) in industrial and organizational psychology from Ohio State University. His research, teaching, and practice center on issues of performance measurement and management, both in teams and in individuals, with particular concern for the validity of workplace judgments, acceptance of feedback, and uses of assessment for team and individual development.

Richard Klimoski is professor of psychology and vice chair of the Department of Psychology at Ohio State University. He received his Ph.D. degree (1970) in psychology and management from Purdue University. His teaching and research interests involve team performance and organizational control systems in the form of performance appraisal and performance feedback programs. He is coauthor (with N. Schmitt) of *Research Methods in Human Resource Management* (1991) and past editor of the *Academy of Management Review*. In 1990, he was elected president of the Society for Industrial and Organizational Psychology.

Joseph E. McGrath is professor of psychology at the University of Illinois, Urbana–Champaign. He received his Ph.D. degree (1955) in social psychology from the University of Michigan. His research interests include small-group processes and performance, temporal and gender issues in social psychology, and research methodology.

Robert M. McIntyre is associate professor of psychology at Old Dominion University, where he is presently serving as the graduate program director of the doctoral program in industrial and organizational pyschology. He received his Ph.D. degree (1978) in psychology from the Pennsylvania State University. He has served as behavioral sciences analyst at Bell Canada in Montreal and as faculty member at Colorado State University and Clarkson University. His research and consulting interests are in the areas of performance assessment, teamwork assessment and development, the measurement of strategic leadership skill, and quantitative methods in test validation.

Debra A. Major is assistant professor of psychology at Old Dominion University. She received her Ph.D. degree (1992) in industrial and organizational psychology from Michigan State University. Her research interests include team leadership and decision making, organizational socialization, and career development.

Karen E. May is a Ph.D. candidate in psychology at the University of California, Berkeley. She is also a senior consultant at

Human Resource Solutions. Her primary research interests are selection, test fairness, work teams, and work-force diversity.

Ben B. Morgan, Jr., is professor of psychology and associate dean of the School of Arts and Sciences at the University of Central Florida. He received his Ph.D. degree (1968) in experimental psychology from the University of Louisville. His research interests focus on issues related to the assessment of human performance, including team performance, crew coordination, and team training. He is a fellow in the American Psychological Association, the American Psychological Society, and the Human Factors Society.

Eduardo Salas is senior research psychologist in the Science and Technology Divison of the Naval Air Warfare Center Training Systems Division. He also has courtesy appointments at the University of South Florida and the University of Central Florida. He received his Ph.D. degree (1984) in industrial and organizational psychology from Old Dominion University. His research interests include team training and performance, training effectiveness, tactical decision making under stress, team decision making, human performance measurement and modeling, and learning strategies for teams. He has coauthored over fifty journal articles and book chapters and has coedited four books.

Douglas J. Sego is a lecturer in management at the School of Business and Management, Hong Kong University of Science and Technology. He received his Ph.D. degree (1994) in organizational behavior from Michigan State University. His primary research interests are training systems, training evaluation, decision making, and utility.

Scott I. Tannenbaum is associate professor of management at the State University of New York, Albany. He is also a principal of the Executive Consulting Group, Inc., a management consulting firm. He received his Ph.D. degree (1986) in industrial and organizational psychology from Old Dominion University. Many of his research and consulting activities have been in the areas of training effectiveness, team performance, organizational change and development, work competencies, human resource information systems, and strategic planning.

Dean Tjosvold is professor of business administration at Simon Fraser University, British Columbia. He received his Ph.D. degree in social psychology (1972) from the University of Minnesota. He has also taught at Pennsylvania State University, was a visiting scholar at the National University of Singapore, and was a visiting professor at the State University of Groningen, The Netherlands. He is widely published in the areas of conflict management, cooperation and competition, decision making, power, and other management issues.

Catherine E. Volpe is senior staff consultant for ESS Corporation. She received her Ph.D. degree (1991) in industrial and organizational psychology from the University of South Florida. She specializes in designing and implementing human resource services, primarily in the areas of training and assessment. Her research interests include team coordination training, individual and group decision making, and the development of training principles to mitigate the effects of stress on decision-making processes.

Kristina Whitney is a Ph.D. candidate in psychology at the University of California, Berkeley. She is also project manager at CORE Corporation. Her research interests include personality and job performance, selection and validation, team effectiveness, and goal setting.

TEAM EFFECTIVENESS AND DECISION MAKING IN ORGANIZATIONS

1

INTRODUCTION: AT THE INTERSECTION OF TEAM EFFECTIVENESS AND DECISION MAKING

Richard A. Guzzo

Historically, the importance of teams to organizations has been recognized with some reluctance but recently has been embraced with enthusiasm. Teams and teaming have become hot topics, almost faddish in recent years, as organizations have come to rely on team-based arrangements to improve quality, productivity, customer service, and the experience of work for their members. Effective decision making has been an ever-present concern in organizations, but as organizations move toward greater decentralization, flatter structures (fewer levels of management), and employee empowerment, the matter of effective decision making has broken free from being a concern solely of the teams at the top of the pyramid and is now important throughout the organization. Teams in organizations make decisions, sometimes because that is their central task and sometimes because they must make decisions on their way to the effective performance of other tasks. This book lives at the intersection of organizational concerns for team effectiveness and decision making.

Team effectiveness and decision making surely seem like two somewhat broad topics to take on in a single book. As research topics, they enjoy rather extensive literatures that only sometimes intersect. As matters of practice, they are addressed in numerous prescriptions that appear in how-to books meant to improve team performance or decision making. This is no how-to book for resolving the complexities of effective team performance and decision making (although chapters throughout the volume do explicitly address practical implications of the facts they report), nor is this book an attempt to align the literatures on team effectiveness and decision making into some singular statement (although chapters throughout the book do draw repeatedly on those two literatures). Instead, this book aims to unify the new knowledge about these two important topics, to advance our knowledge of them, and to frame that knowledge specifically with regard to teams at work in organizations. The surge of research on these topics in recent years provides a backdrop for this book, and the chapters that follow are on the forward edge of that activity.

The Nature of Teams

We make no real distinction between teams and groups in this book. We use these terms interchangeably, perhaps more by necessity than by choice. As a focus of research, groups have long been studied, and teams are newcomers. Much of the research that this book draws on comes under the label of *group dynamics* or *group processes*. That research is quite broad and expansive. We make no attempt to cover it all. Rather, for this book we use what informs us about our specific target of interest: effective task performance by teams working in organizations, teams for whose work decision making is a key component. When we move from the general to the specific, our terminology moves from *groups* to *teams*.

The teams and groups that this book addresses are bounded social units with work to do in larger social systems. The larger social systems of interest are organizations (mainly but not only business and military). A group or a team within an organization is said to be bounded when it has an identifiable membership (that is, members and nonmembers alike clearly know who is a member and who is not) and when it has an identifiable task or set of tasks to perform. Tasks may include monitoring, producing, servicing, negotiating, generating ideas, and other activities. The groups and teams of interest for this book are almost always engaged in rather complex activities that subsume many specific duties or responsibilities. For example, a management team might be engaged in monitoring the business environment, representing an organization to its constituencies, and deciding how to allocate resources. What is critical, however, is that there be task-based interdependence among group members. That is, a group's work must require, to an appreciable degree, that team members interact by way of exchanging information, sharing resources, and coordinating with and reacting to one another in the course of accomplishing the group task. At least a minimal degree of task interdependence is a defining characteristic of the teams of interest. Note, however, that interdependence is best understood as a matter of degree: all work groups in organizations have some interdependence, but some groups have more than others by virtue of technology, position in the organization, choices about how to carry out the work, and other factors.

The teams of interest for this book may sometimes be bounded by space. Some work groups clearly possess their own turf, as is the case for flight crews in an airplane. For other groups, physical separation is not a defining characteristic of existence (for example, a group whose members are in different locations and who communicate with each other electronically). Some groups (such as project teams) may be bounded by time, but temporal boundaries are not critical to all teams addressed by this book. The chapters that follow concern both permanent and transient teams and groups whose members may or may not share physical space.

Thus the teams of interest are bounded social entities with work to accomplish within a larger social system. It is now important to note that these teams can be differentiated in many ways. Some groups may be differentiated by hierarchy (that is, some group members may hold positions in the organization that are superior to other members' positions). In many instances, hierarchical differences among members coincide with who is in charge of the team, but not always. Multifunctional project teams, for example, may bring together members of different rank from quite different parts of the organization (engineering, manufacturing, sales, human resources) but, in carrying out a project, may not necessarily determine leadership responsibilities on the basis of hierarchical difference. Differentiation among members has other bases, too. For example, expertise may be a basis for differentiating among members. Expertise may be accorded by virtue of prior experience and may "come with" members as they enter the team, or it may be a product of who in the group has access to what information at what time during the group's work. Additional bases for differentiation among the members of a group include tenure in the organization, functional background, skills, length of membership in the group, ethnicity, gender, culture, and other factors. As we shall see, an understanding of differentiation by expertise and by personal characteristics is important to our understanding the effectiveness of teams that make decisions as they carry out their work.

The Nature of Decision Making in Teams

Decision making is not the only activity of relevance to team performance, but it is a key activity contributing to team effectiveness and a key activity of interest for this book. Decision making, defined quite broadly, is perhaps best regarded as a bundle of interconnected activities that include gathering, interpreting, and exchanging information; creating and identifying alternative courses of action; choosing among alternatives by integrating the often-differing perspectives and opinions of team members; and implementing a choice and monitoring its consequences. Decision making in teams is quite distinct from individual decision making. In teams, information is often distributed unequally among members and must be integrated, and the integration process may be complicated by uncertainty, by the effects of status differences among members, by the failure of one member to appreciate the significance of the information he or she holds, and so on.

Of particular interest for this book is ongoing, consequential decision making, which often takes place in a context of ambiguity. By *ongoing,* we mean decision activity that is continuous and recurring. Monitoring past decisions is a manifestation of ongoing decision making. *Consequential* decisions are those that are important to the team and to others in the organization in which the team performs. High-stakes decisions are usually associated with teams at the top of an organization, but teams at other levels may also be centers of important decisions. For example, a shipboard team that makes decisions while operating defensive weapons during a naval battle makes highly consequential decisions as it determines whether a potential target is friend or foe and decides on the appropriate action. Ambiguity, of course, is a common feature of decision making. Not all decision making takes place in ambiguity, but much of it does, and ambiguity poses special challenges to the decision-making group. High stakes, ambiguity, compressed amounts of time, heavy work loads, and other factors may become sources of stress that affect the group's ability to perform its task.

Context

A theme that appears repeatedly in this book is the importance of the team's organizational context. Broadly construed, the context in which a team exists is very influential for the team's decision making and performance. Many characteristics of the organizational context may come into play. For example, organizational staffing practices are one aspect of the context. Staffing practices determine the nature of the human resources available to the team. Reward systems are another potentially important aspect of organizational context. Organizational climate, as it concerns such matters as conflict management or risk taking, is also an element of the context surrounding a group's performance. Moreover, other groups are often very important elements of a given group's environment, and the nature of intergroup interactions can be significant for the effectiveness of groups.

Levels of Analysis

Implicit in the foregoing discussion is the idea that team performance and decision making can be — must be — understood from several levels of analysis. One level focuses on the individual. At this level of analysis, emphasis is on the attributes, skills, and psychological and behavioral processes of team members. The individual conflict-management skills of members, their ability to cope with stress, their expertise, their racial or ethnic identities, and other factors are important terms in the equation that explains group performance at this level of analysis.

A second level of analysis focuses on the group as an entity. Here, the contribution of individually held attributes to the group's performance is of less interest. An analysis of group decision making and performance at this level might focus on patterns of intragroup interaction as members exchange information or coordinate their physical efforts as they work.

Yet another level of analysis focuses on the context or environment in which the team performs. Here, such factors as the time pressure inherent in a task may be so examined for their effects on group performance, or the role of organizational systems (staffing, rewarding) may be emphasized. By comparison with the individual and group levels of analysis, this level has received less attention in the literature.

This book is predicated on the assumption that team decision making and performance are too complex to be left to any one level of analysis. This is not to say that some sort of implicit requirement exists for all research and theorizing to be of a multilevel nature (in fact, the chapters in this book tend not to emphasize all the levels of analysis, and we believe that much can be learned from staying within any one level of analysis). Rather, interpretations and theorizing at any one level of analysis should be put forward with the full recognition that

they offer only part of the story and that much remains to be
explained by the operation of factors at other levels of analysis.

Related to levels of analysis is the choice of method one
uses to study teams. The data that appear in this book have
been arrived at by many methods. One very popular data source
has been the experimental study of groups. Other methods include simulation of varying degrees of complexity, naturalistic
observation, interviewing, surveys, and statistical modeling. All
these data sources are represented in the chapters that follow
(and in the literature that they review). As is true for levels of
analysis, there is much of value to be gained through the multiple perspectives afforded by different methods.

Plan of This Book

The chapters of this book present a mix of the general and the
specific, the basic and the applied. Chapter Two presents principles learned from the intensive study of naval tactical teams.
These principles are presented in general terms, and they can
be transferred to many other teams in many other contexts.
Chapter Three addresses the role that a specific technology plays
in a group. The authors review and interpret what is known
about computer-assisted groups — those whose communication
and decision making are supported by electronic means. Chapter
Four addresses two issues — cooperation and conflict — that are
general in the sense that they are part and parcel of the experiences of almost any team in any setting.

Subsequent chapters go into greater depth about a smaller
range of issues. Chapter Five offers an innovative look at team
decision making through the application of a paradigm for research and analysis that originated in the study of individual
decision making. Chapter Six offers an intensive look at new
methods of statistical modeling applied to the study of an old
issue: the intragroup processes that occur as interdependent
members perform group tasks. Chapter Seven also provides a
new look at an old problem: the issue of diversity in teams and
its implications for team effectiveness.

The next two chapters turn to contextual factors. Stress and performance have been investigated largely with regard to individuals. Chapter Eight examines sources of stress and reviews what is known about its relationship to performance in teams. Chapter Nine addresses staffing practices as an influence on team effectiveness. The authors elaborate the connection between organizational staffing practices and team decision making, offering several recommendations for practice.

Chapter Ten also directly addresses an application-oriented issue: the matter of team training. The chapter draws a connection between specification of the competencies required of team members and implementation of training programs to maintain and enhance those competencies. Chapter Eleven concludes the book by briefly reviewing and integrating the preceding chapters and offering a look toward the future.

2

MEASURING AND MANAGING FOR TEAM PERFORMANCE: EMERGING PRINCIPLES FROM COMPLEX ENVIRONMENTS

Robert M. McIntyre, Eduardo Salas

Past and present research on teams is limited in its relevance to field settings. In light of this, we will describe principles learned from research on Naval tactical teams, in the belief that what we have learned about that particular environment bears useful lessons for other organizations employing teams.

Tactical teams within the military exist (1) to help a leader assess a given scenario involving imminent danger or threat, (2) to provide information to the leader in a form that he or she can use in making a decision, and (3) to implement the action implied by the decision that the leader comes to. In this sense, the *tactical team* is a *decision-making team* (see Orasanu & Salas, 1993).

Relevance of This Research

The research base for the present chapter was military teams whose role it is to perform in complex and dynamic environ-

Note: The views expressed herein are those of the authors and do not reflect the opinion of the organization with which they are affiliated. We would like to express our gratitude to Janis A. Cannon-Bowers and Kerry A. Burgess for their comments on earlier drafts.

ments. The primary "product" of the military is defense. If one were to assume that defense is fundamentally and essentially different from the products of other organizations, one might deduce that team research carried out within military organizations has little relevance to other public sector (and all private sector) organizations.

We address this concern in the following way: First, the military depends on teams to carry out its mission, at least as much as any other organization does. The importance of team performance in the military cannot be exaggerated. Therefore, the findings reported here are appropriate for other organizations that depend on team performance to attain their missions and objectives. Second, within the military, teams are used for *tactical* and *strategic* decisions, which ensures that a variety of team functions will be represented. In this sense, the activities carried out by teams resemble those in other, nonmilitary environments. Third, the military is large, complex, and hierarchically arranged, much as most other organizations are (in fact, many other organizations are modeled after the military). In other words, the general context (and perhaps the climate) within which military teams work is similar to that of other organizations. In sum, we argue that, at least with respect to teams, there are substantial similarities between military organizations in which teams operate and other organizations.

Assumptions

In formulating the propositions in this chapter, we began with three assumptions. The first assumption is that team performance, although it is critical to the mission of many organizations, historically has been difficult to define in precise terms. In other words, the ephemeral characteristics of teams and teamwork are at the very heart of problems associated with understanding, managing, and training teams. The second assumption is that there are no definitive answers to questions concerning the nature of teamwork, how it should be managed, and how teamwork skills should be trained (see Salas, Dickinson, Converse, & Tannenbaum, 1992, for a discussion). Some progress has been made (e.g., see Hackman, 1990; Swezey & Salas, 1992), but part of the reason for this state of affairs concerns the unit-of-analysis problem (see the section that follows). The third assumption is that organizations employing teams would derive great benefit from practical guidance (or principles) for managing and training teams, even if this guidance were not based on research using the more widely accepted, "rigorous" paradigms and statistics. That is, the type of work carried out by teams is often so critical to the mission of the employing organization, or even to its survival, that some level of guidance, even preliminary, may be useful for improving team effectiveness.

Operating under these three assumptions, we have combined caution with broad-mindedness in identifying the learning points presented in this chapter. In certain cases, principles were formulated on the basis of behavioral observations. In other cases, the incisive observations of military personnel (primarily team instructors) who participated in the program of research served as a primary basis of our counsel (see Guerette, Miller, Glickman, Morgan, & Salas, 1987). At the practical level, this chapter's lessons are intended to fill a void with respect to how teamwork should be managed, led, measured, and trained. At the scientific level, they should be viewed as testable hypotheses for future research and development in team training and team management.

The Unit-of-Analysis Dilemma

Let us review some rudimentary methodology for the moment. In individual-differences research (the standard fare of psychology), psychologists and other social scientists form hypotheses with regard to some "focal effect" (these usually concern determinants or covariates of individual attributes or characteristics). These researchers also collect data on samples of individuals from specified populations, test their hypotheses, and draw conclusions about the members of the specified populations. The unit of analysis in this type of research is the *individual member* of the population. Statistical procedures are used in this research as tools to help the scientist arrive at a reasonable conclusion with regard to the hypotheses. *Reasonable,* in this context, has come to refer to the scientist's having collected enough data of high enough psychometric quality to rule out competing explanations, especially random chance. A reasonable study, therefore, is one for which the scientist has devised a procedure that will be sensitive to the focal effect while avoiding a high likelihood that random chance is responsible for the effect. This, in a nutshell, summarizes the individual-differences research paradigm. Is this paradigm suitable for carrying out team research?

The answer is a qualified yes. There are important considerations in team research, however. Social scientists whose goal is to study team behavior are attempting to study the behavior of an aggregate of individuals, not necessarily of the individuals themselves. In team research, although teams consist of multiple members, science is interested in making inferences back to the population of *teams,* not to the population of team *members.* In this sense, one can say that the unit of analysis in team research is the *team,* not the individual member.

What does this fact imply with regard to the design of team research? First, the population of many teams, especially intact, permanent teams, is finite and usually relatively small in size. Second, teams found in organizational settings are therefore few in number. Third, large randomly selected samples (the usual requirement of the statistical tools that behavioral science uses) are consequently almost impossible to find.

In the Navy, for example, there may be interest in understanding a team operating within some special class of ship. But suppose that there are as few as twenty-five such ships. The crew on each of ship represents the source of an operational team. Although twenty-five teams may involve as many as 250 individuals or more, the unit of analysis remains the team. Unfortunately, "samples" of twenty-five observations do not accommodate the statistical methods typically used by the social sciences within the individual-differences research paradigm. Ironically, samples consisting of twenty-five operational teams may be considered quite respectable for team research, even though the general social science community has subscribed to the individual-differences paradigm, which often expects powerful statistics on large samples. The result is the common impression that team research is soft, inconclusive, or weak.

One standard response to problems of insufficient sample size is to carry out research in the laboratory on artificial or synthetic tasks that share the essential characteristics of the field setting (see Driskell & Salas, 1992). Accessing sufficient numbers of teams in such settings is not a problem, because no special expertise on the part of research participants is expected, which thereby allows anyone (perhaps after training) to participate as a member of a team.

There are problems with simulations. For example, implementing tasks with high fidelity for teams made up of firefighters, military tactical teams, air crews, or nuclear power plant crews is extremely expensive. Alternatively, the development of less expensive, low-fidelity simulators with high psychological fidelity (that is, simulators in which the essential and underlying knowledge, skills, and abilities are represented) is difficult because of the lack of understanding of the essential knowledge, skills, and abilities required in team tasks.

In short, the unit-of-analysis problem has made serious team research difficult. On the one hand, to follow the now standard individual-differences research paradigm and apply such common tools as linear structural equations analysis is impossible because of the small sample size. On the other hand, laboratory simulations are rejected by organizations and their scientific representatives because of their apparently limited relationship to the real world.

Nature of the Teams Studied

For the purposes of this research, we adopted the following definition of *team* (Morgan, Glickman, Woodard, Blaiwes, & Salas, 1986, p. 3): "a distinguishable set of two or more individuals who interact interdependently and adaptively to achieve specified, shared, and valued objectives." There are two types of teams to be examined in light of this definition: the *tactical decision-making* (TAC-DM) *team,* and the *slower paced, nonemergency decision-making* (SPAN-DM) *team.* (To be more precise, these

two "types" probably represent two ends of a continuum of teams.)
The research on which this chapter was based concerns teams
whose function was to engage in TAC-DM. Much of existing
research in the field, however, concerns SPAN-DM teams. The
TAC-DM team distinguishes itelf from the SPAN-DM counter-
part in different ways. TAC-DM concerns the making of decisions under time pressure and threat. The consequence for error
in tactical decision making is immediate and may be more severe.
By contrast, SPAN-DM often involves long-term consequences
and perhaps economic threat to the organization. Although economic challenge and uncertainty may exist for teams of industrial decision makers, it cannot be considered in the immediate
life-and-death sense appropriate to the tactical environment.

The TAC-DM team, especially the kind treated in this
research, is *intrinsically* a team. It cannot carry out its task without the participation, interaction, and coordination of team
members whose input into the decision is essential to the making of this decision. By contrast, the SPAN-DM team represents
a more loosely knit team. Its function is less team-centered. For
example, individual experts may serve as advisers to a central
decision maker without interacting or coordinating in the ways
that TAC-DM teams must interact and coordinate themselves.
In sum, TAC-DM implies that teamwork is essential to effective performance, whereas teamwork in SPAN-DM might be
thought of as a "nice to have" ingredient. We believe that the
distinction between TAC-DM and SPAN-DM teams provides
one basis for estimating the degree of relevance of the present
chapter. To the extent that one's questions pertain to TAC-DM
teams, this research may have direct relevance. For example,
airline cockpit crews, firefighter teams, surgical teams, nuclear
power plant crews, and special-operations police squads may
benefit directly from the ideas expressed here. To the extent that
one's questions pertain to SPAN-DM teams, this research may
provide indirect relevance and questions for future exploration.

The Team Evolution and Maturation (TEAM) Research Paradigm

The research program from which this chapter emanates is
characterized by several important features. First, it began with

a hypothesized theoretical model that postulated that there are two distinguishable tracks that codevelop over the maturation period of the team. There is the *taskwork* track, which involves the operations-related activities to be performed by the team members. There is also a parallel *teamwork* track, which includes those activities that serve to strengthen the quality of functional interactions, relationships, cooperation, communication, and coordination of team members (see Morgan, Glickman, Woodard, Blaiwes, & Salas, 1986, for details). Second, the TEAM research program took a longitudinal rather than cross-sectional approach to meeting its purposes and goals. This provided the opportunity to monitor teams' *development*—that is, their skill acquisition—over time. Third, the research involved real operational teams in the context of their natural environment. That environment is characterized by rapidly evolving situations, high work loads, time pressure, and the necessity to deal with complex and ambiguous information.

Shortfalls of Prior Research

Past research efforts have concentrated on the taskwork side of the issue, essentially ignoring the critical teamwork side. By contrast, the TEAM research paradigm adopted a holistic perspective on the process of team training and performance. Because its ultimate purpose was to develop methods for improving the training and managing of tactical teams, this research addressed team learning and skills acquisition in toto. This is not to say that the task aspects of team operations were regarded as unimportant. It is to assert that a critical and as yet evaded issue, teamwork itself, became the focal point of investigation.

Descriptions of the Teams Studied

It is useful to understand in a little more detail the operational responsibilities of the teams we observed and measured.

Naval Gunfire-Support (NGFS) Team

The primary responsibility of the NGFS team is to provide gunfire support for ground troops (e.g., Marines) involved in amphibious assaults. For example, if Marines are assigned the task of taking control of a village or city by means of amphibious assault, then the gunfire-support team is responsible for providing firepower as cover while the assault takes place. The NGFS team is also involved in other, related activities (e.g., controlling or disabling certain hostile enemy shore-based positions).

Teams participating in NGFS training are composed of three smaller constituent teams: the three-member bridge team, the eight-member combat information center (CIC) team, and the five-member plot team. The bridge team serves as the interface between NGFS operations and the ship's control operations. The plot team concerns itself with identifying the locations of targets through plotting processes. The CIC team is involved in the actual firing of ordnance. These three constituent teams may or may not be physically separated from one another, depending on the type of combat vessels to which they are assigned.

The CIC team was chosen as the target of observation because it represents the hub of the NGFS team. Experts agreed that a CIC team requires a great (if not the greatest) amount of coordination, communication, and interdependence (Cannon-Bowers, Salas, & Grossman, 1991). In addition, the functions and processes associated with CIC teams in NGFS are characteristic of those belonging to other CIC teams performing different responsibilities. In other words, knowledge of CIC team performance appeared to be generalizable to the performance of other types of teams.

NGFS training involves instruction of intact teams associated with a combat vessel. Members are assigned as permanent members of the NGFS team while serving on the ship. At the time of our investigation, NGFS training consisted of three and a half to four and a half days of simulator exercises. There were five phases of the training, with each phase corresponding to an increasingly difficult exercise. Members of a team sent to training are the same individuals who would be involved at some later time in live-firing exercises on which the ship was to be evaluated. This points to the fact that success in NGFS school has important consequences for the team and the ship.

Data were collected on thirteen military teams (consisting of 121 individuals), a number that represents the teams associated with thirteen ships over approximately a year and a half. (For details on the research effort, see Glickman et al., 1987.)

Antisubmarine Warfare (ASW) Team

The primary task of the ASW team is to detect, track, and defend against enemy submarines. This task is accomplished by means of four constituent teams: an eight-member CIC team, a five-member sonar team, a six-member passive-sonar team, and a two-member underwater/battery plot team. As was the case with NGFS, the CIC team is the hub of the ASW team. The sonar team uses high-energy sound of short duration to determine range and bearing of subsurface vessels by the direction and delay of the return echo. The passive-sonar team is responsible for detecting, classifying, and observing subsurface contacts by using high-tech listening devices to hear the sounds propagated by submarines. The U/B plot team participates in keeping track of enemy submarines and also interfaces with the ship's navigation functions.

In general, ASW team training involves instruction of the intact ASW team associated with a particular combat vessel. During this research, training consisted of four and a half days of simulator exercises with six phases, each of which corresponded to an increasingly difficult scenario.

The phases of training parallel antisubmarine problems of increasing difficulty. In the first problem — single ship/single sub, the simplest — team members are assumed to be aboard a ship whose responsibility is to track a one enemy submarine. In the final, most difficult problem — dual ship/dual sub, high-value unit — team members are assumed to be distributed between two ships. Each subteam must coordinate its activities with the other ship, keeping track of two enemy submarines while providing protection to a third ship, such as an aircraft carrier. As more ships and submarines are involved, the problems become more complex.

Data were collected on eleven ASW teams (consisting of eighty-eight individuals), a number that represents the teams associated with eleven ships over approximately a year and a half. (For details on the research effort, see Glickman, Zimmer, Montero, Guerette, Morgan, & Salas, 1989a, 1989b.)

Guided Missile (GM) Team

The primary task of the GM team was to engage in tactics to detect, track, and defend against enemy surface and subsurface vessels. This task is complex because it relies on incomplete and fuzzy information compiled by members of hierarchically organized teams. In the typical situation, the GM team consisted of eleven members broken up into three constituent teams: the (active-) sonar team, the passive-sonar team, and the plot team. These constituent teams contribute to detecting, tracking, and defending against enemy vessels through the guidance of the plot coordinator, a fire-control computer, and, ultimately, the approach officer.

In some sense, the makeup of the GM team is similar to that of the ASW team. Certain aspects of the GM team environment are different, however. This is particularly evident with respect to the training of these teams. Training is not as structured as it is for the NGFS and ASW counterparts (in fact, it was not required at the time of our research). Submarine officers themselves and GM members have much to say about the nature of the material being imparted and the exercises used in training. Instructors serve as resource persons, rather than teachers, to provide information when a team encounters problems that it cannot easily solve on its own. At the time of our research, training was provided as a service to the submarine community but was not required for certification purposes, as it was in the previously described environments.

At the time of the research, GM training was presented to intact GM teams associated with a submarine. A typical training session lasted four hours, but a submarine team could avail itself of the opportunity for training on more than one occasion while in port.

Ultimately, the goal in data collection at the GM school was to ascertain whether certain observations and findings identified at the other two sites were applicable to this unique variation of team training. Data were collected on thirty-one GM teams (consisting of thirty-four individuals), a number that represents the teams associated with thirty-one ships over approximately two and a half months. (For details on the research effort, see Glickman, Zimmer, Montero, Guerette, Morgan, & Salas, 1989b.)

In sum, three types of teams were under investigation in the TEAM paradigm. These teams performed their tasks in complex environments characterized by rapid information flows, high work loads, high time pressure, intense communication, and a high demand for coordination among team members.

Data Produced by the TEAM Research Paradigm

It may be useful to review the types of data on which this chapter relies. To begin with, open-ended interviews were carried out with instructors at the three sites. The purpose of the interviews was to ascertain the instructors' opinions about what constitutes effective teamwork and what constitutes the appropriate approach to training teams under different circumstances (Guerette, Miller, Glickman, Morgan, & Salas, 1987; Morgan, Glickman, Woodard, Blaiwes, & Salas, 1986; Glickman et al., 1989a, 1989b). All interviews were content-analyzed to identify trends among the instructors' responses.

On the basis of the interviews and direct observations of teams in training, six data-collection instruments were developed for use in this investigation, each one adapted to suit the unique features of the training facility where it was to be used. The instruments are briefly described below. (See Morgan, Glickman, Woodard, Blaiwes, & Salas, 1986, for a thorough description of the instruments.) Three of these forms were completed by the team instructors: the Critical Team Behaviors Form, which was designed to identify important behaviors displayed by the instructor and team members; the Overall Team Performance Form, which required instructors to evaluate overall performance of the teams; and the Individual Performance Summary, designed to evaluate the effectiveness of individual team members in the performance of their assigned duties. The team leader was also asked to complete the Individual Performance Summary.

In addition to the interviews and the data-collection instruments, a self-report questionnaire was developed. This instrument was used to record potentially changing perceptions of the team members. A team demographics form was also developed, to provide information about prior work and training experiences related to the military in general and to the focal operations in particular.

In the NGFS and ASW environments, data collection took place after the morning and afternoon sessions of each training day. (Data collection in GM was different, given the short duration of the training.) Therefore, all forms except the demographics form, which had to be completed only at the beginning of training, were completed after the morning and afternoon sessions. To maximize the completeness and accuracy of their recall, all individuals were asked to give their responses to the questionnaires immediately after the training exercise.

Critical Team Behaviors Form

In order to identify specific effective and ineffective behaviors of team members, the Critical Team Behaviors Form was designed by means of the critical-incident method. Through semistructured interviews that had been conducted with instructors at one of the three sites, behavioral episodes characterizing effective and ineffective teams were identified. From these episodes, specific items were written and sorted by project staff into seven dimensions, which had been identified in the research literature: (1) communication, (2) adaptability, (3) cooperation, (4) acceptance of suggestions or criticism, (5) giving of suggestions or criticism, (6) team spirit and morale, and (7) coordination. The final version of the form was developed after several pilot tests. It contained a total of sixty-eight items and required respondents (usually team instructors) to check off the team behaviors that they had observed and to identify the main actors involved in the episodes.

Overall Team Performance Form

This instrument required instructors to provide an overall appraisal of each team's performance at the end of each session. The form consisted of a 5-point scale ranging from 1 (very good) to 5 (very poor). Descriptive anchors were provided for points 1, 3, and 5. In addition to making the ratings, instructors were asked to list three of the teams' strengths and three of the teams' weaknesses.

Individual Performance Summary

This instrument required the instructors to provide performance ratings of each member of the team on a 5-point scale at the end of each training session.

Team Leader Performance Summary

At the end of each session, team leaders (assigned leaders of the team) also rated individual team members' performance on this form, parallel to the instructors' Individual Performance Summary.

Trainee Self-Report Questionnaire

Each trainee completed a twenty-one-item self-report questionnaire, which was designed to measure the perceptions of trainees regarding individual and team abilities, motivation, and expertise. Designed on the basis of work carried out by James, Gustafson, and Sells (1985), the instrument tapped dimensions associated with the following individual skills: (1) knowledge of duties, (2) motivation, (3) role clarity, and (4) experience and training. The measure also tapped the following teamwork dimensions:

(1) communication, (2) cooperation and coordination, (3) experience and prior training, and (4) power relationships.

Team Demographics Form

This form was designed to determine team members' experience in the military and the particular operations in which members were receiving training. The final version of the instrument was constructed after pilot testing for clarity and consistency of wording.

Data Analyses

All data were collected by means of the questionnaires just described, through interviews with instructors in the three operational training environments, or through direct observation of teams during training. (See Guerette, Miller, Glickman, Morgan, & Salas, 1987; Glickman et al., 1989a, 1989b; McIntyre, Morgan, Salas, & Glickman, 1988; Oser, McCallum, Salas, & Morgan, 1989).

The data varied with respect to accommodating statistical analyses. Certain data (such as critical-behavior data, interview data, and observations) were intractable to sophisticated quantitative analyses yet served as rich sources of information on team processes. In analyzing these data, the researchers looked for evidence of behavioral *trends* that typified team performance. Results of the data analyses are presented below, along with other, more traditional analyses, to support twenty principles in several categories. (It is important to note that other sources also provide support for the principles presented here; Hackman, 1990; Wiener, Kanki, & Helmreich, 1993; Swezey & Salas, 1992.)

Category 1: What Is Teamwork?

Most researchers and supervisors involved in team management and research agree that teamwork is important, that teamwork can make or break the effectiveness of the work group, and that teamwork is critical to the performance of the team. Yet, faced with the problem of defining teamwork, few have provided a clear and direct answer. Recall our adopted definition of *team* (see p. 13). This definition implies that a group's members must interact; must work toward valued, common, specified goals and objectives; and must adapt to circumstances in order to meet these goals and objectives. We believe that a question about the definition of teamwork is a question about the *behavioral indicators* of the three facets of the definition of the word *team:* (1) interaction toward (2) common goals and (3) adaptation to circumstances. In other words, defining teamwork requires an explication of *what a team does* when it is behaving as a team.

Essential Teamwork Behaviors

Our research has shown that teamwork is a *complex* of behavioral characteristics (e.g., see Oser, McCallum, Salas, & Morgan, 1989). Key among these, and perhaps overlooked or underemphasized in past research, are *performance monitoring, feedback, closed-loop communication,* and *backing-up behaviors.* The following sections explain in some detail the meanings of these different aspects of teamwork.

PRINCIPLE 1: *Teamwork means that members monitor one another's performance.*

Both the interview and the critical-behavior data indicate that teamwork requires team members to monitor their fellow members' performance. What are team members monitoring? What is involved in monitoring? The data suggest that effective team members keep track of fellow team members' work while carrying out their own. Keeping track may mean observing combat systems, to ensure that everything is running as expected, and observing fellow team members, to ensure that they are following procedures correctly and in a timely manner.

Lest the reader conjure up the image of team members' spying on one another, it is important to understand that performance monitoring becomes an accepted part of an implicit contract among the team members. It becomes the accepted norm for members to check on one another for the goal of improving the performance of the group. Implicit, then, in this proclivity to monitor others' performance is the prerequisite of establishing a psychological contract of trust among the members. This contract says, in effect, "It is all right for you to watch me. We are all here to maximize the performance of the team." The existence of such a contract was inferred from an examination of the critical-incident data.

PRINCIPLE 2: *Teamwork implies that members provide feedback to and accept it from one another.*

The critical-behavior data, as well as the interview data, support this conclusion. In effect, feedback is a follow-up activity to monitoring. When team members in the process of monitoring recognize effective performance or ineffective performance by their fellow team members, they pass this information on to their fellow team members.

Comments by instructors and observations made by the research staff suggest that there are many instances in which status, rank, or tenure can impede the free flow of necessary feedback (see also Driskell & Salas, 1992). A corollary to this lesson, then, is this: Effective teamwork implies that team members *feel free* to provide feedback. That is, the climate within the group must be such that neither rank nor tenure stands as an obstacle to team members' providing feedback to one another. This kind of freedom is the ideal and is characteristic of high-performing teams. The highest level of teamwork implies the existence of free-flowing feedback.

Furthermore, effective teams engage in tasks with an awareness of their strengths and weaknesses. This characteristic seems to accrue as a result of the group members' providing constructive feedback to one another. It also results from group leaders' modeling a certain receptivity to criticism. That is, when leaders show the ability to accept constructive criticism, they establish a norm that this type of criticism is appropriate.

PRINCIPLE 3: *Teamwork involves effective communication among members, which often involves closed-loop communication.*

Closed-loop communication is a particular type of communication. The term *communication* refers to the exchange of information between a sender and a receiver. Therefore, it is only logical to assert that teamwork involves the exchange of information from one team member to other team members. But, because of the nature of TAC-DM tasks, the exchange of information takes on the particular form of a "closed loop." In one sense, the term *closed-loop communication* defines the exchange of information that occurs in any successful communication. In another sense, *closed-loop communication* describes something particularly important about TAC-DM teamwork, as follows. Information exchange in TAC-DM teams must occur rapidly. Moreover, a TAC-DM team consists of multiple senders and receivers of information. Therefore, the management and organization of information in such a context is an enormous problem at times. In order for information to be exchanged successfully in the context of simultaneous information flow, particular skill is required of the senders to ensure that the information is received as intended. Closed-loop communication involves the following sequence of behaviors: (1) the sender initiates the message; (2) the receiver accepts the message and provides feedback to indicate that the message has been received; and (3) the sender double-checks to ensure that the *intended* message was received.

This type of communication is most readily observable in emergency situations, where the unexpected occurs.

Evidence in support of closed-loop communication skills was provided in a number of ways during data collection. Most often, the interview data with instructors referred to the necessity of "good communication skills" in successful teams. Further probing and examination of the critical-behavior data made it clear that "good communication skills" meant communication in the form of a closed loop.

It is interesting to recognize that closed-loop communication is implicitly addressed in many of the military's formalized communication procedures and protocols. For example, consider the following analysis of the typical task carried out by a TAC-DM team on a military fighting ship:

1. The commanding officer uses a particular set of terms to order his tactical team to launch a certain weapon system. In such situations, this type of command, presented in a particular format, is a stimulus to which the member of the team receiving the command (the receiver) must respond in a particular way.
2. The receiver responds to the command in the prescribed form, tempo, and cadence.
3. Upon hearing the acknowledgment by the receiver, the commanding officer knows that the message was or was not received as intended. The commanding officer—by responding himself in a particular prescribed form—closes the loop on the message, to make sure that what he intended to say was heard.

Communiqués presented in the prescribed form, tempo, and cadence are examples of proceduralized closed-loop communication. The fact that there are prescriptions with regard to the format of communication is evidence that the military implicitly recognizes the importance of closing the communication loop. In other words, at least in some circumstances, procedures can be established to ensure that closed-loop communication takes place.

PRINCIPLE 4: *Teamwork implies the willingness, preparedness, and proclivity to back fellow members up during operations.*

A team's performance monitoring and feedback are necessary conditions of teamwork. However, another ingredient is required for teamwork to truly manifest itself: back-up behavior. This skill is perhaps at the very heart of teamwork, for it makes the team truly operate as more than the sum of its parts. Better teams are distinguished from poorer teams in that their members show a willingness to jump in and help when they are needed, and they accept help without fear of being perceived as weak (see Oser, McCallum, Salas, & Morgan, 1989; Prince & Salas, 1993). This lesson leads to a critical corollary lesson: Team members have the operational expertise to *provide* back-up behavior.

In other words, team members must show competence not only in their own particular technical duties but also in the areas of the other team members with whom they directly interact. Over and over again, experts in the interviews and in the literature on team performance have pointed out that team performance depends on knowing one's job (e.g., Briggs & Johnston, 1967; Salas, Dickinson, Converse, & Tannenbaum, 1992). Further probing of comments like these indicates that knowing one's job really implies knowing the technical tasks of one's own position *and* those of the other team members with whom one interacts.

Enabling Conditions for Teamwork Behaviors

Two related characteristics stand as enabling conditions for the teamwork behaviors just described in lessons 1 to 4. To describe these two characteristics clearly, we ask the reader to recall that we have defined teamwork as the composite of *behavioral* indicators of interaction among team members to reach common goals, as well as adaptation by members to the circumstances faced by the team. We have observed two other characteristics of teamwork that can be thought of as *attitudinal* indicators of interaction toward common goals and adaptation to circumstances. With this background, the principles pertinent to the enabling values can be presented.

PRINCIPLE 5: *Teamwork involves group members' collectively viewing of themselves as a group whose success depends on their interaction.*

This first attitude is best understood as a value shared by team members and pertinent to their membership in the team. It is the team's awareness of itself as a team. When a team has this attitude, each member of the team views himself (all team members were males), when performing within the context of the team task, as a team player, as a part of the team; that is, he sees the team's success as taking precedence over his individual performance. Members of effective teams view themselves as connected team members, not as isolated individuals working with other isolated individuals. Effective teams consist of individuals who recognize that their effectiveness is the team's effectiveness, which depends on the sum total of all team members' performance.

The data for this principle come largely from the instructor interviews, as well as from suggestions by Foushee and Helmreich (1988) and Driskell and Salas (1992). Instructors described the effective team as one "with the right attitude." Instructors consistently indicated that when team members displayed the "right attitude," they viewed their team assignments as extremely important. A common theme among instructors who were interviewed can be summarized in this one comment: "Effective teams take the team assignment seriously." After probing, it was discovered that the thrust of this comment is that people on effective teams see themselves as *team members* first.

The second characteristic value is implied by the first.

PRINCIPLE 6: *Teamwork means fostering within-team interdependence.*

This principle seems simple but is deceptive. A team has been defined as a group of people who interact interdependently. We believe that the definition of *team* implies that the subtasks performed by the team members are interconnected. This means the following: (1) the degree of success on the overall team task depends on the degree of success on each of the subtasks, and (2) the degree of success on one subtask is determined by success on the other subtasks. What does it mean, then, to say that teamwork means to *foster* interdependence? One might assert that a team task either does or does not involve interdependence of tasks.

Here is where a distinction must be made between the *actual interdependence* of subtasks comprising the team task and an *attitude of interdependence* among team members. The latter term refers to the degree to which each team member recognizes that his or her success depends on the success of others. Perhaps the attitude of interdependence held by a team member is akin to role clarity in the sense that it involves understanding one's own team function in relation to others' team functions.

Fostering team interdependence, then, means the team's adopting the value that it is not only appropriate but essential for each team member (regardless of status in the team) to depend on every other team member to carry out the team's mission, on the basis of the actual interrelatedness of the subtasks comprising the overall team task. Contrary to what may take place in the rest of the organization, interdependence is seen as a virtue—as an essential characteristic of team performance—not as a weakness.

Regarding this principle, the interview and critical-behavior data, as well as recent research, suggest a similar message: effective teams not only have an awareness of the importance of their role but also put this into action by fostering within-team interdependence (Cannon-Bowers, Salas, & Converse, 1993; Rouse, Cannon-Bowers, & Salas, 1992). Necessary conditions for this attitude to be shared by team members have already been mentioned: that effective teams contain individuals who know one another's individual jobs, offer to help fellow team members when it is appropriate to help, and depend on one another for this help. All of these assertions were supported by the critical-behavior and interview data (see Glickman et al., 1989a, 1989b; Oser, McCallum, Salas, & Morgan, 1989).

"Ancillary" Teamwork Behaviors

PRINCIPLE 7: *Teamwork is characterized by a flexible repertoire of behavioral skills that vary as a function of circumstances.*

In other words, besides those already mentioned, there is no special set of behaviors comprising teamwork. Analysis of the critical-behavior data indicate that effective teams show the ability to alter their behavior as different situations dictate. For example, in certain circumstances, effective teams have team leaders who engage in what might be described as autocratic behavior. The team leader may demand that certain actions be taken. In other circumstances, much more democratic behavior takes place. The point is that there was no evidence that a single set of specific behaviors makes up teamwork, other than those behaviors outlined above.

A commonly cited characteristic of effective teams is cohesiveness. For example, Likert (1961) states that the members of an effective group are attracted to the group and are loyal to its members, including the leader. In effect, Likert is speaking of an affective attraction among team members, usually known as cohesiveness. The writings of other organizational theorists, such as Blake and Mouton (1964), Argyris (1964), and McGregor (1960), lead to a similar principle: cohesiveness is an important determinant of team effectiveness.

There is danger in being too influenced by this principle or concluding that teamwork is synonymous with cohesiveness, however. We caution against the inference that team members' liking one another, identifying with one another, and feeling comfortable with one another are the sine qua non of teamwork.

Analyses of the military teams' data indicates that at times of high performance demands on the team, teamwork involved a very businesslike orientation toward meeting the performance goal. In such an instance, teamwork may involve the leader's openly reprimanding team members for mistakes and providing direct commands, to accomplish a particular task. The circumstances dictate the particular manifestation of teamwork — positive affect among members at times, interactive management at other times, and autocratic leadership at still others. There seems to be, therefore, a discrepancy between the way the tactical teams in our research performed and the postulate that cohesiveness is a necessary condition of team performance. Parker (1990) addresses this apparent discrepancy by emphasizing that there should be a balance between process behaviors that build and maintain the team (that is, cohesiveness) and activities that promote the completion of basic team tasks. Reflecting similar points that Blake and Mouton (1964) make about effective leadership, Parker's point is that the effective team exhibits production-oriented and people-oriented skills. Our point is that in certain circumstances, teams display production-oriented behavior in preference to cohesiveness.

This is another example of the flexible repertoire that we mentioned above: the effective team displays a repertoire of styles, each of which is more or less suited to particular circumstances (McIntyre, Morgan, Salas, & Glickman, 1988). We have found little evidence for any "most appropriate" style of teamwork in the tactical environment.

What does this say about cohesiveness? Cohesiveness is not a necessary part of TAC-DM teams, if cohesiveness is defined as consistent positive affect. Nevertheless, cohesiveness can be defined in terms of the performance values discussed above—team self-awareness, and within-team interdependence. This definition allows for varying styles and manifestations of affect. In this sense, then, cohesiveness *is* an important ingredient of teamwork in the TAC-DM setting.

PRINCIPLE 8: *Teams change over time.*

While this principle also seems a bit simplistic, it has critical implications for team training. Extensive analyses of the behavioral data suggest that teams change over time (McIntyre, Morgan, Salas, & Glickman, 1988; Oser, McCallum, Salas, & Morgan, 1989). The degree to which they change seems to be determined in part by the degree to which the team members have worked together *as an intact team.* Note that this is not synonymous with work experience, tenure, or time in the military. The critical aspect seems to be whether the team has worked *as* a team.

It may be instructive to review how teams change over time during training. The point has been discussed by McIntyre, Morgan, Salas, and Glickman (1988), who compared more or less effective teams proceeding through six phases during training. In phase 1, team members explored their individual roles, asked for clarification, and checked with other members who experienced uncertainty. In phase 2, the less effective teams continued to struggle with role ambiguity. They failed to communicate necessary information and yet they attempted to assist each other when in need. More effective teams showed less distress concerning role ambiguity. Apparently, due to their greater level of skill, they did not need to make attempts to help one another or check with each other on their required tasks. In phase 3, team members began to communicate more efficiently, check with each other, and ask many questions. On the more effective teams, members tended to ask for help when it was needed, and, in general, were ready to provide information. Less effective teams did not show such tendencies. In phase 4, both the more and the less effective teams showed signs of skill development. Members were freer to check for clarification in their communications, freer to provide and seek feedback, and more likely to engage in closed-loop communication. It appeared that the less effective teams tended not to seek feedback and not to ask for help. In phase 5, the more effective teams showed signs of continued skill development. For example, members of these teams provided feedback and guidance when uncertainties arose and supported each other. Less effective teams did not decline in their behavioral skills, yet they did not show continued skill development. In phase 6, a greater variety of behaviors became evident. Members were more likely to express their feelings toward one another. They seemed to show greater coordination in gathering information, to adapt procedures to conditions, and to check with others when uncertainties arose.

All the ideas expressed by principle 8 suggest a simple corollary: Teamwork not only changes but develops over time. Clearly, the fundamental aspects of teamwork—performance monitoring, feedback, closed-loop communication, backing-up behavior, team awareness, and within-team interdependence—improve over time through experience, practice, and training. Theoretically, this means that teams may vary with respect to their maturity, or level of development, on each of the critical attributes of teamwork. A team may be highly mature with respect to performance monitoring yet less mature with respect to providing feedback or providing back-up support. This principle may help to explain why even very experienced teams show certain deficits in performance. The deficits may exist because certain qualities of teamwork have not been sufficiently developed.

PRINCIPLE 9: *Teamwork and taskwork are distinct.*

How is teamwork distinguished from taskwork? Is the teamwork component of team performance separable from technical aspects of the work?

In our research, the technical aspects of the team operation were regarded as taskwork, and all interactive behaviors among the members were regarded as teamwork. This perspective could have led us to conclude that prescribed task procedures are taskwork, whereas nonprescribed (or emergent) work is teamwork. However, what we learned is that teamwork at times can involve highly technical procedures and activities. In fact, teamwork, as defined above, may very well include prescribed or proceduralized activities, as circumstances dictate. Taskwork is that work done by an individual, or a group of individuals, behaving autonomously rather than interdependently.

Summary: Teamwork

Teamwork is more than the technical accomplishment of the individuals comprising a team or a group. It involves those behaviors that coincide with team members' interacting to achieve desired goals and adapt to circumstances in order to do so. A number of behavioral indicators of team performance have been identified. They include four components (performance monitoring, feedback, closed-loop communication, back-up behaviors) and two performance norms (a team's self-awareness, and the fostering of within-team interdependence). In addition, effective teams are characterized by their changing and developing behaviors and skills. Styles of performance may vary from team to team, or within some teams, from circumstance to circumstance. Teamwork can change and develop over time.

Category 2: Team Leadership

How does one lead in the TAC-DM environment? And what does team leadership mean in the context of TAC-DM teamwork? These questions arise naturally in the effort to coming to a better understanding of teamwork.

Role of Team Leaders

This category of principles concerns the role of team leaders during formal training and, by inference, during tactical decision making. It should be noted that the term *team leader* is used in a broad rather than restricted sense. Hence, for example, even though in certain TAC-DM contexts there is a single assigned team leader who is ultimately responsible for decisions made by the team, other senior team members and those assigned as assistants to the leaders are also considered team leaders because they all are expected to provide team leadership and management.

PRINCIPLE 10: *Team leadership makes a difference with respect to the performance of the team.*

This principle may seem rather obvious, yet it is intended to communicate what may be forgotten at times: team leaders serve as models for their fellow team members. In other words, if they openly engage in teamwork — that is, monitor, provide and accept feedback, and provide and accept back-up behaviors — other team members are likely to do the same. The critical-behavior data, the self-report data, and the interview data all confirm this finding. In fact, several instructors stated that team leaders "are critical" and have "tremendous influence on teams," and that when team leaders are poor, so are teams (see Burgess, Riddle, Hall, & Salas, 1992).

PRINCIPLE 11: *Team leaders vary on level of expertise in the team operation and on readiness to lead a team.*

From interviews with instructors, it was discovered that when team leaders are ill prepared with regard to the technical operations of the team, or with regard to serving as team leader, a certain disorder results among team members. A team leader's lack of readiness can communicate to the other team members that there is little significance attached to the team, to the team task, or to team training. By contrast, when a team leader is sufficiently well versed in the technical aspects of the team task and in the leadership function itself, team members have a sense of directedness and a sense that their assignment is important.

PRINCIPLE 12: *Team leaders must "know their stuff" and be willing to listen to other team members who have special expertise.*

This principle speaks to the issue of the security and self-confidence that a team leader must feel in carrying out the team leader's role. Team leaders must have access to the technical details of a team operation. This access eventuates from their own personal knowledge and experience, as well as from the knowledge and experience of other team members who have special expertise.

The data suggest that if a team leader feels insecure, he may feign a level of expertise that he does not possess. Further, if a team leader is unduly concerned about saving face, he may show resistance to seeking help and accepting feedback or advice from team members of lower rank. Both kinds of resistance are counterproductive to teamwork.

PRINCIPLE 13: *Team leaders serve as models of teamwork.*

Concerning back-up behavior, for example, one interview comment indicated that the "type of supervisor" influences whether helping behavior among team members starts from the beginning of team training. Supporting the same idea, some instructors noted that experienced supervisors "help everyone out." Another comment indicated that a leader must stress that it is acceptable for junior team members to correct him if these individuals think that he is wrong. This shows the influence that the team leader has on both monitoring and feedback. In combination, these data illustrate how important it is for a team leader to serve as a role model for teamwork.

PRINCIPLE 14: *An important part of a team leader's job is to provide feedback.*

Instructors emphasized that an important part of the effective team leader's role is to provide feedback and recommendations for improvement. Some data indicate that this feedback derives from a knowledge of the technical and operational details.

PRINCIPLE 15: *The style of the leader moderates the degree of successful feedback to the team.*

To impart the full sense of this principle, some background comments are necessary. In the environments where this research was carried out (and, presumably, in other parts of the military), researchers occasionally encountered team leaders who displayed a number of characteristics that noticeably interfered with team effectiveness. These characteristics were (1) a proclivity to micromanage, (2) a tendency toward an autocratic style of managing team members, and (3) a very strong sense of over-confidence with regard to their mastery of the technical aspects of the team tasks. We refer to this complex of characteristics as the *tough leadership style.* (It is beyond the scope of this chapter to explore all of the characteristics of this type of leader or leadership style, but the behaviors and characteristics just mentioned are the most commonly noted ones.) Instructors indicated that it was difficult to provide constructive criticism to individuals displaying the tough leadership style. These individuals often rejected feedback, showed resistance to it, or in some way become defensive with regard to it. Thus it appears that the tough leadership style has negative effects that hamper team development and performance. Consider a number of possible consequences. First, under tough leadership, critical information from outside the team may be screened from the team because the leader finds it unacceptable or unnecessary. Second, team members may resist providing feedback or back-up help to the leader, or even to each other, for fear of reprisals. Third, the tough leadership style may cause team orientation to deteriorate. These are just a few consequences of the tough leadership style.

PRINCIPLE 16: *Team leaders who are respected by team members are effective.*

Several comments indicated that when team members did not like team leaders, they tended not to support them or help them. One comment indicated that team members who did not like a team leader would not "work hard to make him look good." The real lesson here is that team leaders should be vigilant with regard to the respect they command. The leader's loss of the team members' respect leads to the risk of alienated team members, which leads in turn to a failure in teamwork. Loss of other team members' respect is a problem that the leader must manage in order to maintain the team's effectiveness.

Summary: Team Leadership

One requirement for the team leader is a certain level of competence in the operational details of the team task. But even the most effective of team leaders cannot possibly possess all the knowledge, skills, and abilities of all the team members. Where his technical competence is low, he must rely on his team members to support the team. In a sense, the team leader should be the consummate team member: his concern should be the success of the *team,* not of himself. The team leader serves as a model of teamwork among the team members. For example, by openly depending on the specialized expertise of team members, by openly accepting criticism and feedback, and by providing positive and negative feedback to other team members, he encourages a climate for the same type of behavior among all team members. The team leader should be cautious about his leadership style and the degree to which he is liked. What we call the tough leadership style, as well as lack of respect from other team members, may obstruct the development of teamwork.

Category 3: Individual Team Members' Roles

This section concerns the behaviors, levels of skill, and levels of preparation that individuals need to ready themselves for teamwork. Some lessons appear to be more military-specific than previous lessons. Therefore, whenever appropriate, an effort is made to relate the lessons to circumstances in other organizations.

Role of Team Members

PRINCIPLE 17: *Team effectiveness requires individual team members to acquire a certain level of competence in their specific assigned team tasks, before the team training itself.*

Consistently, instructors pointed out that there are kinds of knowledge, skill, and ability that team members should acquire before team training begins. It is usually left to the initiative of the team member himself to amass these competencies. In certain instances, the acquisition of the prerequisite knowledge and skills results from formal training. In others, it results from experience.

In nonmilitary organizations, the principle may pertain to the knowledge, skills, and abilities that are assumed to be prerequisites for engaging in team tasks of almost any sort. That is, the acquisition and mastery of individual task skills is a necessary condition for serving as an effective team member.

PRINCIPLE 18: *There is often no system for ensuring that individual team members will attain the prerequisite knowledge and skills.*

Data indicated that the work environment provided few incentives to motivate or facilitate individual's acquisition of the prerequisite knowledge before team training. In fact, there was a perception among some individuals who took the initiative to prepare ahead of time that they were being "punished," because their prior preparation meant that they were working "double duty": preparing for team training, and performing their other (collateral) jobs.

This principle may well extend to nonmilitary jobs. For example, consider the prior preparation that ad hoc teams in industry bring with them to assigned team tasks. Are there similar concerns with respect to these types of teams, whose members retain their formal responsibilities in addition to the new responsibilities of team tasks? We know of many anecdotes that say that such a problem can enter the nonmilitary workplace as well. Perhaps the real lesson here is this: unless there is a system in place for ensuring that individuals acquire and retain the prerequisite knowledge, skills, and abilities, teamwork is not to be expected.

PRINCIPLE 19: *Some teams pass through team training on the strength of a few individuals' effort, and not as a result of teamwork.*

This principle seems important to articulate, despite the fact that the evidence for it was relatively sparse. The principle says that dependent teams slip through the system because of the outstanding performance of a few highly prepared or experienced members. Whatever the explanation of this phenomenon, it can have serious consequences for an organization. For example, how will a team fare when its star performer is either missing or overloaded?

All organizations employing teams, not just the military, must prepare for the possibility that team members will shirk the individual responsibility to prepare for team tasks and attain the prerequisite levels of knowledge, skill, and ability.

PRINCIPLE 20: *Team members need to know the tasks of those others with whom they interact during team operations.*

To truly participate in teamwork, it is important for team members to have acquired a certain level of competence in the *general* team tasks, and a high degree of competence in those tasks that are closely linked to their own. Here, the phrase *closely linked* refers to the situation of team members whose functional contributions to the team task depend on other team members.

The point of this principle is that team members can engage in the critical aspects of teamwork (monitoring, feedback, and back-up behaviors) to the extent that they know *what* they are monitoring, know *what* to feed back to team members, and know *how* to provide back-up support.

Summary: The Role of Team Members

The principles in this section support the unsurprising conclusion that team members must acquire individual competence before effective teamwork can take place. Despite the obvious need for individual competence, however, individuals are often torn between team-related and other responsibilities. Within the Navy, this conflict involves carrying out on-board duties in addition to the responsibilities of a team member. In nonmilitary organizations, similar kinds of conflicting demands also prevail.

Management, then, is faced with the important challenge of creating a system that reinforces the development of team-related prerequisites. This requires, first, that team-related prerequisites be known; second, that the team task be analyzed in sufficient detail for cross-training of team members to be implemented; and, third, that management recognize and control the frequent tendency of teams to depend inordinately on their strongest member(s).

Where Do We Go from Here?

Developing detailed propositions for future research goes beyond the scope of this chapter. However, we offer a number of questions that may stimulate further research on team performance in organizations. The intent of these questions is to maintain the recent burst of interest in and research on team performance and to motivate social scientists and practitioners alike to continue building our understanding of how better to manage, train, and foster teamwork in industries and organizations.

On the Nature of Teamwork

Although our understanding of teamwork is richer now, several critical questions remain unanswered:

1. What is the role of organizational context in fostering teamwork? Does organizational context moderate the relationship between teamwork and team performance? Does organizational climate or culture determine the level or type of teamwork that exists at the work-group level?
2. Does the importance of teamwork vary as a function of the

predictability of the task demands? Does teamwork have a greater impact in emergencies than in everyday circumstances? Is teamwork a more important skill in environments where crises occur relatively frequently than in environments where crises are few?

3. What is the role of coordination in teamwork? How does coordination pertain to the constructs and characteristics that we observed in our research? (Because of the abstract nature of coordination, and because of the many ways in which the concept can be defined, we found relatively little direct support for coordination beyond the usual idea that an effective team is one that is coordinated. Paradoxically, coordination may be the most frequently cited quality of effective team performance.)

On Developing Teamwork Skills

The existence of behaviorally based constructs provides the basis for assessing teamwork and for designing interventions and training to improve teamwork. However, there are questions that need to be answered:

1. Where should an organization place its resources with respect to training teams? Should the organization pay primary attention to task competence or to teamwork skill? Should there be equal emphasis on both?

2. What specific training interventions can be developed to enhance team performance in organizations? What criteria should be used to select these? How would we know that they worked?

Team Leadership

In general, we found that leaders make a difference in team performance. They play an important role in modeling teamwork and setting the ground rules for team members to successfully engage in teamwork processes. Questions remain, however:

1. What is the significance of task expertise for team leaders? Is it a prerequisite for being a team leader? Can an expert in teamwork serve as a team leader even when his or her task expertise is minimal?
2. Is team leadership something different from leadership in general? If so, what knowledge, skills, abilities, and other characteristics are required? What behaviors comprise team leadership per se? Under what conditions do these behaviors emerge? Are there environmental or task variables that lead to team-leadership behavior?
3. What are the roles of the organizational context and the culture on team leadership? Is a team leader's effectiveness influenced by the climate or the culture of the organization?

On Team Members' Roles

This category of lessons provided some interesting insights into the nature of the individual's readiness to carry out the team task and his effectiveness as a team member. Being an effective team member means more than knowing one's job or knowing about teamwork, but questions naturally arise:

1. What is the relationship between task competence and team-skill competence? Can a team that is highly skilled in team-work readily take on new team tasks? Or does the individual task competence of each team member determine the effectiveness of the team?
2. Is the level of teamwork displayed within an organization under the control of the individual member of the team and the organization? In other words, is it sufficient to focus on individuals within the organization to build teamwork skills? Or does the organizational reward structure ultimately determine the degree of effectiveness of teamwork skill throughout the organization?

Conclusion

The principles in this chapter provide the basis for a *theory of teamwork*. Other scientists have said that there is "nothing more practical than a good theory." A theory of teamwork, from this chapter's behavioral perspective, has the practical advantage of going beyond the generalities that we often find in the business press.

But are theories very practical for organizations? We believe they are not only practical but also necessary. In their attempts to implement or improve team-based performance, organizations need to think specifically about how organization members can effectively serve in the capacity of team members. This requires a conscious effort on the part of the organization to develop an understanding of teams and teamwork. In point of fact, it requires the incorporation of a theory of teamwork into the organization's operating philosophy. Teamwork will take place within the organization to the extent that the organization fosters it and builds on it in all aspects of its human resource management functions.

References

Argyris, C. (1964). *Integrating the individual and the organization.* New York: Wiley.

Blake, R., & Mouton, J. S. (1964). *The managerial grid.* Houston: Gulf.

Briggs, G. E., & Johnston, W. A. (1967). *Team training: Final report, February 1966–February 1977* (NTDC Report No. 1327-4). Orlando, FL: Naval Training Device Center.

Burgess, K. A., Riddle, D. L., Hall, J. K., & Salas, E. (1992, March). *Principles of team leadership under stress.* Paper presented at the meeting of the Southeastern Psychological Association, Knoxville, TN.

Cannon-Bowers, J. A., Salas, E., & Converse, S. A. (1993). Shared mental models in expert team decision making. In N. J. Castellan, Jr. (Ed.), *Current issues in individual and group decision making* (pp. 221–246). Hillsdale, NJ: Erlbaum.

Cannon-Bowers, J. A., Salas, E., & Grossman, J. D. (1991, June). *Improving tactical decision making under stress: Research directions and applied implications.* Paper presented at the International Applied Military Psychology Symposium, Stockholm, Sweden.

Driskell, J. E., & Salas, E. (1992). Can you study real teams in contrived settings? The value of small-group research to understanding teams. In R. W. Swezey & E. Salas (Eds.), *Teams: Their training and performance* (pp. 101–124). Norwood, NJ: Ablex.

Foushee, H. C., & Helmreich, R. L. (1988). Group interaction and flight crew performance. In E. L. Wiener & D. C. Nagel (Eds.), *Human factors in aviation* (pp. 189–225). San Diego, CA: Academic Press.

Glickman, A. S., Zimmer, S., Montero, R. C., Guerette, P. J., Campbell, W. J., Morgan, B. B., Jr., & Salas, E. (1987). *The evolution of teamwork skills: An empirical assessment with implications for training* (NTSC Report No. 87-016). Orlando, FL: Naval Training Systems Center.

Glickman, A. S., Zimmer, S., Montero, R. C., Guerette, P. J., Morgan, B. B., Jr., & Salas, E. (1989a). *The evolution of teamwork skills: A comparative assessment.* Unpublished technical report.

Glickman, A. S., Zimmer, S., Montero, R. C., Guerette, P. J., Morgan, B. B., Jr., & Salas, E. (1989b). *The evolution of teamwork skills: Further tests of generalizability.* Unpublished technical report.

Guerette, P. J., Miller, D. L., Glickman, A. S., Morgan, B. B., Jr., & Salas, E. (1987). *Instructional processes in team training* (Tech. Rep. No. 87-017). Norfolk, VA: Old Dominion University, Center for Applied Psychological Studies.

Hackman, J. R. (Ed.). (1990). *Groups that work (and those that don't): Creating conditions for effective teamwork.* San Francisco: Jossey-Bass.

James, L. R., Gustafson, S. B., & Sells, S. B. (1985). *Final report: Development of effective leaders: The need to consider situational specificity versus cross-situational consistency* (Contract No. NC0014-80-C-0135). Arlington, VA: Office of Naval Research, Group Process Program.

Likert, R. (1961). *New patterns of management.* New York: McGraw-Hill.

McGregor, D. M. (1960). *The human side of enterprise.* New York: McGraw-Hill.

McIntyre, R. M., Morgan, B. B., Jr., Salas, E., & Glickman, A. S. (1988). *Teamwork from team training: New evidence for the development of teamwork skills during operational training.* Paper presented at the Interservice/Industry Training Systems conference, Orlando, FL.

Morgan, B. B., Jr., Glickman, A. S., Woodard, E. A., Blaiwes, A., & Salas, E. (1986). *Measurement of team behaviors in a Navy environment* (NTSC Report, No. 86-014). Orlando, FL: Naval Training Systems Center.

Orasanu, J. M., & Salas, E. (1993). Team decision making in complex environments. In G. Klein, J. Orasanu, R. Calderwood, & C. E. Zsambok (Eds.), *Decision making in action: Models and methods* (pp. 327-345). Norwood, NJ: Ablex.

Oser, R., McCallum, G. A., Salas, E., & Morgan, B. B., Jr. (1989). *Toward a definition of teamwork: An analysis of critical team behaviors* (NTSC Report No. 89-004). Orlando, FL: Naval Training Systems Center.

Parker, G. M. (1990). *Team players and teamwork: The new competitive business strategy.* San Francisco: Jossey-Bass.

Prince, C., & Salas, E. (1993). Training and research for teamwork in the military aircrew. In E. Wiener, B. Kanki, & R. Helmreich (Eds.), *Cockpit resource management* (pp. 337–366). San Diego, CA: Academic Press.

Rouse, W. B., Cannon-Bowers, J. A., & Salas, E. (1992). The role of mental models in team performance in complex systems. *IEEE Transactions on Systems, Man, and Cybernetics, 22,* 1296–1308.

Salas, E., Dickinson, T., Converse, S. A., & Tannenbaum, S. I. (1992). Toward an understanding of team performance and training. In R. W. Swezey & E. Salas (Eds.), *Teams: Their training and performance* (pp. 3–29). Norwood, NJ: Ablex.

Swezey, R. W., & Salas, E. (1992). Guidelines for use in team-training development. In R. W. Swezey & E. Salas (Eds.), *Teams: Their training and performance* (pp. 219–245). Norwood, NJ: Ablex.

Wiener, E., Kanki, B., & Helmreich, R. (Eds.). (1993). *Cockpit resource management.* San Diego, CA: Academic Press.

3

COMPUTER-ASSISTED GROUPS:
A CRITICAL REVIEW OF
THE EMPIRICAL RESEARCH

Andrea B. Hollingshead, Joseph E. McGrath

Our world is filled with technological devices intended to help humans pursue their goals. Among those devices are many designed to improve work in groups. Most of those are electronic in form and relatively new.

Even our brief experience with such systems makes it apparent that electronic enhancements in work groups are not an unmixed blessing. Simultaneously, they reduce some barriers to effective group performance and impose others. They do so by altering the informational, temporal, and interactional processes by which groups do their work. Put another way, it seems clear that various forms of technological enhancement *interact with* various individual, group, task, and situational conditions to yield major effects — some good, some bad — on the quality and speed of group task performance and on the processes by which groups carry out their tasks.

The putative advantages that accompany technological enhancements derive from (1) their potential for improving information access and information-processing capability and (2) their potential for expanding opportunities for group members

to participate without regard to temporal and spatial impediments (that is, group members do not all have to be in the same
place or to be operating at the same time in order to work col-
laboratively). The putative constraints imposed by such technological enhancements arise from the more or less drastic reduction that such enhancements impose on the number and variety
of modalities of communication (for example, loss of nonverbal, paraverbal, and social-status cues), with a consequent reduction in the "richness" of the information transmitted by those
media (Daft & Lengel, 1986).

 While much has been written about the impact—positive
and negative—of electronic technology on how groups can and
do work, the empirical literature assessing such potentials is
limited and relatively scattered. This chapter reports the results
of a systematic review of published empirical studies (including two unpublished doctoral dissertations from our research
program) assessing the impact of computer-mediated interaction on groups. The first section lays out some crucial features
of computer-mediated systems that affect how groups do their
work. The second section describes the sample of studies and
points out some methodological limitations of the body of literature. The third section discusses substantive results of our systematic review of empirical research on these systems.

 Three other reviews of literature relevant to this topic have
appeared recently (Kraemer & King, 1988; Kraemer & Pinsonneault, 1990; McLeod, 1992), the later a quantitative meta-
analysis. Each of these specifies a somewhat different topical focus, and thus each deals with overlapping but not identical bodies
of literature. Each of those reviews arrives at some of the same
conclusions we did, but each also presents some differences in
viewpoints, conclusions, and interpretations. Our review has
the advantage of a more recent cutoff date, and hence a much
larger body of empirical studies.

Important Features of Computer-Assisted Groups

Groups can use computers in many aspects of their work. For
example, a group can use computers as tools to provide a rich

and detailed data base to one or more of its members, to provide a structured format within which task performance takes place, and/or to provide the means for communication among members. These three functions of computers — information access and processing, performance structuring, and communication — may or may not go together. For example, each member of a given group may have access to vast bodies of information via computer data bases, but group members may still communicate with one another entirely in direct (unmediated) face-to-face form. By contrast, sets of individuals who have never met may interact in ways that are similar to what we ordinarily mean by "meetings" or "discussions" or "collaborations," doing so entirely by means of computer-mediated text (and/or graphic) messages, but the computer system they are using may not provide any of them access to any special information beyond that carried in the group's own communication activities. Elsewhere (McGrath & Hollingshead, 1993), we have dealt with electronic systems that serve the information-access and performance-structuring functions for work groups, as well as with those that perform the communication function. The work presented here focuses on computer mediation of communication within work groups.

Dispersion of Members Over Space and Time

One relevant distinction in regard to such systems is whether a group's members are together in space or geographically dispersed. That distinction is used as a simple dichotomy in much of the literature, but actual uses of computer technology in groups are less clear. Some computer-mediated work involves groups whose members are all in the same room and who therefore could (but may or may not) conduct some of their communication face to face. Other computer-mediated groups involve interaction of members who are in different places and therefore could not use face-to-face communication during meetings.

Group work that extends over time raises even more complications. For example, a set of coauthors who build a joint product over a matter of months may do a lot of the work via computer-mediated text messages but may nevertheless do some of the work in face-to-face meetings (or via other communications media, such as phone or mail). Conversely, collaborators who are working primarily in direct, face-to-face mode may from time to time communicate with one another via electronic mail. In both cases, collaborators almost certainly will do a lot of the basic composition and editing of text "off line"—that is, working alone, not in interaction with collaborators by any medium of communication.

The temporal dimension is also frequently reflected in the literature as a simple dichotomy between groups working synchronously versus asynchronously in time. The actual temporal distribution of group work again presents a somewhat more complicated picture than that. There are three main temporal forms in which group work may be carried out.

I. Single Meeting. Either a computer-mediated or a face-to-face group may have only a single meeting, during which group members communicate (by direct or mediated means) primarily in an each-to-all fashion (with little or no each-to-some communication occurring during the meeting).

II. Series of Meetings. Either a computer-mediated or a face-to-face group may have a series of meetings, each held at a specific time and using some communication system, during which communication among members is primarily in the each-to-all mode. Members of such groups may or may not have each-to-some communication with other members between meetings. If they do, it may or may not be by the same communication system used during the meetings.

III. Temporally Distributed Meeting. A computer-mediated group (but not a face-to-face group) can also use a temporally distributed "meeting" in which members communicate in each-to-all fashion via some computer-mediated communication system (for example, e-mail). Members make their individual contributions in a temporally asynchronous pattern, distributed over a considerable period of calendar time. Such a group may or may not have additional each-to-some communications (either by mediated or by direct communication).

The theory underlying our work argues that groups are to be considered as continuing, intact social systems engaged in one or more relatively macro projects, any one of which is likely to extend beyond the temporal boundaries of a single meeting (McGrath, 1990, 1991). There are some actual groups that do exist only for a single meeting—and, heaven knows, groups in most research studies are of that kind. But many natural groups have a life that extends beyond a single meeting on a single topic. Thus the second temporal form is both more prevalent and more theoretically crucial than the first, but it is studied far less often.

The third temporal form reflects one of the major putative advantages of computers in group work—namely, certain forms of technological enhancements of work groups permit them to interact via computers, asynchronously (as in the use of bulletin-board and e-mail technologies) and to carry out collaborative work even when members do not work at the same time. Such an asynchronous group has neither a single meeting at a single point in time nor multiple meetings at specified points of time, with distinct nonmeeting intervals between them. Rather, the "single meeting" of such a group is itself distributed over an extended period of calendar time. Any one member is likely to be engaged with the group's business during some (but by no means all) of that time. In such a case, each member has considerable "between" times during which he or she is not engaged in formal, each-to-all communication with the other members of the group via the computer-mediated system. Each-to-some communication among subsets of members of the group, by any of a range of media, may take place during these "between" times. These temporal distinctions, as well as the spatial ones, are reflected in our categorization of the empirical studies reviewed here.

Variations in Task Type

Another dimension on which group work varies, and which is seldom adequately reflected in the research literature of the field, is the variation among work groups that stems from differences in kind and difficulty level of group tasks. Most experimental studies of groups use an arbitrarily selected task of convenience. Most field studies use whatever specific tasks the extant groups are doing. Neither of these approaches gives much thought to how task factors may alter the impact of the technological enhancements being studied, yet on theoretical grounds there is reason to expect a strong interactive relation between task type and technological enhancements in effects on group process and performance.

A task-classification schema presented in earlier work (McGrath, 1984) is shown as Figure 3.1. That schema proposes that any group task can be categorized as belonging to one or another of four main types (each with two subtypes). The four main task types, related to each other as the four quadrants of a circumplex structure, are identified by the main performance process that each entails: *to generate* (ideas or plans), *to choose* (a correct answer or a preferred solution), *to negotiate* (conflicting views or conflicting interests), and *to execute* (in competition with an opponent, or in competition against external performance standards).

From the information-processing perspective, these task types differ in terms of the degree to which effective performance on them depends only on the transmission of information among members of the group or also requires the transmission of values, interests, personal commitments, and the like. They differ, that is, in the degree of "media richness" (Daft & Lengel, 1986) required for their accomplishment. It is likely that the effects of any given form of computer mediation will depend on the type of task that the group is doing (as well as on various characteristics of the group itself).

Prior Structuring of Information and Action

All forms of computer mediation, to some degree, place limits and structure on the communication process itself, necessarily limiting the channels and modalities by which members can communicate with one another and, to some extent, limiting the

Figure 3.1. Group Task Circumplex.

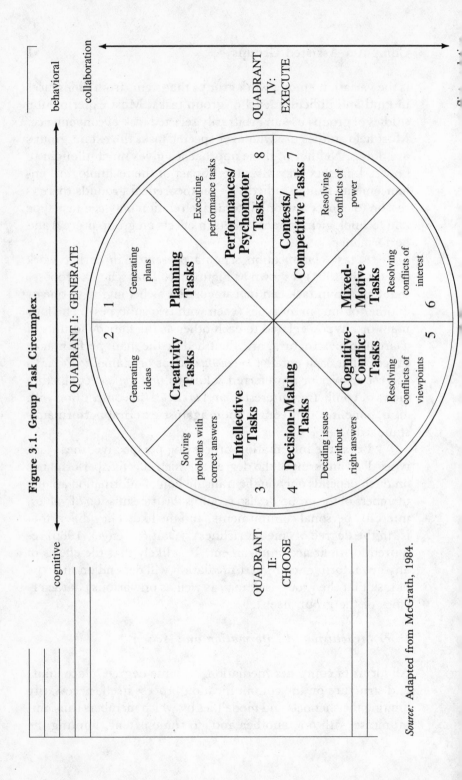

cognitive — behavioral

collaboration

QUADRANT I: GENERATE

QUADRANT IV:
EXECUTE

8 Executing performance tasks

Performances/ Psychomotor Tasks

7 Resolving conflicts of power

Contests/ Competitive Tasks

1 Generating plans

Planning Tasks

6 Resolving conflicts of interest

Mixed- Motive Tasks

2 Generating ideas

Creativity Tasks

5 Resolving conflicts of viewpoints

Cognitive- Conflict Tasks

3 Solving problems with correct answers

Intellective Tasks

4 Deciding issues without right answers

Decision-Making Tasks

QUADRANT
II:
CHOOSE

Source: Adapted from McGrath, 1984.

syntactical forms by which members can communicate via those available channels. Even unmediated face-to-face groups impose some limitations and structuring on group communication processes and other aspects of group work, often by implicit but powerful social norms (McGrath, 1990).

Some technological enhancements also limit and structure the group's performance in one or another of several ways: by removing one or more of the performance processes from the group's performance responsibility; by structuring the amount and form of information available to the group; and/or by structuring the form and sequence of responses by which the group can do its work. Group decision-support systems exemplify such task structuring. They often embed tools for structuring the generation of ideas, for setting an agenda, for attaining consensus, and so on, in addition to providing a system by which group members can communicate with one another. Furthermore, such systems sometimes impose highly constrained response formats on the group — for example, requiring members to pick a single answer from a set of preestablished alternatives, rather than allowing the group to generate its own alternatives, modify and combine them with one another, and then choose its own form and pattern of response by which to convey that choice. Any systematic analysis of the impact of computer mediation on groups must take account of the impact of such prior structuring of group task activity, as well as the modifications of group communication, that arise from use of any given computer-mediation system.

The quadrants of the task circumplex shown in Figure 3.1 help organize the forms in which the task performance of work groups can be constrained by prior structuring (by either computer-based media or "manual" means). Most of the forms of task structuring used in computer-mediated groups have to do with structuring the processes underlying one or more of the four quadrants.

Quadrant I. Some forms of task structuring involve procedures that structure how the group goes about its *generating* activities — brainstorming, goal-setting procedures, agenda setting, or procedures for acquiring alternatives, ideas, goals, plans, and so on.

Quadrant II. Other forms of task structuring involve procedures that structure how the group goes about its *choosing* activities — procedures for aggregating and weighting preferences, for facilitating "rational" choices among "right" answers, for selecting and using algorithms to determine "satisficing" or "optimizing" solutions, and for choosing among alternative preferences.

Quadrant III. Still other forms of task structuring involve procedures that structure how the group goes about its *negotiating* activities — multiattribute utility analysis, negotiation-structuring protocols, procedures for resolving conflicting interests, or voting procedures to force resolution of conflicting views.

Quadrant IV. Yet other forms of task structuring involve procedures that structure how the group carries out its *executing* activities — procedures that require the group to generate its product in a specified response form (such as a rank ordering or a probability estimate), that limit the modalities of response to be used in generating the product, that constrain response sequences, or that set criteria for the timing, quality, and form of the product.

We took the extent and form of prior task structuring into account in our categorization of studies, by distinguishing between systems that involved only mediation of within-group communication and those that also entailed structuring of group task performance. Following our earlier usage of terms (McGrath & Hollingshead, 1993), we labeled the former *group communication support systems,* or GCSS, and we labeled the latter *group performance support systems,* or GPSS. We chose GPSS rather than the more conventional label of *group decision support systems,* to emphasize the point that not all the types of tasks involved are decision tasks as expressed in the circumplex model (see Figure 3.1).

A Model for Analysis of Effects in Computer-Aided Groups

Many factors affect the flow of work in groups, including features of the task and communication systems, features of the group members and the group as a system, and the interaction of all of those factors in context. Therefore, it is useful to construct a conceptual model of the problem at hand, a model that will encompass the full panoply of relevant variables placed in functional relation to one another, so as to provide a framework for organizing and interpreting empirical findings. Such a model is presented in Figure 3.2. The model construes the problem in terms of a sequence of four panels of variables. The first panel consists of three major classes of input factors that form the basic constituents of work groups in context: group and member characteristics; tasks, projects, and purposes; and communication systems. The second panel is a set of variables that reflects the prevailing operating conditions under which a given group is carrying out a given purpose on a given occasion (for example, whether group members are anonymous, or whether there is time pressure). These serve the methodological function of mediating or moderating variables. Next is a set of indices that reflects ongoing group activity while the group is doing its work. Methodologically, these are process variables and can be regarded both as outcomes variables and as antecedents of other outcome variables. Finally, there is a set of variables that reflects subsequent conditions — for the group, for its task, and for its members — that result from the group's work. Methodologically, these are outcome variables, explicit or implicit criteria for evaluation of the effectiveness of the communication system and/or other input factors. The entries in the panels of variables in Figure 3.2 are intended to be illustrative. They are drawn both from the research literature on groups and from the literature on computer-mediated task performance and are certainly not exhaustive.

In light of the preceding discussion, it is clear that attempts to study how communication technologies affect work in groups must take account of far more than the simple question

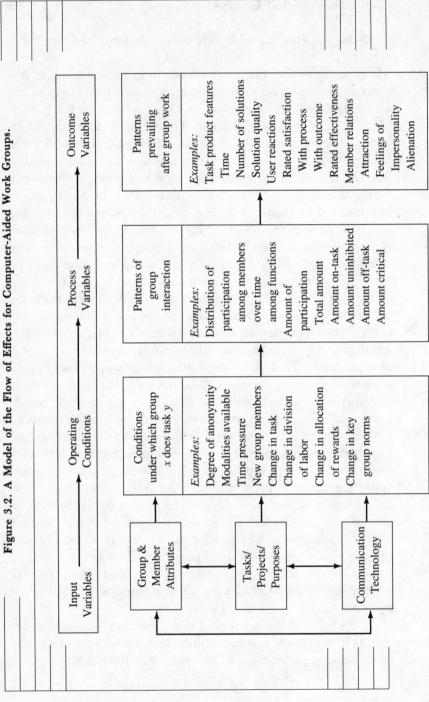

Figure 3.2. A Model of the Flow of Effects for Computer-Aided Work Groups.

of whether the group does or does not have access to computers. The impact of communication technologies depends on both the time and the space distributions of the group's work, on the nature and quality of the tasks in which they are engaged, on the degree to which various portions of the group's work is prestructured, and on the various characteristics of the group, its members, and its context. In the next section, we will examine the results of empirical studies in this area, to determine the extent to which that body of work deals effectively with the many relevant factors.

Empirical Literature on Computer-Mediated Groups

We gathered all the bibliography we could find about effects of communication technologies on work in groups — soliciting preprints and reprints, searching the tables of contents of the past five or ten years for over fifty journals, and searching reference sections of obtained articles. We found and catalogued, in an elaborate coding schema, over 250 studies (see McGrath & Hollingshead, 1994). For the analyses presented here, we selected catalogued articles that presented (1) empirical evidence about (2) task performance of groups that had (3) some form of computer enhancement. That total turned out to be fifty articles encompassing about 150 "findings." A *finding*, here, is a statement, backed by appropriate logical and statistical information, that there is (or is not) an empirical relationship between one or more independent and one or more dependent variables.

Classification of the Empirical Studies

The empirical studies we found fit into three main temporal categories:

I. *Studies of groups with different communications media, for a single meeting.* The preponderance of studies ($n = 42$) is in this category. Most of these studies were conducted in the laboratory, using ad hoc groups. They are further subdivided into thirteen studies using a GCSS and twelve studies using a GPSS, in both cases comparing computer-supported groups with face-to-face groups. Category I also subsumes twelve studies of decision-room groups and two studies of computer conferences that did not include face-to-face comparisons, as well as three studies that compared decision-room groups to physically dispersed groups, but with no face-to-face comparison.

II. *Studies of groups with different communications media, for a series of meetings.* Four of these studies compared computer-supported groups with face-to-face groups (two used GCSS, one used GPSS, one used GCSS and GPSS). One study examined decision-room groups, with no face-to-face comparison.

III. *Studies of groups using different communications media throughout an extended time period* ($n = 3$). These all studied computer groups versus other media (phone, mail). One was done with a between-groups design; two had within-groups designs.

Table 3.1 lists the studies in each of these three categories. Table 3.2 aggregates across studies and summarizes the results by dependent variable. Exhibit 3.1 describes each study in more detail (types of participants; size of groups; number of groups; type of research strategy used—lab experiment, field experiment, field study, case study; type of task performed, as shown in Figure 3.1; descriptions of empirical findings).

Methodological Limitations of the Literature

We take seriously the idea that empirical relationships involving computer-aided groups should be regarded at the outset as a *joint* function of all the factors implied in the model shown in Figure 3.2. That is, if we want to know about or predict group performance, for example, then it does matter who the members are, how they are organized as a group, what task they are doing, what technology they have to do it with, and under what operating conditions they are working. It also matters what aspect

Table 3.1. Empirical Studies of Computer-Supported Groups.

I. *Single Meeting*
  A. *Face-to-Face Versus Computer-Supported Groups (25 Studies)*
    1. *GCSS (13 Studies)*
      Arunachalam (in press)
      Daly (1993)
      Dubrovsky, Kiesler, & Sethna (1991)
      Hiltz, Johnson, & Turoff (1986)
      Hiltz, Turoff, & Johnson (1988)
      Hollingshead (1993)
      Kiesler, Zubrow, Moses, & Geller (1985)
      McGuire, Kiesler, & Siegel (1987)
      Siegel, Dubrovsky, Kiesler, & McGuire (1986)
      Smith & Vanecek (1988)
      Smith & Vanecek (1990)
      Straus & McGrath (in press)
      Weisband (1992)
    2. *GPSS (12 Studies)*
      Gallupe, Bastianutti, & Cooper (1991)
      Gallupe, Dennis, Cooper, Valacich, Bastianutti, & Nunamaker (1992)
      Gallupe, DeSanctis, & Dickson (1988)
      George, Easton, Nunamaker, & Northcraft (1990)
      Ho & Raman (1991)
      McLeod & Liker (1992)
      Poole & DeSanctis (1992)
      Poole, Holmes, & DeSanctis (1991)
      Steeb & Johnston (1981)
      Valacich, Paranka, George, & Nunamaker (in press)
      Watson, DeSanctis, & Poole (1988)
      Zigurs, Poole, & DeSanctis (1988)
  B. *Decision-Room Groups (No Face-to-Face Comparison) (12 Studies)*
    Adelman (1984)
    Connolly, Jessup, & Valacich (1989)
    Dennis, Heminger, Nunamaker, & Vogel (1990)
    DeSanctis, Poole, Lewis, & Desharnais (1991)
    Dickson, Lee, Robinson, & Heath (1989)
    Easton, George, Nunamaker, & Pendergast (1990)
    Jessup, Connolly, & Galegher (1990)
    Nunamaker, Vogel, Heminger, Martz, Grohowski, & McGoff (1989)
    Sambamurthy & Poole (1992)
    Valacich, Dennis, & Connolly (in press)
    Valacich, Dennis, & Nunamaker (1991)
    Vogel & Nunamaker (1988)
  C. *Computer Conference Groups (No Fact-to-Face Comparison) (2 Studies)*
    Hiltz, Johnson, & Turoff (1991)
    Lea & Spears (1991)

Table 3.1. Empirical Studies of Computer-Supported Groups, Cont'd.

    D. *Groups in Decision Room Versus Dispersed Groups (3 Studies)*
        Bui, Sivansankaran, Fijol, & Woodburg (1987)
        Gallupe & McKeen (1990)
        Jessup & Tansik (1991)
II. *Series of Meetings*
    A. *Face to Face Versus Computer (4 Studies)*
        1. *GCSS*
           Hollingshead, McGrath, & O'Connor (1993)
           Walther & Burgoon (1992)
        2. *GPSS*
           Chidambaram, Bostrom, & Wynne (1991)
        3. *GCSS & GPSS*
           Jarvenpaa, Rao, & Huber (1988)
    B. *Decision-Room Groups (No Face-to-Face Comparison) (1 Study)*
        Zigurs, DeSanctis, & Billingsley (1991)
III. *Extended Time Period*
    Groups Using Computers Versus Other Media (3 Studies)
        A. *Between-Groups Design (1 Study)*
           Eveland & Bikson (1989)

        B. *Within-Groups Design (2 Studies)*
           Finholt, Sproull, & Kiesler (1990)
           Sproull & Kiesler (1986)

---

of task performance (decision time, production rate, quality) is being assessed. Given that premise, to make meaningful statements about the effects of, say, a computer-based communication system on task or product quality, we must be able to specify several sets of things:

- How such relationships vary with (or do not vary over) a number of group and member characteristics. (Does group size matter? Are CEOs just like college students?)
- How such relationships vary with (or do not vary over) task types. (Are brainstorming, decision, and planning tasks all affected in the same way, and to the same degree, by a given feature of the group's communication system?)
- How such relationships depend on (or do not depend on) the task structuring that accompanies computer use.

Table 3.2. Summary of Empirical Findings.

Interaction Process
Distribution of Participation Among Members
More equal with computer-supported groups (9); no difference (4)
More equal with computer-supported groups in which status differences
had been reduced (1)
Amount and Content of Participation
Computer Groups
Less overall participation (10); no difference (2)
More uninhibited communication (7); no difference (3)
More communication displaying positive affect (2)
Less argumentation (2)
Less social pressure (2); more (2); no difference (5)
More task-irrelevant communication (2)
More task-relevant communication (3); no difference (2)
Less socioemotional communication (2); more (1)
Less speculation (1)

Computer Groups with Anonymity
More critical communication (2)
More supportive communication (1); no difference (1)
Degree of Consensus
Computer-supported groups had more (4)
More with a facilitator or designated leader (2)
More with a higher level of support (level 2 GDSS versus level 1
GDSS) (1)
Level of Conflict
Computer-supported groups had more than manual groups (groups with
nonelectronic decision-support systems) (3)
Conflict Management
Better in computer-supported groups (1)
Better in manual groups (1), and better in manual groups during the two
initial sessions, but better in computer-supported groups during the two final
sessions (1)
Leadership: Computer Groups
Less likely to have emergent leadership (2)
More likely to have decentralized leadership (1), and less likely to have
stable leadership (1)
Interpersonal Relations: Computer Groups
Deemphasized personal relations and experienced less interpersonal
attraction (2), but no significant differences over time (1)
Choice of Media
Members used computers (e-mail) for work-based communication, and
face-to-face communication for substantive consensus decisions (1)
Teams used GPSS to aid group decisions when technology was introduced
early rather than late in group development (1)

Table 3.2. Summary of Empirical Findings, Cont'd.

Task Performance
Task Completion (or Decision) Times: Computer Groups
   Longer task times (13); no difference (1)
   Dispersed groups took longer (1), shorter (1) time than groups in a
   decision room
Solutions: Computer Groups
   More solutions (13); no difference (1)
   More task-solution proposals (3)
   More correct solutions (1) but more errors (3)
   Computer groups with anonymous members had more solutions than
   computer groups whose members were not anonymous (3)
   Computer groups instructed to be critical had more unique solutions than
   computer groups not so instructed (1)
   Larger computer groups had more ideas than did smaller computer groups (5)
Performance (or Decision) Quality: Computer Groups
   Better quality (7); poorer (8); no difference (6)
   Poorer initially but no differences after three weeks (1)
   Manual groups higher than GDSS, and both higher than unstructured
   face-to-face groups (3)
   Computer-mediated groups were less likely to discuss the most important
   case attributes (2)
   Better solutions for dispersed groups than for decision-room groups (1);
   no difference (1)
   Better solutions for groups with more flexible (compared to less flexible)
   GDSS (1)
Decision Shift: Computer Groups
   More (3); no difference (2)
Consensus: Computer Groups
   Less likely to reach consensus (2); no difference (3)
   Less able to reach consensus when they had *both* a leader and feedback
   than when they had *either* (1)

Performance and Task Type
Idea-Generation Tasks: Computer Groups
   Better than face-to-face groups (4); no difference (4)
Intellective Tasks: Computer Groups
   Worse than face-to-face groups (5); better (1); no difference (2)
Decision-Making Tasks: Computer Groups
   Better than face-to-face groups (2); worse (1); no difference (4)
Negotiation Tasks: Computer Groups
   Worse than face-to-face groups (2)

User Responses
Judgments of Satisfaction and Effectiveness
In Studies with No Noncomputer-Group Comparisons
   Satisfaction: high for computer groups (5)
   Judgments of effectiveness: high for computer groups (4)

Table 3.2. Summary of Empirical Findings, Cont'd.

In Studies with Noncomputer Comparison Groups: Computer Groups
  Satisfaction with process lower (6); higher (4); no difference (3)
  Satisfaction with outcome lower (2), higher (1)
  Judgments of self, others: more negative (3)
  Judgments of effectiveness: lower (3); no difference (2)
  Computer groups had lower satisfaction with structured decisions than
  with unstructured decisions (2)
Other User Reactions: Computer Groups
  Higher level of anxiety (1)
  Feeling of less freedom to participate (1); no difference (1)
  Less accuracy in perceptions of group interaction (1)
  Less perceived evaluation apprehension (2)
  Less perceived production blocking (2)

The requirement for such specifications in turn implies that, in order to make strong generalizations based on the empirical literature, the literature will have to include studies that systematically vary (1) important group and member characteristics, (2) task types and other task characteristics, and (3) communications media. Moreover, some of those studies will have to deal with the same set of dependent variables across group, task, and media conditions.

We recognize that such a systematic body of information is an ideal; it certainly does not describe the body of literature at hand. Instead of these ideal conditions, we found a body of literature that reflects several rather serious limitations and confounds. First, however, let us call attention to a very important point that can easily get lost in any critical treatment of an aggregate body of literature, such as the one presented here: *the methodological criticisms given here about confounds and so on are* not *directed at the soundness of the methodology or the conceptualization of any given study.* Indeed, certain sets of studies within this body of literature are exemplary in those respects. In any case, most of the criticisms do not apply to individual studies but rather to *aggregate* bodies of work; that is, they have to do with the conditions and measures that are *missing* from *sets* of studies, not with the conditions or measures that are *present* in (or absent from) any *given* study. But the pursuit of scientific knowledge is

Exhibit 3.1. Annotated Bibliography.

Adelman, L. (1984). Real-time computer support for decision analysis in a group setting: Another class of decision-support systems. *Interfaces, 14,* 75–83. Category IB. Case study. Task types 1, 2, 4. One work group in an organization. Work group: strongly supported final decision and took action within one week after exercise.

Arunachalam, V. (in press). Computer-mediated communication and structured interaction in transfer pricing negotiation. *Journal of Information Systems.* Category IA1. Lab experiment. Task type 3. Sixty three-person groups of undergraduates. Computer groups: lower decision quality (with structured better than unstructured), more uninhibited participation, longer time to agreement in computer and/or manual (i.e., structured face-to-face).

Bui, T., Sivansankaran, T., Fijol, Y., & Woodburg, M. (1987). Identifying organizational opportunities for GDSS use: Some experimental evidence. *Transactions of Seventh Conference on Decision Support Systems,* San Francisco, CA, 68–75. Category ID. Lab experiment. Task type 2. Twelve three-person groups of MBA students. Dispersed groups (versus decision-room groups): better-quality decisions, less time to decisions, no effect on number of solutions or on satisfaction.

Chidambaram, L., Bostrom, R. P., & Wynne, B. E. (1991). The impact of GDSS on group development. *Journal of Management Information Systems, 7*(3), 3–25. Category IIA2. Lab experiment. Task type 4. Twenty-eight five-person groups of undergraduate business students. Initially, face-to-face groups had higher cohesiveness and managed conflict better than GDSS groups, but this pattern reversed itself in the final two weeks.

Connolly, T., Jessup, L. M., & Valacich, J. S. (1989). Effects of anonymity and evaluative tone on idea generation in computer-mediated groups. *Management Science, 36,* 689–703. Category IB. Lab experiment. Task type 2. Twenty-four four-person groups of business students. Groups with anonymous members: more total comments, critical comments, and supportive comments. Groups with critical versus supportive confederate had more unique solutions but lower satisfaction.

Daly, B. (1993). The influence of face-to-face versus computer-mediated communication channels on collective induction. *Accounting, Management & Information Technology, 3*(1), 1–22. Category IA1. Lab experiment. Task type 4. Sixty-four four-person groups of undergraduates. Computer groups: more equally distributed but lower amount of participation, longer time to decisions, more errors, but no difference in number of correct solutions; rated others as less helpful and self as more anxious, nervous.

Dennis, A., Heminger, A., Nunamaker, J., & Vogel, D. (1990). Bringing automated support to large groups: The Burr-Brown experience. *Information and Management, 18*(3), 111–121. Category IB. Case study. Task types 1, 2, 4. One work group in an organization. Work group: high levels of satisfaction, and rated meetings as extremely effective.

DeSanctis, G., Poole, M. S., Lewis, H., & Desharnais, G. (1991). Using computing in quality team meetings: Initial observations from the IRS–Minnesota Project. *Journal of Management Information Systems, 8*(3), 7–26.

Exhibit 3.1. Annotated Bibliography, Cont'd.

Category IB. Field experiment. Tasks unspecified. One hundred thirty-six GDSS-supported meetings of ten quality teams in an organization over seven months. GDSS was introduced at different times in group life. The earlier in group's life the GDSS was introduced, the more the group used it, and the more the group used its more advanced (level 2) functions. System used for task- and process-related activities. Satisfaction ratings were high (no comparison groups).

Dickson, G., Lee, J., Robinson, L., & Heath, R. (1989). Observations on GDSS interaction: Chauffeured, facilitated, and user-driven systems. In R. Blanning & D. King (eds.), *Proceedings of the Twenty-second Annual Hawaii International Conference on System Sciences, 3,* 337–343.
Category IB. Lab experiment. Task type 4. Chauffeured and facilitator-driven GDSS achieved higher degrees of consensus than user-driven GDSS.

Dubrovsky, V. J., Kiesler, S., & Sethna, B. N. (1991). The equalization phenomenon: Status effects in computer-mediated and face-to-face decision-making groups. *Human-Computer Interaction, 6,* 119–146.
Category IA1. Lab experiment. Task type 4. Twenty-four four-person groups consisting of college freshmen and MBAs. Computer groups: more equal distribution of participation across status inequalities.

Easton, G., George, J., Nunamaker, J., & Pendergast, M. (1990). Using two different electronic-meeting system tools for the same task: An experimental comparison. *Journal of Management Information Systems, 7*(1), 85–100.
Category IB. Lab experiment. Task types 1, 2, and 4. Ten six-person groups of students. Groups with more flexible GDSS: better decision quality, more unique solutions; no effect for satisfaction, consensus.

Eveland, J. D., & Bikson, T. K. (1989). Work group structures and computer support: A field experiment. *ACM Transactions on Office Information Systems, 6,* 354–379.
Category IIIA. Field experiment. Task types 1, 4. One thirty-nine member standard group and one forty-member computerized group of retirees and workers of an organization. Computerized group: broader participation, fluctuating leadership, and more satisfaction with process. Standard group: less participation, greater centralization, and stable leadership.

Finholt, T., Sproull, L., & Kiesler, S. (1990). Communication and performance in ad hoc groups. In J. Galegher, R. Kraut, & C. Egido (eds.), *Intellectual Teamwork: Social and Technological Foundations of Cooperative Work.* Hillsdale, N.J.: Erlbaum.
Category IIIA. Field experiment. Task types 1, 2, 4. Seven seven- to ten-person software development teams of advanced undergraduate students; e-mail used to partition work, face-to-face preferred for substantive consensus decisions. Groups that used e-mail more: higher task quality (as judged by instructor), and more equal participation.

Gallupe, R. B., Bastianutti, L. M., & Cooper, W. H. (1991). Unblocking brainstorms. *Journal of Applied Psychology, 76*(1), 137–142.
Category IA2. Lab experiment. Task type 1. Forty four-person same-sex groups of students. Computer groups generated more ideas.

Gallupe, R. B., Dennis, A. R., Cooper, W. H., Valacich, J. S., Bastianutti, L. M.,

Exhibit 3.1. Annotated Bibliography, Cont'd.

& Nunamaker, J. F. (1992). Electronic brainstorming and group size. *Academy of Management Journal, 35,* 350–369.
Category IA2. Two lab experiments conducted at different universities. Task type 2. Experiment I compared two-, four-, and six-person groups; experiment II compared six- and twelve-person groups. All groups composed of undergraduates taking business courses. Experiment I: four- and six-person (but not two-person) computer groups produced more nonredundant ideas and had higher-quality products than face-to-face counterparts. Computer groups perceived less production blocking and evaluation apprehension, with the difference stronger for larger groups. Satisfaction decreased with group size, but not different across media for two-person groups. Experiment II replicated these findings for six- and twelve-person groups.

Gallupe, R. B., DeSanctis, G., & Dickson, G. (1988). Computer-based support for group problem solving: An experimental investigation. *MIS Quarterly, 12*(2), 277–296.
Category IA2. Lab experiment. Task type 4. Seventy-two three-person groups of MBA students. GDSS groups: more alternatives, better decision quality, longer time to decision, lower satisfaction with process and with outcome.

Gallupe, R. B., & McKeen, J. (1990). Enhancing computer-mediated communication: An experimental study into the use of a decision-support system for face-to-face versus remote meetings. *Information and Management, 18,* 1–13.
Category ID. Lab experiment. Task type 4. Eighteen three-person groups of undergraduates. GDSS groups: took longer than face-to-face groups, and remote groups took longer than proximate groups. No effects for decision quality. Remote groups less satisfied, but no satisfaction effect for GDSS.

George, J., Easton, G., Nunamaker, J., & Northcraft, G. (1990). A study of collaborative group work with and without computer-based support. *Information Systems Research, 1*(4), 394–415.
Category IA2. Lab experiment. Task type 4. Thirty six-person groups of MIS undergraduates. GDSS groups: longer time to decision, less consensus, more equal participation, no difference in decision quality, and less likelihood of emergent leadership occurring.

Hiltz, S. R., Johnson, K., & Turoff, M. (1986). Experiments in group decision making, 1: Communications process and outcome in face-to-face versus computerized conferences. *Human Communications Research, 13*(2), 225–252.
Category IA1. Lab experiment. Task types 3, 4. Thirty-two five-person groups of undergraduates. Computer groups: less total communication, less agreement, proportionately more task-oriented communication, more equal participation; no difference in decision quality.

Hiltz, S. R., Johnson, K., & Turoff, M. (1991). Group decision support: The effects of designated human leaders and statistical feedback in computerized conferences. *Journal of Management Information Systems, 8,* 81–108.
Category IC. Lab experiment. Task types 2, 4. Twenty-four five-person groups of managers and professionals. Decision quality better with designated leadership, worse with statistical feedback; less participation with statistical feedback; no differences in satisfaction.

Hiltz, S. R., Turoff, M., & Johnson, K. (1988). Experiments in group decision

Exhibit 3.1. Annotated Bibliography, Cont'd.

---

making, 3: Disinhibition, deindividuation, and group process in pen-name and real-name computer conferences. *Decision Support Systems, 5,* 1–16. Category IA1. Field experiment. Task type 4. Eighteen five-person groups of managers. No differences for amount or number of uninhibited remarks for consensus; more conservative decisions in pen-name computer condition.

Ho, T. H., & Raman, K. S. (1991). The effects of GDSS and elected leadership on small-group meetings. *Journal of Management Information Systems, 8,* 109–134. Category IA2. Lab experiment. Task type 5. Forty-eight five-person groups of undergraduates. Manual (nonelectronic support) groups had higher consensus; no main effects for equality of influence; a significant negative correlation between premeeting consensus and equality of influence for GDSS groups (but not for manual or unsupported face-to-face).

Hollingshead, A. B. (1993). *Information, influence and technology in group decision making.* Unpublished doctoral dissertation, University of Illinois, Urbana–Champaign. Category IA1. Lab experiment. Task type 3. Eighty three-person same-sex groups of undergraduates. Face-to-face groups with a rank-ordering task were more likely to get correct answer. Face-to-face groups: more comments, less time to decision. Computer-mediated groups: higher proportion of normative influence, and lower proportion of informational influence attempts; lower proportion of speculation, and higher proportion of socioemotional comment.

Hollingshead, A. B., McGrath, J. E., & O'Connor, K. M. (1993). Group task performance and communication technology: A longitudinal study of computer-mediated versus face-to-face work groups. *Small Group Research, 24*(3), 307–334. Category IIA1. Experimental simulation. Task type 2, 3, 4, 6. Twenty-two three- and four-person groups of students in an advanced undergraduate psychology class took part in a workshop that was part of that class. The workshop consisted of weekly two-hour sessions for thirteen weeks. Computer-mediated groups had poorer task performance than face-to-face groups initially, but after three weeks there were no task-performance differences. When face-to-face groups were shifted to computer condition for two weeks, midway through the study, they experienced similar detrimental performance effects, which suggests that newness to the medium, not newness of the group, underlies those performance weaknesses. Overall, there were no media differences on generate and decision tasks (types 2 and 4); face-to-face groups performed better on intellective and negotiation-based tasks (types 3 and 6).

Jarvenpaa, S. L., Rao, R. S., & Huber, G. P. (1988). Computer support for meetings of medium-sized groups working on unstructured problems: A field experiment. *MIS Quarterly, 12*(4), 645–666. Category IIA3. Lab experiment. Task type 4. Three teams of seven software designers. Decision quality: e-bulletin board best, GCSS second best, no support (i.e., face-to-face) third. No effects for participation, satisfaction with process.

Jessup, L., Connolly, T., & Galegher, J. (1990). The effects of anonymity on GDSS group process with an idea-generating task. *MIS Quarterly, 14*(3), 312–321. Category IB. Lab experiment. Task type 2. Twenty four-person groups of undergraduates. Groups with anonymous members: more total comments, more critical comments; no difference in number of supportive comments.

Exhibit 3.1. Annotated Bibliography, Cont'd.

Jessup, L. M., & Tansik, D. A. (1991). Group problem solving in an automated environment: The effects of anonymity and proximity on group process and outcome with a group decision-support system. *Decision Sciences, 22,* 266–279. Category ID. Lab experiment. Task type 2. Twenty four-person groups of undergraduates. Most solutions in anonymous/dispersed groups, least in identified/proximate. Satisfaction highest for anonymous/dispersed and identified/proximate groups.

Kiesler, S., Zubrow, D., Moses, A. M., & Geller, V. (1985). Affect in computer-mediated communication: An experiment in synchronous terminal-to-terminal discussion. *Human Computer Interaction, 1,* 77–104. Category IA1. Lab experiment. A "get acquainted" task. Forty two-person groups of undergraduates. Computer groups: less inhibited participation, less positive evaluation of others; no effect on physiological arousal, emotion, or self-evaluation.

Lea, M., & Spears, R. (1991). Computer-mediated communication, deindividuation, and group decision making. *International Journal of Man-Machine Studies, 34,* 283–301. Category IC. Lab experiment. Task type 4. Forty-eight three-person groups of freshman psychology students. For dispersed groups (using e-mail), when group identification was salient, participants showed more choice shift than did those in an individual-salience condition, exchanged fewer words (but more social remarks) and shorter messages, with a smaller proportion of remarks related to the task; participated less equally and perceived less disagreement among themselves.

McGuire, T. W., Kiesler, S., & Siegel, J. (1987). Group and computer-mediated discussion effects in risk decision making. *Journal of Personality and Social Psychology, 52,* 917–930. Category IA1. Lab experiment. Task type 4. Sixteen three-person groups of managers/administrators. Face-to-face groups performed in accord with choice-shift literature and prospect theory. After group discussion, they were more risk-averse for gains, risk-seeking for losses. Computer groups did not shift. They also showed less argumentation.

McLeod, P. L., & Liker, J. K. (1992). Electronic meeting systems: Evidence from a low-structure environment. *Information Systems Research, 3*(3), 195–223. Category IA2. Lab experiment. Task types 2, 4. Thirty-four four- or five-person groups of students. Computer groups: more task-related and fewer socioemotional comments, better performance on intellective task, worse performance on judgmental task, less satisfaction on judgmental task; no difference on intellective task; no difference on equality of participation.

Nunamaker, J., Vogel, D., Heminger, A., Martz, B., Grohowski, R., & McGoff, C. (1989). Experiences at IBM with group support systems: A field study. *Decision Support Systems: The International Journal, 5*(2), 183–196. Category IB. Field study. Task type varied by group. Three hundred eighty-seven employees of an organization, ranging from plant managers to shop-floor personnel, participated in groups ranging from four to ten persons (average size eight). Groups used GDSS with three major modules. Participants agreed that the system provided process effectiveness and reported being very

Exhibit 3.1. Annotated Bibliography, Cont'd.

satisfied; estimated man-hour savings averaging 55 percent. Participation seemed to be more equally distributed. No face-to-face comparisons were made.

Poole, M. S., & DeSanctis, G. (1992). Microlevel structuration in computer-supported group decision making. *Human Communication Research, 19*(1), 5–49. Category IA2. Lab experiment. Task type 4. Eighteen three- to five-person groups of students. GDSS groups that used the system as designed (faithful appropriation) had greater change in consensus and better outcomes. High and low consensus-change groups did not differ in amount of conflict. Increased restrictiveness of GDSS reduced action to control GDSS and increased action devoted to working on system products.

Poole, M. S., Holmes, M., & DeSanctis, G. (1991). Conflict management in a computer-supported meeting environment. *Management Science, 37*(8), 926–953.
Category IA2. Lab experiment. Task type 4. Forty three- and four-person groups of MIS and MBA students. No differences in participation or in consensus change. Conflict and conflict-management behaviors varied across structure and communications media.

Sambamurthy, V., & Poole, M. S. (1992). The effects of variations in capabilities of GDSS designs on management of cognitive conflict in groups. *Information Systems Research, 3,* 224–251.
Category IB. Lab experiment. Task type 4. Forty-eight groups (of approximately five members) of undergraduate students. Groups using a level 2 GDSS (both communications support and decision structuring) experienced more conflict than groups using a level 1 GDSS (communication support only). Groups using a computerized level 2 GDSS were significantly more capable of confronting conflict and resolving it positively than groups using an equivalent manual form of communication and consensus structures.

Siegel, J., Dubrovsky, V., Kiesler, S., & McGuire, T. W. (1986). Group processes in computer-mediated communication. *Organizational Behavior & Human Decision Processes, 37,* 157–187.
Category IA1. Three lab experiments. Task type 4. Experiment I: Eighteen three-person groups of undergraduates. Experiment II: twelve three-person groups of undergraduates. Experiment III: eighteen three-person groups of undergraduates. Computer groups: more equal participation, fewer remarks, more uninhibited behavior, longer time to decisions, more decision shift from initial individual opinions; equally task-oriented, but larger proportion of remarks were proposals. The computer technologies had essentially the same decision-making outcomes.

Smith, J., & Vanecek, M. (1988). Computer conferencing and task-oriented decisions: Implications for group decision support. *Information and Management, 14,* 123–132.
Category IA1. Lab experiment. Task type 3. Sixty-six dyads of undergraduates. Computer groups: deviated more from correct answer, shared less information, had fewer correct reasons for eliminating wrong answers, considered fewer important attributes in their decisions, perceived less progress, and perceived less freedom to participate.

Smith, J., & Vanecek, M. (1990). Dispersed-group decision making using non-

Exhibit 3.1. Annotated Bibliography, Cont'd.

---

simultaneous computer conferencing: A report of research. *Journal of Management Science, 7*(2), 71–92.
Category IA1. Lab experiment. Task type 3. Seventeen five-person groups of volunteers from professional organizations and corporations. Seven groups worked on an asynchronous system (two-week limit). The other ten worked face to face (one-hour limit). Face-to-face groups shared more of the important information, had more correct reasons for eliminating wrong answers, and perceived more progress. No differences between media for perceived freedom to participate or for deviations from the correct answer.

Sproull, L. S., & Kiesler, S. (1986). Reducing social-context cues: Electronic mail in organizational communication. *Management Science, 32*(11), 1492–1512.
Category IIIA. Field study. Task type not specified. Five hundred thirteen workers in R&D and business-product organizations; e-mail behavior was more undifferentiated by status and more uninhibited.

Steeb, R., & Johnston, S. C. (1981). A computer-based interactive system for group decision making. *IEEE Transactions on Systems, Man, and Cybernetics, 11*(8), 544–552.
Category IA2. Lab experiment. Task type 4. Ten three-person groups of students. GDSS groups: better quality of decisions, longer decision times, higher satisfaction with process and outcome.

Straus, S., & McGrath, J. E. (in press). Does the medium matter? The interaction of task type and technology on group performance and member reactions. *Journal of Applied Psychology*.
Category IA1. Lab experiment. Task types 2, 3, 4. Seventy-two three-person same-sex groups of undergraduates. Computer groups: less total communication; higher proportion of task communication, disagreement, and positive interpersonal acts; more equal participation; no difference in negative interpersonal acts; lower levels of interpersonal attraction and satisfaction. Face-to-face groups: more productive on all three task types, and higher-quality task products on intellective and decision tasks, but there were no media differences in task-product quality for the idea-generation task.

Valacich, J., Dennis, A., & Connolly, T. (in press). Idea generation in computer-based groups: A new ending to an old story. *Organizational Behavior and Human Decision Processes*.
Category IB. Four lab experiments. Task type 2. In the first three experiments, three-, four-, six-, nine-, twelve-, and eighteen-person groups were compared to nominal groups of comparable sizes. In those studies, large groups (twelve- and eighteen-member groups) using a computer system had more nonredundant ideas than equivalent-sized nominal groups; decline in average idea quality with group size for both electronic and nominal groups. In the fourth experiment (using eight nine-person groups), standard computer groups were compared with computer groups in which the technology was modified so that only one member could type at a time (to reflect the kinds of production blocking in face-to-face brainstorming groups). Standard groups: more nonredundant ideas.

Valacich, J. S., Dennis, A. R., & Nunamaker, J. F. (1991). Group size and anonymity effects on computer-mediated idea generation. *Small Group Research, 23*(1), 49–73.

Exhibit 3.1. Annotated Bibliography, Cont'd.

Category IB. Lab experiment. Task type 2. Approximately twenty-five three- and nine-person groups of advanced undergraduate business students. Large groups produced more nonredundant ideas and had higher total quality of ideas. Anonymity of members had no effect on idea generation. Identified groups had higher satisfaction and perceived effectiveness. Small-identified groups made fewest critical remarks, were most satisfied, and had highest perceived effectiveness.

Valacich, J. S., Paranka, D., George, J. F., & Nunamaker, J. F. (in press). Communication concurrency and the new media: A new dimension for media richness. *Communication Research.*

Category IA2. Lab experiment. Task type 2. Twenty five-person groups of advanced undergraduate business students. Groups using electronic communication channels generated more and better ideas than groups using verbal communication channels. Dispersed groups did not differ from proximate groups on any idea-generation measures. No differences between conditions on satisfaction.

Vogel, D., & Nunamaker, J. (1988). Health service group use of automated planning support. *Administrative Radiology.*

Category IB. Case study. Task type 1, 2, 4. One work group in an organization. Satisfaction: high levels. Effectiveness: participants said they did as much in one morning as they would have done in two days. No within-group or between-group comparisons were made.

Walther, J. B., & Burgoon, J. K. (1992). Relational communication in computer-mediated interaction. *Human Communication Research, 19*(1), 50–88.

Category IIA1. Lab experiment. Task type 4. Thirty-two three-person groups of undergraduates. Three decision tasks over a five-week period. For the computer groups, ratings of one another's composure/relaxation, informality, receptivity/trust, and social (versus task) orientation rose over time.

Watson, R., DeSanctis, G., & Poole, M. S. (1988). Using a GDSS to facilitate group consensus: Some intended and unintended consequences. *MIS Quarterly, 12,* 463–478.

Category IA2. Lab experiment. Task type 4. Eighty-two three- and four-person groups of MIS students. GDSS groups: worse decision quality than manual (structured but not electronic) groups, but better than face-to-face unstructured groups; no effects on consensus; less satisfaction with process.

Weisband, S. (1992). Group discussion and first advocacy effects in computer-mediated and face-to-face decision-making groups. *Organizational Behavior and Human Decision Processes, 53,* 352–380.

Category IA1. Lab experiment. Task type 4. Twenty-four three-person groups of undergraduates. Computer groups: more implicit and explicit proposals, social pressure, uninhibited behavior, task-irrelevant remarks, and fewer arguments. Computer groups took longer to reach decision. No difference in choice shifts.

Zigurs, I., DeSanctis, G., & Billingsley, J. (1991). Adoption patterns and attitudinal development in computer-supported meetings: An exploratory study with SAMM. *Journal of Management Information Systems, 7*(4), 51–70.

Category IIB. Lab experiment. Task type 1. Eight four- and five-person groups.

Exhibit 3.1. Annotated Bibliography, Cont'd.

Some groups adopted and some rejected a GDSS technology. Reasons for rejection included resistance, inadequate learning, perceived mismatch of technology and task, real and perceived system inadequacies, and external events.

Zigurs, I., Poole, M., & DeSanctis, G. (1988). A study of influence in computer-mediated group decision making. *MIS Quarterly, 12*(4), 625–644. Category IA2. Lab experiment. Task type 4. Thirty-two three- and four-person groups. No difference in overall amount of influence, although there were differences in patterns of influence behavior. GDSS groups: more equal distribution of influence, more communication related to procedures, less communication related to goal orientation or integration.

---

necessarily a cumulative enterprise. Even if an entire literature is made up of methodologically and conceptually sound studies, it nevertheless can have serious limitations (confounds) when regarded as a whole. Such is the case here.

Ignoring of Group and Member Factors. The studies reviewed here pay virtually no attention to any group or member characteristics. Groups vary in size (although they are mostly quite small). Little is said about composition with respect to *any* characteristics (gender, task experience or competence, length of membership in the group, and so on). To aggregate over studies in this body of literature requires us to assume that studies with participants drawn from radically different populations (college students, company executives) are essentially comparable.

Nonsystematic Coverage of Time/Space and Task Distinctions. The research to date has certainly not covered, in any systematic way, the various spatial and temporal arrangements and types of group tasks, as discussed above, nor has it compared various forms of computer-mediated groups with face-to-face groups and with one another. There are relatively few studies within any one of the space/time combinations, and there are none at all in some of them. Most of the studies involve a single, relatively short meeting of ad hoc groups performing a single, experimenter-assigned task.

Methodological Clustering of Studies. The body of literature suffers from a major confounding of several important facets. The research tends to be in "clusters"; that is, if we regard the studies done by researchers trained in or working out of a given research locale or "lab" (Carnegie-Mellon University, or the University of Minnesota, or the University of Arizona) in the aggregate, then many of those studies are likely to make use of (1) the same spatial and temporal form of the technology, (2) the same type of research strategy (lab experiment, or case study), (3) the same task type (brainstorming, or group decision), often using the same specific task within that type, and (4) a particular set of dependent variables (distribution of participation, or time to decision). What is more, the complex of studies done in a given research locale may well be the only group of studies using a particular combination of conditions and measures. Together, these limitations and confounds add up to some serious impediments to the generalization of findings. In the face of these deficiencies, we must summarize and interpret the research results with great caution.

Summary and Discussion of Empirical Findings

The findings presented in Exhibit 3.1 are summarized, one dependent variable at a time, in Table 3.2, where the numbers in parentheses represent the number of studies for which a given finding was obtained. The summary largely overlooks the confounding of results with respect to research locale, research strategy, task type, and dependent variables. It also overlooks the variations in group and member characteristics that have largely been ignored in this research area. The modal finding for *every* dependent variable, over the fifty studies, is "not tested." Even for distribution of participation over members and decision times, which are the two most widely studied variables, more than half of the studies did not test them.

If this set of findings is regarded as the extant body of knowledge about these variables, and if we wish to interpret the findings optimistically (in an "overall weight of the evidence" manner), then we can draw the following cautious conclusions.

Amount of Interaction or Participation

Use of a computer-aided communication system (a GCSS) in a work group is likely to lead to a pattern of participation that, overall, is less in amount but more equally distributed among members. Apparently, there is more equal participation in computer-aided groups, although there are some exceptions (most studies simply do not report on that variable). In virtually all cases, the equalization of participation occurs because there is a great reduction in the total number of acts in computer-mediated (as compared with face-to-face) interactions. Thus the computer does not simply reduce the participation of loquacious group members or simply increase the participation of quiet group members; it does not "democratize" group discussion, as some researchers have implied. Rather, it reduces participation for *all* participants.

In computer groups, there is less argumentation. Nevertheless, in computer groups there may be more uninhibited communication ("flaming"), especially in computer conferences, and more positive socioemotional communication. There seems to be both more task-relevant and more task-irrelevant communication, as well as relatively more influence attempts. (It is not clear how all these reported participation results—increases in many categories, but decreases in the overall amount of communication—can be true at the same time; perhaps the answer lies in the fact that most of the participation evidence is presented in terms of relative rates or proportions.) Computer systems may expose conflicts more effectively, but they may or may not have structuring procedures that help groups work through conflicts over time. All these studies have ignored how group process is distributed over time and over the group's functions, modes, and tasks.

Task Performance

Groups with computers, in spite of generating less participation or communication, take longer to carry out a given task than do face-to-face groups, at least on early task trials, before group members have much experience with the technology. These groups are also less likely to reach consensus (but they have a higher degree of consensus if they do reach consensus).

The effects of computers on quality of task performance appear to depend on the task type. Computer groups produce more ideas of higher quality on idea-generation tasks. Face-to-face groups tend to have higher-quality products on intellective and negotiation-related tasks. Longitudinal research suggests that this relationship may be attenuated over time as group members adjust to the task, to the technology, and to one another. Several studies show that a manual version of the same task (with the high task structuring of GPSS, but without electronic communication) yielded even higher-quality decisions than did GPSS with computer, decisions that in turn were of higher quality than in the "no structure" face-to-face condition. This suggests that it may be *task structure*, rather than computer mediation, that influences decision quality on these tasks. Task structure may include procedures that simplify the handling of complex information, procedures that explicate the agenda (thus making the group process more organized), and procedures that expose conflict and help the group deal with it.

User Responses

Regarding user responses, one further distinction needs to be noted: when a comparison group is used (computer versus face-to-face groups, for example), results for satisfaction and user-rated effectiveness are equivocal, about evenly split among findings of higher, lower, and no difference for computer groups. When no comparison group is used (for example, in studies using only groups in a decision room), researchers almost always find high levels of satisfaction and of user-rated effectiveness.

In almost all small-group research, performed either in the laboratory or in field settings with groups not using electronic technology, most participants report attitudes toward (that is, satisfaction with) their groups that are relatively far toward the positive end of the rating scales. To interpret the responses of computer-assisted groups as reflecting high satisfaction, without also making comparisons to noncomputer group conditions, may give us less information about user satisfaction than about systematic biases in respondents' use of rating scales. Note, too, that the term *effectiveness* has highly variable meanings in user-rating studies. In one study, *effectiveness* turns out to refer to "more equal participation."

Users may or may not like using the computer. Their attitudes may depend on their expectations before using the system, their stakes in the game, previously existing norms in the group, and/or their own experience with the system. These reactions may or may not get more favorable over time.

Conclusion

It is apparent that any generalization drawn from these results is very shaky. Each individual study may be methodologically strong and sound (although some are not), but the body of literature as a whole is burdened with a triple or quadruple confounding of communication system, task type, and research strategy. Furthermore, the literature virtually ignores all group and member variables. Finally, there is wide variation in dependent variables, and they tend to cluster within the confounded task-media-strategy clusters.

The vast majority of the research on which these conclusions are based is static; that is, it involves ad hoc groups using computer systems for a single session, often for the first and only time, as compared with face-to-face groups (whose members have been using their "technology" all their lives). There is no reason for us to be confident that any of these findings, even those that are apparently robust over studies, will be robust over time and over increased experience with the technology. Indeed, the findings of the few studies that have measured the performance of computer-mediated groups over time suggest that the static findings will not prove to be dynamically robust.

As already noted, to some extent this area currently has a half-dozen or so separate bodies of evidence — separate clusters of "facts" deriving from separate subbodies of work performed in different research settings and dealing with different communication media, different tasks, and different dependent variables. The problem is not that those sets of facts disagree; rather, it is that they cannot be compared because they deal with different parts of the domain and do so in different research languages. What this area of research needs, we believe, is not just more careful experiments showing some positive or negative impact of computer technology on work in groups. It needs more programmatic research, providing a theory-guided, multivariate, longitudinal approach that can explore all the variables in this domain more systematically than has been the case so far. Much more research is needed on what happens when advanced technology, designed to help groups do their work, is actually put to use by work groups in their day-to-day activities. We have had rapid developments in technological systems and an outpouring of thoughtful, insightful conceptualizations of these matters, but empirical research to assess the usefulness of the technology has not kept pace.

The impact of technology on groups depends on myriad conditions and factors. How well a given group with a given technology fulfills its intended purpose depends not only on what functions the technological system is intended to serve but also on the attributes of the group and its members, on the type of task the group is doing, on the operating conditions under which the members are working, and on interactions among features of the group, the task, the technology, and the context.

The impact of technology on group process and performance also operates in dynamic interdependence with key features of the group, task, and situation and is therefore contingent on the detailed, specific history of the particular group, its task, and its circumstances. Group technology can have an impact on each of several key functions — internal and external communication, information access and processing, consensus generating and conflict resolution, and task performance. Technology can aid or hinder the group in its performance of processes that lie at the core of group existence — its development of norms, its members' participation patterns, and its members' satisfaction with themselves, their group, and its work. The technology can become an integral part of the meaning of the group as a continuing, dynamic, functional social system. We need to carry out research on those systems that is both more comprehensive and more systematic than what we have done so far, and that explores key issues within a long-term, context-embedded research paradigm.

References

Daft, R. L., & Lengel, R. H. (1986). Organizational information requirements, media richness, and structural design. *Management Science, 32,* 554–571.

Kraemer, K. L., & King, J. L. (1988). Computer-based systems for cooperative work and group decision making. *ACM Computing Surveys, 20*(2), 115–146.

Kraemer, K. L., & Pinsonneault, A. (1990). Technology and groups: Assessments of the empirical research. In J. Galegher, R. Kraut, & C. Egido (Eds.), *Intellectual teamwork: Social and technological foundations of cooperative work* (pp. 373–404). Hillsdale, NJ: Erlbaum.

McGrath, J. E. (1984). *Groups: Interaction and performance.* Englewood Cliffs, NJ: Prentice-Hall.

McGrath, J. E. (1990). Time matters in groups. In J. Galegher, R. E. Kraut, & C. Egido (Eds.), *Intellectual teamwork: Social and technical foundations of cooperative work* (pp. 23–61). Hillsdale, NJ: Erlbaum.

McGrath, J. E. (1991). Time, interaction, and performance (TIP): A theory of groups. *Small Group Research, 22*(2), 147–174.

McGrath, J. E., & Hollingshead, A. B. (1993). Putting the "group" back into group support systems: Some theoretical issues about dynamic processes in groups with technological enhancements. In L. M. Jessup & J. S. Valacich (Eds.), *Group support systems: New Perspectives* (pp. 78–96). New York: Macmillan.

McGrath, J. E., & Hollingshead, A. B. (1994). *Groups interacting with technology.* Newbury Park, CA: Sage.

McLeod, P. L. (1992). An assessment of the experimental literature on the electronic support of group work: Results of a meta-analysis. *Human Computer Interaction, 7*(3), 257–280.

4

COOPERATION THEORY, CONSTRUCTIVE CONTROVERSY, AND EFFECTIVENESS: LEARNING FROM CRISIS

Dean Tjosvold

Kenny Sawyer, director of human resources at Dorsey Trailers, has this to say about a flood that engulfed the plant: "The experience taught me about the incredible power of the human spirit. The flood did a lot more to pull us together than it did to push us apart. It was one heck of a team-building exercise." Like Sawyer's, teams are often asked to solve complex problems and accomplish challenging tasks (Hackman, 1990). Physicians, nurses, and technicians experiment with new life-extending surgical operations. Firefighters must contend with the vagaries and dangers of fires in warehouses and in refineries. Command-and-control teams try to integrate conflicting information about events in the battle zone. American engineers and production specialists coordinate with British marketers to penetrate the German market. These teams cope with emerging situations where some elements are unique and cannot be fully anticipated. They operate under time pressure: being late can mean failure, even disaster.

Teams have always had to deal with crises, but more teams than ever must now operate in complex environments,

where crises are an ever-greater possibility. Rather than usher-
ing in an era of leisure and stability, our technological and economic progress has made us vulnerable (Driskell & Salas, 1991).
Political uncertainties in Europe quickly affect markets in North
America. Shootings of employees bring modern violence and
social fragmentation into our offices. Hurricanes and earth-
quakes wreak havoc on concentrated urban and seashore development. Through the sabotage of hackers, natural disasters,
and minor technical problems, disrupted computer systems halt
company operations. The rapidly changing marketplace, the
need to downsize, the pace of mergers and acquisitions, and
government deregulation foster risk and uncertainty.

  An underlying reason for our increased vulnerability to
crises is that we have become much more interdependent, so
that problems "over there" have become problems "here." Research and development, marketing, and production must work
together intensely to make a company synergistic and competitive. They share each other's mistakes and tragedies, as well as
successes. Companies are struggling with the demands of developing international strategic alliances. The computer systems
and fax and telephone lines used to keep in touch with dispersed,
diverse organizations expose our intensified interdependence and
vulnerability.

  Our interdependence, which makes us so vulnerable, also
holds the potential for us to manage our crises. The most fundamental way a group and organization can prepare for crises
is through developing committed, spirited teamwork. To cope
successfully with crises, people must work hard and skillfully
to use structures, relevant information, and procedures. To do
that, they must feel like and be able to act as members of an
effective team. This investment in cooperative teamwork not
only pays off in dealing with crises but also helps the team accomplish its assignment.

  A crisis of confidence is the most taxing of all crises because, as it questions the integrity and trustworthiness of one's
partners, it undercuts problem solving and crisis handling. A
crisis with a *trusted* other becomes defined as a mutual challenge
that both must confront together; a crisis with a *suspected* col-

league becomes a fight over who is to blame. Suspicious, hostile partners in a joint venture continually worry that they are being exploited and that their efforts will come to nought. People in a crisis of confidence often find it most difficult to confront their suspicions, and they begin to withdraw from the partnership.

Traditionally, teams have been considered too slow and cumbersome to deal with crises; strong, directive leadership is what has been said to be needed. But experienced managers and researchers have argued that special task forces are vital mechanisms for dealing with a wide range of organizational crises (Landon, 1991; Leonard, 1991a, 1991b; Overman, 1991a, 1991b; Pauchant, Mitroff, & Ventolo, 1992). Companies should develop a structure that identifies the people who will serve as a crisis task force to facilitate communication and make decisions, so that employees believe that there will be a way to get through the turmoil. The team members should use crisis drills to practice how to cope and work together. They need up-to-date, easily accessed information on how to reach employees, suppliers, and emergency services at any time of the day or night. They should have alternatives to computerized technologies for operating the business.

In addition to a crisis task force, many work groups need to prepare themselves as teams to deal with crises. A specific crisis cannot be predicted, but groups should realize that a crisis can always happen.

Many managers are aware, although often only implicitly, of the importance of strong relationships in handling crises. They frequently fail to invest in developing these relationships, however, because they have only vague ideas about the nature of productive teamwork and how to develop it. They hope that everyone will pull together in a time of adversity. This chapter uses cooperation theory and constructive controversy to suggest an ideal of effective teamwork and how it can be developed. Experimental studies have documented the causal relationships proposed by this approach; questionnaire studies provide evidence that these findings can be generalized to field settings; and interview studies have shown how cooperative goals and constructive controversy are critical for marketing products, implementing technology, responding to customers' complaints, handling grievances, and performing many other organizational tasks (Tjosvold, 1993a, 1993b, 1991b, 1990c). Studies have also explicitly demonstrated the utility of cooperative goals and constructive controversy for handling crises (Tjosvold, 1984, 1990a, 1990b).

Potential and Pitfalls of Teams

Evidence continues to mount that groups have the potential to solve complex, difficult problems effectively. Many studies have also identified significant barriers to group effectiveness.

Managers have increasingly argued that teamwork is critical to solving pressing organizational problems. Many studies support such a conclusion (Hill, 1982; Johnson & Johnson, 1989). For example, groups, as compared to individuals, can provide more accurate ratings of job performance after a time delay (Martell & Borg, 1993). Especially for an intellectual task based on a correct answer, as compared to a judgment task, a group is able to recognize the answer so that "truth wins" (Laughlin, VanderStoep, & Hollingshead, 1991). The presence of even one group member with insight into the answer typically results in the whole group's becoming committed to this response. Groups can perform at least to the level of the most knowledgeable member, even though who this member is varies from one problem to another.

Yet groups cannot be expected to be superior to individuals for all tasks. Pooling the results of individuals working alone has usually resulted in more ideas than group brainstorming, although groups appear to be better at evaluating these ideas (Diehl & Stroebe, 1991). Groups are potentially beset by numerous obstacles and barriers that prevent identifying and combining the ideas and energy of group members. Many researchers are most impressed with the difficulties of group work and the prevalence of process losses, so that groups seldom function at maximum effectiveness and, indeed, may often be ineffective (Sheppard, 1993). For example, group members may be tempted to engage in social loafing and reduce their efforts

(Karau & Williams, 1993). Making tasks more visible and making individuals accountable can reduce social loafing (George, 1992), as can the belief that others may not be willing to do the task (Williams & Karau, 1991).

Experience and skills in working together are critical (Watson, Michaelsen, & Sharp, 1991). For example, assigning high expectations has been found to help brainstorming groups generate new ideas (Paulus & Dzindolet, 1993). Through experience, groups can come to recognize the individual expertise necessary to solve some problems (Libby, Trotman, & Zimmer, 1987). The confidence that they have the needed information and expertise helps groups solve problems (Stasser & Stewart, 1992). Being familiar with each other can also aid members in their performance (Goodman & Leyden, 1991).

Evidence clearly indicates that groups are not invariably effective (Weldon, Jehn, & Pradhan, 1991). Putting people into one room and calling them a group does not mean that they can function effectively together. Expecting groups to be superior on all tasks is not justified. Groups must be well structured and managed if they are to solve organizational problems effectively and efficiently. Cooperation theory has proved useful in identifying major conditions that must be created to realize the potential of groups and overcome barriers. For example, as described in the following section, cooperation theory was able to identify when flight crew members were able to handle threats efficiently.

Handling Threats to Airplane Safety

The first officer was apprehensive as the 737 began its descent. Thunderstorms surrounded the plane. He did not have a clear view of the runway, and he had little experience with the electronic equipment. Fortunately, the other pilot was very supportive and reassured the first officer that the runway was free and the plane was on course. Working as a team and trusting each other's abilities, the two of them landed the plane safely.

As the 747 descended, the captain was preoccupied with auto land. He should have realized that the plane was not on the right glide path, because air traffic control had not given clearance to descend. The first officer tried diplomacy by telling the captain the plane's altitude, but this information did not trigger any response from the captain. When the plane reached eight hundred feet, the first officer began yelling commands at the captain, who followed them. The first officer made all the captain's decisions, including talking to the passengers. The first officer realized that his hesitation in dealing with the captain's preoccupation had put the plane in grave danger.

As these two examples illustrate, teamwork is critical in maintaining the margin of safety in the sky (Tjosvold, 1990b). It has long been recognized that flight crew members must be trained, skilled, and responsible in order to fulfill their individual roles. But cockpit and cabin crews must also effectively communicate information, discuss ideas, and coordinate efforts to cope with danger (Blake, Mouton, & McCause, 1989; Cooper, White, & Lauber, 1980; Engen, 1984; Foushee, 1984).

Confronting Safety Problems Together

Tjosvold (1990b) found many examples of flight crew members working together to minimize threats to airplanes. These examples were coded into categories to identify the major ways in which crew members worked together effectively and ineffectively:

1. *Crew members exchanged information to identify and solve problems.* For example, a flight attendant noticed a small engine fire and reported it quickly to the captain. The captain checked his instruments, and the second officer inspected the engine. They soon discovered the cause of the fire and proceeded without further incident.

2. *Crew members discussed ideas to create the best solution to a problem.* For example, the captain informed the flight attendant

that there had been a bomb threat. They kept calm and shared their information. Together they discussed how to tell the passengers that they would not be disembarking at the terminal. They decided to tell the passengers that there were technical difficulties at the terminal.

3. *Crew members demonstrated teamwork by following procedures and instructions from superiors.* After a wing engine failed upon takeoff, the captain and the officers carried out their respective duties. At the captain's command, the second officer proceeded without hesitation to secure the engine, while the first officer monitored and advised air-traffic control and obtained approach clearance. They landed the plane safely.

4. *Crew members gave information and identified a problem so that the right person could solve it.* After one of a DC8's four engines failed, everyone gave the captain information. He decided that poor weather precluded returning, and that it was too early to dump fuel. Everyone felt free to make suggestions and asked the captain to explain his delay in dumping fuel. Everyone agreed that he was making the right decision.

Failing to Coordinate

The same study (Tjosvold, 1990b) also identified situations in which failure to communicate and work together had left a plane vulnerable:

1. *Crew members sometimes did not follow procedures, but this was unintentional.* For example, when smoke was detected in the washroom, the first officer took initiative but should not have done so without instructions from the captain.

2. *People deliberately ignored advice and insisted on doing things their own way.* The captain was "behind the plane" in not thinking about approach and landing. However, he insisted on proceeding with the second leg of the flight, despite poor weather conditions and lightning. The first officer recorded his opposition to the flight on the flight recorder.

3. *Crew members were unable to discuss their opposing views openly.* The captain ordered the first officer to take the plane down a couple of hundred feet, then down another hundred feet,

and so on, with no apparent reason or explanation. The first officer followed these orders without questioning them. After the flight, the crew wondered what had happened and how the first officer had kept his cool. The captain apologized for his actions but did not attempt to explain them.

4. *Flight personnel ignored and were indifferent to their responsibilities.* The first officer was very nonchalant when confronted by the captain about his failure to check the fuel load and baggage loading.

5. *Crew members failed to communicate instructions and identify problems in a timely manner.* The captain did not inform the flight attendants, who were busy serving a meal, that the plane was ahead of schedule. When the attendants realized that the plan was descending, they did not have time to secure the equipment, make the normal landing checks, or get into their jumpseats.

Crew members have important ways of working together, but they can also interfere and obstruct. What makes the difference? When did flight crew members work together productively, and when did they fail to coordinate? The study indicates that when crew members believed that they had cooperative rather than competitive or independent goals, they were much more likely to coordinate their efforts effectively. They were then much more prepared to discuss their ideas openly and directly, so that they could manage crises together. Figure 4.1 illustrates these results, as well as what happens when goals are perceived as competitive.

Cooperation Theory and Constructive Controversy

In the 1940s, Morton Deutsch argued that how people believe their goals are related is a useful way to understand the dynamics and consequences of interaction. He later extended cooperation and competition to the analysis of inevitable frustrations, disappointments, and other conflicts (Deutsch, 1949, 1973, 1980, 1990). Hundreds of studies have developed this theory and shown it to be an elegant, powerful way of understand-

Figure 4.1. Cooperation and Competition.

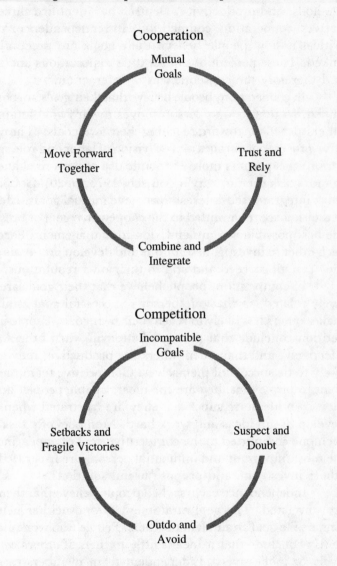

Cooperation

Mutual
Goals

Move Forward
Together

Trust and
Rely

Combine and
Integrate

Competition

Incompatible
Goals

Setbacks and
Fragile Victories

Suspect and
Doubt

Outdo and
Avoid

ing interdependence and conflict (Deutsch, 1980, 1990; Johnson & Johnson, 1989; Tjosvold, 1986a, 1986b, 1991b).

Interaction can take on very different characteristics. People's beliefs about how they depend on each other drastically affect their expectations, communications, problem-solving methods, and productivity. Deutsch has identified three alternatives: cooperation, competition, and independence. What is critical is how people believe their goals are predominantly linked. These perceptions affect their expectations and actions and therefore the consequences of interaction.

In cooperation, people believe that their goals are positively linked, so that as one person moves toward goal attainment, others also move toward reaching their own goals: "The cooperative process encourages more division of labor and role specialization; this permits more economic use of personnel and leads to more task productivity" (Deutsch, 1973, p. 20). Cooperative work integrates self-interest to achieve mutual goals. Members of a task force, committed to the cooperative goal of presenting the best possible recommendation to management, encourage each other to investigate solutions and develop proposals so that they can all succeed and add to their own reputations.

In competition, people believe that their goals are negatively related, so that one person's successful goal attainment makes others less likely to reach their own goals. People in competition conclude that they are better off when others act ineffectively, and that when others are productive, they are less likely to be successful themselves. Competitive team members want to prove that they are the most capable people, and that their own ideas are superior. They are frustrated when others develop useful ideas and work hard. Members of a task force, each one committed to the competitive goal of appearing to be the most important and influential person, are frustrated when others investigate and propose useful solutions.

Independence occurs when people believe that their goals are unrelated. The goal attainment of one neither helps nor hinders the goal attainment of others. People who work independently conclude that it means little to them if others act effectively or ineffectively. Independent team members care little whether others develop useful ideas or work hard. Independent work creates disinterest and indifference.

Whether people believe that their goals are predominantly cooperative, competitive, or independent profoundly affects their

orientation toward others. In cooperation, people want others
to act effectively and expect others to want them to be effective
because this is in each person's self-interest. They trust that their
risks and efforts will be supported and reciprocated. These three
"pure" work patterns are used here to illustrate the theory of
people working together. In reality, however, work situations
never completely correspond to a single pattern, but it is assumed that the dominant pattern will have the most influence
on interactions between participants (Tjosvold, 1986a).

The theory does not make the unreasonable assumption
that people are inevitably altruistic. It assumes only that people can understand how cooperative goals promote their own
welfare by promoting others' interests. The hypothesized effects
of competition do not rest on the assumption that people are
naturally mean-spirited and aggressive. It is necessary to conclude only that people are self-interested, and that when they
perceive the incompatibility between their goals and those of
others, they expect that what helps others will harm them.

The dynamics of cooperation and competition have been
shown to affect attitudes and productivity. A meta-analysis
confirms that cooperative experiences, as compared to competitive experiences, reduce prejudice, increase acceptance of others,
and heighten morale (Johnson, Johnson, & Maruyama, 1983).
Traditionally, competition has been assumed to motivate productivity. However, meta-analyses clearly indicate that cooperation induces higher achievement and productivity, especially
on more complex tasks and problems that benefit from the sharing of information and ideas (Johnson & Johnson, 1989; Johnson, Maruyama, Johnson, Nelson, & Skon, 1981).

Studies document that people in cooperation share information, take one another's perspectives, communicate and influence effectively, exchange resources, and assist and support
one another (Johnson & Johnson, 1989). But what is the nature of this productive interaction? It can be characterized as
constructive controversy (Tjosvold, 1985, 1989a, 1991a). Contrary
to the common assumption that cooperative goals promote har-
mony and avoidance of conflict, the theory of constructive controversy proposes that open discussion of opposing views is most

Figure 4.2. Dynamics of Cooperative Controversy.

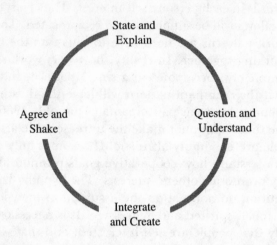

critical for making cooperative situations productive (see Figure 4.2). It is under competitive and individualistic conditions that people are more likely to avoid conflict and, if that proves too impractical, to try to win the fight or dissolve the relationship.

People in cooperation, recognizing that it is in everyone's self-interest to promote everyone else's effectiveness, freely speak their minds and reveal their frustrations (Van Berklom & Tjosvold, 1981). Protagonists welcome these confrontations and realize the importance of working out settlements, so that they can continue to assist each other. They work for mutually beneficial solutions that maintain and strengthen the relationship. They explore each other's perspectives, creatively integrate their views, and are confident that they will continue to work together for their mutual benefit. As a result of these positive dynamics, they are prepared to discuss future conflicts.

Controversy dynamics aid decision making. Because people understand opposing ideas and information and have taken each others' perspectives into account, they are able to see the limitations of their own views and to incorporate other arguments. They combine the most reliable information and the best ideas to make a high-quality decision that they are willing to implement (Tjosvold, 1982; Tjosvold & Deemer, 1980; Tjosvold & Field, 1984).

Decision makers in cooperation express controversy openly, consider opposing views without bias, and arrive at effective, integrated solutions (Tjosvold, 1982; Tjosvold & Deemer, 1980). By contrast, people who are in competition and are determined to win and outdo each other are apt to have closed minds. They reject opposing positions and the people arguing them, refuse to incorporate other ideas into their own decision making, and fail to reach agreements.

The negative dynamics found in competition and independence typically restrict information and resource exchange, distort communication, and escalate or avoid conflict. These patterns in turn frustrate productivity (except on some simple tasks), intensify stress, and lower morale. Independence and competition both encourage the avoidance of conflict.

Competitive goals make managing conflict very difficult and often lead to escalating, debilitating fights. With competitive goals, people suspect that self-interest will lead to mutual frustration. They fear ridicule and doubt that others are interested in their feelings and frustrations. Although they often prefer to avoid conflict, especially with their bosses and others who have authority and power, the underlying problems continue to frustrate them. If they do decide to confront their antagonists, they often do so in a tough, dominating manner, which escalates the conflict. Whether they choose to avoid or confront conflict, they usually feel that they have lost and only hope that others have lost more.

As suggested by the theory and as documented by studies, cooperative goals make it more likely that opposing views will be revealed and effectively discussed (Tjosvold, 1985, 1991a). This research has also helped identify the kinds of interactions that result from cooperative goal interdependence and contribute to constructive controversy:

1. People who discuss their controversies cooperatively and constructively elaborate their views and ideas thoroughly. They openly express their opinions and frustrations.

2. They search to understand the other's perspective. Feeling uncertain about the correctness and completeness of their own views and positions, they ask each other questions. They open-mindedly listen to the other's position and put themselves in the other's shoes.
3. They work for their mutual benefit and see themselves and others as "in this together."
4. They try to influence each other and are themselves open to being influenced. Decision makers who want to influence others and are open to being influenced use controversy advantageously.
5. They show respect for other people and avoid embarrassing and insulting them. This cooperative approach to controversy is also strengthened when people influence each other without trying to dominate or force each other.
6. They try to integrate others' views and ideas to create solutions that are mutually advantageous.

To maintain a cooperative approach to controversy, decision makers discuss their differences without appearing to challenge others' competence (Tjosvold, 1983). People who feel that they are weak (or appear weak and ineffective) reject opposing positions and feel competitive.

Overview of Research Support

Hundreds of studies have documented the dynamics and results of cooperative and competitive interdependence (Johnson & Johnson, 1989). Experimental, questionnaire, and organizational studies have specifically investigated controversy with cooperative and competitive contexts.

Experimental Evidence

Experimental studies have documented the causal links among cooperation, controversy, and problem solving. People confronted with opposing views have been found to feel uncertain about the most adequate solutions; they doubt that their own positions are correct (Tjosvold, 1982; Tjosvold & Deemer, 1981, 1980; Tjosvold & Johnson, 1977, 1978; Tjosvold, Johnson, & Fabrey, 1980; Tjosvold, Johnson, & Lerner, 1981). Given this uncertainty about the adequacy of their own positions, they have been found to be curious and to seek to understand opposing views. For example, people in controversy, compared to situations in which controversy is avoided, ask more questions and demonstrate greater interest in understanding opposing perspectives. They recall more opposing arguments, identify the reasoning that others are using, and predict the reasoning that others will use on new issues more frequently than people do who have similar views.

Developing a cooperative context for controversy has been found to be useful in creating the willingness to consider and incorporate opposing views (Tjosvold, 1982; Tjosvold & Deemer, 1980; Tjosvold & Johnson, 1978; Tjosvold, Johnson, & Fabrey, 1980; Tjosvold, Johnson, & Lerner, 1981). When people are trying to use controversy for cooperative ends and show mutual respect, the discussion of opposing views can be used to develop new and more effective decisions that are responsive to several points of view.

Generalization of Findings

Questionnaire studies have documented that these dynamics hold for decision making in organizations (Barker, Tjosvold, & Andrews, 1988; Tjosvold & Tsao, 1989). For example, managers answered questions to indicate whom they involved in making important successful and unsuccessful decisions, and they answered a fifteen-item questionnaire measuring how openly and cooperatively the decision makers were in discussing opposing views (Tjosvold, Wedley, & Field, 1986). Following the recommendations of the Vroom-Yetton model was modestly associated with successful decision making and accounted for about 4 percent of the variance. Discussing opposing views openly and cooperatively accounted for more than 40 percent of the variance on effective decision making.

Cooperative goals and constructive controversy have been found to contribute greatly to the effectiveness of self-managing teams (Alper & Tjosvold, 1993). For example, a midwestern manufacturing plant that had implemented a self-managing team structure five years earlier, was interested in using cooperation theory to analyze its self-managing teams. The 540 employees, involved in sixty-five teams, completed a questionnaire based on cooperation theory. (The teams were responsible for scheduling, housekeeping, safety, purchases, accident investigation, and quality.) Teams characterized by highly cooperative goals discussed opposing views openly and skillfully. These teams were also rated by themselves, their team leaders, and their supervisors as more careful, productive, and innovative than were teams with more competitive and independent goals and with less open discussion of conflicting positions. These high correlations suggest that cooperative goals and constructive controversy very much contribute to stronger teamwork and improve the performance of self-managing teams.

Serving Customers

Studies have extended research to show the vital role of the dynamics and outcomes of cooperation and constructive controversy in a wide range of decision making within organizations. For example, coordinated action is needed to respond to customers' problems successfully; often the employee who hears a complaint cannot solve the problem alone. Cooperative goals and cooperative controversy helped employees in the customer service division of a large telecommunications company combine their ideas and actions to deal successfully with customers' complaints. When employees from different departments cooperated, customers were well served, the company's image was enhanced, time and materials were efficiently used, and employees felt more confident about themselves and their work relationships. By contrast, competitive interactions wasted time and materials, damaged the company's reputation, and undermined future work. Open and cooperative discussion of viewpoints also helped managers from diverse departments assist engineers in winning contracts and improving productivity within a large consulting firm (Tjosvold, 1988).

To use their networks successfully, salespeople have developed cooperative goals and used controversy to structure specific price and service agreements and facilitate their effective implementation (Tjosvold, Meredith, & Weldwood, in press). Serving customers is not accomplished through the skill and flair of individual salespersons (Wong & Tjosvold, in press). For example, to market high technology effectively, service, training, engineering, and technical personnel must coordinate with one another and with salespersons (Tjosvold & Wong, 1992). Cooperative goals promote the open, lively discussions that result in integrated, creative solutions that solve problems and create value for customers (Tjosvold, Dann, & Wong, 1992).

Cooperative goals and cooperative controversy also contribute to the development of constructive relationships with customers. In high-quality relationships, salespersons are helpful both before and after a sale. They disclose themselves as people and indicate that they want to maintain a relationship in the future that will lead to repeat business.

A recent study documents the value of cooperative teamwork in working with customers (Wong & Tjosvold, in press). Twenty-five salespersons of a large international airline, and forty travel agents and managers in charge of corporate travel, described specific interactions. When the sales representatives and their customers believed that their goals were cooperatively related, they trusted that they could rely on each other, felt accepted, and avoided trying to dominate. They went out of their way to assist each other, give information, and explain issues. They explored their different views to solve problems and used their conflicts to strengthen their relationships. In cooperation, salespersons and clients felt good about their interaction, made progress solving problems and getting tasks accomplished, worked efficiently, formed stronger work relationships, and had confidence that they could work successfully in the future. Cooperative interactions enhanced sales and reputations.

By contrast, salespersons and clients with competitive and independent goals tended to be suspicious, avoided open and constructive discussion of ideas and differences, and attempted to dominate others. They had negative feelings, failed to make

much progress on tasks, worked inefficiently, weakened their
relationships, and had doubts about future collaboration. They
refused to listen and accommodate, lost sales, and felt disap-
pointed and embarrassed.

Research supports the argument that cooperative relationships with customers are critical because they bind customers
to the company, provide useful information on the company's
products and services, and lead to reliable, repeat business.
When sales representatives and customers develop strongly
cooperative goals, they manage conflicts, solve problems, and
form positive expectations of future encounters. Cooperation
and skillful use of controversy appear to be useful for service
both inside and outside the organization (Tjosvold, 1993b).

Organizational Innovation

Organizations must innovate so that they are prepared to serve
customers in the future with high-quality products at competitive prices. Faculty members and employees of a large postsecon-
dary educational institution were interviewed about when they
were able to solve problems in new and creative ways and when
they were frustrated and unable to develop new approaches
(Tjosvold & McNeely, 1988). When they discussed their opposing views openly and forthrightly and considered all views,
they were able to develop innovative solutions. When they discussed issues competitively from only one point of view and were
unable to incorporate different views, they failed to make progress and developed solutions low on quality and creativity.

Managers have long complained that employees resist new
technological innovations and that, as a consequence, invest-
ments do not produce the expected productivity increases. Less
recognized is the fact that in order to use the technology, employees must identify problems and discuss solutions. Cooperative employees of a retail chain were able to use new scanning
technology efficiently because they exchanged information and
hammered out ideas about how to solve the many problems that
the technology had created (Tjosvold, 1990b).

Many companies rely on performance appraisal systems to promote employee development. Less recognized is the fact that the utility of performance appraisal depends in large part on the effective discussion of opposing views about the employees' performance and plans for improvement. Managers with bosses who dealt with conflicts cooperatively, rather than handling them competitively or avoiding them, gave high ratings on quality of feedback, felt more motivated to work hard, were more committed to performance appraisal, and were confident that they could work well with their bosses in the future (Tjosvold & Halco, 1992).

With cooperative goals, people have been found to discuss problems and controversies openly and constructively and to assist and influence each other effectively. Meta-analyses support the proposition that cooperative goals and interactions contribute to productivity and morale. Studies have documented that constructive controversy contributes substantially to solving a wide range of important problems that confront organizations. This rich theoretical and empirical foundation is beginning to be used for understanding and developing teamwork and positive uses of conflict in organizations (Tjosvold, 1989b, 1991a, 1991b, 1993a, 1993b; Tjosvold & Tjosvold, 1991).

Developing Cooperative, Spirited Teamwork

There is no set program for action that helps teams, especially those operating in complex environments, accomplish their tasks. The management of crises certainly cannot be planned or programmed; beyond some general prescriptions (identifying an emergency task force, having the necessary information), teams and organizations must be free to respond to unique situations and cope as best they can. But there is a great deal of work that groups and organizations can do to prepare themselves for solving critical problems and managing crises. As we have seen, people who believe that they have strongly cooperative goals, and that they can discuss their differences openly and constructively, are much more able to respond to the unique features

of a problem or a crisis and to develop suitable plans. The time
to develop spirited teamwork is *before* a deadline or crisis. Indeed, teams should expect difficulties and crises. Investing in
team relationships is a concrete way of getting prepared to handle
them. The studies showing that cooperative goals and constructive controversy contribute to problem solving, even in complex, time-pressured situations, ties a great deal of research and
knowledge to the practical problem of crisis management. Research has underscored various ways to develop cooperative goals
and constructive controversy.

Cooperative Goals

Cooperative unity cannot be taken for granted. Even a vision
to serve customers does not guarantee it. Employees may believe that they should compete against each other, to show the
boss that they are most able to serve customers, or they may
want to prove to themselves that they are better than others.
Cooperative work at times seems impractical and costly. Employees would rather work on their own individual tasks than
take time from a busy day to coordinate. The costs of scheduling another meeting and rearranging vacation time are often
very immediate, whereas the benefits of working together to develop a new program are more distant.

　　Nor can unity be decreed. It is not enough for managers
to talk about how employees should cooperate, or to blame them
for not cooperating. People must come on their own to the conclusion that what is good for one is good for all, and that success for one is success for all. Moreover, one person cannot
cooperate alone. Everybody must see the positively related goals
and be willing to work together to accomplish them.

　　Cooperative goals are easier to establish within a small
group than in an organization as a whole. General organizational
missions and visions are often too distant and unmotivating.
Research indicates that making organizational goals concrete
and tangible through gainsharing can strengthen cooperative
unity. For example, a large utility agreed to split equally the
savings generated by employee involvement and by employees'

participation in solving problems (Petty, Singleton, & Connell, 1992). During the year of the plan, improvements on nine out of ten measures of productivity were superior to results for a division that was not part of the gainsharing program. Managers and employees attributed their success to improved teamwork.

To conclude that they have cooperative goals, people use various cues and information, including the following (Tjosvold, 1992):

1. *Commitment to serving customers.* People in the organization and on the team understand that good service demands coordinated effort. To serve customers well requires development, engineering, production, service, and sales employees to pull together.
2. *Assignment of a task and demand for one product.* The team as a whole is to develop a new product or solve a customer-related problem. The manager wants team members to integrate their ideas and develop one solution. Each team member signs off on the team's output, indicating that she or he has contributed and supports it. Then the group assigns responsibility to members for coordinating different aspects of the solution.
3. *Promotion of group learning.* All group members are expected to improve their skills in working with people, selling, and operating machinery and to help each other learn. The manager chooses one team member at random to demonstrate learning, and the team is rated on that basis.
4. *Challenging tasks.* Team members will be highly motivated to accomplish probable but difficult tasks and will recognize that they need everyone's ability and support to do so.
5. *Demonstration of how the resources necessary for success are distributed among group members.* Team members realize that, as individuals, they cannot try to accomplish the task alone but must pool their resources.
6. *Assignment of complementary roles.* One employee is asked to record ideas, another to encourage full participation, still another to be a devil's advocate and challenge common views, and yet another to observe and provide feedback in order to help the group reflect on its functioning.

7. *Accountability for unproductive groups.* Managers confront a failed team and impose some shared consequence, rather than singling out an individual to blame.
8. *Praise of the team as a whole for its success.* The manager recognizes all members of the team, and their accomplishments are written up in the company newsletter.
9. *Rewarding of individuals on the basis of group performance.* Each team member receives a monetary bonus, based on the team's success.
10. *Encouragement of team identity.* Teams devise and publicize their own names and symbols. Members focus on their common characteristics and backgrounds. Team members discuss their feelings and the values that they consider important, and they develop personal relationships (Kramer & Brewer, 1984).

Constructive Controversy

Issues and decisions come in such great variety that there is no one particular way that they should be approached. A first rule, however, is that the team must be flexible and use the approach appropriate to the situation. A leader or coordinator can dispense with minor issues efficiently; some decisions are not worth the effort of exploring in great depth, and previous solutions can reasonably be applied. At times, too, decisions must be made quickly, with little or no consultation. But an effective team approaches important, ongoing issues, such as a crisis, through constructive controversy. The team should dig into issues, create alternatives, and choose a high-quality solution that solves the problem and strengthens the group. Members use constructive controversy to explore issues and create alternatives.

To be used successfully, controversy must reaffirm the team's cooperative goals. Controversy, used in a win-lose, competitive way, or in a way that questions people's abilities and motives, tears teams apart and creates one-sided, ineffective solutions. Skillfully discussed, controversy increases trust and unity.

Teams explore issues thoroughly by protecting and stimulating diverse views. They search opposing ideas and integrate them to create workable solutions. Strategies include the following:

1. *Establish norms for openness.* Everyone is encouraged to express his or her opinions, doubts, uncertainties, and hunches. Ideas are not dismissed because they first appear too unusual, impractical, or undeveloped. Protect rights: the rights of dissent and free speech reduce fear of retribution for speaking out.
2. *Assign opposing views.* Coalitions are formed and given opposing positions to present and defend. One person is assigned to take a critical role by attacking the group's current preference.
3. *Use the golden rule of controversy.* Discuss issues with others as you want them to discuss those issues with you. If you want people to listen to you, then listen to them.
4. *Consult relevant sources.* Articles, books, consultants, and experts can provide experiences and ideas to help the group decide which course of action is superior. Include diverse people. Independent people with different backgrounds, expertise, opinions, outlooks, and organizational positions are likely to disagree.
5. *Show personal regard.* Criticize ideas rather than attacking an individual's motivation or personality. Avoid insults and implications that challenge another's integrity, intelligence, or motives.
6. *Combine ideas.* Team members avoid "either my way or your way" thinking and try to use as many ideas as possible to create new, useful solutions.

The Leader's Role

Developing teamwork, like crisis handling itself, requires both strong leadership and teamwork. But the strong leadership role in this case is much different from the "take charge and make all the decisions" role traditionally considered critical in complex situations and crises. Leaders take the initiative to nurture people and their relationships by constructing the cooperative team organization needed to achieve a vision. Employees must be willing and able to follow this lead, as characterized by the following attributes:

1. *Shared conviction.* Managers and employees first get exposure to the cooperative framework and gain a sense of its power and usefulness. Reading this chapter or other relevant books and articles, getting involved in discussions about teamwork, attending seminars and presentations, and talking to people already using teamwork and the cooperative model can get people to explore the issues further. Full debate can uncover ideas and reservations about teamwork and help people consider the pros and cons of teamwork and understand why teams must be well managed if they are to be successful.

2. *Common knowledge base.* Team members learn about cooperation and constructive controversy and begin to decide how they can apply them. They are on the same wavelength in their commitment to strengthening the team, and they have a shared set of aspirations for it, although they may have opposing ideas of how specifically to create a cooperative, conflict-positive team. Working in groups, managers and employees learn and teach each other about the framework and about how cooperation and constructive controversy reinforce each other.

3. *Mutual work.* At workshops and meetings, the team takes joint action to strengthen itself and the company. Workshop participants form task forces that report recommendations for how the team members can strengthen the team's vision, feel more united, and use their opposing ideas thoroughly. They work to achieve a living, workable consensus on the company's direction. They structure job assignments, rewards, and norms to strengthen unity. They use conflict to identify and solve problems. Task forces and other groups use their team skills to explore specific business issues, make decisions, and implement solutions.

4. *Continuous development.* Recognizing the need to continue investing in their groups and organizations (or risk creating suspicion and unresolved hostility), team members commit themselves to dealing with conflicts directly and openly. They schedule regular sessions to reflect on how they are working together and on how they can strengthen their cooperative goals.

Research Directions

Theory, research, and practice suggest important questions that ought to be explored. Studies are needed to document more clearly the value of competition and independence, as well as to understand the processes of how goal interdependence is achieved and how cooperation theory could be applied to non-Western and cross-cultural settings.

Competition and Independence

Competitive and independent work surely has an important role in organizations. Cooperative work is not always more appropriate and more effective than competition or independence. Managers and employees must take a contingency perspective and develop the goal interdependence most effective for a given situation. Most researchers, myself included, would agree with this perspective. The problem is that research has not very successfully documented situations in which competition and independence actually are effective.

Some studies suggest that competition and independence are more productive than cooperation for simple tasks, such as decoding. Indeed, it would not be effective management practice to assign a team of people to do what an individual working alone can do well. As a whole, however, the research has not consistently identified the types of tasks in which competition and independence are generally superior (Johnson & Johnson, 1989), nor have our investigations of a wide range of organizational issues identified which ones are more effectively addressed through competition and independence. Future research is needed to identify the tasks and circumstances where competition and independence are superior and then to document these in actual organizations.

One reason for the failure to document the superiority of competition is that there has not been much research using cooperation theory to explore interorganizational dynamics. Competition surely has an important role to play in the free-market system, yet research can shed some light on these issues because reality is not very close to the ideology of competition. For example, Japanese and American automakers have successfully completed joint ventures. In his analyses, Porter (1990, 1985) argues that competitors should cooperate to maintain an effective industry structure, and that in many world-class industries competitors and suppliers have worked together to create a competitive advantage for a nation. Competition appears to have limited value for relationships with customers and suppliers. Entrepreneurs have been shown to develop cooperative goals and constructive controversy with a whole network of people in order to build their businesses (Tjosvold & Weicker, 1993).

Antecedents

Group tasks, shared rewards, a common identity, complementary resources, distributed information, and a sense of community and reliance are major antecedents of cooperative goals. However, the processes by which people combine these elements in making the decision for goal interdependence needs more clarification. Managers and employees are confronted with a wide range of information, and they must sort through and organize it to reach their conclusions. Since most situations are mixed, rather than pure, the cues are not consistent. Some suggest competition; some, cooperation; others, independence.

Research is needed to investigate how human resource and industrial relations systems affect cooperative teamwork. Gainsharing seems to be able to strengthen common cooperative goals for an organization (Petty, Singleton, & Connell, 1992; Ross, Hatcher, & Collins, 1992). Research could specify how promotion and grievance systems and labor-management negotiations affect cooperative goals and constructive controversy.

Cross-Cultural Settings

Research support for cooperation and constructive controversy has been developed largely in North American and, to some extent, European settings. Some studies suggest that this framework is useful and accounts for considerable variance in problem-solving effectiveness for Chinese populations (Tjosvold & Chia, 1989; Tjosvold, Lee, & Wong, 1992; Tjosvold & Tsao, 1989) and for Dutch populations (Kluwer, De Dreu, Dijkstra, Van der Glas, Kuiper, & Tjosvold, 1993). But much more research is needed before the theory can be used in settings outside North America. In the global economy, more and more teams will be multicultural and will involve people from different nations. Research could document the extent to which cooperative goals and constructive controversy can guide these emerging teams.

Research on cooperation and constructive controversy has been additive and cumulative, but this research does suggest vital new questions that need to be explored. Attention has focused on comparing cooperation and competition, but the dynamics and outcomes of independence are less well understood. Our knowledge could be refined by an examination of how, for example, highly cooperative situations differ from slightly cooperative ones.

Conclusion: Meeting the Challenge

A crisis is a test of a group or organization. Handled well, the crisis strengthens the team. It makes members more confident and better prepared to handle future crises. Handled poorly, the crisis makes people suspicious, and they become reluctant to contribute to the team. They may look elsewhere for more reliable, credible partners. To prepare for a crisis, a group can develop itself as an effective cooperative team that confidently uses its members' various ideas and views efficiently.

During the crisis, team members combine their energies and efforts to coordinate effectively. They integrate their ideas and views to hammer out solutions that will help them get through the crisis (Cosier & Schwenk, 1990; Eisenhardt, 1989; Eisenhardt & Bourgeois, 1988). Decision makers remain vigilant,

rather than hypervigilant or indifferent (Mann & Janis, 1989).
Despite the stress, leaders remain open to the information of
employees as they explore how to cope (Driskell & Salas, 1991).
They resist the temptation to reject those with opposing views
and to impose "groupthink" despite pressing deadlines (Aldag
& Fuller, 1993; Kruglanski, 1986; Kruglanski & Webster, 1991).
In this way, for example, members of the Israeli government,
under the stress of seeing Israeli citizens held for ransom at Entebbe, explored opposing opinions, searched for disconfirming
information, and made decisions responsive to several values
(Maoz, 1981).

After a crisis, team members reflect on their handling of
it and ask how they did and did not work cooperatively and use
controversy. They celebrate their successes and use their short-
comings as opportunities to strengthen teamwork.

Crises have the potential of bringing people together as
people realize how much they depend on each other (Overman,
1991b; Landon, 1991). However, the handling of a crisis must
reinforce the cooperative community, where people are committed to each other's success.

Some managers and organizations get addicted to crises
because these push petty rivalries to the back and bring people
together. Such a strategy is risky, however, because people who
do not believe that they can pull together with others will look
for independent solutions. Continual cries of "Crisis!" are also
liable to be met eventually with disillusionment, cynicism, and
withdrawal.

No amount of preparation can ensure that a complex
problem or a crisis will be handled well, but developing strong,
spirited teamwork is a very valuable way to prepare. Then it
is more likely that people, confronted with a tough challenge,
will work together to meet it rather than blame each other and
seek independent solutions. Even if the crisis is not handled successfully, a strongly cooperative team is less likely to look for
scapegoats and more prepared to confront future obstacles.

Development of spirited teamwork requires a long-term
view. Investment in relationships does not pay off in increased
profits overnight, nor does it give the same immediate sense of

achievement that successfully coping with a present crisis does. Commentators have long complained that North American managers do not have a long-term view of the value of fostering teamwork. One reason for their short-term focus is that most managers have only a vague understanding of the nature of productive teamwork in organizations and of how it can be developed.

The research-based model of teamwork outlined in this chapter can help realize the benefits of interdependence as well as cope with its vulnerabilities. Interdependence has been shown to enhance productivity and to lay the groundwork for solving problems and managing crises. A strong cooperative team is viable protection against a crisis of confidence and ensures that teammates will come through when the chips are down.

References

Aldag, R. J., & Fuller, S. R. (1993). Beyond fiasco: A reappraisal of the groupthink phenomenon and a new model of group decision processes. *Psychological Bulletin, 113,* 533–552.

Alper, S., & Tjosvold, D. (1993). *Cooperation theory and self-managing teams on the manufacturing floor.* Unpublished manuscript. Simon Fraser University.

Barker, J., Tjosvold, D., & Andrews, I. R. (1988). Conflict approaches of effective and ineffective managers: A field study in a matrix organization. *Journal of Management Studies, 25,* 167–178.

Blake, R. R., Mouton, J. S., & McCause, A. A. (1989). *Organization by design.* Reading, MA: Addison-Wesley.

Cooper, G. E., White, M. D., & Lauber, J. K. (Eds.) (1980). *Resource management on the flightdeck:* Proceedings of a NASA industry workshop (NASA Technical Report No. CP-2120). Moffett Field, CA: National Aeronautics and Space Administration — Ames Research Center.

Cosier, R. A., & Schwenk, C. R. (1990). Agreement and thinking alike: Ingredients for poor decisions. *Academy of Management Executive, 4,* 69–74.

Deutsch, M. (1949). A theory of cooperation and competition. *Human Relations, 2,* 129–152.

Deutsch, M. (1973). *The resolution of conflict.* New Haven, CT: Yale University Press.

Deutsch, M. (1980). Fifty years of conflict. In L. Festinger (Ed.), *Retrospections on social psychology* (pp. 46–77). New York: Oxford University Press.

Deutsch, M. (1990). Sixty years of conflict. *International Journal of Conflict Management, 1,* 237–263.

Diehl, M., & Stroebe, W. (1991). Productivity loss in idea-generating groups: Tracking down the blocking effect. *Journal of Personality and Social Psychology, 61,* 392–403.

Driskell, J. E., & Salas, E. (1991). Group decision making under stress. *Journal of Applied Psychology, 76,* 473–478.

Eisenhardt, K. M. (1989). Making fast strategic decisions in high-velocity environments. *Academy of Management Journal, 32*(3), 543–576.

Eisenhardt, K. M., & Bourgeois, L. J., III. (1988). Politics of strategic decision making in high-velocity environments: Toward a midrange theory. *Academy of Management Journal, 31,* 737–770.

Engen, D. (1984). Cockpit-cabin communications. *SF Accident Prevention Bulletin, 41,* 1–3.

Foushee, H. C. (1984). Dyads and triads at 35,500 feet: Factors affecting group process and aircrew performance. *American Psychologist, 39,* 886–893.

George, J. M. (1992). Extrinsic and intrinsic origins of perceived social loafing in organizations. *Academy of Management Journal, 35,* 191–202.

Goodman, P. S., & Leyden, D. P. (1991). Familiarity and group productivity. *Journal of Applied Psychology, 76,* 578–586.

Hackman, J. R. (1990). *Groups that work (and those that don't): Creating conditions for effective teamwork.* San Francisco: Jossey-Bass.

Hill, G. W. (1982). Group versus individual performance: Are n + 1 heads better than one? *Psychological Bulletin, 91,* 517–539.

Johnson, D. W., & Johnson, R. T. (1989). *Cooperation and competition: Theory and research.* Edina, MN: Interaction Books.

Johnson, D. W., Johnson, R. T., & Maruyama, G. (1983). Interdependence and interpersonal attraction among heterogeneous and homogeneous individuals: A theoretical formulation and a meta-analysis of the research. *Review of Educational Research, 53,* 5–54.

Johnson, D. W., Maruyama, G., Johnson, R. T., Nelson, D., & Skon, L. (1981). Effects of cooperative, competitive, and individualistic goal structures on achievement: A meta-analysis. *Psychological Bulletin, 89,* 47–62.

Karau, S. J., & Williams, K. D. (1993). Social loafing: A meta-analytic review and theoretical integration. *Journal of Personality and Social Psychology, 65,* 681–706.

Kluwer, E., De Dreu, C.K.W., Dijkstra, S., Van der Glas, F., Kuiper, A., & Tjosvold, D. (1993). Doelinterdependentie en conflicthantering in profit-en non-profit organisaties [Goal interdependence and conflict management in profit and nonprofit organizations]. *Toegepaste Social Psychologie,* (pp. 208–218). Eburon: Delft, The Netherlands.

Kramer, R. M., & Brewer, M. B. (1984). Effects of group identity on resource use in a simulated common dilemma. *Journal of Personality and Social Psychology, 46,* 1044–1057.

Kruglanski, A. W. (1986, August). Freeze-think and the *Challenger. Psychology Today,* pp. 48–49.

Kruglanski, A. W., & Webster, D. M. (1991). Group members' reactions to opinion deviates and conformists at varying degrees of proximity to decision deadline and environmental noise. *Journal of Personality and Social Psychology, 61,* 221–225.

Landon, L. W. (1991, November). "We didn't fall through the cracks." *HR Magazine,* pp. 48–50.

Laughlin, P. R., VanderStoep, S. W., & Hollingshead, A. B. (1991). Collective versus individual induction: Recognition of truth, rejection of error, and collective information processing. *Journal of Personality and Social Psychology, 61,* 50–67.

Leonard, B. (1991a, November). Battling natural disaster. *HR Magazine,* pp. 50–52.

Leonard, B. (1991b, November). What luck really means. *HR Magazine,* pp. 53–55.

Libby, R., Trotman, K. T., & Zimmer, I. (1987). Member variation, recognition of expertise, and group performance. *Journal of Applied Psychology, 72,* 81–87.

Mann, L., & Janis, I. (1989). Decisional conflict in organizations. In D. Tjosvold & D. W. Johnson (Eds.)., *Productive conflict management: Perspectives for organizations* (pp. 16–45). Minneapolis: Team Media.

Maoz, S. (1981). The decision to raid Entebbe: Decision analysis applied to crisis behavior. *Journal of Conflict Resolution, 25,* 677–707.

Martell, R. F., & Borg, M. R. (1993). A comparison of the behavior-rating accuracy of groups and individuals. *Journal of Applied Psychology, 78,* 43–50.

Overman, S. (1991a, November). After the smoke clears. *HR Magazine,* pp. 44–46.

Overman, S. (1991b, November). "You may not be able to deal with this." *HR Magazine,* pp. 46–47.

Pauchant, T. C., Mitroff, I. I., & Ventolo, G. F. (1992). The dial tone does not come from God! How a crisis can challenge dangerous strategic assumptions about high technologies: The case of the Hinsdale telecommunication outage. *Academy of Management Executive, 6,* 66–79.

Paulus, P. B., & Dzindolet, M. T. (1993). Social influence processes in group brainstorming. *Journal of Personality and Social Psychology, 64,* 575–586.

Petty, M. M., Singleton, B., & Connell, D. W. (1992). An experimental evaluation of an organizational incentive plan in the electric utility industry. *Journal of Applied Psychology, 77,* 427–436.

Porter, M. (1985). *Competitive advantage.* New York: Free Press.

Porter, M. (1990). *The competitive advantage of nations.* New York: Free Press.

Ross, T. L., Hatcher, L., & Collins, D. (1992). Why employees support (and oppose) gainsharing plans. *Compensation & Benefits Management, 8,* 17–27.

Sheppard, J. A. (1993). Productivity loss in performance groups: A motivation analysis. *Psychological Bulletin, 113,* 67–81.

Stasser, G., & Stewart, D. (1992). Discovery of hidden profiles by decision-making groups: Solving a problem versus making a judgment. *Journal of Personality and Social Psychology, 63,* 426–434.

Tjosvold, D. (1982). Effects of the approach to controversy on superiors' incorporation of subordinates' information in decision making. *Journal of Applied Psychology, 67,* 189–193.

Tjosvold, D. (1983). Social face in conflict: A critique. *International Journal of Group Tensions, 13,* 49–64.

Tjosvold, D. (1984). Effects of crisis orientation on managers' approach to controversy in decision making. *Academy of Management Journal, 27,* 130–138.

Tjosvold, D. (1985). Implications of controversy research for management. *Journal of Management, 11,* 21–37.

Tjosvold, D. (1986a). Dynamics of interdependence in organizations. *Human Relations, 39,* 517–540.

Tjosvold, D. (1986b). *Working together to get things done: Managing for organizational productivity.* Lexington, MA: Heath.

Tjosvold, D. (1988). Cooperative and competitive interdependence: Collaboration between departments to serve customers. *Group & Organization Studies, 13,* 274–289.

Tjosvold, D. (1989a). Interdependence and conflict management in organizations. In M. A. Rahim (Ed.), *Managing conflict: An interdisciplinary approach* (pp. 41–50). New York: Praeger.

Tjosvold, D. (1989b). *Managing conflict: The key to making your organization work.* Minneapolis: Team Media.

Tjosvold, D. (1990a). Cooperation and competition in restructuring an organization. *Canadian Journal of Administrative Sciences, 7,* 48–54.

Tjosvold, D. (1990b). Flight crew collaboration to manage safety risks. *Group & Organization Studies, 15,* 11–19.

Tjosvold, D. (1990c). Making a technological innovation work: Collaboration to solve problems. *Human Relations, 43,* 1117–1131.

Tjosvold, D. (1991a). *Conflict-positive organization: Stimulate diversity and create unity.* Reading, MA: Addison-Wesley.

Tjosvold, D. (1991b). *Team organization: An enduring competitive advantage.* New York: Wiley.

Tjosvold, D. (1992). *Antecedents of cooperation and competition: Evidence from 15 organizations.* Unpublished manuscript. Simon Fraser University.

Tjosvold, D. (1993a). *Learning to manage conflict: Getting people to work together productively.* New York: Lexington Books.

Tjosvold, D. (1993b). *Teamwork for customers: Building organizations that take pride in serving.* San Francisco: Jossey-Bass.

Tjosvold, D., & Chia, L. C. (1989). Conflict between managers and employees: The role of cooperation and competition. *Journal of Social Psychology, 129,* 235–247.

Tjosvold, D., Dann, V., & Wong, C. L. (1992). Managing conflict between departments to serve customers. *Human Relations, 45,* 1035–1054.

Tjosvold, D., & Deemer, D. K. (1980). Effects of controversy within a cooperative or competitive context on organizational decision making. *Journal of Applied Psychology, 65,* 590–595.

Tjosvold, D., & Deemer, D. K. (1981). Effects of control or collaborative orientation on participation in decision making. *Canadian Journal of Behavioural Science, 13,* 33–43.

Tjosvold, D., & Field, R.H.G. (1984). Managers' structuring cooperative and competitive controversy in group decision making. *International Journal of Management, 1,* 26–32.

Tjosvold, D., & Halco, J. A. (1992). Performance appraisal: Goal interdependence and future responses. *Journal of Social Psychology, 132,* 629–639.

Tjosvold, D., & Johnson, D. W. (1977). The effects of controversy on cognitive perspective taking. *Journal of Educational Psychology, 69,* 679–685.

Tjosvold, D., & Johnson, D. W. (1978). Controversy within a cooperative or competitive context and cognitive perspective taking. *Contemporary Educational Psychology, 3,* 376–386.

Tjosvold, D., Johnson, D. W., & Fabrey, L. (1980). The effects of controversy and defensiveness on cognitive perspective taking. *Psychological Reports, 47,* 1043–1053.

Tjosvold, D., Johnson, D. W., & Lerner, J. (1981). The effects of affirmation and acceptance on incorporation of an opposing opinion in problem solving. *Journal of Social Psychology, 114,* 103–110.

Tjosvold, D., Lee, F., & Wong, C. L. (1992). Managing conflict in a diverse workforce: A Chinese perspective in North America. *Small Group Research, 23,* 302–332.

Tjosvold, D., & McNeely, L. T. (1988). Innovation through communication in an educational bureaucracy. *Communication Research, 15,* 568–581.

Tjosvold, D., Meredith, L., & Weldwood, R. M. (in press). Implementing relationship marketing: A goal interdependence approach. *Journal of Business & Industrial Marketing.*

Tjosvold, D., & Tjosvold, M. M. (1991). *Leading the team organization: How to create an enduring competitive advantage.* New York: Lexington Books.

Tjosvold, D., & Tsao, Y. (1989). Productive organizational collaboration: The role of values and cooperative goals. *Journal of Organizational Behavior, 10,* 189–195.

Tjosvold, D., Wedley, W. C., & Field, R.H.G. (1986). Constructive controversy, the Vroom-Yetton model, and managerial decision making. *Journal of Occupational Behavior, 7,* 125–138.

Tjosvold, D., & Weicker, D. W. (1993). Cooperative and competitive networking by entrepreneurs: A critical-incident study. *Journal of Small Business Management, 31,* 11–21.

Tjosvold, D., & Wong, C. L. (1992, June). *Cooperative conflict and coordination to market technology.* Paper presented at the meeting of the International Association of Conflict Management, Minneapolis.

Van Berklom, M., & Tjosvold, D. (1981). The effects of social context on engaging in controversy. *Journal of Psychology, 107,* 141–145.

Watson, W., Michaelsen, L., & Sharp, W. (1991). Member competence, group interaction, and group decision making: A longitudinal study. *Journal of Applied Psychology, 76*(6), 803–809.

Weldon, E., Jehn, K. A., & Pradhan, P. (1991). Processes that mediate the relationship between a group goal and improved group performance. *Journal of Personality and Social Psychology, 61,* 555–569.

Williams, K. D., & Karau, S. J. (1991). Social loafing and social compensation: The effects of expectations of co-worker performance. *Journal of Personality and Social Psychology, 61,* 570–581.

Wong, C., & Tjosvold, D. (in press). Goal interdependence and quality in services marketing. *Psychology & Marketing.*

5

RAISING AN INDIVIDUAL DECISION-MAKING MODEL TO THE TEAM LEVEL: A NEW RESEARCH MODEL AND PARADIGM

Daniel R. Ilgen, Debra A. Major,
John R. Hollenbeck, Douglas J. Sego

As the 1980s ended and the 1990s began, a great deal of attention was focused on work teams. For example, *Time* featured a cover story in October 1990 titled "The Right Stuff: Does U.S. industry have it? With teamwork and new ideas, GM's Saturn aims to show that the American manufacturers can come roaring back." A *Fortune* cover story in the same year was titled "Who Needs a Boss? Not the employees who work in self-managed teams. They arrange schedules, buy equipment, fuss over quality—and dramatically boost the productivity of their companies."

Several factors contributed to the interest. Economic setbacks in U.S. manufacturing provided an impetus for introspection, with a search for sources to which to attribute a perceived decline in the productivity of the U.S. work force. Not surprisingly, this search led to comparisons with international competitors, in an attempt to discover what they were doing right. Rightly or wrongly, one of the commonly held beliefs was that a major competitor, Japan, was successful in part because teamwork seemed to be stressed over individualism in Japanese organizations.

This, along with highly publicized work-redesign projects that organized production around work teams (such as the Volvo manufacturing plant in Sweden and General Motors' Saturn plant), led to heightened interest in teams at work.

Highly visible team failures became a second source of interest in teams. At least two civilian airline accidents resulted from breakdowns in the team routines of cockpit crews. In one case, preflight procedures failed to detect an error that should have been obvious. In another case, there was reason to suspect that casual conversation among crew members prior to takeoff distracted the crew from carefully attending to the preflight routine. And in the most publicized of all team errors, a command-and-control team of the *Vincennes,* a U.S. Naval vessel stationed in the Persian Gulf in July 1988, mistakenly identified an Iranian commercial airliner as a hostile military aircraft and shot it down.

Common to all teams is the need to make team decisions. The establishment of teams in the workplace shifts decision-making responsibility for many decisions from supervisors and middle management to teams of workers directly involved with the organization's primary objective — the production of goods or services. Cockpit crews and command-and-control teams coordinate information and then make decisions critical to the operation of the aircraft or unit. In all cases, information is processed by individuals and shared among them in some fashion. Decisions or judgments are then rendered and represent the results of collective team actions. One clear message from all of the recent interest in teams is that there is a strong need for better understanding of team functioning and decision making in all kinds of situations and conditions, particularly conditions of high stress. It is in the spirit of this latter conclusion that this chapter was written.

Team Decision Making: Definitional Issues

Teams

Research on issues related to teams appears in the literature under the headings *teams* or *small groups,* with a far larger proportion of the work falling under the latter heading. From a review of the small-group research, McGrath (1984) concludes that virtually all definitions of the term *small group* include three attributes: two or more individuals, interaction among group members, and interdependence among them in some way. To these three, McGrath adds that a small group exists in some time frame; that is, it has a past, a present, and a future. Both the past and anticipation of the future will influence the present behaviors of small-group members. Left unanswered is the question of how small "small" is. Most would agree that a small group is small enough so that all group members can be aware of each other, but the exact limits on size depend on other factors, such as the nature of the task or the amount of interaction. We, too, will leave the size limit open, with a lower-bound exception: dyads are often considered teams. We have chosen to exclude them because there are a number of important team processes that do not occur in dyads, such as coalition formation and complex patterns of status and communication. We recognize that the exclusion of dyads is arbitrary, but it is consistent with the types of team problems that we have chosen to address.

From our perspective, teams share the foregoing characteristics with small groups, with one additional characteristic: teams exist for some task-oriented purpose. They design buildings, plan fundraising campaigns, play basketball games, and so on. Typically, they do not exist for purely social reasons. One might consider four or five good friends who gather every Friday after work to be a small group, but rarely would such a group be considered a team. Teams have explicit goals and, with few exceptions, the members of a team have some level of awareness of the team goals. Thus, when we speak of teams in work-oriented organizations, we add yet another defining characteristic: shared goals. The definition of *team* that most closely captures what we will assume for our discussion is taken from Morgan, Glickman, Woodard, Blaiwes, and Salas (1986), who state that teams are "distinguishable sets of [more than two] individuals who interact interdependently and adaptively to achieve specified, shared and valued objectives" (p. 3).

Team Decision Making

Decision making falls within a family of loosely related theoretical perspectives and research paradigms known as *information processing* (Lachman, 1987). These theories are concerned with how individuals select and process information to be used either in the present or later to make decisions. The complexities of individual decision making are enormous, both in terms of the nature of the information available to individuals and in the way people process information by attending, coding, storing, recalling, and combining it to reach decisions.

All individual decision-making models or theories share two basic assumptions. The first of these is that individuals base their decisions on some finite set of elements, often called *cues*. The word *finite* must be qualified, however. Such sets of information are often finite only in the sense of the individual's use of them. In actuality, there may be an infinite number of dimensions of information that have some relevance to a decision, but individuals may treat them as if they were finite, or at least probabalistically finite. The second assumption is that individuals combine these cues in some fashion to reach decisions. Beyond these two assumptions, the commonality among models breaks down, often on the basis of assumptions about what will constitute the criteria for judging the quality of a decision. Two decision-making models dominate, one based on the use of conditional probabilities (the Baysean model) and the other based on a regression model with weights for cues and the combination of cues (the Brunswik lens model). The team decision-making model to be developed later in this chapter is an adaptation of the lens model. In the lens model, it is assumed that some set of cues exists that is relevant to a particular decision, either individually or in interaction, that the weights for the cues and their interactions are known or can be discovered.

As if individual decision making were not complex enough, team decision making adds a number of other complexities. Although the decision itself can be raised to the level of the team by simple analogy, the fact remains that team decisions are still made by members of the team working together. Thus, team decision making is a multilevel phenomenon that must take into account individual and team processes. At the individual level, each team member may reach a decision on the basis of some consideration of a set of cues and their weights. Within the team, however, individual members may have information about different cues. Individuals within the team may also have different weights for the same cues. The nature of the distribution of knowledge about cues and their weights, as well as the nature of the interaction among the team members in the decision process, is in part a function of previously established roles and individual differences. Consider for a moment the decision to purchase a new production robot, a decision to be made by a team that includes a design engineer, a manager of the production unit that will use the robot, a purchasing agent, and a person who is to be trained to operate the robot. Together, they are to make a team decision about what robotic system to purchase. In such a situation, expertise is distributed among the team members, with no one member possessing all the relevant information. In addition, even when team members have access to the same information, they may evaluate or weigh it much differently. For example, a purchasing agent and a line manager on the same team may have very different views about the importance of price in the final decision, even when they both have access to the same price information. They also have different areas of expertise, and so they can address different domains of the problem. Such a situation is an example of *team decision making under conditions of distributed expertise*. In sum, when decision making moves to the team level, there are both individual and team-level constructs that are derived from the decision process itself.

In addition to decision-making constructs, there are other uniquely team-level constructs that have an impact on decisions and have no individual-level analogues. Such constructs as trust in others, cooperation, coordination, and power or status differences among team members exist within teams. The team-level variables may affect team decisions either directly or in interaction with individual variables. For example, the power or status of an individual may have a direct effect on a team's decision, by increasing the weight given to the judgments of people in high-power positions, where trust among members may interact with the mean ability level of the team so that under conditions of high trust and high ability the team does well but does not do well under low trust, regardless of the mean ability level. Clearly, team-level variables do affect team decisions.

In the remainder of this chapter, we shall focus on decisions that are made by teams — that is to say, although individuals on the team do contribute to the decision, the decision that is reached is attributed to the team, rather than to any individual or individuals on the team. The way team members contribute to the team decision will vary according to the team decision-making structure, but it is assumed that more than one of the team members' judgments will be expressed and, in some fashion, will contribute to the overall decision. Before we turn to the development of our team decision-making model, we will briefly (and selectively) review the past research on team decision making, as background for the approach taken here.

Past Approaches to Team Decision Making

A great deal of work exists on team decision making. Much of it appears under the heading *group decision making*. Regardless of the label, if the work involves a set of individuals who interact interdependently and adaptively to reach some decision, we have considered it to be team decision making for the purpose of our discussion. We took the liberty of referring to the collectives as *teams*, even when the authors labeled them *groups*, if the collectives fit our definition of teams.

Team Decision-Making Criteria: Internally Referenced

Virtually all the research on team decision making is concerned with some outcome of the decision-making process. Outcomes can be classified into two sets. One set is concerned with outcomes of the decision making *process*, or the feelings and reactions of the team members that result from reaching decisions in teams. In a sense, these outcomes are referenced internally (internal to the team itself). The other set deals with the quality of the decision, as judged against standards or criteria external to the team. The vast majority of the research deals with internally referenced criteria; that is, the primary concern of most of this research is with team decision-making *processes*. Information flow in teams, as a function of such things as the extent to which it is common to all members (Stasser & Titus, 1985); the use of available information (Argote, Seabright, & Dyer, 1986); use of feedback (Tindale, 1989) — these are just a few examples of some of the process factors studied. Two examples of internally referenced work are addressed below.

Consensus. This is one of the most commonly investigated internal criteria (Davis, 1992) and is perhaps most thoroughly researched in the jury decision-making literature (see Gerbasi, Zuckerman, & Reis, 1977; Penrod & Hastie, 1979; Stasser, Kerr, & Bray, 1982; Stasser, Kerr, & Davis, 1989). Typically, in this research, a particular consensus rule is described or proposed, and teams (real or mock juries) are observed with respect to the extent to which they use the rule and with respect to the factors that influence their use of the rule. Other consensus research has varied the composition of teams and looked at the effect of the homogeneity or heterogeneity of team members on selected individual-difference variables. Liddell and Slocum (1976) studied the effects of the degree of personality and role compatibility on team decision-making effectiveness. They assessed group members with respect to the amount of control desired and the amount bestowed on them by role requirements. Compatible groups, defined as those in which high-control individuals were able to have the most influence and low-control ones were not required to exert influence, made faster decisions and fewer errors on a symbol-identification task.

Coalition Formation. A related line of research concentrates on the nature of the coalitions that are formed among team members who have to reach a decision and the effects of such coalitions on the decisions that are made. (See Komorita, 1984, for an excellent review of the coalition-formation literature.) In coalition-formation research, members of teams are required to make choices, and the variable of interest is who aligns with whom to reach a decision. Individual team members are typically viewed in terms of the resources that they possess and the power that they wield within the team as a result of these resources. As is the case with most of the internally referenced criteria, the decision reached by the team is of less interest than is the way in which the team reaches that decision.

Team Decision-Making Criteria: Externally Referenced

In contrast to internally referenced criteria are externally referenced ones that focus on the quality of decisions resulting from the team decision-making process. In this case, some external standard exists for evaluating the decision that is reached. With respect to the quality of their decisions, teams are studied against the standard itself, relative to other teams, or relative to an equal number of *individuals* working on the task alone. Examples of the latter type of study are research that compares the quality of team decisions made by consensus (where all team members reach agreement) to the quality of individual decisions (see Argote, Devadas, & Melone, 1990; Yetton & Bottger, 1982) or research that looks at decision quality as it is related to the nature of team consensus (see Castore & Murnigham, 1978; Sniezek & Henry, 1989, 1990).

When the task of a team has a major decision component, and when the performance of the team is a function of the quality of team decisions, the research on team performance fits into the category of externally referenced criteria for team decisions. Only research in which team performance is judged according to some preestablished quality standards fits into this category. The work of Laughlin and his colleagues is a good example of such research (Laughlin, 1980; Laughlin & Adamopolus, 1980, 1982; Laughlin, Kerr, Davis, Halff, & Marciniak, 1975; Laughlin, Kerr, Munch, & Haggarty, 1976). For instance, Laughlin, Kerr, Davis, Halff, and Marciniak (1975) used a difficult English-vocabulary test to examine the performance of teams consisting of two to five members. The test had objectively correct answers, and the researchers found that a "truth wins" process was the best representation of the groups' decision processes; that is, once the correct answer was proposed, a group typically reached consensus. Similar results were obtained in studies using a more extensive verbal-achievement test (Laughlin, Kerr, Munch, & Haggarty, 1976) and a verbal analogies test (Laughlin & Adamopolus, 1980).

In spite of the dominating interest in team performance and the fact that decisions are likely to play a major role in the performance of many teams, there is very little work that combines the two areas. Typically, when the interest is in performance, decision making is assumed to be of interest but is not assessed. It is assumed that if the team performed well, good decisions were made, and that if it did not, then the decision-making issues may or may not have been handled well. Often, however, when decision making is the focus, subsequent team performance resulting from the decision is not investigated. Assessment of the decision or of the way the decision was made completes the investigation, with no evaluation of the quality of the decision. As we will argue, there is now some shifting of this limited outlook on team decision making.

Shifts in Approaches to Team Decision Making

More recently, we have seen heightened interest in teams that make important decisions and in actual decisions that have externally referenced criteria. As already mentioned, much of the interest has been stimulated by things "gone wrong"—a failing economy, airline accidents, military mistakes, and so forth. In all cases, the decisions were evaluated against external criteria that left no doubt about what was good or bad.

Case Studies

Hackman (1990) includes a number of examples of teams and team research that fit the current focus. For example, Denison and Sutton (1990), in their contribution, describe a case in which operating-room nurses were structured into teams. Increased participation in decision making, opportunities for cross-training, and greater flexibility were among the noted advantages of teamwork. In another case, Eisenstat (1990) discusses the start-up of a manufacturing team, touching on several variables that influenced its success, such as managerial support, availability of expert advice, and a motivating task. For both Denison and Sutton (1990) and Eisenstat (1990), external criteria provide the rationale for looking at the teams. Assuming that the current trend toward increased use of teams in important organizational roles will continue, research on teams making critical decisions should increase.

Cockpit Crews

Foushee (1982, 1984) has conducted extensive research with the National Aeronautics and Space Administration (NASA). He has found that members of crews with higher error rates are more uncertain when responding to task demands, experience greater frustration or anger, more frequently report being embarrassed, and tend to disagree among themselves more frequently (Foushee, 1982). Gregorich, Helmreich, and Wilhelm (1990) have developed an attitudinal instrument directed specifically at cockpit crews, to be used for measuring attitudes in order to understand the team processes likely to affect decision making in this critical setting under normal and stressful conditions.

Teamwork

Morgan, Glickman, Woodard, Blaiwes, and Salas (1986) have begun an equally important line of research aimed at defining and measuring team behaviors. Working inductively from the literature, and also from data gathered in extensive interviews, they have identified critical dimensions of teamwork. Then, with an instrument based on what was learned, teams constructed for the purpose of training were evaluated, to assess the impact of teamwork dimensions on the quality of team performance in tasks requiring decisions.

The three kinds of research just cited fit into the domain of *team research with externally referenced criteria*. They also deal with team decision-making processes. In our opinion, they address several interesting and important team decision-making issues.

At the same time, although team decision making plays an important role in all these areas, the approach to the problem has been from the perspective of teams, rather than from that of decision making. As a result, clear development of the decision-making issues for teams is lacking in this work.

One way to address this shortcoming is to attempt to apply the extensive literature that does exist on decision making to the team setting. As indicated earlier, this work is primarily focused on individuals, not teams, and so a necessary task is to interpret our knowledge of individual decision making with respect to the demands known to face teams. We address that task in the remainder of this chapter.

Common Threads

The actors, settings, and problems faced by teams have dominated interest, both practically and theoretically, in the last few years. They differ widely, but there are a number of similarities among them. First, teams are usually composed of members who have a common goal but bring different knowledge and skills to team subtasks. Not all team members know or understand all phases of the team's task, but they work together with the others to produce an integrated action. Thus, for example, a television news team, with reporters who know little about operating cameras and camera operators who do no reporting, can produce excellent news stories. Differential expertise, applied to subtasks within the team and integrated into a team decision, has been described as *distributed decision making with teams of differential expertise* (Vaughan, 1990) and is an important part of most of the teams of interest in the late 1980s and beyond.

A second overarching similarity among the teams of interest is that they operate in high-stakes environments. In the case of cockpit crews, lives depend on their actions. In almost all cases, the teams have a number of complex tasks that must be performed in coordination with others, often under severe time and resource constraints.

Third, continuity and interdependence must be maintained in most of the teams of interest; they do not function in isolation. Decisions made at one time must be integrated with the past history of the team, and the potential future consequences of actions cannot be ignored, since the team members often must continue to work together. The teams of interest also tend not to be isolated from other persons, teams, and organizations. They are typically immersed in a complex web of interdependence.

In our approach to team decision making, we try to keep in mind the characteristics common to the teams of interest. In particular, we address teams that focus on overall performance, where *differentiated members* combine resources to make and implement *ongoing decisions* in *high-stakes environments* characterized by ambiguity, high work loads, time constraints, and systems embeddedness.

A Model of Team Decision Making

Individual Decision Making

Stevenson, Busemeyer, and Naylor (1990), in a comprehensive and insightful review of individual judgment and decision making, point out that a wide variety of models of individual judgment and decision making represent two general orientations. One orientation is prescriptive or normative. It is the approach typically taken by management scientists, engineers, and statisticians. Models are developed, and decisions are judged against the models, with the "correct" decisions representing those that fit the models best. The prescriptive or normative nature of the work attempts to train or in other ways to aid the decision maker to bring decisions more in line with the model (to make the "right" decisions). The second orientation is descriptive and is more likely to be adopted by psychologists, political scientists, and sociologists. In this case, the task is more that of learning how people make decisions and then building models of that decision process. Such models are not presumed to be correct, in the sense of being "right," but are judged on the degree to which they fit the decisions that people make. Stevenson, Busemeyer, and Naylor (1990) argue that decision making requires an interdisciplinary approach, which integrates prescription and description, but they limit their attention to descriptive models. Like Stevenson, Busemeyer, and Naylor (1990), we endorse an integration of prescriptive and descriptive approaches to decision making, but we also build our model on a descriptive one from the individual-decision and judgment literature. (In the decision-making literature, the terms *decision* and *judgment* are typically used interchangeably. In this chapter, to avoid confusion, we shall not make a distinction between the two and shall use the term *decision* when we mean either a decision or a judgment. In other writings, we have argued that there are special cases where a distinction between the two terms is useful, but those cases will not be addressed here. See Hollenbeck et al., in press.) We shall return to some prescriptive issues after presenting the model.

The individual model chosen for adaptation to group decision making is a correlational model developed by Brunswik in the 1940s and the 1950s (Brunswik, 1940, 1943, 1955, 1956) and called the Brunswik lens model by many since that time (see Figure 5.1).

The model construes decisions as resulting from the evaluation of a finite set of cues, or predictors, represented by the vector of Xs in the center of the figure. Each X represents a value on some cue dimension. For example, if the decision involved the selection of a job applicant from a number of candidates, X_1 might be previous experience, and the value (X_{1i}) might be time in years. From the set of predictors, there are two sets of decision-making rules. Each set is represented by a function (typically linear), where the cues are combined and weighted to lead to a decision. In the job-applicant selection example, the decision would be that of selecting the applicant, and the function would be the description of the combination rule for weighting all the cues to make a select-or-reject decision on each applicant. In Figure 5.1, the shaded region represents one function, and the unshaded represents another. The symbols r_i' and r_i represent the weights of the cues in the respective functions, with respect to the contributions of the cues to the final decision.

The shaded portion of the figure represents the set of predictors (X_1 through X_n), a criterion (Y_d'), and a set of linear

Figure 5.1. Brunswik Lens Model of Decision Making.

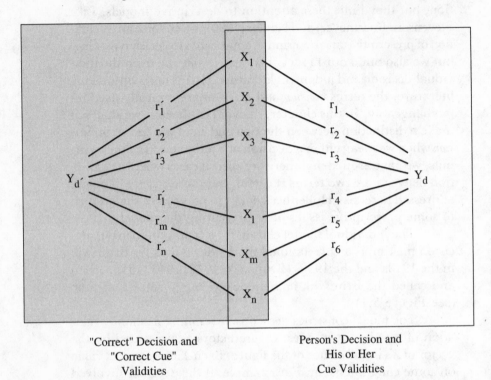

<table>
<tr><td>"Correct" Decision and
"Correct Cue"
Validities</td><td>Person's Decision and
His or Her
Cue Validities</td></tr>
</table>

Source: Adapted from Blum & Naylor, 1968, p. 456.

weights (r_1' through r_n') for the predictors of the criterion. For the typical research paradigm using the model, the linear model relating predictors or cues to the criterion is known. That is to say, if the model were used as shown to study selection decisions, decision makers would be presented with a number of applicants, each with values on each of the *n* cues, and the researcher would have created, a priori, a particular functional relationship between the cues and the criterion. For the given problem, the a priori model is considered the "correct" model to which the decision maker's choices would be compared. Individuals would then be presented with a number of applications and asked to make selection decisions.

With the combination of the known cue values represented by the applicants and the decision maker's decisions regarding each applicant, the linear equation for the way the decision maker used the cues to make decisions could be generated. This is represented by the weights (r_1 through r_n) in the unshaded area of Figure 5.1. Finally, on the basis of a number of comparisons within or across the "correct" model and the decision maker's model, some interesting theoretical and practical questions can be addressed. For example, if X_1 represents previous experience in a selection problem, a comparison of r_1' to r_1 will provide information about whether the decision maker puts more or less weight on previous experience than the a priori model says he or she should. Although there are a large number of ways the model is used, many comparisons constructed within it, and many cues generated, Figure 5.1 provides a basic construal of some of the primary elements of the model.

The decision model outlined in Figure 5.1 is based on the assumption that individuals are rational decision makers who obtain information on the relevant set of cues for any particular decision, assign weights to the cues, and reach decisions. Under ideal conditions, decisions can be shown to follow the model quite closely. Under most conditions, however, the gap between the "correct" model (on the left) and actual decisions (on the right) is not small. A large body of research offers explanations for the gap between the two models. Much of it relies on the assumption that human information-processing abilities are limited. As a result, people simplify the decision process.

March and Simon's notion (1958) of "satisficing" rather than "optimizing" is based on the observation that people cannot search all alternatives (that is, cannot identify all cues or observe all combinations of cue values) and select the best alternative. Rather, they search until they have found one (or two, or a few) that clears the criterion of acceptability, and then they select that alternative. Similarly, Kahneman and Tversky (1973) have stimulated a great deal of research on biases in decision making that resulted from the simplifying strategies they labeled *heuristics*. Their descriptive research aims at identifying and labeling heuristics and describing the types of effects that particular heuristics have had on actual decisions. Much of the recent work on individual decision making has focused on heuristics and other decision biases, on the assumption that the information-processing demands of most decisions are far from simple and are often beyond human capacity, thus requiring individuals to simplify the process.

A Team Lens Model

Brehmer and Hagafors (1986) argue that when an organization is faced with a complex decision problem, the most common way of simplifying it is to assign the complex decision to a staff of experts. The experts divide the larger problem into a number of subproblems, each of which is assigned to another expert. The Brehmer and Hagafors model (1986), presented in Figure 5.2, is a special case of such a situation, in which the complex problem represented by the column of cues is subdivided into sets of two cues assigned to each of three individuals. These individuals reach individual decisions in their own areas of expertise (in the areas represented by the two cues

Figure 5.2. The Brehmer and Hagafors Model of Staff Decision Making.

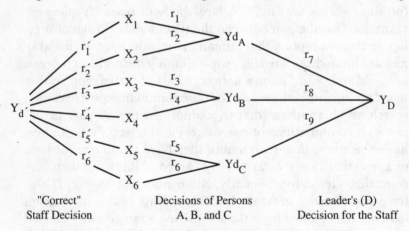

"Correct"   Decisions of Persons   Leader's (D)
Staff Decision   A, B, and C   Decision for the Staff

Source: Adapted from Brehmer & Hagafors, 1986, p. 183.

assigned to them). Their decisions serve as inputs (cues) for the leader, who makes a decision for the staff. Under such conditions, the subordinates make a decision on two cues, and the leader needs only to consider the three decisions from his or her subordinates' cues for reaching a decision for the staff.

In a laboratory study designed only to be illustrative of some empirical issues that could be addressed in the model, Brehmer and Hagafors (1986) varied the validity of the initial set of cues and the validity of the subordinates' decisions. Only leaders were used as subjects, and subordinates' decisions were experimentally manipulated: each leader was provided with decisions supposedly made by subordinates, who had seen particular cue values. A number of interesting findings resulted. For example, if one subordinate made less valid decisions than the other two, then the leaders, presented with the cues themselves rather than with the subordinate's decision, underutilized the cues that were the responsibility of the less reliable subordinate. The interesting general finding, in our opinion, was the fact that it was not easy for leaders to learn how to make good decisions under the staff-structure condition. It was not at all clear that the hierarchical structure simplified the decision process for the leader. Clearly, there is a lot more to be learned. Unfortunately, little has been done to study staff decisions, either under the simple model represented in Figure 5.2 or under more complex ones that match a wider set of staff and team situations.

A Distributed Decision-Making Model of Team Decision Making

The Model

By their own admission, Brehmer and Hagafors (1986) present a very limited team adaptation of the social judgment model of individual decision making. In particular, it is limited to team decisions (labeled "staff decisions" by the authors) in which subordinates have exclusive access to a limited subset of information (cues) and team leaders base team decisions only on the inputs of their subordinates. In addition, to our knowledge, the one study based on the model was limited to how team leaders learned to make decisions. While team learning is an extremely important part of team decision-making processes, it is not the only important one.

Our goal was to build on a lens-type model of decision making, both by modifying the basic structure in ways that would represent team decision making when expertise is distributed across members and by extending the team processes of interest beyond those of learning. To describe the team model, we begin with the characteristics of a hierarchical team and build a decision-making structure onto it.

Figure 5.3 illustrates a hierarchical decision-making team with four members. Such teams have three primary characteristics. The first of these is hierarchy: team members are not of equal status. In the illustration, member D is of higher status than the other three members reporting to him or her; the other three members do not differ in formal status.

The second characteristic is that the primary task of the team is to make decisions. In the case illustrated here, each of

Figure 5.3. Hierarchical Decision Making on a Four-Person Team.

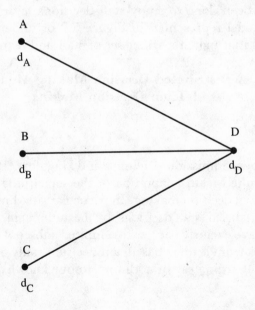

the subordinate members reaches a decision or judgment (d_A through d_c), and the subordinate's recommendation is passed on to the leader, who also makes a decision (d_D). Typically, and as is the case in Figure 5.3, the leader's decision represents the decision of the team. Figure 5.4 builds on the hierarchy shown in Figure 5.3 by introducing a new construct: distributed expertise. The distribution of expertise is represented by the allocation of critical information about the decision to individuals on the team. The pattern of distribution represents the expertise system. On the far left of Figure 5.4 is a column of cues (*X*s). As was the case at the individual level, each *X* is a vector element, where the elements (X_1) represent specific values on the dimension for each of the decisions. Expertise is represented in the figure by the association of information with individuals. Individuals' areas of expertise are construed to be described by the pieces of information to which each person has access. In Figure 5.4, person A is an expert in the knowledge domain represented by X_1 and X_2, and so on.

Note that it is not necessary for information to be the unique property of one person. In Figure 5.4, information on dimension 2 is available to persons A and B, and the leader has direct knowledge about both 1 and 6, even though those dimensions are also known by persons A and C, respectively. Although it is not necessary for all information to be available to only one team member, it is also not acceptable for all the members of the team to have direct access to all the relevant information. In other words, when everyone knows all the information without having to get some of it from other team members, the level and nature of expertise is not considered to be distributed.

Figure 5.4 introduces the third important characteristic of a team: a communication structure. By definition, communication structures exist among persons. The one illustrated in the figure shows person A being able to communicate directly only with the leader, person D; persons B and C can communicate directly with the leader and with each other. Finally, the leader communicates directly with each of A, B, and C. On this team, it is still possible for all persons to communicate with all the others, but for person A the communication with persons B and C is indirect; that is, A must go through D to get messages

Figure 5.4. A Communication Structure for a Four-Person Team.

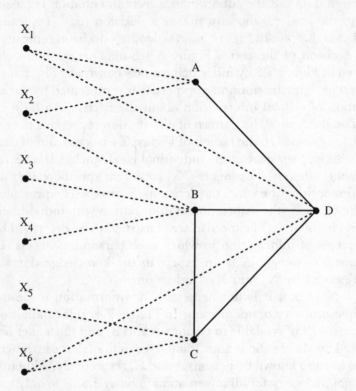

to and from the other two subordinates, and persons B and C must do the same to get messages to A.

According to our model, the combination of the communication system with the expertise system provides the structure within a team for potential access to information by each team member. Take, for example, person B in Figure 5.4. This person may obtain information on X_2, X_3, and X_4 directly. The person is one step removed from information on X_5 and X_6; he or she can ask person C for that information (assuming that person C honors person B's request) and, for X_6, the same can be done through the leader. Finally, person B can obtain information on X_1 indirectly, by going through two persons — first the leader, who can then go through person A to get the information and relay it back to B. A similar two-step indirect path exists from B through the leader and person C to information on X_5. In most cases, however, it would appear to be more efficient to get that information by going directly to person C.

With Figure 5.4, we have incorporated distributed expertise into a team hierarchy in such a way as to provide a structure for describing how information becomes available to team members for making decisions. The availability of information relevant to a team decision represents a necessary but not sufficient condition for reaching a decision. The remainder of the process involves the decision itself. In particular, the concern is with how the information is used by the team to reach a decision and with the quality of the decision. In order to evaluate the latter, decision-making research typically has used decisions whose quality can be evaluated against established criteria.

Figure 5.5 introduces the decision process into the combination of the hierarchy (Figure 5.3) and the expertise and communication systems (Figure 5.4). As in the first two figures, six dimensions of information are used to reach a decision (X_1 through X_6). Working left from the Xs, the "correct" decision is represented by Y_d'. The lines between the dimensions of information and the decision represent the extent to which each one of the dimensions is related (contributes) to the decision. In the individual decision-making literature using the Brunswik lens model, a linear-regression model is used to relate dimensions to decisions. Regression weights are chosen and then sets of cues and decisions are generated to match the chosen model. The team construal of the decision model represented in Figure 5.5 is exactly analogous to this. Here, a set of cue values is generated, along with a set of decisions, in order to fit a model, and the model generated from the same set of cues presented to the group is represented in the left-hand portion of Figure 5.5. The Y_d' is the "correct" decision, to which the team's decision can be compared.

The right-hand portion of Figure 5.5 represents decisions made on the team. As illustrated, there are two sets of decisions. The first of these includes the decisions made by persons A, B, and C, symbolized by Y_{dA}, X_{dB}, and Y_{dC}. The figure illustrates the case in which all six sets of information are used

Figure 5.5. Hierarchical Decision Making
on a Four-Person Team with Distributed Expertise.

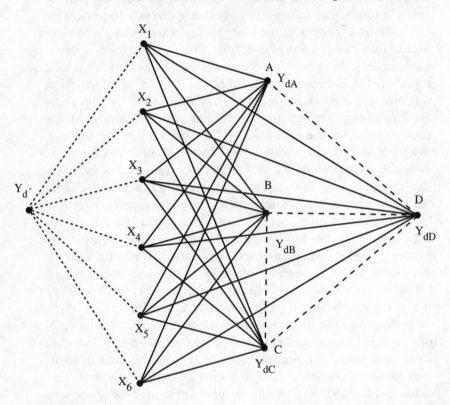

by each team member to make a decision. Each team member's decision can be represented or captured by regressing the individual's decisions on the cues presented to him or her. The second decision is that of the leader. This decision has the potential for being a little more involved than the subordinates' decisions in a group structured in the hierarchical fashion illustrated. One way for the leader to make a decision is exactly the same as for the subordinates; that is, the leader can base his or her decision on a linear combination of the six cues. Unlike the subordinates, however, in the configuration illustrated in Figure 5.5 the leader has access to the decisions of each of the subordinates, in addition to access to cue information. Thus the subordinates' decisions are analogous to cue dimensions for a decision by the leader based on three cues. Therefore, the leader's decision can be modeled as a function of the three subordinates' decisions. The leader's decision can also be modeled as a function of the individual cues. Within the team decision-making model presented here, one way to evaluate the accuracy of either the leader's/team's decision and/or the decisions of the team members is to compare them to the decisions already judged most appropriate — specifically, to compare Y_{dA}, Y_{dB}, Y_{dC}, or Y_{dD} to Y_d'.

This completes the conceptual framework of our model for decision making in hierarchical teams with distributed expertise. Onto this framework can be mapped a large number of team and individual constructs that are likely to play a major role in team decision making. For example, it can be argued that at the individual level, team members' abilities will affect the decisions of both the persons and the team. At the team level, such constructs as conflict, coordination, cooperation, and climate have been shown to be important. Our research on teams incorporates these and other individual and team constructs to study team decision making when the decision-making task is modeled by the structures introduced in the last three figures.

An Experimental Paradigm

To study team decision making under conditions of distributed expertise, a four-person team exercise was developed (see Hollenbeck, Sego, Ilgen, & Major, 1991, for a complete description of the task). On the task, each team member is assigned a specific role and is responsible for reaching a decision. Early work with the task involved role playing a command-and-control unit in a naval setting, with responsibility for monitoring an airspace and making decisions about unidentified aircraft entering airspace unannounced. As is clear in Hollenbeck, Sego, Ilgen, and Major (1991), although a naval task is used, it can be easily modified to deal with a wide variety of team decision tasks where team members hold different roles (such as a four-person task force comprising an engineer, a union representative, a production manager, and a purchasing agent who are to make decisions about the purchase of industrial robots). The general team program goes by its acronym, TIDE[2] (Team Interactive Decision Exercise for Teams Incorporating Distributed Expertise).

For illustration purposes, consider a configuration of TIDE[2] that was used in an initial study. The simulation assigned people to four roles within a team, with three of the roles subordinated to the fourth. The three subordinate roles were to monitor a "sea screen" for unidentified aircraft. One subordinate was supposedly located on land at a coastal air defense (CAD) station, another on a cruiser, and a third in a reconnaissance aircraft (AWAC). The team leader was located on an aircraft carrier. When an unidentified aircraft came into the area, all were to gather information about it, reach independent decisions about what to do, and send their decisions to the team leader, who would reach a decision for the team regarding the reaction to the unidentified aircraft. The decision was expressed in terms of the level of threat that the team believed the unidentified aircraft represented. Training on the task provided the leaders with specific information about how the level of threat was to be determined. In the jargon of the model, the training specified the cues and the way the cues should be weighted in deciding on the level of threat. Thus, while the purpose of the individual use of the lens model described earlier was to discover the way in which individuals learn how to combine cues, in this case team members were told how to do it. The focus here was on how well they used the rules they had been taught.

Nine types of information (cues) were available to the teams, including such data as speed of the aircraft, its angle of flight with regard to the team's location, and its altitude. The types of information are represented by the numerals in Figure 5.6. In particular, each subordinate had direct access to five pieces of information, two of which were also available to one of the other subordinates (but not to both) and one of which was available to the leader (but to no other subordinate). Thus, for example, the person in the AWAC could directly measure 1 through 5, but he or she had direct access exclusively to no item, shared access to item 3 with the leader, and shared access

Figure 5.6. Allocation of Nine Cues to Four Roles in a
Team Decision-Making Simulation Exercise.

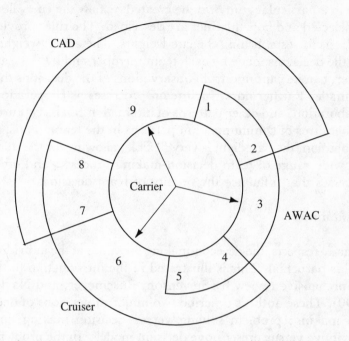

with the cruiser to items 4 and 5. For the person on the AWAC
to learn about the values of other cues (6, 7, 8, or 9), he or she
had to communicate with one of the persons who had that information, and that person had to share it. Expertise was defined
by the cues to which a person had direct access and, therefore,
by some degree of control over which other team members
learned about this information.

All team interaction went on through a networked computer system. An unidentified aircraft appeared on the screen
of all four team members simultaneously. Team members were
to interact with each other and then make decisions, which would
be sent to the leader for the overall team decision. Once a decision was made for the team, the decision appeared on the screens
of all members, along with feedback regarding the quality of
the decision, based on rules that had been taught before the
exercise.

A wide variety of team decision-making problems can be investigated with this paradigm. The ecological validity of the cues in a particular study can be created by how the cue values are selected and how the rules are described. The rules provide the basis for establishing the cue weights. The actual weights, and the decisions made by each team member and by the team leader, can be captured from observations of the decisions that are made. Furthermore, such team processes as cooperation, collaboration, and other patterns of interaction can be captured by measures of communication patterns in the team. Thus, in our opinion, the paradigm is very flexible, allowing for the study of a wide range of team decision-making processes and other processes that influence the quality of team decisions.

Potentialities

In many respects, the decision-making literature at the individual level is parochial. This is illustrated in the introduction to the comprehensive review by Stevenson, Busemeyer, and Naylor (1990). These authors describe two major dimensions of decision making: problem solving versus decision making, and descriptive versus prescriptive decision models. In the problem-solving case, persons confronted with a problem must generate the issues or dimensions on which they will seek information; then they must reach a decision regarding their approach to the problem. For decision making, the information set is fixed, and individuals make decisions or choices based on a fixed set. Although it is readily accepted that decision making is a subset of problem solving, and that many more problems are likely to be of the problem-solving than of the purely decision-making nature, there tends to be little integration among the works in problem solving with those in decision making. In terms of sheer volume of research, the decision-making work far outweighs that in problem solving, despite the reverse in terms of naturally occurring events. A similar isolation exists between the second major dimension of decision making, descriptive versus prescriptive decision models. In the former case, interest is in observing decisions and fitting the observed behavior as well as possible to a particular model. In the latter case, a model is selected, and behaviors are observed and then fit to the model as closely as possible, on the assumption that the model represents a good way to make decisions. As Stevenson, Busemeyer, and Naylor (1990) point out, the emphasis in each area is very different, and the researchers involved in each area tend to come from different disciplines — social and behavioral sciences for the descriptive models, and engineering and mathematics for the prescriptive ones.

We are suggesting that the model presented here provides a means for studying the broader issues of problem solving with some of the precision used in decision-making research. In addition, the model can be used in both a prescriptive and a descriptive fashion. Problem solving exists to the extent that individual experts have the freedom to choose whether to access particular pieces of information, rather than being presented with all the information. Problem solving also occurs to the extent that teams evolve strategies to deal with making decisions. In the latter case, teams develop patterns of interaction, in terms of who speaks to whom about what information, and they create problem-solving strategies to reach decisions. At the same time, when a team has a decision-making task with external criteria for correctness (that is, when ecological validity can be determined), the decision-making variables can be studied within the framework of problem solving — a framework that, we would argue, is far more frequently encountered by teams than is the strictly decision-making framework.

By studying team decision making over time within the above paradigm, both prescriptive and descriptive elements of decision making can be integrated. Problems with known solutions (judgments) and strategies for reaching decisions can be studied over time in a descriptive sense, to see how teams perform decision tasks. Through training and other means of structuring the problem, prescriptive processes can be presented to teams, and the teams' performance can be evaluated against them.

We believe that the model, coupled with the experimental paradigm, also allows for the use of a wider variety of research methods than has been typically encountered from any one decision-making perspective. Ford, Schmitt, Schechtman, Hults, and Doherty (1989) make the common distinction between structural or statistical modeling in decision making, where the focus is on the relationship between information (cues, inputs) and decision responses, and process models that work to discover how decision makers get from inputs to outputs. They correctly point out that the two foci are rarely integrated into the same research studies, and yet the two approaches are potentially complementary, not mutually exclusive. The paradigm presented here offers the opportunity for such integration. On the one hand, the ability to create decision structures for teams allows for the evaluation of the effectiveness of structural models for capturing the decisions of teams that are presented with a number of tasks with known cues and cue values. On the other hand, it allows for capturing the processes used by the teams to reach those decisions, by measuring the intermediate steps taken as team members interact to share information about cues and other information.

Team Decision Making and Levels of Analysis

Ultimately, we are concerned with the decisions of teams that are embedded in larger organizational systems. The embeddedness of individuals in teams, and of teams in organizations, necessarily raises both conceptual and methodological issues related to levels of analysis. For a long time, those in the organizational sciences treated levels in a rather cavalier fashion. For the most part, the issues were simply ignored. However, Roberts, Hulin, and Rousseau (1978) and others (Dansereau, Alutto, Markham, & Dumas, 1982; James, 1982; Roberts & Burstein, 1980) have demonstrated that failure to consider level of analysis for constructs and measures can have serious consequences. The problem of levels is particularly important in the present case, where constructs at one level (in this case, at the level of the individual) are being translated into team-level phenomena; and yet teams are still composed of individuals, even though they are acting as some form of collective.

Rousseau (1985) presents an excellent description of the types of biases that are confronted when multiple levels of analysis are involved in research and theorizing. She also provides a taxonomy for the constructs that are most frequently of interest in research confronted by multiple levels, and her taxonomy is what most interests us here. In particular, she describes three forms of models for constructs that arise in cross-level research and theory, as when the interest is in decisions made by teams (one level) of individuals (another level) acting in concert. The first form encompasses *composition models*. These specify functional relationships between variables, where the variables themselves are conceptually located at different levels, and where the constructs at each level are functionally similar although not necessarily identical. In the case of team decision making, we have argued that the decision process at both the individual and the team level involves the consideration of cues. The cues are weighted by the decision maker, and the weights function similarly but not identically at the individual and the team level. At the team level, for example, the leader's decision is based on weights that are influenced by judgments about the reliability and validity of the subordinates whose judgments the leader uses as cues for his or her decision. In this sense, there are compositional issues as one moves from individuals to teams. These issues, if ignored, can be misleading; for example, it can certainly be misleading to assume that team decision processes regarding cue weights are simple analogues of individual ones.

Rousseau's second form of cross-level models involves hypothesized functional relationships between a variable at one level and a variable at another. These are termed *cross-level models* by Rousseau. Numerous examples of such cases exist for team decision making, such as the introduction of team members' abilities into models predicting the quality of team decisions. In this case, abilities are individual characteristics, which by definition are at the level of the person, whereas team performance is a team output.

The third form encompasses the multilevel models. In these cases, the relationship among variables is predicted to be generalizable from one level to the other. Again, many of the relationships described earlier (between cues, weights and decisions, or choices) assumed that the nature of a relationship observed at the individual level would be generalizable to the level of the team.

The importance of the levels-of-analysis issue is that, according to the nature of the model that is being assumed for the constructs of interest, there are both methodological and conceptual questions that must be taken into account in order to avoid biases and misinterpretation of results. Since team decision making by its very nature involves at least three levels (individuals, aggregates of individuals, and tasks or environments), issues of levels cannot be ignored. Therefore, as research is generated on the basis of this or any other model, levels must be considered. Fortunately, both conceptual (Rousseau, 1985) and empirical (Dansereau, Alutto, & Yammarino, 1984; Hollenbeck, Ilgen, & Sego, 1994; Ostroff, 1993) advances have improved our ability to address the levels issues that have been ignored in much of the earlier work on teams.

Conclusion

If one accepts, as we do, that many situations today and in the near future will require people to work in teams where members combine resources to make and implement decisions in high-stakes environments, then it is critical that we understand the decision-making capabilities of teams. Such an understanding is necessary for constructing teams whose members have the skills and abilities to carry out team tasks. It is also necessary to understand team functioning in order to construct team tasks so that task demands are within the capabilities of the persons working on teams. Finally, if individuals are to be trained to operate in teams, or if decision aids are to be developed to foster the effectiveness of teams operating in the kinds of environments just mentioned, then there must be a body of knowledge that guides the development of task design, training, and decision aids.

Although a great deal of work exists on both decision making and team functioning, this work is limited in the extent to which it speaks to the issues of teams operating in the types of environments that are of interest here. There are a number of reasons for these limitations. First, the vast majority of studies on decision making are limited to individual rather than team decision making. Second, when teams are studied, much of the work focuses on internal team processes, without regard for team performance. Often when teams are asked to perform tasks, performance on the tasks is used only as a condition for observing team process; task performance is not of interest. Finally, when models of team performance are built, they often deal with specific performance situations that have limited generalizability to teams in ongoing organizational settings of interest here, or tasks are very abstract and quite far removed from the tasks of ongoing teams. Excellent models of team performance that tend to fit into the two sets just mentioned are represented by work on jury decision making (Davis, Holt, Spitzer, & Stasser, 1981) and by the work of Laughlin (Laughlin & Adamopolis, 1982).

Recent research on cockpit crews (Foushee, 1982, 1984; Hackman, 1987; Gregorich, Helmrich, & Wilhelm 1990), problem-solving groups (Gersick, 1989), and training teams (Morgan, Glickman, Woodard, Blaiwes, & Salas, 1986) involves team members who make decisions in settings that more closely approximate those identified as the focus of our concern. Nevertheless, although this research is a better match as to setting, it trades off setting for precision in construct measurement and model development. Such trade-offs are inherent in behavioral research (Runkel & McGrath, 1972), and well-reasoned positions can be made for either extreme, but these reasons should not preclude attempts to combine some of the advantages of both.

The model and the research paradigm presented here represent a compromise between the two extremes. The model itself provides a structure for guiding research that studies team decision making under conditions where external standards exist. Furthermore, the model fits the decision-making tasks of a number of diverse teams. The task simulation based on the model provides a setting for investigating hypotheses derived from either the model or from situational conditions faced by teams of the type we have described.

Like any other model or paradigm, those proposed here also represent trade-offs. For example, one loses the precision of the decision-making models that restrict the decision domain to those situations where all cue values and their distributions are known. Also lost is the breadth of concern for emerging team constructs that could be observed on tasks for which no standards of performance are known. Moreover, some of the naturally occurring events that are likely to be important for any team operating in a real-life environment are lost when a team simulation is used. At the same time, given the importance of understanding decision making in the kinds of teams important in modern organizations, the model and the paradigm fill a crucial vacuum by capitalizing on some of the advantages of model-driven research in the laboratory and by simulating critical field conditions. More research is currently being conducted on the model, using the paradigm.

References

Argote, L., Devadas, R., & Melone, N. (1990). The base-rate fallacy: Contrasting processes and outcomes of group and individual judgment. *Organizational Behavior and Human Decision Processes, 46,* 296–310.

Argote, L., Seabright, M. A., & Dyer, L. (1986). Individual versus group use of base-rate and individuating information. *Organizational Behavior and Human Decision Processes, 38,* 65–75.

Blum, M., & Naylor, J. C. (1968). *Industrial psychology: Its theoretical and social foundations.* New York: HarperCollins.

Brehmer, B., & Hagafors, R. (1986). Use of experts in complex decision making: A paradigm for the study of staff work. *Organizational Behavior and Human Decision Processes, 38,* 181–195.

Brunswik, E. (1940). Thing constancy as measured by correlation coefficients. *Psychological Review, 47,* 69–78.

Brunswik, E. (1943). Organismic achievement and environmental probability. *Psychological Review, 50,* 255–272.

Brunswik, E. (1955). Representative design and probabilistic theory in a functional psychology. *Psychological Review, 62,* 193–217.

Brunswik, E. (1956). *Perception and the representative design of experiments.* Berkeley: University of California Press.

Castore, C. H., & Murnigham, J. K. (1978). Determinants of support for group decisions. *Organizational Behavior and Human Performance, 22,* 75–92.

Dansereau, F., Alutto, J. A., Markham, S. E., & Dumas, M. (1982). Multiplexed supervision and leadership: An application of within and between analysis. In J. G. Hunt, V. Sedaran, & C. Schriesheim (Eds.), *Leadership beyond establishment views* (pp. 157–192). Carbondale: Southern Illinois University Press.

Dansereau, F., Alutto, J. A., & Yammarino, F. (1984). *Theory testing in organizational behavior: The variant approach.* Englewood Cliffs, NJ: Prentice-Hall.

Davis, J. H. (1992). Some compelling intuitions about group consensus decisions, theoretical and empirical research, and interpersonal aggregation phenomena: Selected examples, 1950–1990. *Organizational Behavior and Human Decision Processes, 52,* 3–38.

Davis, J. H., Holt, R. W., Spitzer, C. E., & Stasser, G. (1981). The effects of consensus requirements and multiple decisions on mock juror verdict preferences. *Journal of Experimental Social Psychology, 17,* 1–15.

Denison, D. R., & Sutton, R. I. (1990). Operating-room nurses. In J. R. Hackman (Ed.), *Groups that work (and those that don't): Creating conditions for effective teamwork* (pp. 293–308). San Francisco: Jossey-Bass.

Eisenstat, R. A. (1990). Fairfield Coordinating Group. In J. R. Hackman (Ed.), *Groups that work (and those that don't): Creating conditions for effective teamwork* (pp. 19–35). San Francisco: Jossey-Bass.

Ford, J. K., Schmitt, N., Schechtman, S. L., Hults, B. M., & Doherty, M. L. (1989). Process tracing methods: Contributions, problems, and neglected research questions. *Organizational Behavior and Human Decision Processes, 43,* 75–117.

Foushee, H. C. (1982). The role of communications, sociopsychological, and personality factors in the maintenance of crew coordination. *Aviation, Space, and Environmental Medicine, 53,* 1062–1066.

Foushee, H. C. (1984). Dyads and triads at 35,000 feet: Factors affecting group process and aircrew performance. *American Psychologist, 39,* 886–893.

Gerbasi, K. C., Zuckerman, M., & Reis, H. T. (1977). Justice needs a new blindfold: A review of mock jury research. *Psychological Bulletin, 84,* 323–345.

Gersick, C.J.G. (1989). Marking time: Predictable transitions in task groups. *Academy of Management Journal, 32,* 274–309.

Gregorich, S. E., Helmreich, R. L., & Wilhelm, J. A. (1990). The structure of cockpit management attitudes. *Journal of Applied Psychology, 75,* 682–690.

Hackman, J. R. (1987). Group-level issues in the design of training issues for cockpit crews. *Cockpit Resource Management Training* (NASA Report No. CP2455). Moffett Field, CA: National Aeronautics and Space Administration, Ames Research Center.

Hackman, J. R. (1990). Conclusion: Creating more effective work groups in organizations. In J. R. Hackman (Ed.), *Groups that work (and those that don't): Creating conditions for effective teamwork.* San Francisco: Jossey-Bass.

Hollenbeck, J. R., Ilgen, D. R., & Sego, D. J. (1994). Repeated measures regression and mediational tests: Enhancing the power of leadership research. *Leadership Quarterly, 5,* 3–23.

Hollenbeck, J. R., Ilgen, D. R., Sego, D. J., Hedlund, J., Major, D. A., & Phillips, J. (in press). The multilevel theory of team decision making: Decision performance in teams incorporating distributed expertise. *Journal of Applied Psychology.*

Hollenbeck, J. R., Sego, D. J., Ilgen, D. R., & Major, D. A. (1991). *Team interactive decision exercise for teams incorporating distributed expertise (TIDE²): A program and paradigm for team research* (Tech. Rep. No. 91-1). Michigan State University, Department of Management and Psychology.

James, L. R. (1982). Aggregation bias in perceptions of agreement. *Journal of Applied Psychology, 67,* 219–229.

Kahneman, D., & Tversky, A. (1973). On the psychology of prediction. *Psychological Review, 80,* 237–251.

Komorita, S. S. (1984). Coalition bargaining. *Advances in Experimental Social Psychology, 18,* 183–245.

Lachman, R. (1987). Information processing theory. In R. J. Corsini (Ed.), *Concise encyclopedia of psychology* (pp. 589–591). New York: Wiley.

Laughlin, P. R. (1980). Social combination processes of cooperative problem-solving groups on verbal intellective tasks. In M. Fishbein (Ed.), *Progress in social psychology: Vol. 1* (pp. 67–103). Hillsdale, NJ: Erlbaum.

Laughlin, P. R., & Adamopolus, J. (1980). Social combination processes and individual learning for six-person cooperative groups on an intellective task. *Journal of Personality and Social Psychology, 38,* 941–947.

Laughlin, P. R., & Adamopolus, J. (1982). Social decision schemes on intellective tasks. In H. Brandstatter, J. H. Dais, & G. Stocker-Kreichgauer (Eds.), *Group decision making* (pp. 81–102). San Diego, CA: Academic Press.

Laughlin, P. R., Kerr, N. L., Davis, J. H., Halff, H. M., & Marciniak, K. A. (1975). Group size, member ability, and social decision schemes on an intellective task. *Journal of Personality and Social Psychology, 31,* 522–535.

Laughlin, P. R., Kerr, N. L., Munch, M. M., & Haggarty, C. A. (1976). Social decision schemes of the same four-person groups on two different intellective tasks. *Journal of Personality and Social Psychology, 33,* 80–88.

Liddell, W. W., & Slocum, J. W. (1976). The effects of individual-role compatibility upon group performance: Extension of Schutz's FIRO theory. *Academy of Management Journal, 19,* 413–426.

McGrath, J. E. (1984). *Groups: Interaction and performance.* Englewood Cliffs, NJ: Prentice-Hall.

March, J. G., & Simon, H. A. (1958). *Organizations.* New York: Wiley.

Morgan, B. B., Jr., Glickman, A. S., Woodard, E. A., Blaiwes, A., & Salas, E. (1986). *Measurement of team behaviors in a Navy environment* (NTSC Report No. 86-014). Orlando, FL: Naval Training Systems Center.

Ostroff, C. (1993). Comparing correlations based on individual level data and aggregated data. *Journal of Applied Psychology, 78,* 569–582.

Penrod, S., & Hastie, R. (1979). Models of jury decision making: A critical review. *Psychological Bulletin, 86,* 462–492.

The right stuff (1990, October 10). *Time,* pp. 74–84.

Roberts, K. H., & Burstein, K. (1980). Issues of aggregation. In K. H. Roberts & K. Burstein (Eds.), *New directions for methodology in the social sciences: Vol. 6.* San Francisco: Jossey-Bass.

Roberts, K. H., Hulin, C. L., & Rousseau, D. M. (1978). *Developing an interdisciplinary science of organizations.* San Francisco: Jossey-Bass.

Rousseau, D. M. (1985). Issues of level in organizational research: Multilevel and cross-level perspectives. In L. L. Cummings & B. M. Staw (Eds.), *Research in organizational behavior: Vol. 7* (pp. 1–37). Greenwich, CT: JAI Press.

Runkel, P. L., & McGrath, J. E. (1972). *Research on human behavior: A systematic guide to method.* Troy, MO: Holt, Rinehart & Winston.

Sniezek, J. A., & Henry, R. A. (1989). Accuracy and confidence in group judgment. *Organizational Behavior and Human Decision Processes, 43,* 1–28.

Sniezek, J. A., & Henry, R. A. (1990). Revision, weighting, and commitment in consensus group judgment. *Organizational Behavior and Human Decision Processes, 45,* 66–84.

Stasser, G., Kerr, N. L., & Bray, R. M. (1982). The social psychology of jury deliberations: Structure, process, and product. In N. L. Kerr & R. M. Bray (Eds.), *The psychology of the courtroom* (pp. 221–256). San Diego, CA: Academic Press.

Stasser, G., Kerr, N. L., & Davis, J. H. (1989). Influence processes and consensus models in decision-making groups. In P. B. Paulus (Ed.), *The psychology of group influence* (2nd ed.) (pp. 279-326). Hillsdale, NJ: Erlbaum.

Stasser, G., & Titus, W. (1985). Pooling of unshared information in group decision making: Biased information sampling during discussion. *Journal of Personality and Social Psychology, 48,* 1467-1478.

Stevenson, M. K., Busemeyer, J. R., & Naylor, J. C. (1990). Judgment and decision making theory. In M. D. Dunnette & L. M. Hough (Eds.), *Handbook of industrial and organizational psychology: Vol. 2* (pp. 283-374). Palo Alto, CA: Consulting Psychologists Press.

Tindale, R. S. (1989). Group versus individual information processing: The effects of outcome feedback on decision making. *Organizational Behavior and Human Decision Processes, 44,* 454-473.

Vaughan, W. S., Jr. (1990). *Toward a science of command and control: Challenges of distributed decision making.* Unpublished paper. Arlington, VA: Office of Naval Research, Cognitive and Neural Sciences Division.

Who needs a boss? (1990, May). *Fortune,* pp. 52-60.

Yetton, P. W., & Bottger, P. C. (1982). Individual versus group problem solving: An empirical test of a best-member strategy. *Organizational Behavior and Human Performance, 29,* 297-321.

6

INNOVATIONS IN MODELING AND SIMULATING TEAM PERFORMANCE: IMPLICATIONS FOR DECISION MAKING

Michael D. Coovert, J. Philip Craiger,
Janis A. Cannon-Bowers

Individuals interested in the study of team performance have traditionally relied on standard methods of measuring and modeling the performance of individuals in teams. In this chapter, we introduce several methodological tools often overlooked by psychologists. These methods include Petri nets, simulation and modeling strategies, artificial intelligence, neural networks, fuzzy sets, and expert systems. Our intent is not to be exhaustive in describing the strategies but rather to provide the reader with a feel for the techniques. If we are successful, psychologists will consider the use of one or more of these techniques with future applied and theoretical problems they encounter.

It is apparent that teams are becoming increasingly important to modern organizations (Hackman, 1990). For this reason, a number of issues regarding teams and team performance have been the subject of considerable study in recent years. Unfortunately, there still exist a number of unresolved issues regarding the investigation and understanding of teams and team processes. Central to these is the problem of analyzing and measuring team performance. The purpose of this chapter is to describe several techniques that may be useful in studying teams, but are often overlooked by practitioners and researchers. To this end, we will first delineate what we believe are the challenges in understanding team performance, and then we will describe a variety of modeling techniques and show how these may be useful tools for studying team performance.

Issues in Team Performance

As noted, a number of issues in the team area require further study. Before describing these, we must first make explicit the types of teams that are our focus. We define a team, in keeping with other chapters in this volume, as a set of two or more individuals who interact interdependently to accomplish a shared objective. This definition would include many types of work teams, such as firefighting teams, police units, research-and-development teams, product-development teams, and the like.

It should be noted that our conception emphasizes interdependence as a key factor in distinguishing a team from a group (see Swezey & Salas, 1992, for a more detailed discussion of this distinction). The notion of interdependence is a crucial one here because it suggests that team members must interact with each other in a prescribed manner in order to accomplish a task. That is, interdependence necessitates interaction among team members. Furthermore, this must be coordinated interaction if a goal or task is to be accomplished by the team. Therefore, in order to understand a team, we must understand not only the behavior of the individuals who comprise the team but also the points at which team members must interact and the nature of these interactions. Only then can we determine the relationship between these interactions and the team's effectiveness. This assertion implies that a full understanding of the nature of team performance requires the availability of methods that will allow a systematic assessment and modeling of the nature and quality of team members' interactions. The following sections describe in more detail the associated challenges.

Analyzing and Measuring Team Performance

There is no doubt that teams are complex entities. They subsume all the factors typically of interest in understanding individual performance (knowledge, skills, abilities, motivation, expertise, preferences), with additional concerns that stem from the fact that team members must interact with one another in a coordinated manner. In fact, understanding *when* and *how* team members interact may be a key to describing team performance in a meaningful way. Moreover, coordinated behavior has a sequential or temporal component; that is, individual tasks often need to be performed in a particular order. We introduce the notion of *team process* as a label to incorporate these various factors. The term is being used here to refer to the behavioral, procedural, and temporal phenomena that describe a team's functioning.

In order to identify, train, and maintain effective performance in work teams, it is necessary to understand team process. That is, we must understand how, when, and why team members interact as they do, as well as the relationship between these interactions and team effectiveness. Methods for analyzing teams in order to gain this understanding of team process are not well developed at this point. Traditional job-analysis methods are useful for some purposes, but they generally fail to provide the necessary detailed information (a notable exception is the work by Levine, Penner, Brannick, & Coovert, 1988). Methods and tools for analyzing team process are needed so that it will be possible to document how effective teams interact and to develop measurement and training systems for teams.

In dealing with teams whose members must respond quickly, operate in stressful environments, or are confronted with large amounts of information, simply tracking interactions among members can be difficult. For example, when a military command-and-control team is confronted with a potentially hostile contact, team members must quickly gather, process, assess, integrate, and communicate a large amount of information in support of a tactical decision. In this case, things happen

so quickly that simply recording the team process—the interactions among members—is difficult and labor intensive.

Once recorded, team members' interactions must be analyzed, so that effective patterns of interaction can be discovered.
This is more difficult than it sounds. A team strategy (a set of
behaviors and interaction patterns initiated by the team in
response to situational demands) can include multiple team
members acting in parallel, can occur over a specified period
of time, and can incorporate one or more seemingly complex
sequences of interaction among members. Moreover, team processes are dynamic and evolve over time. A team may initiate
different strategies according to its members' histories and past
experiences of working together. Traditional analysis techniques
in the area of team performance are not equipped to recognize
these strategies.

To summarize, the complexity of teams and team process
requires that new methods and tools be developed to aid in the
analysis of team functioning. Such methods are necessary so
that an understanding of how team behavior affects team effectiveness can be gained.

Measuring Team Performance

A closely related problem in the team area concerns measuring
team process and performance. Obviously, in order to select,
train, and maintain teams, a scheme to measure team process
is necessary. Such a measurement system would be able to
describe interactions among team members so as to capture the
moment-to-moment changes that occur. Beyond this, an effective measurement system would describe which team process
is effective and why. That is, it would provide causal information (why things happened as they did) and diagnostic information (what went wrong in a particular team). This type
of system could provide a basis for delivering feedback to a team.
Finally, the ability to index or quantify team performance would
be desirable, so that meaningful comparisons between teams
could be made. The ability to measure and quantify team performance rests on the ability to capture and describe it. As noted

earlier, simply tracking performance in a dynamic team environment can be difficult. Beyond this, a method to determine the effectiveness of particular behaviors, processes, and strategies does not exist. Therefore, just as methods to analyze team performance are lacking, methods to measure team process are also in need of development.

Performance Modeling

It has been asserted recently that performance-modeling technologies may be useful as a means of analyzing and measuring team performance (Coovert & McNelis, 1992). Performance-modeling techniques incorporate a host of mathematical and graphic approaches that have been shown to be useful for modeling various aspects of behavior (Murata, 1989). To date, the potential offered by these techniques in analyzing and measuring team performance is only beginning to be realized. The following sections describe several performance-modeling methods that may be useful as strategies for analyzing and measuring team performance. It is our intention to describe these in sufficient detail to interest researchers who might like to apply them to the team area. Where appropriate, we direct readers to sources that provide more detailed information regarding the techniques.

Simulation and Modeling

The remaining sections of this chapter provide an introduction to alternative methodologies for studying team performance. We discuss four techniques that we have employed as alternatives to the conventional experiment and quasi-experiment, including Petri nets, production rules, fuzzy logic, and artificial neural nets. These methods, although originally developed for use in engineering (Petri nets) and artificial-intelligence research (production rules, fuzzy logic, and artificial neural networks), have common characteristics that allow the psychologist to apply them to nonmechanical systems—what we will call *dynamic behavioral systems*.

On the basis of our experiences, we have included what

we feel are the most important facets of each of the strategies, as well as enough background information for the reader to gain a fundamental understanding of how each strategy can be applied to team research. Although the topics are oriented toward computer science and engineering, our presentations assume that the reader has no prior experience in either area. We have tried to adapt our presentation to the researcher or practitioner who is conducting team research and who wishes to add to his or her methodological toolbox. We should also be explicit about what this chapter is *not* intended to be: namely, an exhaustive tutorial on simulation and modeling, an exhaustive tutorial on any of the strategies, or a tutorial on artificial-intelligence programming. Readers interested in a deeper understanding of these topics may consult the references. Before we continue, it is essential to understand a fundamental idea: a team can be conceptualized in terms of systems theory.

Teams as Systems

According to Bertalanffy (1968), "General system theory should be, methodologically, an important means of controlling and instigating the transfer of principles from one field to another, and it will no longer be necessary to duplicate or triplicate the discovery of the same principles in different fields isolated from each other" (p. 80). For Simon (1969), "Resemblance in behavior of systems without identity of the inner systems is particularly feasible if the aspects in which we are interested arise out of the organization of the parts, independently of all but a few properties of the individual components" (p. 21). A *system* is an aggregation of interacting objects whose behavior is influenced—is shaped—by its need or desire to achieve its goals. Characteristics commonly associated with systems include a hierarchical structure, labor specialization, component interaction, information transfer, and feedback. Because of the inherent complexity of systems, as well as the complexity of structure and behavior, systematic study of these phenomena is difficult. Bertalanffy (1968) calls this the *systems problem*—that is, the difficulty of applying traditional scientific methods (what he calls "classical analytical procedures") to the study of a system's behavior. According to Bertalanffy, traditional analytical methods are limited to those phenomena where (1) interactions among the underlying parts of the phenomenon are trivial and (2) relationships among the system's components are best expressed with a linear function. The behavior of most systems, however, does not meet these criteria, given that their behavior is adaptive (shaped by goal orientation) and dynamic (involving changes in system structure and behavior). Consequently, traditional methodologies are inherently limited in their ability to capture the complexity and dynamics of most system behavior. Bertalanffy did, however, delineate a number of methodologies that, he argues, are flexible enough for the study of systems. These include computer simulations, set theory, graph theory, net theory, cybernetics, automata theory, decision theory, and information theory.

Simon (1969) argues that system similarity can be defined in terms of the organization of the components comprising a system, rather than in terms of its physical structure; it is the organization of the system, coupled with the system's need to adapt to environmental conditions and attain its goals, that gives rise to the system's behavior.

One of the commonalities between Bertalanffy's and Simon's work that is relevant to the study of team performance is that the isomorphism of the *abstract structures* comprising systems allows us to employ similar strategies to study dissimilar systems. That is, abstract structures — including hierarchical structure, labor specialization, component interaction, information transfer, and feedback — are the structures comprising the systems that determine the system's behavior. The main theme weaved throughout this chapter is that teams can be conceptualized in terms of systems theory and are therefore amenable to study with methods previously employed for mechanistic systems.

Perhaps the most defining characteristics of teams are (1) that they are adaptive (that is, their behavior is shaped by their need to adapt to their goals and environmental conditions) and (2) that they are dynamic (that is, the need to adapt creates bidirectional relationships between the task environment and team behavior). Whether an organization modifies its product line and sales structure to reflect changing consumer needs, or a military team modifies its battle tactics because of changing battle conditions, the behavior of the dynamic system is a function of its goal orientation (to increase profits or defeat an enemy). Every organization exists for some purpose, and in its quest for goal attainment, the systems must adapt to the often volatile task environment. For the purposes of this chapter, we use the term *dynamic behavioral system* synonymously with the word *team*. As this chapter unfolds, we will show how computer simulations provide the industrial psychologist with the ability to represent the most complex real-world dynamic behavioral systems to any arbitrary level of complexity. Along the way, we hope to show why computer simulations are an ideal methodology for studying team behavior.

Computer Simulations for Prediction and Description of System Behavior

Four techniques that we review here are Petri nets, production rules, fuzzy logic, and artificial neural networks. Although hundreds of volumes have been devoted to the in-depth study of each of these subjects, space limitations preclude anything but the simplest introduction of each topic here.

We will begin by presenting a brief overview of computer simulations. Then we will discuss properties of simulations that provide the industrial psychologist with a means of analyzing and measuring team performance. For each technique, we provide an example and a hypothesis amenable to testing with a computer simulation. We evaluate the adequacy of each method for the study of team performance on the basis of two criteria.

The first criterion concerns the ability to describe dynamic behavior. Does the technique allow us to describe, to arbitrary levels of complexity and detail, the structures inherent in the phenomenon that influence the behavior of the system (that is, can the computer model be an adequate *isomorphic* representation of a team)? Describing team behavior is important when there are structures, whether physical or behavioral, that we wish to model explicitly, such as team formation (a physical structure), lines of communication (behavioral and physical structures), or lines of authority (behavioral structures).

The second criterion concerns the ability to provide estimates of behavioral outcomes. Does the technique allow us to make predictions about the behavior of the system across a broad range of possible behavioral outcomes (that is, can computer simulations provide an adequate *paramorphic* representation of team behavior)? To what extent does each strategy allow us to predict the outcomes of team behavior? Does the strategy allow an adequate level of prediction at various levels of analysis? The answers to these questions depend, of course, on the interests of the researcher. We will, however, attempt to deduce when any of the strategies is the best one for any condition. Our aim is to illustrate how computer simulations provide an almost unlimited ability to describe the structure and predict the outcomes of a dynamic behavioral system.

Computers as Methods

Although the terms are often used interchangeably, *computer model* and *computer simulation* are distinct yet related concepts. A computer model can be thought of as an abstract description of a system, consisting of its most salient features — a computerized metaphor for an abstract theory or system (Nielsen, 1991; Winston, 1989). By contrast, a simulation involves the systematic study of the behavior of a computer model under varying conditions. Thus a simulation implies a model, but not vice versa. A computer model is static. It serves as a description of some abstract theory or system. By contrast, a simulation is inherently dynamic. Model variables are manipulated, so that the researcher can assess changes in the system caused by the interactions of the model's intrinsic structures. (Note the similarity between the manipulation of behavioral variables in the traditional psychology experiment and the manipulation of abstract model variables in simulation.)

Reliable Results and Method Convergence

Why should an industrial psychologist be interested in computer simulation? Do we really need another method for studying human behavior? Haven't we extended the traditional psychological experiment or quasi-experiment to its limit? We are not calling for the demise of the traditional psychological methods. Rather, it is our opinion that industrial psychologists can employ these methods to complement psychological experiments. Our experience also shows that computer simulations provide several advantages not afforded by traditional methodologies:

- Alternative methods can be used to "triangulate on the referent" (Campbell & Fiske, 1959). We have stronger evidence of the reliability of our findings if they generalize across populations, time, *and* methods, thus providing evidence that the results are not method-bound.
- A computerized theory forces us to specify precisely all the important variables, the relationships among them, and the directional influences.
- A computerized theory forces us to think about problems in new ways, which may result in novel answers and approaches to old, intractable problems (Winston, 1989).
- Computer simulations allow unequalled flexibility in the creation and testing of theories of an almost unlimited complexity.
- "Computer programs exhibit unlimited patience, they require no feedback, and they do not bite" (Winston, 1984, p. 2).

Concerning team research, we see two primary advantages of computer modeling. It forces the researcher to think precisely and globally about the nomological network of latent relationships implied by his or her theory, and it allows the researcher to explore complex models and theory that might be difficult if not impossible to research in real life.

An illustration will help clarify our argument. Let us say we have a number of hypotheses that we would like to test about how task and worker characteristics interact to affect productivity. We have identified ten variables that, we hypothesize, affect productivity (p): feedback (fbk), task variety (tv), task identity (ti), cognitive ability (ca), motivation (m), training (t), experience (e), role overload (ro), role conflict (rc_1), and role clarity (rc_2). Once we have identified the problem domain and the model variables, we must specify the causal relationships among the variables. For instance, we may want to evaluate two methods of representing the causal relationships among these variables. If the variables are scaled continuously, we might specify this relationship through a combination of linear and nonlinear mathematical functions, specified in the form of an equation:

$$f(p) = ca^2 \times \frac{\sqrt{ti}}{m} \times \log(e) + \frac{tv + ti}{2} - \frac{ro + rc_1 + rc_2}{3} \times \sqrt[3]{fbk \times t}$$

Once the hypothesis is identified, we can manipulate the independent variables (any of the variables on the right side of the equation) while holding the other variables constant and note the effects of the various manipulations of the independent variables on production. So far, it should be noted that the stages required to develop and run a simulation are, in the abstract, very similar to the stages required in the traditional psychological experiment.

The nonlinear equation above specifies precisely the mathematical relationship between productivity, task, and worker characteristics. Unfortunately, we do not often (if ever) have a theoretical basis for inferring the mathematical functions underlying human behavior to such a precise degree. Rather, we might have knowledge about how variables influence other variables at magnitudes of a more general scale. For instance, we might partition our variables into quasi-continuous categories, such as low, medium, and high. If our variables are quasi-continuous, we might use production rules to specify relationships among variables. A production rule is a method of representing knowledge that can be employed in computer programs, allowing us to map from one domain (task and worker characteristics) to another domain (predictions about productivity) based on previous hypotheses about the relationships among the variables in the domain. To illustrate:

- If motivation is high and cognitive ability is medium or high, then productivity will be high.
- If task variety is low and cognitive ability is low, or motivation is low, then productivity will be low.
- If task variety is medium and task identity is medium or low, and cognitive ability is high or medium, and motivation is medium or high, then productivity will be high or medium.

Note that linear and nonlinear relationships can be represented quite flexibly via production rules. According to the complexity of the theory, the researcher can explicate a model describing complex hypotheses, using a few rules or well over a hundred. One difference between the two methods of representing hypotheses is that the natural-language composition of the rules makes it much easier for researchers to understand the general implications of the model (presumably at the cost of precision). We argue, however, that this cost is artificial. Reduced precision has little if any detrimental effect on our ability to represent hypotheses and make predictions, since most behavioral measures of work (and, indeed, psychological measures in general) are latent in nature — unobservable hypothetical variables. Measures of latent variables (job satisfaction, organizational commitment, altruism) are man-made measures of convenience and have no intrinsic objective nature. Therefore, we lose little information by using quasi-continuous categories to quantify the variables of interest, and we gain much in terms of our ability to communicate our hypotheses.

Simulations and Assumptions

An important consideration is that inferences drawn from a model are influenced by the assumptions that serve as the basis for the model. Of course, the assumptions included in the model will depend on the researcher's interests. Consequences of failure to incorporate the appropriate assumptions into a model range from the need to "tweak" (modify) the model to the inability to veridically represent even robust aspects of interest. To illustrate, before the Persian Gulf War, allied military strategists predicted that the Iraqis might set fire to the thousands of oil wells in Kuwait, as an act of sabotage. A number of renowned scientists theorized about the global effects of these fires. On the basis of computer simulations, they postulated that the fires would create clouds of oil-laden soot that would rise into the atmosphere, causing catastrophic climatic changes around the world. The military strategists' predictions did come true. Almost a thousand oil wells were set afire, and most of them burned uncontrolled for well over a year. The results were dissimilar to those predicted, however. Why was there this disparity between the predicted and the actual results? Although it cannot be proved conclusively, one explanation involves the ubiquity of a nonlinear natural phenomenon (Kosko, 1992). It is well known that atmospheric variables are tremendously nonlinear, with an almost infinite number of causal mechanisms interacting on a grand scale. If an important assumption is not included, results may not reflect reality. (Researchers in the hard sciences, incidentally, have developed a new science, *chaos theory,* that focuses on nonlinear relationships between naturally occurring phenomena. Chaos theory is based on the belief that relationships between many if not most naturally occurring phenomena demonstrate how small changes in the initial state of a system may lead to tremendously large differences in later states. This is commonly called "sensitive dependence on initial conditions"; see Gleick, 1987, and Lorenz, 1963.)

Petri Nets

Three Special Issues

One of the most beautiful things we have ever beheld was a stream of crystal-clear water cascading down a lush green mountain over moss-covered rocks. In the background, we saw leafy trees and bushes emerging from the rock-covered earth. The rocks jutted this way and that. In the center of it all was the water rushing, over and around the protruding rocks, but always rushing downward to meet the river.

Perhaps even more beautiful is a human being engaged in a complex task. Consider an Olympic gymnast. Her body twists and contorts as she moves fluidly and effortlessly through myriad positions, each one more complex than the last.

Or consider a team of individuals engaged in a complex activity, such as a game of basketball. Each player performs a set of fluid and dynamic actions. And, like the mountain stream, the team has a dynamic, fluid behavior all its own.

In fact, a good deal of the splendor of such scenes is due to the dynamic nature of the actors and actions. Unfortunately, psychologists and others have been lacking in the ability to model this type of behavior. Too often, we are forced to examine values on some static variable (or on a set of static variables) and, using all the imagination we can muster, to envision how a change in one variable might affect other parameters of the system. What would happen to the stream if I moved that boulder over here? What if a tree five inches in diameter fell across it there?

Another encumbrance we are forced to endure is consideration of the system from just one perspective when, for various theoretical and applied reasons, it would be useful to examine it from many perspectives. Consider again the basketball team. It could easily be one unit of analysis—but so could the guards, the forwards, and various combinations of each group with the center. We might also consider each individual and then model how routine (and nonroutine) behaviors are performed. The point is that, very often, our interest in modeling and understanding complex behavior does not lend itself to comparisons of mean or even covariance structures. When we are confronted with a complex system of interest (such as a team), it would be helpful to have a tool or method that could do at least three things. First, it should allow the construction of a meaningful representation of the system at multiple levels of abstraction (multiple levels within a hierarchy). Second, the methodology should allow for the ability to run dynamic simulations in order to verify the system, validate the system, and make changes to the system and have the model reflect the impact of those changes. Third, the technique should allow for the explicit representation of such team behaviors as coordination.

Highlights of Petri Nets

Petri nets are a very useful and powerful modeling tool. The methodology was proposed by Petri (1962) as a general-purpose modeling tool for asynchronous systems. Since that time, Petri nets have been the focus of much research aimed at embellishing and extending their capabilities.

Petri nets are graphic and mathematical. The graphic aspect makes them a useful tool for representing a system in a manner that nearly anyone can understand and therefore allows them to be employed by a wide group of individuals. Systems that have been successfully modeled by Petri nets have such diverse characteristics as being asynchronous, concurrent, nondeterministic, distributed, and stochastic. As a mathematical tool, algebraic equations, state equations, or other models are established that control the behavior of the system. The mathematical underpinnings of the nets allow for rigorous analyses of various types.

There are a few special types of Petri nets, but we will not differentiate among them in this chapter. Rather, our purpose is to make the reader comfortable with the process of constructing the representation of a system, using as few basic constructs and rules as necessary. Readers interested in special issues are encouraged to seek out the literature on the topic of interest and to employ various software packages (Alphatech, 1992; Chiiola, 1990; Metasoftware, 1992; Perceptronics, 1992) for the analysis of their models.

Basic Components

The basic components of Petri nets are quite few, yet we can use these limited building blocks to construct and represent very complex and powerful models. There are three basic elements of a Petri net. The first is the representation of an active component of the system that we are modeling. *Active* components are represented as rectangles or squares. They might also be used to represent agents or events and are generally referred to as *transitions*. *Passive* components are represented as circles. They also represent channels, preconditions, or postconditions and are generally referred to as *places*. *Connections* between active and passive system components are made through arrows, with the direction of an arrow indicating the direction of the relationship (for example, the flow of information). An active component connected to a passive component, and the passive component connected to a subsequent active one, is represented as follows: $\square \rightarrow \bigcirc \rightarrow \square$. Formally, the structure of a Petri net is a bipartite directed graph, $G = [P, T, A]$ where $P = \{p_1, p_2, \ldots, p_n\}$ is a set of finite places, $T = \{t_1, t_2, \ldots, t_m\}$ is a set of finite transitions, and $A = \{P \times T\} \cup \{T \times P\}$ is a set of directed arcs. The set of input places of a transition (t) is given by $I(t) = \{p|(p,t) \in A\}$, and the set of output places of transition (t) is given by $O(t) = \{p|(t,p) \in A\}$. A more complete definition presents a Petri net as $PN = (P, T, F, W, M_o)$ where $P = (p_1, p_2, \ldots, p_m)$ is a finite set of places, $T = (t_1, t_2, \ldots, t_n)$ is a finite set of transitions, $F \subseteq (P \times T) \cup (T \times P)$ a set of arcs representing flow relations, $W:F \rightarrow \{1, 2, 3, \ldots\}$ specifies a weight function, $M_o:P \rightarrow \{1, 2, 3, \ldots\}$ specifies the initial marking (e.g., places with tokens and how many tokens). A net structure $N = (P, T, F, W)$ without a specific initial marking is denoted by N. The initial marking of a Petri net is denoted by $(N, M\text{-}0)$.

An Illustration

Let us consider the everyday task of going to a grocery store to do some shopping. We can construct a model of that task with an individual as the active component of the system and the shelves of the grocery store as the passive component (see Figure 6.1). The individual as the active component is represented as the rectangle, and the passive shelves of the store are depicted by the circle. The upper arc describes the individual going to the shelves, and the lower arc represents the products moving to the individual.

Figure 6.1. A Simple Model of Shopping.

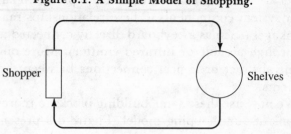

We now increase the detail of the model and represent the act of shopping. In Figure 6.2, the first activity represents a shopper entering the store and locating a shopping cart. The subsequent passive component indicates that the shopping cart has been procured. The second active component represents the desired items being placed in the cart, with the subsequent passive component indicating that all the desired items have been obtained. The final active component represents the individual checking out and leaving the store. In addition to being a more complex representation of the shopping process, Figure 6.2 presents a rule regarding the construction of Petri nets: active components are connected only to passive components, and passive components are connected only to active components. (The reason for this restriction concerns the mathematics behind the analysis of the nets. The interested reader is encouraged to pursue the appropriate literature; see Reutenauer, 1990.) The arrows

Figure 6.2. An Elaboration of the Shopping Model.

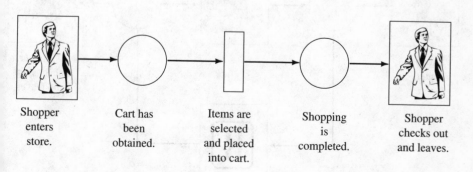

| Shopper enters store. | Cart has been obtained. | Items are selected and placed into cart. | Shopping is completed. | Shopper checks out and leaves. |

in the net are also important in that they represent relationships between system components. These relationships may be explicit linkages (such as a keyboard directly connected to a computer through a cable or infrared emitter). More often, they represent abstract or logical connections between the system components.

We now use these same building blocks to represent two extensions of our shopping model. Figure 6.3 presents shopping in a store with different aisles. After we have entered the store and obtained a cart, we may proceed down either the aisle for dairy products or the aisle for prescriptions (but not the aisle for fish — note the direction of the connecting arrows). Once we have gone down either the dairy or the prescription aisle, we may proceed down the fish aisle *or* we may check out. If we go down the fish aisle, we must then go through either the dairy

Figure 6.3. A Further Elaboration of the Shopping Model.

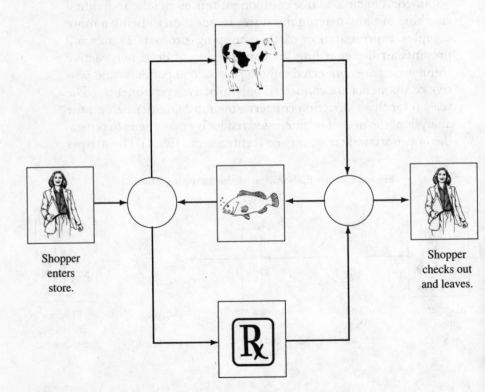

Shopper
enters
store.

Shopper
checks out
and leaves.

or the prescription aisle prior to checking out. It is interesting to note that this model implies an efficient design for shoppers who need just dairy or just prescription products, or for shoppers who need all three products, obtained in the given order, but it is not efficient for shoppers who need only fish.

A second extension (see Figure 6.4) allows suppliers to enter the store and restock the shelves after the store closes. The new active element represents the suppliers, and an arrow connects them to the first passive element. The round-headed arc (touching on the figure of the shopper) is called an *inhibitor arc* and is used here to represent the fact that if it is after hours, shoppers are kept from entering so that the suppliers can restock the store. In this representation, suppliers restock the shelves in the same way as shoppers remove items.

Figure 6.4. Final Elaboration of the Shopping Model.

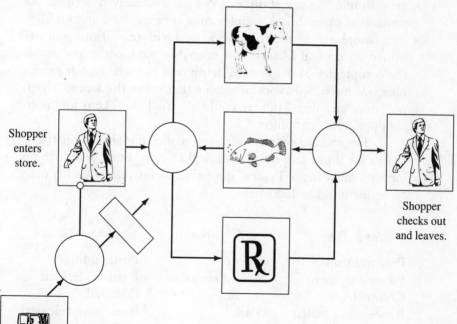

Dynamic Representations

As a graphic tool, a Petri net is similar to a flow chart or block diagram, and it is this visual component that makes it an excellent tool for communication. But these nets go beyond flow charts and block diagrams in that they incorporate *tokens,* which are used to simulate dynamic and concurrent activities of a system. Tokens reside in places and move throughout the net as transitions "fire." (The "firing" of a transition is controlled by rules associated with that transition. In the simplest case, a transition is enabled and "fires" as soon as a token resides in the place that precedes it.) A token is used to represent an abstract or nonabstract entity within a model. In Figure 6.3 we have several tokens of different types, representing a shopper entering, the products available in each aisle, and the shopper leaving. Figure 6.4 adds a new token type, to represent suppliers.

The rules that govern the "firing" of transitions range from very simple to very complex. We have already described the simplest of cases. More complex rules state more complex things. The complexity of the rules associated with transitions is determined by several factors, but probably the most important is the complexity of the system being represented. In our examples, we have two types of tokens that enter the store, "shopper" and "supplier," but we could also include tokens for "nonshopper" and "shoplifter."

Depending on the purpose of the model we construct, places for input and output, as well as transitions, will take on various meanings. Typical applications for places and transitions include the following:

Input Places	*Transitions*	*Output Places*
Precondition	Event	Postcondition
Passive element	Active element	Passive element
Channel	Agency	Channel
Resources needed	Task	Resources released
Buffer	Processor	Buffer
Condition	Clause in logic	Conclusion

Multiple Meaningful Perspectives

We mentioned earlier that a useful tool or methodology should help us represent the system of interest in a meaningful manner and from multiple perspectives (or levels of abstraction). We now describe how those models can be constructed, using the *replenishment-at-sea task* as an example. This task (Hogan, Sampson, Raza, Millar, & Salas, 1987) simulates a frequent U.S. Navy task of transferring supplies at sea from a supply ship to a receiving ship (see Figure 6.5). In the laboratory, the supply ship resides on one table and is separated by approximately thirty centimeters of "ocean" from the receiving ship, which is on a second table. Two methods exist for transferring cargo between the ships. The first uses a battery-operated, remote-controlled crane on the receiving ship. The second method employs two towers, one on each ship, each equipped with a pulley and a rope. The supply ship, manned by its operator, has three containers for holding cargo, two platforms, and a net. Each container has a separate weight capacity and can be attached to either the crane or the pulley. Holds on the supply ship are loaded with blocks of various sizes and colors, cylinders, and metal bars representing fuel, ammunition, food, supplies,

Figure 6.5. Replenishment at Sea.

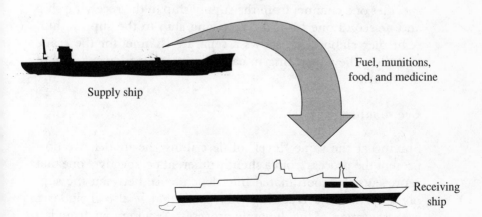

Fuel, munitions, food, and medicine

Supply ship

Receiving ship

and spare parts. The operator has three duties: attaching the platforms to the pulley and the crane, loading cargo onto the platforms, and helping the pulley operator move the pulley back and forth between the two ships. The receiving ship is manned by two individuals, a pulley operator and a crane operator. The pulley operator, in addition to moving the pulley with the supply ship's operator, helps the crane operator unload and store cargo that arrives on the receiving ship. The crane operator also assists the pulley operator in the unloading and storing. The overall objective of the task is to transfer as much cargo as possible within a specified time.

Petri Net Representation

Construction of a Petri net to represent any complex system usually consists of a sequence of models, beginning with the general, moving through a process of continual refinement, and stopping at the appropriate level of detail. The simplest meaningful description of the replenishment-at-sea task is given in the top panel of Figure 6.6. The supply and receiving ships are each represented as one agency, and a transfer channel exists between them. The center panel of Figure 6.6 shows an elaboration or refinement of the model. (An elaboration of places is denoted by a broken circular or oval line; an elaboration of a transition is denoted by a broken square or rectangle.) This elaboration specifies one channel from the supply ship to the receiving ship and a second one from the receiving ship to the supply ship. A further elaboration shows a separate channel for the crane and the pulley operating in each direction (see lower panel of the figure).

Coordination

Staying at the same "level" of describing the model, we now present the process from a slightly different perspective, one that represents the coordinated interdependence between the supply ship and the receiving ship (note that it also includes a representation of the dynamic process). As you move from left

Figure 6.6. Three Representations of Replenishment at Sea.

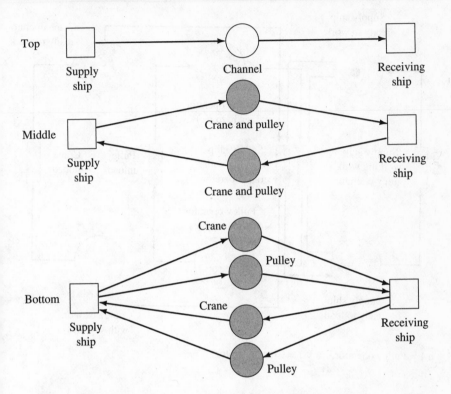

to right in Figure 6.7, note the correspondence to the supply ship's operator, the pulley operator, and the crane operator, respectively. The tokens in the upper three places of the net indicate that the conditions are met for each of the three individuals to work. The second and third transitions from the left indicate that the supply ship is working with either the pulley or the crane operator, respectively. If the "supply ship working with pulley operator" transition fires, then the tokens are removed from the "supply ship ready to work" and "pulley operator ready to work" places and are deposited in the "supply ship ready to load" and "pulley operator with supplies" places. In the real world, this transition represents the two individuals cooperating together to operate the pulley. The subsequent "firing" of transitions would represent the supply ship's operator loading

Figure 6.7. Operators Represented as Separate Subnets.

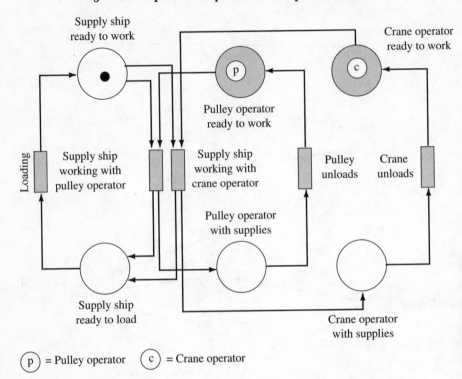

supplies and the pulley operator unloading supplies, respectively. When the supply ship's "loading" is completed, the token is placed back in the "supply ship ready to work" transition, and the operator can work with the crane operator (or again with the pulley operator, if the token indicates that the pulley operator is ready).

It is important to note that we are not describing underlying rules embedded in the transitions that would govern behavior in the real situation. These, of course, would be included in a real simulation-and-analysis model and would contain information about such things as length of time to load and unload supplies and what to do in case of a conflict inherent in the net. (There is such a conflict now. The supply ship can work with either the pulley operator or the crane operator. When working with the pulley operator, however, it is not possible to work with the crane operator, since the precondition "supply ship ready to work" is no longer enabled. The reason is that the token has moved to "supply ship working with pulley operator.")

Two Alternative Representations

We could also represent the process by reducing the number of places and/or transitions through the addition of more control at the transition level. One such change is depicted in Figure 6.8. Two places have now been removed, and the crane and the pulley are depicted as tokens themselves, but we retain separate arcs for each. Figure 6.9 depicts the general case in which the crane and the pulley are individual tokens and in which the logic at the second and third transitions controls which token

Figure 6.8. Operators Represented as Tokens,
Retaining Separate Channels.

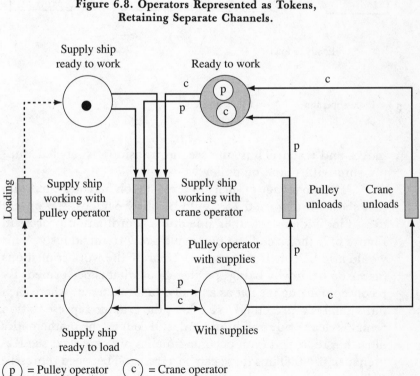

Figure 6.9. Operators Represented as Tokens, with One Common Channel.

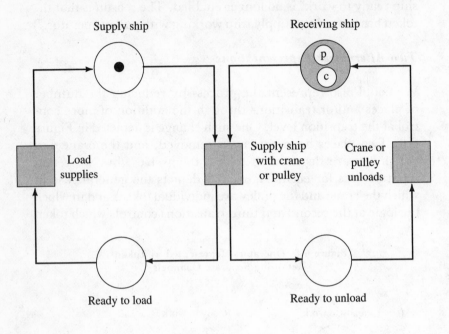

moves and when. Thus, the second transition is labeled "supply ship with crane or pulley."

The advantage of such a representation, as contrasted with that shown in Figure 6.7, should be fairly evident. If we were to add individuals to either side of the coordination process in Figure 6.7, the size of the net would grow tremendously. This would also be true if we were to elaborate the work transitions (as we do below) by being specific about what is performed. By reconceptualizing the net as an individual-token net, where each individual is represented as a token, the graphic representation remains clean and straightforward. (Of course, the mathematics of such a representation become much more complex; see Reutenauer, 1990. Thus there can be a trade-off between representational elegance and the underlying mathematics that represent the model. Fortunately, most computer programs that implement complex Petri nets assist the modeler with this trade-off.)

An Additional Elaboration

Figure 6.10 presents one further elaboration at the team level. The figure clearly illustrates the tasks that each team member must perform individually and makes explicit those tasks where interaction with other team members must occur. We now briefly describe each position's representation. The left portion of the figure depicts the supply ship, and that position has three tasks. The first two, loading the supplies and attaching and unattaching the different platforms to the crane and the pulley,

Figure 6.10. Alternative Representation of Operator Roles.

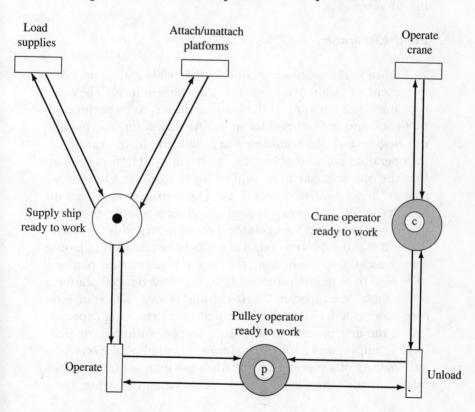

are independent of the other team members. The current marking of the net shows a token in the place, and so the supply ship's operator is ready to perform any of the tasks. (The term *marking* refers to the places in the net where tokens either reside or do not reside; see Murata, 1989, for details and implications.) At the bottom-left portion of the figure, the transition labeled "operate" is shared by the supply ship and the pulley operator. This transition removes a token from the enabling place for each and returns it when the two operators have finished operating the pulley. The transition explicitly indicates the interdependence between these two positions. The place for the pulley operator also enables the two tasks of the pulley operator. The crane operator's two tasks are represented on the right side of the figure, with the independence of operating the crane made explicit, as is interdependence (with the pulley operator) during the unloading of supplies.

Final Elaboration

In Figure 6.11, we describe one further elaboration, in order to present a portion of a job at the task-element level. The operator starts the job at p_1. If the loading duty is to be performed, t_1 "fires," and control resides in p_2. At this point, the loading can begin, and two transitions are enabled. In the case of t_2, the operator realizes that loading can begin; t_3, if it "fires," means that the operator has to be told to begin loading. Once either t_2 or t_3 "fires," control moves to p_3. The transition t_4 represents a choice point. If the correct platform is *not* available, then control moves to p_4, and the operator communicates with the receiving ship that the desired platform needs to be sent over (t_5); once communication is finished (p_5) the operator waits for the platform to be sent over before progressing to p_6. If the desired platform *is* available, then loading begins straightaway. The transition t_7 represents a decision about the platform's reaching capacity. When the first piece is to be placed on the platform, the platform is empty, and a token resides in p_7, enabling the selection and loading of a piece of cargo. After the item is placed on the platform, the token is back in p_6. This chain of events, from

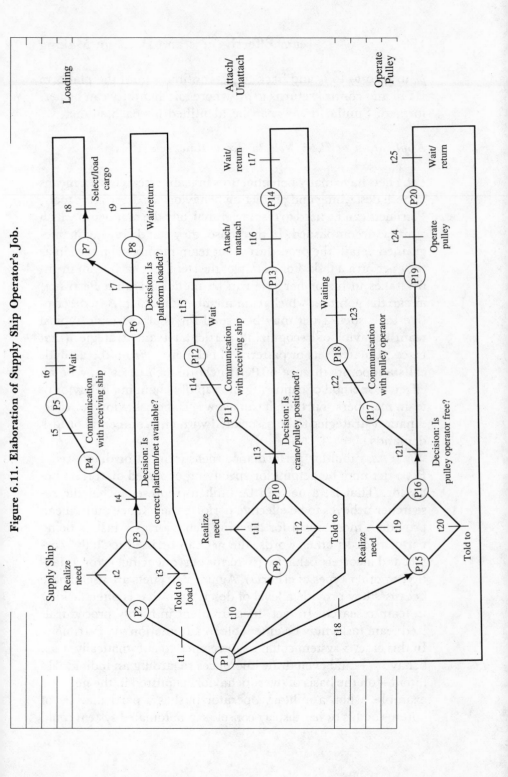

Figure 6.11. Elaboration of Supply Ship Operator's Job.

p_6 to t_7 to p_7 to t_8 and back to p_6, continues until the platform is full and control returns to p_1, where another duty can be performed. Similar details can be identified for each subnet.

Application of Petri Nets to Team Research

Petri nets have many potential uses in team research, as a means of both describing and predicting behavior. As descriptive tools, Petri nets can be used to display graphically the manner in which a task is accomplished. In this sense, they can delineate, in fine-grained detail, the procedures that team members engage in as they perform a task. For example, the steps that each team member takes in his or her role can be modeled with a Petri net, as can the points at which team members interact. As a descriptive tool, such a net may be useful for characterizing typical team behavior or recognizing particular team strategies (that is, coordinated sets or patterns of behavior). From the analytical standpoint, the use of Petri nets in such cases may be an effective method of capturing the rapidly changing behavior of team members. Further, it can allow specific behavioral or coordination strategies to be associated with environmental or task demands.

As a tool for performance measurement or diagnosis, a Petri net may be helpful for specifying expected or correct behavior. That is, a net can be built to represent what the researcher believes to be effective performance. Once built, it can provide a mechanism for tracking behavior as a task is being performed. In other words, the net can be used to "tally" correct and incorrect behavior (in terms of sequencing, error, quantity, or other types of criteria). Again, Petri nets are useful here because they provide a level of description that is often lacking in team research. In fact, measurement in highly proceduralized team tasks may be amenable to automation via Petri nets. In this case, a system could be developed to automatically track behaviors — and even draw inferences regarding an individual's intent — on the basis of overt behaviors captured in the net. For example, when a military operator pushes a particular set of buttons on his or her display console, an automated system could use the Petri net to *infer* an intention to shoot a missile. In a training scenario, such information could be used to provide feedback regarding the appropriateness of that behavior.

Petri nets may also be used for predictive purposes. A number of analytical strategies exist that can help evaluate the efficiency of a net. These are too detailed to describe here, but suffice it to say that several methods exist that would allow a researcher to examine questions about the structure of the behavior described in a net, the efficacy of the relationships in a net, and the overall effectiveness of the net (Jensen & Rozenberg, 1991).

Artificial Intelligence, Computer Modeling, and Team Behavior

We now discuss alternative modeling techniques that have their roots in artificial intelligence (AI). First, however, we provide a very brief review of artificial intelligence because of its commonality to the remaining methods.

Artificial Intelligence

There have been numerous definitions of AI, but we prefer a concise one: "the automation of intelligent behavior" (Luger & Stubblefield, 1989, p. 1). Essentially, AI is an area of computer science that focuses on the development of computer programs that can perform tasks that are normally associated with intelligent human behavior. Research has typically focused on such areas as natural-language understanding, vision processing, speech recognition, robotics, and expert systems.

AI has an eclectic theoretical foundation, with many of its ideas based on mathematics, formal logic, engineering, philosophy, and psychology. Much of the original focus of AI research was on the development of computer programs that could solve problems over a wide variety of domains. However, years of slow progress indicated that the programs would have to be limited to smaller domains (see Newell & Simon, 1972). The 1970s and 1980s saw greater acceptance of AI systems by the general public, and the number of AI programs used in private industry increased dramatically during the last decade. The standard results of these programs show a tenfold increase in productivity (Feigenbaum, McCorduck, & Nii, 1989).

Recently, there has been some sharing of resources between those using simulations in their research and researchers on artificial intelligence. Researchers employing computer simulations use AI techniques for their knowledge-representation paradigms, whereas AI researchers employ simulations for their power and realism (Widman, Loparo, & Nielsen, 1989).

Production Rules

Undoubtedly, the most widely used form of knowledge representation employed in AI programs is the form that involves *production rules*. Most of the problem-solving tasks we encounter daily can be represented naturally in the form of rules, as follows:

1. If it is raining and you have no raincoat, then drive to store and buy one.
2. If you need to drive to the store and your car is low on gas, then fill up your gask tank.
3. If you need to fill up your gask tank and you have no money, then go to the nearest bank machine (or ATM).
4. If you go to the ATM and get some money, then fill up your gask tank and drive to the store.

A production rule is a two-part structure, consisting of an antecedent clause (*if*) and a consequent clause (*then*). *If* the antecedent conditions of a rule are satisfied — *if* the conditions exist in the task environment — *then* the rule "fires," and its consequent clause is *instantiated* (activated). Thus, as in the example above, *if* it is raining *and* you have no raincoat, *then* the first rule "fires": you must go to the store to purchase a raincoat. Note that these four rules form a natural problem-solving chain: the "firing" of the first rule might lead to the "firing" of the second, and so on. This is called *forward-chaining*, or representing problems in terms of moving from initial conditions to a goal state (Winston, 1989). Production rules are a flexible and natural approach to representing knowledge, from the simplest every-day problems to the most complex problem domains. They are most commonly associated with the most successful of all AI applications, expert systems.

Expert Systems. An expert system is a computer program that contains the knowledge of one or more experts. As such, an expert system is able to simulate the decision-making ability of a human expert (Hall & Kandel, 1986). Because of the extensive knowledge encoded in these programs, they are also often called *knowledge-based systems*. Expert systems have been developed for variety of purposes, including medical diagnosis (Buchanan & Shortliffe, 1984; Cios, Shin, & Goodenday, 1991), proving of mathematical theorems (Winston, 1989), configuration of mainframe computers (Luger & Stubblefield, 1989), recognition of human speech (Erman, Hayes-Roth, Lesser, & Reddy, 1980), assistance in the location of oil (Lindsay, Buchanan, Feigenbaum, & Lederberg, 1980), and integration of incremental-fit indices from covariance structural-modeling solutions (Craiger & Coovert, 1991).

How "expert" are expert systems? MYCIN, an expert system used by physicians to assist in the diagnosis of blood disorders, was tested against a number of medical experts in the field. An initial evaluation found only 70 percent agreement between the experts' diagnoses and MYCIN's. Most of the differences, however, were found to be in diagnosis of the severity of the disorder, not in the disorder itself. After modification, later evaluation showed a 92 percent agreement rate between the physicians and MYCIN (Buchanan & Shortliffe, 1984). This finding may suggest that people, either implicitly or explicitly, use *if-then* rules when making decisions.

Production Rules and Team Performance. To illustrate the application of rules to team research, we can apply production rules to the replenishment-at-sea task. Let us say that we are interested in how the behavior of the supply ship's operator influences both the pulley and the crane operator, and vice versa. The following rules can be used to represent a tiny portion of the overall simulation:

1. If both the pulley and the supply ship operator are using the pulley, then neither one is free.
2. If the crane operator is moving the crane, then the crane operator is not free.
3. If the pulley and crane operators are both free, then the pulley or the crane can be loaded.
4. If the pulley is empty, then load the pulley.
5. If the pulley is free, then communicate to the crane operator and communicate to the ship's operator.
6. If the crane is empty, then load the crane.
7. If the crane is loaded and the crane operator and the supply ship's operator are free, then move the crane to the supply ship.
8. If the load is lost, then report to your superior.

The antecedent clauses of the rules contain information on the task environment and critical team behaviors — some behaviors appropriate, some inappropriate — and the other side contains the consequences of the behavior for the task environment. Note that these rules are able to define complex bidirectional relationships between team members and the task environment. The behavior of team members changes the task environment, which then requires changes in the behavior of the team members to adapt to the new goal or task conditions.

Why do we include inappropriate behavior in our simulation? If we were studying teams by means of traditional methods, it would be difficult if not impossible to study the effect of inappropriate behavior on team performance (except in the context of a contrived task in a controlled experimental setting). With a simulation, however, we can specify ranges of behavior and develop hypotheses as changes in behavior influence the team's performance. In our simulation, there is almost unlimited flexibility in our ability to specify conditions and predictions with production rules.

Suppose that we are also interested in the effects of coordination on the time it takes to complete a task. We can model the effects of coordination by including temporal information in the rules, thereby gaining the ability to estimate the effects of various behaviors on efficiency and productivity:

9. If the pulley load is greater than three hundred pounds, then average time to task completion is 1.25 minutes, and neither operator is free.

10. If the crane operator is moving the crane and the crane load is greater than two hundred pounds and less than maximum, then the average time to task completion is .75 minutes, and the crane operator is not free.

11. If the pulley is loaded and the supply ship's operator is free and the crane is not on the supply ship, then move the crane to the other ship, and the average time for the move will be 1.25 minutes.

12. If the pulley operator drops the load or the supply ship's operator drops the load, then assess a performance penalty of seven minutes.

We have included average performance times for tasks and a penalty for poor performance. This allows the researcher to quantify (and assess the effects of) both appropriate and inappropriate behavior. By implementing a time variable, the researcher may also discover significant nonlinear relationships that may not be obvious or even discoverable with traditional methods. For example, the researcher may find that, in general, task performance is not negatively affected by nonoptimal loading of the pulley or the crane; however, small changes at critical points may cause the rest of the task structure to break down.

Production Rules for Prediction and Description of Team Behavior. Given a few hundred such rules, one can describe even the most complex relationships among individual team members, entire teams, and the environments in which they perform. Because they are implemented in natural language, and because of their plasticity in modeling even the most intricate behavioral networks, production rules are an attractive means of describing team structures.

By developing a priori theory as to possible outcomes of team behavior, one can contrast the a priori theory with actual results. This is one of the strengths of computer simulations: explicitly coding behaviors, dependencies, and consequences forces one to be more critical of the necessary ingredients of the theory, including all relevant causal mechanisms. Omission of a single essential ingredient may not be missed in traditional means of specifying psychological hypotheses; but, when ingredients are coded into a computer model, small deviations quickly become apparent. Thus production rules are also attractive as a means of predicting team outcomes.

Application of Production Rules to Team Research. How can production rules be used in team modeling and simulation? A researcher may state a hypothesis about team behavior as follows: *Time pressure and collective efficacy will interact in such a way that teams low in collective efficacy will be more prone to the impact of time pressure than will teams high in collective efficacy.* The same hypothesis, stated in terms of production rules, could encourage the researcher to specify the phenomenon in more detail:

1. If collective efficacy is high and time pressure is high, then the team's performance will be moderate.
2. If collective efficacy is low and time pressure is high, then the team's performance will be low.
3. If collective efficacy is low and time pressure is low, then the team's performance will be moderate.
4. If collective efficacy is high and time pressure is low, then the team's performance will be high.

Obviously, specifying the implications of a hypothesis in this way is a matter of course in conducting experiments. The value of production rules, then, may be that they provide a framework and a format in which hypotheses can be specified. Moreover, they are predictive statements and, as such, lend themselves to testing.

Acknowledging Reality: The Role of Uncertainty in Task Environments. Since real situations are characterized by varying degrees of uncertainty, it may be desirable to incorporate into the model a measure for the uncertainty inherent in the task environment. By *uncertainty,* we mean the imperfect correlation between a set of inputs and outputs: although the conditions specified in the antecedent clause may exist, the consequent clause may not apply every time; given a specified set of antecedent conditions, we may find that a particular consequence exists only 80 percent of the time.

Uncertainty is a ubiquitous phenomenon, and incorporating it into a simulation correctly acknowledges that real-world phenomena involve uncertainty. This is almost certainly the default condition in the task environments where teams operate. A surgical team, for example, is often unsure about the cause of certain symptoms (a reason for exploratory surgery). A combat team is not always sure, even with the best surveillance, of the enemy's location, strength, or battle plan. A sales team, even with the best marketing research, is not sure about the needs or desires of consumers.

We often express the degree of uncertainty in a task environment in linguistic terms: "Doctor, there is a *good* chance that the cause of the symptoms is staphylococcus." "General, we are *fairly certain* that the enemy will attack at dawn." "If we do not capture at least 15 percent of the market, there is a *very poor* chance of this product's surviving in the marketplace." Uncertainty can be a thorn in the side of any research. It exists in abundance and therefore should not be ignored or ascribed to "random error." Failing to acknowledge and account for uncertainty means failing to acknowledge the real circumstances under which teams operate.

Fuzzy Set Theory

Tasks involving vague and incomplete information, ambiguous cues, and the like — that is, tasks involving uncertainty — are tasks that humans handle efficiently. Driving a car is just such a task. We could never get from home to the grocery store if we required a continuous stream of feedback on the exact physical measurements necessary for driving: "Turn the steering wheel to $1°18'53''$. Apply 4.04 pounds of pressure to the accelerator. Begin deceleration when speed reaches 22.6 miles per hour."

Instead we use approximations of these behaviors: "Turn the steering wheel *a little* to the right. Press *very lightly* on the gas pedal. As you begin to approach the speed limit, *slow down*." Most people of driving age would be able to follow these instructions without too much difficulty, despite their imprecise and vague nature. Indeed, most of the tasks we perform can be and are described in uncertain, imprecise, vague, and even ambiguous terms, and we find that we have little difficulty understanding and carrying out instructions.

Things break down, however, when we provide a computer with this type of instruction. Computers are unable to function in an environment of inexactness. Anyone who has ever coded even a small program knows what a small "bug" can do to the outcome. Why are computers poorer than people at these types of tasks? It is primarily because computers were developed to handle the types of problems at which humans are not good (such as adding up huge columns of numbers and sorting large lists of data).

Mathematical Representation of Vagueness. Most real-life situations involve vague, ambiguous, and inexact information cues, but we often describe or categorize these situations in precise, crisp terms. Zadeh (1965) developed *fuzzy set theory* as a mathematical means of quantifying the vagueness and the linguistic inexactness inherent in many real-world environments. Fuzzy set theory is now commonly employed in computers as a means of providing them with the ability to represent and reason with vague and imprecise information.

Fuzziness should not be confused, as it often is, with *stochastic uncertainty*. The latter term refers to our inability to predict future events because of random processes. (Some would argue that random processes are a fiction: it is our inability to account for 100 percent of causal mechanisms that creates randomness.) For example, our inability to predict the roll of a die is due to small variations in such variables as the trajectory and velocity of the die and the texture of the surface where it lands. Fuzziness, however, concerns our inability to describe phenomena precisely in linguistic terms. For example, our inability to describe precisely how we drive from point A to point B, how we catch a ball, or how we form words may be seen as a problem stemming from linguistic inexactness — semantic difficulties arising from our inability to put complex descriptions of behavior into words. A primary extension of fuzzy sets has been to *fuzzy logic,* which is a method of reasoning with fuzzy sets.

Fuzzy Logic and a Fuzzy Example. To illustrate the concept of fuzziness, consider a situation where you are asked to rate a co-worker's job performance. Informally, you might be asked, "How would you rate Susan's job performance?" What kind of terminology are you likely to use? Some reasonable terms are *poor, fair, average, good,* and *excellent.* Or you might say that Susan is "a *very good* worker" or a "*somewhat poor* worker." Formally, you might be asked to evaluate Susan's work with a Likert scale whose anchors are "*much better than* the average worker," "*about the same as* the average worker," and "*much worse than* the average worker." When you hear these imprecise terms, are you thrown into a quandary about how to interpret them? Usually not: if you are familiar with the job and know that Susan is an excellent worker, then you probably have a fairly reasonable idea of what kinds of behavior Susan exhibits at work.

Why is it that people do not use more precise terminology when describing phenomena? It is probably because precision is not required for a satisfactory decision (this is what Simon refers to as "satisficing") and would probably even be detrimental, eventually causing cognitive overload. People are able to forgo precision without much cost because most people understand (within limits, of course) what others mean by the terms *good, not very good,* and so on. Humans appear to have the ability to understand that inexact terms correspond to, or map, exact real-world measures (although somewhat imperfectly).

Scientists are still unsure why people are able to extrapolate from vague information, and the answer to this question is outside the scope of the present chapter. The questions we would like to address are these: At what exact place of the continuum on a rating scale should a worker be considered *good?* Where does *very good* begin? How much difference is there between *very good* and *poor?* These are very important questions. Careers are made and broken on the basis of performance evaluations.

Recall that in classical set theory, mutually exclusive categories do not overlap, by definition. That is, in a performance rating, someone cannot be both a *good* and a *very good* worker. Told that Susan is a *good worker* and a *very good* worker, most people would feel somewhat uncomfortable. Nevertheless, we will now show why it is not unreasonable to consider her both a *good* and a *very good* worker, by showing how fuzzy set theory can be applied to this situation. Table 6.1 shows membership grades (values) on a five-point behaviorally anchored rating scale. The membership grades (cell values) specify how representative an element is of a category; the higher the membership grade, the more representative the value is of that category. For example, a rating of 5.0 is most representative of the fuzzy set *very good*, whereas a rating of 1.0 is most representative of the fuzzy set *poor*. The performance rating of 3.0 falls somewhere in between; it is most representative of the fuzzy set *average* and is equally representative of the fuzzy sets *good* and *fair*.

Table 6.1. Performance Ratings and Fuzzy Set Grades of Membership.

Performance Rating	Very Good	Good	Average	Fair	Poor
1	0.0	0.0	0.3	0.5	1.0
3	0.1	0.5	1.0	0.5	0.1
5	1.0	0.7	0.2	0.0	0.0

Note the seeming contradiction: someone receiving a rating of 3.0 falls into each of the fuzzy sets (evaluation categories); however, the membership grade of 1.0 in the fuzzy set *average* indicates that the worker is most likely an average worker, and only half as likely to be considered a good or fair performer. We argue that this is much more justified than the typical case. Someone receiving a mean rating of 2.99 might be categorized as a good worker; someone else receiving a mean rating of 3.01 might be considered a very good worker. This makes little sense, but this type of categorization does allow us to acknowledge that even though the first worker receives a slightly lower rating, the two workers are very close in terms of performance. Fuzzy logic allows us to acknowledge this closeness by allowing grades of memberships across *each* of the categories. Note that by using fuzzy logic, we can represent the uncertainty in our evaluations of a person's performance by allowing multiple grades of membership across overlapping fuzzy sets.

Fuzzy Logic and Team Behavior. Perhaps the most important attribute of fuzzy logic is that it allows researchers to imitate *approximate reasoning*—that is, "inference of a possibly imprecise conclusion from a set of possibly imprecise premises" (Giarratano & Riley, 1989, p. 320). Fuzzy logic has also been proposed as the only form of inference that will allow the computer to imitate commonsense reasoning, an attribute previously attributed only to human beings. (The study of approximate reasoning, especially with regard to team decision making, has a number of consequences that we will discuss shortly.)

The implications of this line of reasoning for modeling and simulating team behavior are important. Consider the typical environment in which complex problems present themselves. The defining characteristic of these situations is undoubtedly the existence of uncertainty—the inability to represent accurately all the available task-relevant information. In fact, it is not unreasonable to suggest that the more critical the problem, the more complex the network of causal relationships, and the higher the inherent uncertainty.

How do we apply fuzzy logic to the problem of analyzing and measuring team performance? We can incorporate fuzzy logic into our rules, as a means of representing our uncertainty about how environmental conditions will influence team performance. Systems that employ a combination of production rules and fuzzy set theory are called *fuzzy systems* (Hall & Kandel, 1986). For example, we might hypothesize that wind velocity and wave height are environmental conditions critical to the task of transporting supplies across ships *while the ships* are moving. What hypotheses might we offer regarding the effects of wind velocity and wave height on a ship's position? Because the interaction of these variables is difficult if not impossible to specify with 100 percent confidence, we can make predictions about these effects and include fuzzy indices as a means of acknowledging this uncertainty:

1. If wind speed is low and wave height is moderate, then ship speed should be moderate.
2. If wind speed is moderate and wave height is moderate, then ship speed should be moderate or low.
3. If wind speed is very high and wave height is moderate, then ship speed should be low.

The primary difference between the function of the typical rule-based system and the fuzzy system is that in the former, the most applicable rule "fires"; in the latter, all rules will "fire." Let us explain. When the measures of the input variables (wind velocity and wave height) and are put into the system, they will be in continuous form (real numbers). Membership functions are employed to map from the continuous measurements to the membership grades for each of the fuzzy categories. Figure 6.12 illustrates three membership functions for the fuzzy variable "wind velocities."

Wind velocity has been partitioned into three fuzzy sets: *low, moderate,* and *high*. Three membership functions allow us to take a real value for wind speed and map that value to each of the fuzzy sets. The membership function defined for the fuzzy set *low* approximates a sigmoidal distribution. The *moderate* set approximates a leptokurtic Gaussian distribution. The *high* set roughly approximates a log distribution.

Three values of wind velocity are also defined: A (10 miles per hour), B (20), and C (75). According to the tenets of fuzzy logic, each value will have a membership grade in each of the categories. To determine these membership grades, we move directly up from the point on the abscissa until it bisects each distribution, and then we move horizontally to the ordinate, to determine the fuzzy membership grade. For point A, the membership grade for the fuzzy set *low* is approximately 0.85, and 0.0 for both the *moderate* and *high* sets. The membership grades of 0.85, 0.0, and 0.0 indicate that 10 miles per hour is most

Figure 6.12. Membership Functions Defining Fuzzy Sets for Wind Velocity.

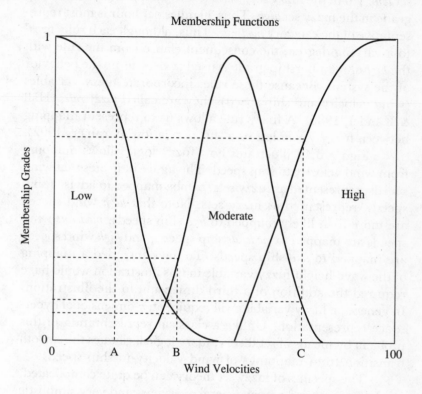

probably in the fuzzy set *low*. For point B, we move up vertically and bisect the first distribution, the fuzzy set *low*. Moving
horizontally to the ordinate, we find that B's membership grade
is approximately 0.07 for the fuzzy set *low,* and approximately
0.20 for *moderate* and 0.0 for the fuzzy set *high*. Point C has a
membership grade of approximately 0.12 in the fuzzy set *moderate,* and approximately 0.70 in the fuzzy set *high*. Thus B is most
representative of the fuzzy set *moderate,* and C is most representative of the fuzzy set *high*.

Consider for the first input a wind velocity of 50 miles
per hour. (For now we will ignore the variable of wave height,
since it is constant across the three rules.) Using the membership
functions defined in Figure 6.12, we find that a wind velocity

of 50 miles per hour has a membership grade of 0.0 in the fuzzy set *low*, 1.0 in the fuzzy set *moderate*, and a very tiny membership grade in the fuzzy set *high*. Thus 50 miles per hour is most representative of the category *moderate*. Thus, although each rule "fires" to a varying degree, the consequent clause from the rule with the *highest* membership grade is used to determine the behavior of the system. Because these rules incorporate fuzzy variables (wind velocity and ship speed), they are called *fuzzy rules* (Hall & Kandel, 1986). A fuzzy rule allows us to represent mapping between fuzzy variables, or a "fuzzy relation" (Craiger, 1992).

Figure 6.13 illustrates how fuzzy logic allows mapping from wind velocity to ship speed. The figure indicates that wind speeds, represented as fuzzy sets, can be mapped to advised ship speeds, represented as fuzzy sets. Note that *high* wind speeds are more than likely mapped to *low* ship speeds, *moderate* wind speeds are mapped to *moderate* ship speeds, and *high* wind speeds are mapped to *low* ship speeds. To have included a mapping of the wave-height fuzzy variable in this illustration would have required the addition of a third dimension to the illustration. In general, *n* fuzzy variables will require an *n*-dimensional hyperspace representation. Unlike a classical representation of this problem by means of set theory, fuzzy logic facilitates the smooth transition from mappings of wind velocity to ship speeds.

The specifics of fuzzy set theory can be quite complicated. We have presented a very general overview, and very simplistic examples, to impart feeling for how uncertainty can be incorporated into a computer simulation. We refer the interested reader to Kosko (1992) for further understanding of fuzzy set theory.

Application of Fuzzy Logic to Team Research. Like production rules, the principles of fuzzy logic can aid team researchers by providing a tool with which to describe and predict team behavior. As a descriptive tool, fuzzy logic offers a way to specify in detail the behavior of individual team members and of the team as a whole. Furthermore, as a predictive tool, fuzzy logic has the added value of being able to summarize the anticipated behavior of a team, even given the naturally occurring uncertainty. For example, fuzzy logic could help a researcher

Figure 6.13. Fuzzy Rule Mapping Wind Speed to Ship Speed.

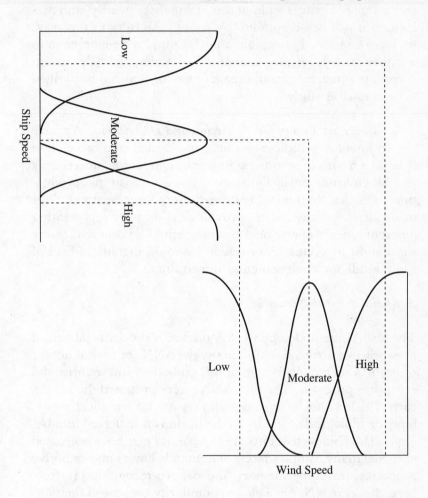

predict the outcome of task demands on strategy changes in a military command-and-control team. More specifically, one could posit that if time pressure is low, then team members will exercise explicit coordination by discussing strategy changes with one another, and performance will be acceptable. If time pressure is moderate, then team members will exercise explicit coordination by discussing strategy changes with one another, and performance will be poor. If time pressure is high, then team

members will exercise implicit coordination by making necessary strategy changes without discussing them overtly, and performance will be acceptable. By stating the rules in this way,
we have attempted to explain a fairly complex phenomenon in
a rather straightforward manner. Moreover, the rules all incorporate predictions about team behavior that can be verified
with empirical study.

Fuzzy Set Theory for Prediction and Description. We have
shown how fuzzy indices can be incorporated into production
rules as a means of acknowledging and representing uncertainty
in task environments. Thus, even more than simple production rules that do not include uncertainty indices, simulations
incorporating fuzzy indices provide flexibility for representing
different types of operational environments. We believe that any
simulation involving team research should include indices of
some kinds for environmental uncertainty.

Artificial Neural Networks

The last AI methodology we will discuss is the artificial neural
network. An artificial neural network (ANN, or neural net for
short) is a metaphor for the brain, embodied in the form of a
computer program. The first ANNs were proposed during the
early 1940s as a means of describing, in mathematical terms,
how the biological structure of the brain is transferred into behavior (McCullouch & Pitts, 1943). Neural nets have been used
to model many complex facets of human behavior and cognitive
processes, including memory and pattern recognition (Grossberg, 1982). ANNs have gained popularity because of their applications outside biological and behavioral modeling, including applications for predicting stock prices, diagnosing diseases
(Caudill, 1990), and classifying jobs (Dobbins & Coovert, 1992).
    The distinctive and defining attribute of ANNs is their
capability of learning the relationships between a set of input
patterns and an associated set of output patterns. Once the ANN
has learned these relationships, it is able to generalize across
new, never-before-seen input stimuli. Therefore, a rough anal-

ogy can be drawn between ANNs and traditional statistical methods, such as multiple regression. The primary difference is that ANNs are model-free estimators (Kosko, 1992): the model hypothesized to "cause" the distributions in the data are not prespecified; rather, the ANN employs an adaptive procedure to capture the relationships underlying the data. Thus ANNs are able to approximate arbitrarily complex mathematical functions. To understand how ANNs learn via adaptation, we must first describe the physical structure of an ANN.

Processing Elements and Interconnections. The structure that represents the ANN is called its *architecture*. One can think of the ANN's architecture as being analogous to the physical architecture of the brain—neurons connected to other neurons via dendrites and axons.

Figure 6.14 illustrates a very simple architecture: a three-layer ANN. The bottom layer of processing elements (PEs) repre-

Figure 6.14. Three-Layer Neural Network.

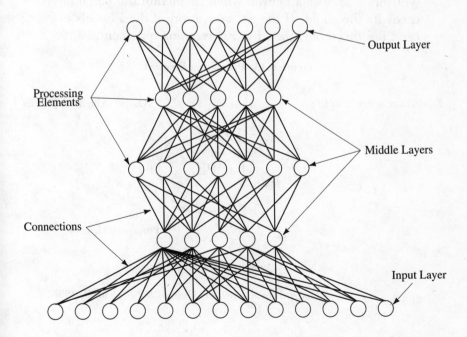

sents the *input layer* (for the independent variables). The middle layer is often called the *hidden* or *middle layer,* and the top layer represents the *output layer* (for the dependent variables). The simplest architecture consists of an input and an output layer, but a single hidden layer greatly increases the net's ability to approximate arbitrarily complex mathematical functions.

PEs and interconnections between the PEs serve as the building blocks of an ANN. PEs are the computer equivalent of the neuron. Figure 6.15 illustrates the basic PE. Each PE has an associated mathematical function that determines the activation of the PE. The activation of the PE at time *t* is determined by the inputs of each of the PEs connected to the PE (lower-level PEs) and the current activation of the PE. Each input connection has an associated weight. The activation of each PE is calculated by multiplying the weight by the associated input and summing across these values. The PE's output is therefore a function of the PE's activation.

Like real neurons, PEs can be either excitatory or inhibitory. If the activation of the PE exceeds a certain threshold, it will "fire," as does a neuron when its membrane potential exceeds its threshold. If the net activation of the PE fails to exceed the threshold, then the PE remains quiescent.

Figure 6.15. Processing Element.

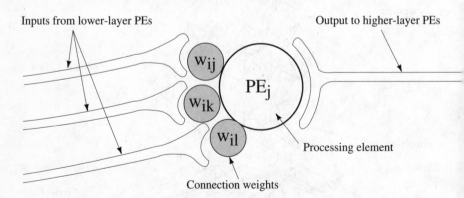

Inputs from lower-layer PEs

Output to higher-layer PEs

w_{ij}

PE_j

w_{ik}

w_{il}

Processing element

Connection weights

Source: Adapted from Rumelhart, Hinton, & McClelland, 1987.

Learning. A common characteristic of learning rules is that they are based on the minimization of the difference between the ANNs output and the actual output associated with the input (characterized as the net's *error*). The most frequently used learning rule is the *back-propagation algorithm,* named for the way in which the error from the outer layer is propagated backwards through the middle layer(s) to calculate the error generated by the middle-layer PEs (Rumelhart, Hinton, & Williams, 1986).

Learning consists of updating the weights of the PEs so that the difference between the net output and the actual output associated with the input (the error) is minimized. Learning takes place over many training sessions. A training session consists of an input pattern and an associated output pattern. Each of the input patterns is submitted to the ANN. Using the current set of weights, the ANN formulates its best prediction of what the associated output pattern should be. According to how accurate the ANN's predictions are, weights on the PEs are revised via the error-reducing algorithm so that the error value derived from the difference between the ANN's prediction and the actual output pattern is minimized.

The number of training sets necessary for a specified level of accuracy will depend on a number of things, including the complexity of the relationships between the input and output patterns and the ANN's architecture. The ability of the ANN to learn complex relationships is so powerful that a number of researchers are currently working on autonomous vehicles — cars that maneuver without human guidance (Caudill, 1991).

Characteristics. Perhaps the most interesting ability of ANNs is their capacity to solve the same kinds of problems that humans do (abstract problems, such as recognizing faces and recognizing incomplete patterns). Another defining feature of ANNs is that "knowledge is encoded as patterns of connectivity across processing elements" (Hinton, McClelland, & Rumelhart, 1986, p. 49). Thus the entire net represents the knowledge, as opposed to the individual elements, of the net. The final difference is that algorithmic (traditional) programs perform instructions sequentially (one at a time), whereas an ANN performs them in parallel, allowing for much quicker processing. Because of the final two characteristics (parallel processing and distributed knowledge), the programming of ANNs has often been called *parallel distributed processing* (Hinton, McClelland, & Rumelhart, 1986). It should be apparent that the ability to learn, distributed knowledge, and parallel processing are attributes of the human brain.

ANNs in Team Research. Let us take an example used in the previous section, with the same environmental and task conditions, and predict how these will interact to influence task performance. For the ANN to learn these relationships, we must have access to a data base that contains measures on the environmental and task variables, as well as associated outputs (such as measures of performance). Each case consists of measures on five input variables — wind velocity, wave height, team training, team experience, and team motivation — and a measure of performance (such as the time needed to complete a particular task). The measures can be scaled continuously, quasi-continuously, or categorically (ANNs are scale-friendly). As in cross-validation, we should partition the sample into a training set and a holdout sample (for example, 75 percent and 25 percent, respectively). The training set is provided so that the neural net can extract information about the relationships between the variables; the holdout sample is used after training, as a means of testing how well the ANN learned these relationships and how well it is able to generalize to new cases. Like traditional statistical methods, the better defined the relationships, the easier it is for the ANN to learn. The ANN architecture will consist of five input PEs, a single middle layer containing two PEs, and a single output PE.

We present 75 percent of the cases to the ANN. Using the initial set of weights, the ANN predicts what the output should be. The difference between the actual and the estimated output is employed to revise the weights, so that the error is reduced. This continues until the ANN meets a criterion set by the researcher. To test how well the neural net has learned these relationships, we then present the 25 percent of holdout cases to the ANN. The final mean square error (sum of squared deviations across the holdout cases) can be used as an indicator of how well the ANN can generalize to never-before-seen cases; the smaller the error, the more able it is to generalize. If the ANN indicates that it can generalize, then we can use the ANN as a "black" box, to predict the performance of teams.

ANNs for Prediction and Description. A major limitation is that, by contrast with the other strategies, we cannot draw an explicit analogy between any real-world structure (team formation, lines of communication) and any structure in the ANN. One characteristic of the ANN is that knowledge is represented as patterns of connectivity across the PEs, and these patterns of connectivity are what impedes the drawing of a strict analogy between real-world structures and our model. Thus ANNs, although adept at approximating complex mathematical functions, serve as "black boxes": we put information into the system and receive output information, but the means by which the ANN represents knowledge (in a distributed manner) precludes us from specifying or understanding with any real precision exactly what input leads to what output.

ANNs are ideal for predicting team outcomes, however. A common goal of team research is to predict team decisions on the basis of members' knowledge of certain task-environment variables. An ANN could be created that would associate initial sets of conditions (input patterns) to performance outcomes (output patterns). In this circumstance, an ANN could be composed either for the entire team or for individual team members. The net could then be trained to associate the input patterns to outcomes (team performance). The disadvantage is that because of the way knowledge is stored, it is difficult if not impossible to determine how important each input is in influencing the outcome.

If a model does not imply that team structure affects team behavior, then it is not important to represent structure in the model of the team, and ANNs are applicable and appropriate.

If, however, the model does postulate that the structure of the problem has an effect on behavior, then it may be extremely difficult if not impossible to represent such structure adequately with an ANN.

Conclusion

Psychologists are in a very enviable position. Given our orientation and training, we are able to address a wide variety of theoretical and practical problems that cut across all of human behavior, as well as the systems humans interact with. We are often able to make contributions to theory and practice. We are also fortunate because we have a wide variety of methodological tools that we can employ to address problems. Unfortunately, however, we tend to look only for solutions to problems that lend themselves to our methodological approaches. For example, we restrict ourselves to viewing problems only from the perspective of the *outcomes* of the tools we have. We also conceptualize problems in terms of solutions based on a comparison of mean or covariance structures. If the problem cannot be formulated in that manner, we often try to force a fit into that perspective. Complex problems may need a lot of pushing and pulling.

This chapter has been an attempt to increase awareness regarding the scope of tools available to industrial and organizational (I/O) psychologists. The tools described here have a fairly rich life in other disciplines (computer science, engineering) and in subdisciplines of psychology. We hope that I/O psychologists will consider employing one or more of the tools described here.

Petri nets are a very powerful graphic and mathematical modeling tool. One of their real strengths is the ability to generate multiple representations of the same problem and then build on one or more of those representations through successive elaborations or refinements. If you are facing a situation of parallel operations or conflict, or if you need to represent a problem with multiple levels of abstraction, Petri nets are an ideal choice. Models can be analyzed through traditional techniques or with statistical tools (which are, perhaps, more comfortable for psychologists).

Fuzzy logic has the potential for greatly extending our ability to develop all types of models. Fuzzy logic even allows us to define degrees of membership in a team. Thus, an individual is not classified as being exclusively in or out of a particular team; rather, he or she can be thought of as being more in certain teams than in others.

Artificial intelligence, including expert systems and artificial neural networks, provide very powerful mathematical and conceptual metaphors for modeling team behavior. Neural networks might be considered if you are interested in developing a cognitive model of individual or team actions. These nets perform best when the problem is nonlinear or when the task is one of classification. Expert systems provide the ability to symbolically model individual or teams, as well as the ability to explicitly define (and test) a theory of behavior in terms of the code of the system. We encourage those of you working in areas related to team measurement and performance to consider the appropriateness of all the methodologies described here.

References

Alphatech, Inc. (1992). *Modeler.* Burlington, MA.

Bertalanffy, L. (1968). *General systems theory: Foundations, development, applications.* New York: George Braziller.

Buchanan, B. G., & Shortliffe, E. H. (1984). *Rule-based expert systems: The MYCIN experiments of the Stanford heuristic programming project.* Reading, MA: Addison-Wesley.

Campbell, D. T., & Fiske, D. W. (1959). Convergent and discriminant validation by the multitrait-multimethod matrix. *Psychological Bulletin, 56,* 81–105.

Caudill, M. (1990). *Neural network primer.* San Francisco: Miller Freeman.

Caudill, M. (1991). Driving solo. *AI Expert, 6,* 26–30.

Chiiola, G. (1990). *GreatSPN.* University di Torino, Torino, Italy.

Cios, K. J., Shin, I., & Goodenday, L. S. (1991). Using fuzzy sets to diagnose coronary artery stenosis. *Computer, 24,* 57–63.

Coovert, M. D., & McNelis, K. (1992). Team decision making and performance: A review and proposed modeling approach employing Petri nets. In R. W. Swezey and E. Salas (Eds.), *Teams: Their training and performance* (pp. 247–280). Norwood, NJ: Ablex.

Craiger, J. P. (1992). *A heuristic procedure for mapping knowledge, skills, and abilities to tasks.* Unpublished doctoral dissertation, University of South Florida, Tampa.

Craiger, J. P., & Coovert, M. D. (1991). Fuzzy fit-index training systems (FFITS): An intelligent system for interpreting and integrating covariance structure modeling solutions. *Applied Psychological Measurement, 15,* 292.

Dobbins, A., & Coovert, M. D. (1992, May). *In search of the holy grail for job classification.* Paper presented at the meeting of the Society for Industrial and Organizational Psychology, Montreal.

Erman, L., Hayes-Roth, F., Lesser, V., & Reddy, D. (1980). The HEARSAY II speech understanding system: Integrating knowledge to resolve uncertainty. *Computing Surveys, 12,* 213–253.

Feigenbaum, E. A., McCorduck, P, & Nii, H. P. (1989). *The rise of the expert company.* New York: Vintage.

Giarratano, J., & Riley, G. (1989). *Expert systems: Principles and programming.* Boston: PWS-Kent.

Gleick, J. (1987). *Chaos: Making a new science.* New York: Penguin.

Grossberg, S. (1982). *Studies of mind and brain.* Boston: Reidel.

Hackman, J. R. (Ed.). (1990). *Groups that work: (and those that don't): Creating conditions for effective teamwork.* San Francisco: Jossey-Bass.

Hall, L. O., & Kandel, A. (1986). *Designing fuzzy expert systems.* Koln, Germany: Verlag TUV Rheinland.

Hinton, G. E. (1992). How neural nets learn from experience. *Scientific American, 267,* 144–151.

Hinton, G. E., McClelland, J. L., & Rumelhart, D. E. (1986). Distributed representations. In D. E. Rumelhart and J. L. McClelland (Eds.), *Parallel distributed processing: Explorations in the microstructure of cognition.* Cambridge, MA: MIT Press.

Hogan, R., Sampson, D., Raza, S., Millar, C., & Salas, E. (1987). Research with small groups: Two realistic tasks. *Technical Report,* Naval Training Systems Center, Orlando, FL.

Jensen, K., & Rozenberg, G. (Eds.) (1991). *High-level Petri nets: Theory and application.* Berlin: Springer-Verlag.

Kosko, B. (1992). *Neural networks and fuzzy systems: A dynamic systems approach to machine intelligence.* Englewood Cliffs, NJ: Prentice-Hall.

Levine, E. L., Penner, L. A., Brannick, M., & Coovert, M. D. (1988). *Analysis of job/task analysis methodologies for team training design* (NTSC Technical Report No. 86-D-001-0296). Orlando, FL: Naval Training Systems Center.

Lindsay, R. K., Buchanan, B. G., Feigenbaum, E. A., & Lederberg, J. (1980). *Applications of artificial intelligence for organic chemistry: The DENDRAL project.* New York: McGraw-Hill.

Lorenz, E. (1963). Deterministic nonperiodic flow. *Journal of Atmospheric Sciences, 20,* 130–141.

Luger, G. F., & Stubblefield, W. A. (1989). *Artificial intelligence and the design of expert systems.* New York: Benjamin Cummings.

McCullouch, W. S., & Pitts, W. (1943). A logical calculus of the ideas immanent in nervous activity. *Bulletin of Mathematical Biophysics, 5,* 115–133.

Metasoftware. (1992). *Design CPN.* Boston, MA.

Murata, T. (1989). Petri nets: Properties, analysis, and application. *Proceedings of the IEEE, 77,* 541–580.

Newell, A., & Simon, H. A. (1972). *Human problem solving.* New York: Wiley.

Nielsen, N. R. (1991). Application of artificial intelligence techniques to simulation. In P. A. Fishwick and R. B. Modjeski (Eds.), *Knowledge-based simulation: Methodology and application.* New York: Springer-Verlag.

Perceptronics. (1992). *Percnet/hsi.* Woodland Hills, CA.

Petri, C. A. (1962). Kommunikation mit automaten [communication with the machine]. Schriften des IIM Nr. 2, Institute for Instrumentelle Mathematik, Bonn. Technical Report RADC-TR-65-377 (1966). New York: Griffiss Air Force Base.

Reutenauer, C. (1990). *The mathematics of Petri nets.* Englewood Cliffs, NJ: Prentice-Hall.

Rumelhart, D. E., Hinton, G. E., & McClelland, J. L. (1987). A general framework for parallel distributed processing. In D. E. Rumelhart and J. L. McClelland (Eds.), *Parallel distributed processing: Explorations in the microstructure of cognition.* Cambridge, MA: MIT Press.

Rumelhart, D. E., Hinton, G. E., & Williams, R. J. (1986). Learning internal representations by error propagation. In D. E. Rumelhart and J. L. McClelland (Eds.), *Parallel distributed processing: Explorations in the microstructure of cognition.* Cambridge, MA: MIT Press.

Simon, H. A. (1969). *The sciences of the artificial.* Cambridge, MA: MIT Press.

Swezey, R. W., & Salas, E. (Eds.). (1992). *Teams: Their training and performance.* Norwood, NJ: Ablex.

Widman, L. W., Loparo, K. A., & Nielsen, N. R. (1989). *Artificial intelligence, simulation, and modeling.* New York: Wiley.

Winston, P. H. (1989). *Artificial intelligence.* Reading, MA: Addison-Wesley.

Zadeh, L. A. (1965). *Fuzzy sets: Information and Control, 8,* 338–353.

7

UNDERSTANDING THE DYNAMICS OF DIVERSITY IN DECISION-MAKING TEAMS

Susan E. Jackson, Karen E. May,
Kristina Whitney

Changing work-force demographics and new organizational forms are increasing the diversity of work teams in general and decision-making teams in particular. Given these environmental changes, work teams that are diverse in terms of sex, race, ethnicity, national origin, area of expertise, organizational affiliation, and many other personal characteristics are increasingly common.

Diversity may lead to a variety of different consequences for decision-making teams. Consider, as a hypothetical example, an academic selection committee searching for a department chair. The members' diverse perspectives would undoubtedly influence the decision process. If managed well, their discussions might eventually result in the hiring of a Nobel laureate. If badly mismanaged, others at higher levels might usurp the selection committee's choice of a new leader.

The purpose of this chapter is to present a framework for understanding the dynamics of diversity in work teams. We first describe the types of diversity that characterize today's work teams. Next, we present a general framework for analyzing how

204

diversity influences work teams, their individual members, and their employing organizations. This framework identifies the basic dimensions of diversity, delineates several possible consequences, and describes the processes that shape the consequences of diversity. We use this framework to guide our subsequent discussion of the dynamics of diversity in work teams in general and in decision-making situations in particular. Finally, we conclude with a brief discussion of some of the implications of our analysis, for both research and practice.

The Nature of Diversity in Decision-Making Teams

The Changing Work Force

The changing demographics of the U.S. labor force account for increasing gender diversity, cultural diversity (including cultural differences due to race and ethnicity), and age diversity.

Gender Diversity. Women are entering the labor force in growing numbers. By the year 2000, the work force is expected to be almost completely gender-balanced. When this balance point is reached, the work force as a whole will be maximally diverse with respect to this attribute. Furthermore, gender-based segregation in the workplace is declining. Although they are still seldom seen in corporate board rooms, women currently represent more than 35 percent of the administrative and managerial workforce (Selbert, 1987). Consequently, all but the highest-level decision-making teams in organizations are likely to be characterized by substantial gender diversity.

Domestic Cultural Diversity. As the 1980s drew to a close, the U.S. Department of Labor was projecting rapid increases in the cultural diversity of the labor supply (Johnston & Packer, 1987). Only 58 percent of new entrants into the labor force were expected to come from the "majority" population of white native-born Americans. The remaining 42 percent were expected to be mostly immigrants (22 percent), followed by approximately equal numbers of African Americans and Hispanic Americans. These national trends are striking, yet they understate the truly dramatic regional changes occurring in Hawaii, California, Texas, New York, and Florida, where the growth in the Asian American, Hispanic American, and immigrant populations is especially rapid. In California, for example, racial diversity is fast approaching the point at which no single group will represent a majority.

National immigration figures understate the extent of cultural diversity in other ways as well. The immigrant population itself has become more diverse as Asians and Latinos from many countries join the once-predominant European immigrants. There are growing numbers of second- and third-generation U.S. citizens who continue to have strong ties to another national culture (see Fugita & O'Brien, 1991; Mydans, 1991). And, although the proportion of African Americans has remained relatively stable, their employment patterns have shifted considerably, resulting in higher degrees of racial integration in clerical, technical, and skilled crafts jobs ("Race in the Workplace," 1991).

Age Diversity. Descriptions of work-force demographics usually emphasize the fact that the average age of the work force is increasing but give little attention to indications that the distribution of ages (variance) represented in the work force is also changing. Yet, given several other trends, employees of greatly different ages are more and more likely to find themselves working side by side. The shrinking rate of growth in the labor pool is pushing employers to hire at both extremes of the age distribution, with the result that both student interns and former "retirees" are being hired to fill vacant positions (Bolick & Nestleroth, 1988). Furthermore, as middle-aged women enter or reenter the work force, they often find themselves working in entry-level jobs traditionally filled by younger employees. Finally, as organizations allow the higher education of younger employees to substitute for the job experience that previous cohorts of employees had to accrue in order to be promoted, relatively young employees are found more often in higher-level jobs. Consequently, within each level of the organizational hierarchy, age diversity is replacing the homogeneity associated with traditional age-based stratification.

New Organizational Forms

Teams are becoming more diverse, not only because of changing work-force demographics but also because of the development of new organizational forms. The globalization of the business economy and the formation of interdepartmental and interorganizational alliances are two forces shaping these new organizational forms.

Global Operations. The globalization of the business economy has received much recent attention in the United States. As trade barriers are removed and competition intensifies, many U.S. companies are beginning to expand their operations in order to take advantage of foreign labor and consumer markets. For smaller companies, foreign activities may be limited to a single joint venture or to offshore production or distribution systems that involve one or two other countries. For larger corporations, foreign offices may be in over one hundred different countries (see Fulkerson & Schuler, 1992). The presence of international affiliations, although not inevitable, is likely to lead eventually to the formation of teams of people with diverse cultural backgrounds, including management teams, design teams, operation teams, and marketing teams (Adler & Ghadar, 1991; Kanter, 1991; Von Glinow & Mohrman, 1990), all of which engage in decision-making activity.

Interdepartmental and Interorganizational Alliances. In order to succeed in an increasingly competitive domestic and global environment, many organizations are utilizing teams to pursue new business strategies that emphasize quality, innovation, and speed. Such work teams often bring together employees from previously segregated areas of the company, creating occupational and knowledge-based diversity. For example, R&D teams bring together experts from a variety of knowledge backgrounds with the expectation that, in combination, they will produce more creative thinking and innovation.

In addition, teams may be used to bring together employees from two or more organizations. For example, in order to improve the quality of their finished products, manufacturers may include their suppliers as part of a product-design team, and in order to ensure that the finished product appeals to their customers, they may include the end users on the team. Such alliances require subunits from different organizations to coordinate their activities. In doing so, they produce teams that must develop modes of operating that fit with the differing corporate cultures in which the subunits are embedded (Hofstede, 1991; Kanter, 1989).

Corporate (and subunit) cultures shape expectations for behavior and guide interactions among interdependent employees. During a typical day, they are an unnoticed medium for carrying out activities. But when corporate norms, habits, and routines are not shared by all the members of an interdependent team, they become more salient, creating both opportunities for innovation and threats to effective team functioning.

In today's business environment, work teams are becoming both more common and more diverse, intensifying the importance of understanding the dynamics of work-team diversity. Of particular importance to this chapter is diversity within decision-making teams. Organizations are rapidly restructuring to take advantage of the potential benefits of diverse decision-making teams, making the assumption that the liabilities of such teams are worth the risk (or can be successfully avoided). Many of the specific assets and liabilities of work teams arise directly out of diversity. To be effective, diverse decision-making teams must carefully manage their assets and liabilities. Doing so presumes a thorough understanding of how and why diversity affects the behavior of teams and their members.

Framework for Analyzing the Dynamics of Diversity

Given the complex nature of diversity and its consequences, it is useful to rely on a heuristic as a guide to discussion. Our discussion in this chapter is guided by the heuristic of a theoretical framework that identifies primary constructs and connects them to form a meaningful territorial map. Within this framework, diversity is placed as a construct that appears early in the causal chain of phenomena considered. The focus is on the consequence of diversity, rather than on its determinants or its role as a contextual or moderating variable (see Levine & Moreland, 1990).

General Causal Model

In keeping with an open-systems perspective, we assume that the constructs in the taxonomy are nodes in a complex, multilevel, dynamic nomological net. Numerous reciprocal and complex interrelations exist among the primary constructs. The general pattern of these interrelationships and the presumed causal linkages are illustrated graphically in Figure 7.1. The general causal model acknowledges the importance of macro-

**Figure 7.1. General Causal Model for
Understanding the Dynamics of Diversity in Work Teams.**

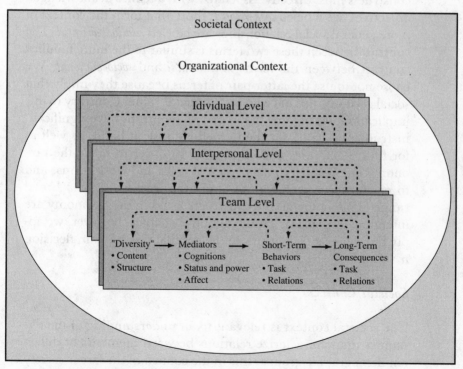

© Susan E. Jackson

level phenomena that characterize the embedding societal and organizational contexts. Although a full discussion of these is beyond the scope of this chapter, the importance of societal- and organizational-level phenomena should not be ignored (for more detailed discussions, see Cox, 1993; Ibarra, 1993; Nkomo, 1992).

Taxonomy of General Constructs

The taxonomic component of our framework, shown in Table 7.1, organizes constructs into four general categories that correspond to their presumed roles in the general causal model: aspects of diversity, mediating states and processes, short-term behavioral manifestations, and longer-term consequences. Within each general category, constructs are arrayed vertically, to reflect three levels of analysis: individual, interpersonal, and team. The constructs most directly associated with a team's acknowledged objectives are labeled *task-related;* those that form the context of more general social relationships are labeled *relations-oriented.* The contrast between these two terms is similar to the more familiar contrast between the terms *instrumental* and *socioemotional.* We chose not to use the latter pair of terms because they imply that social relationships have no instrumental value. Contrary to this implication, we assume that social relationships have significant instrumental value for the immediate task at hand, as well as for future activities and objectives. In order to make the taxonomy applicable to many types of tasks and work teams, and to encourage researchers to apply the framework to a broad range of phenomena, the constructs listed in the taxonomy are intentionally general. Throughout this chapter, however, we apply our general framework to the specific task of team decision making.

Societal Context

The societal context is relevant to an understanding of the dynamics that characterize relations between members of different demographic groups. It is in the context of the larger society that individuals are socialized to exhibit behaviors "appropriate" to their membership in demographic groups, and it is in this context that individuals first learn to respond differentially to members of different demographic groups (see Maccoby & Jacklin, 1974; Jacklin, 1989). In addition, events in society— including new legislation, local politics, and nationally organized demonstrations—can stimulate changes in intergroup relations in the workplace (see Alderfer, 1992; Sessa, 1992).

Organizational Contexts

Organizational contexts also influence relations among members of work teams. For example, some organizations intentionally or unintentionally socialize members in different subunits to compete with employees from other units (other functional areas, business units, or geographical locations). Others emphasize cooperation and weak interunit boundaries (Tichy & Sherman, 1993). Human resource management practices, such as selection systems, training programs, and methods of appraisal, also can shape team composition and team dynamics (see Sundstrom, DeMeuse, & Futrell, 1990). For example, "managing diversity" and cross-cultural training interventions are often designed to sensitize employees to the norms and behavior patterns of various cultures, in the hope of improving interactions among employees. Affirmative action programs are often designed to reduce segregation within organizations.

The Team-Organization Interface

Organizations impinge on work teams, and they also absorb the effects of work teams. Of particular relevance here is the extent to which organizations are affected by the longer-term individual, interpersonal, and team consequences identified in Table 7.1.

The literature on organizational behavior suggests several means by which organizations can be affected by the longer-term consequences of work-team diversity. For example, in his description of the consequences of organizational demography,

Table 7.1. Taxonomy of General Constructs in a Framework for Understanding Diversity in Work Teams.

Aspects of Diversity: Content and Structure	Mediating States and Processes	Short-Term Behavioral Manifestations	Longer-Term Consequences
	Level of Analysis: Individual		
Readily Detectable Attributes Task-related: organizational tenure, team tenure, department/unit membership, memberships in task-relevant external networks, formal credentials, education level Relations-oriented: sex, culture (race, ethnicity, national origin), age, memberships in formal organizations (religious, political), physical features Underlying Attributes Task-related: knowledge, skills, abilities (cognitive, physical), experience Relations-oriented: social status, attitudes, values, personality, behavioral style, extrateam social ties	Task-Related Information processing (e.g., attention, recall) Learning (e.g., discovery, creativity) Task-based information Power to control tangible resources Power to control human resources Relations-Oriented Social cognitive processes: stereotypes and schema-based expectancies Affective responses: attraction, anxiety, fear, guilt, frustration, discomfort	Task-Related Seeking, offering, receiving work-related information, tangible resources, human resources Initiating/responding to influence attempts Relations-Oriented Seeking, offering, receiving social information and/or support	Task-Related Personal performance (speed, creativity, accuracy) Satisfaction with performance of self and team Acquisition of knowledge and skills regarding technical aspects of task, managing human and tangible resources Establishment of position in work-communication networks Relations-Oriented Acquisition of interpersonal knowledge and skills regarding interpersonal aspects of task Establishment of position in social-communication networks (within team and in external environment) Satisfaction with social relationships

Level of Analysis: Interpersonal

	Task-Related	Task-Related	Task-Related
Interpersonal (dis)similarity in terms of readily detectable and underlying attributes Dyadic Individual-to-subgroup Individual-to-team	Differences in task-based cognitions Expertise-based status differentials Differences in power over tangible and/or human resources Relations-Oriented Social familiarity Diffuse status differentials Differences in social cognitions Differences in affective responses	Exchanges, negotiations, consolidation of task-related information, tangible resources, or human resources Relations-Oriented Exchanges/consolidation of social information and/or support	Power balance Relations-Oriented Status hierarchy Balance of interpersonal accounts (political debts, credits) Solidification of friendship coalitions

Level of Analysis: Team

	Task-Related	Task-Related	Task-Related
Team composition: heterogeneity versus homogeneity of readily detectable and underlying attributes Special configurations Presence of "tokens" Presence of small minority faction Bipolar team composition	Shape of expertise-based status hierarchy Patterns of task-based cognitions Shape of power distributions for control of tangible and/or human resources Relations-Oriented Stage of team socialization Shape of diffuse social-status hierarchy Patterns of social cognitions Patterns of affective responses across team members	Task-related communication networks Allocation and use of tangible and human resources Influence networks Relations-Oriented Friendship-based communication networks	Team performance (speed, accuracy, creativity) Team satisfaction with performance Team learning about technical aspects of task and management of tangible and human resources Relations-Oriented Membership stability Adoption of social structure (norms and roles, influence networks, friendship networks)

Pfeffer (1983) argues that conflict associated with heterogeneity, in terms of organizational tenure, results in fragmented organizations that are difficult to manage. By contrast, the higher turnover rates that seem to occur in heterogeneous teams and organizations may lead to increases in organizational innovation, adaptation, and performance because fresh perspectives are brought (see also Schneider, 1987). The perspective of organizational demography also draws attention to the interorganizational consequences of turnover. For example, it has been argued that interorganizational mobility will tend to make organizations more similar to each other because ideas and information are transmitted through the process (Baty, Evan, & Rothermel, 1971). In addition, interorganizational mobility is associated with interorganizational communication and coordination (Pfeffer & Leblebici, 1973). The implication of this is that, to the extent that interorganizational coordination is important for success, organizations characterized by team heterogeneity should be successful in this domain. This seems to be the driving principle behind many newer types of interorganizational network structures (see Kanter, 1989).

Articles appearing in the popular press point to the potential value that work-force diversity can add to organizations, as the impetus behind recent efforts to manage diversity more effectively. Often implicit in such reports is the assumption that an organization's bottom line is influenced by the extent to which employees from different backgrounds can work together toward organizational goals. This assumption corresponds to a shift away from viewing diversity as primarily a social issue to viewing it as a strategic business imperative (Copeland, 1988; DeLuca & McDowell, 1992; Jackson & Alvarez, 1992; Solomon, 1989; Thomas, 1990). It is supported by anecdotal data related to such interventions as Digital Equipment's Valuing Differences Program. Top management at Digital reports that managing diversity effectively leads to such consequences as a solid reputation as one of the best places to work, an empowered work force, greater innovation, increased productivity, and a competitive advantage in global competition (Walker & Hanson, 1992). This assumption — that diversity influences organizational outcomes through its impact on the longer-term consequences included in our taxonomy—has not been specifically tested by rigorous scientific research. Nevertheless, it is reasonable to expect that both task-related and relations-oriented consequences within work teams accumulate to affect bottom line indicators of organizational effectiveness.

Team Decision Making in the Context of Our General Framework

The advantage of a framework composed of fairly general constructs is its potential for broad applicability, but the price paid is that specific constructs relevant to particular topics may not appear explicitly. For example, the relevance of the constructs that comprise Table 7.1 to the phenomenon of team decision making is not transparent. To realize the value of this taxonomy of general constructs for an understanding of diversity in decision-making teams, constructs in the taxonomy need to be translated into the language commonly used to describe a specific phenomenon.

Decision making includes numerous activities for which reseachers have developed an array of teams. In particular, researchers who adopt an issue-processing perspective for studying decision making tend to cast a very wide net when identifying relevant phenomena. This perspective characterizes much of the field-based research literature on managerial decision making (see Dutton, 1988; Jackson, 1992a; Janis, 1989) and contrasts sharply with the narrower view of decision making often adopted by researchers working in laboratory settings (see McGrath, 1984).

There are two distinguishing characteristics of the issue-processing perspective. First, it recognizes as integral to decision making many activities that precede a decision (environmental scanning, problem sensing, formulation, and framing) and that follow the making of a decision (decision announcements, implementation, evaluation, and readjustments), in addition to core decision-making activities (generating alternatives, evaluating alternatives, and resolution). Second, it recognizes that political (nontask) agendas coexist with decision agendas.

Behavior necessarily reflects both types of agendas. The taxonomy of constructs shown in Table 7.1 captures this duality with its inclusion of constructs that are primarily task-related and constructs that are primarily relations-oriented.

Throughout this chapter, our description of the role of diversity in team decisions adopts the strategic issue-processing perspective. In addition, it assumes the following:

1.   Interdependent team members are working on projects that they believe are relevant to organizational functioning.
2.   The decision activity represents a substantial portion of the team members' responsibilities, although it need not be their only responsibility.
3.   Members interact face to face in a context that allows some degree of intimacy.
4.   Team members have a fair amount of autonomy regarding the process of decision making (that is, the decision does not involve the routine application of heuristic rules, and authority is not vested completely in a leader).
5.   Team effectiveness is at least minimally valued by team members, although team members are not assumed to agree about the appropriate criteria for judging effectiveness.
6.   The team does not yet have a long (and therefore unique) life history.

In cases where these conditions do not hold, the dynamics that occur may be substantially different. Unfortunately, there is almost no research that considers how diversity affects teams under different conditions.

The Concept of Diversity

The term *diversity* has little history within the behavioral sciences and is not (yet) a scientific construct. Instead, it is an everyday term that sprang to life rather recently, nourished by widespread media coverage of the "managing diversity" activities that organizations are adopting in response to changing work-force demographics. Nevertheless, the body of social science research relevant to understanding the dynamics of diversity in organizations is large, although it is widely dispersed across subdisciplines that neither cross-reference each other nor have a common terminology (see Ferdman, 1992). For integration of the available scientific evidence into a single framework, the conceptual territory of interest must be identified and labeled. In particular, the umbrella term *diversity,* which we use in a general sense to indicate the presence of differences among members of a social unit, must be dissected into a set of more precise terms. In Table 7.1, terms that refer to both the content and the structure of diversity appear in the far-left column.

The Content of Diversity: Individual Attributes

As explained below, diversity is a compositional construct that does not exist at the individual level of analysis. Nevertheless, the individual level of analysis is included as an aspect of diversity because individual differences in various attributes, when present in a team, department, or organization, create diversity. That is, individual attributes reflect the *content* of diversity; by contrast, the configuration of attributes within a social unit reflects the *structure* of diversity.

Within our framework, individual attributes are categorized as either readily detectable or underlying, and as either task-related or relations-oriented. *Readily detectable* attributes can be quickly and consensually determined with only brief exposure to a target person. Generally, they are immutable. Readily detectable attributes that are *task-related* include organizational and team tenure, department or unit membership, membership in task-relevant external networks, formal credentials, and educational level. Those labelled *relations-oriented* include sex, culture (race, ethnicity, national origin), age, membership in formal (religious or political) organizations, and physical features.

Underlying attributes are more subject to construal and more mutable. *Task-related* underlying attributes include knowledge, skills, abilities (cognitive and physical), and experience. *Relations-oriented* underlying attributes include social status, attitudes, values, personality characteristics, behavioral style, and extrateam social ties. Both readily detectable and underlying attributes contribute to the *total* diversity present in a team.

Task-Related Attributes. To date, studies of how team diversity (in general) influences team decision making have emphasized the cognitive aspects of decision making, including identifying and ranking decision objectives, searching for information, generating alternative solutions, and analyzing the potential consequences of possible decisions. A relatively rational process is assumed; cognitive biases and errors in information processing may interfere, but it is presumably the human cognitive apparatus that is the major source of such interference. From this perspective, diversity within a decision-making team is recognized as important primarily because it is associated with the resources available during the decision-making process — especially task-related cognitive resources.

Researchers often assume that readily detectable attributes are associated with underlying attributes that are task-related (Hambrick & Mason, 1984; Lawrence, 1991). For example, a cross-functional design team that included a purchasing manager, a marketing manager, design engineers, production engineers, and a customer-service representative (diversity with respect to unit membership) would be expected to make better design decisions than a more homogeneous team because task-related underlying attributes (such as knowledge, skills, and abilities, or KSAs) are assumed to be associated with unit membership. Associated with these KSAs would be a broader distribution of task-related cognitions, which in turn would stimulate information seeking and exchange, as well as task-related negotiations and resource allocation.

Relations-Oriented Attributes. Contrasting with a rational and instrumental explanation for how diversity can affect decision making is a second perspective, which acknowledges the more emotional (political), relations-oriented aspects of team life. This perspective reflects the fact that observed decision-making processes seldom seem to fit the idealized, coolly rational processes just described. Instead, emotions run hot. Personal affiliations, self-serving behavior, and politics are common, and the resulting decision processes are often muddled at best (see Janis, 1989; Lindblom, 1959). Available resources may not be fully identified and used by the team (Bottger & Yetton, 1988) and the final decision may be shaped as much by unstated individual and interpersonal objectives as by the team's formally stated task objective.

The relations-oriented phenomena present throughout our taxonomy are an essential aspect of the context within which the task-related phenomena unfold. At all levels of analysis, relations-oriented phenomena are affected by the pattern of readily detectable, relations-oriented attributes (gender, ethnicity, age) that characterize the team. Readily detectable attributes play a special role in shaping the dynamics of diversity because they elicit many of the social cognitive processes and affective reactions that guide team interactions (see Berger & Zelditch, 1985; Devine, 1989; Stephan, 1985; Turner, 1987).

The Structure of Diversity

Readily detectable and underlying attributes do describe the dimensions of diversity in terms of content, but it is equally important to consider the structure of diversity. Terms for referring to the structure of diversity differ across levels of analysis, from *interpersonal (dis)similarity* to *team composition.*

Interpersonal (Dis)similarity. Similarity is a relational construct that compares the attributes of two entities. In a social system, the two entities compared can be individuals, subgroups within a team, whole teams, or some combination of these. In this chapter, however, we focus mostly on the degree to which an *individual* and some second entity differ in terms of various attributes (hence the term *interpersonal (dis)similarity*). Most extant research addresses dissimilarity between two individuals. (Some authors, however—such as Tsui & O'Reilly, 1989, and Tsui, Egan, & O'Reilly, 1992—have used the term *relational demography* to refer to interpersonal dissimilarity.) Nevertheless, each unique component of interpersonal similarity has the potential to explain some of the dynamics within diversity teams (see Jackson, Stone, & Alvarez, 1993, for a discussion of how individual-team dissimilarity may affect the process of socialization).

Team Composition. At the team level of analysis, numerous configurations of attributes are possible, and so several terms are needed to refer to the structure of diversity. In the psychological literature, *composition* is an umbrella term for referring to configurations of attributes within small groups (Levine & Moreland, 1990), and we adopt this terminology here.

One of the most frequently studied aspects of composition is *team heterogeneity,* which refers to the degree to which members of a team as a whole are similar (homogeneous) or dissimilar (heterogeneous) with respect to individual-level attributes. Several different statistical formulae are available for assessing the degree of heterogeneity in a team. All yield indices that take on low values when all members have a common attribute. The indices take on higher values to the extent that (1) individuals' attributes are dissimilar to each other, (2) there is equal (versus disproportionate) representation across different values of an attribute, and (3) there are many (versus fewer) possible values associated with the attribute.

Along the continuum of homogeneity-heterogeneity, a few configurations of attributes have attracted special attention. One such configuration is the presence of a demographic "token" or "solo" member (see Kanter, 1977). This configuration exists when a nearly homogeneous team includes a single dissimilar member (a lone male on a team of females; a lone accountant on a team of sales personnel). Two other psychologically distinct configurations are the presence of a small minority faction (two members who are similar to each other but distinctly different from the other members of a team) and a bipolar team composition, with two equal-size coalitions (a team composed of 50 percent employees from headquarters and 50 percent employees from a subsidiary). Such configurations can be particularly influential in affecting team dynamics (see Kerr, 1992).

Linking Diversity to Longer-Term Consequences

The conceptual framework presented in this chapter is intended to serve as a stimulant and guide to future research aimed at improving our understanding of how diversity influences work-team dynamics in general and team decision making in particular. The framework presumes that empirical linkages exist between the causal input constructs (at the left in Figure 7.1 and Table 7.1) and the outcome constructs (at the right in Figure 7.1 and Table 7.1). In this section, we introduce the longer-term consequences for all three levels of analysis. Then we review the empirical evidence concerning the linkage between diversity and team consequences. (A subsequent section will describe intermediate linkages, which serve as explanations for why and how team diversity is translated into various longer-term consequences.)

Overview of Longer-Term Consequences

Figure 7.1 and Table 7.1 maintain a distinction between short-term behavioral manifestations, which are assumed to be quite dynamic and subject to change during task performance, and the eventual longer-term consequences of such behaviors, which are presumed to be more enduring. Reflecting a sequencing of effects through time, this distinction calls attention to our assumption that work teams are held accountable for completing tasks. Formal documentation is more likely for these longer-term consequences—especially at the level of team consequences—than for the more ephemeral short-term behaviors. At a point of closure, teams may intentionally pause to reorganize for new tasks, or they may move on to new tasks in an almost seamless continuation. In either case, longer-term consequences are the remnants of a team's past that are carried forward, informally or in institutionalized form, as the team and its members engage in new tasks.

Individual Consequences. For individuals, longer-term consequences arise from experiences within the team, as well as from experiences with external contacts. The primary task-related consequences for individuals concern personal performance (including speed, creativity, and accuracy); feelings of satisfaction (which may reflect evaluations of one's own performance or the performance of other team members); acquisition of knowledge and skills (including those of a technical nature and those related to the management of tangible and human resources); and established positions within work communication networks (including those within the team and those that reach beyond the team and into the larger organizational and professional communities). Relations-oriented consequences for individuals concern acquisition of interpersonal knowledge and skills (such as knowledge about how to negotiate, exercise influence, or build support); establishment of one's position within social communication networks (including those within the team and those external to the team); and feelings of satisfaction with established social relationships.

Interpersonal Consequences. At the interpersonal level of analysis, the longer-term consequences of diversity are presumed to be primarily relations-oriented, rather than task-related. Nevertheless, the task-related exchanges and negotiations that are engaged in to bring a previous task to closure may have lingering consequences for new tasks. In particular, two parties may have negotiated terms for expending human and financial resources, terms that place contingencies around future resource expenditures; such an agreement has the potential to change the balance of power between the parties involved. Similarly, the process of carrying out a task can have longer-term relations-oriented consequences, including a new or reestablished status hierarchy for the two entities involved, a new or reestablished balance of interpersonal accounts (political debts and credits), and solidified friendship coalitions that are carried forward.

In order to assess whether and how these individual and interpersonal consequences are affected by team-level diversity, cross-level research designs and analysis are necessary (see Rousseau, 1985). Unfortunately, such research is rare. Nevertheless, one recent study is directly relevant to the question of how team diversity affects the longer-term individual consequences listed in our taxonomy. In a study of top management teams, a set of seven indicators of team heterogeneity has been found to explain a significant amount of variance in individual turnover, even after controlling for how similar an individual was to the group as a whole (Jackson et al., 1991). This finding underscores the value of including constructs at each of the three levels of analysis included in our taxonomy for conducting studies intended to improve our understanding of the behaviors of individuals in organizational contexts.

Task-Related Team Consequences. For the team as a whole, task-related consequences involve team performance, team satisfaction, and team learning. Team performance is particularly important at the team level because it is likely to have a major impact on how the organization responds to the team and its members. Within the context of the team itself, the team's satisfaction with performance may also have an enduring impact: dissatisfaction may prompt restaffing and reorganization, whereas satisfaction may either energize the team or induce complacency. In addition, regardless of whether a team performs well and regardless of its eventual level of satisfaction, the process of carrying out a task provides opportunities for task-based learning. Such learning, whether related to technical matters or to the management of tangible and human resources, may be an especially important determinant of the team's future effectiveness.

Empirical Evidence Linking Diversity to Longer-Term Team Consequences

Task-Related Team Consequences. The majority of the existing research that is directly relevant to task-related team consequences focuses on the link between team composition and team performance. We have found no empirical studies that examine the linkage between team diversity and other longer-term, task-related consequences, such as team satisfaction with performance or team learning.

Several reviews of basic research that relates team diversity to creative decision making (and that was conducted mostly in laboratory settings) support the conclusion that team heterogeneity improves performance in terms of decision quality (Filley, House & Kerr, 1976; Hoffman, 1979; McGrath, 1984; Shaw, 1981). This effect has been found for diversity of many types, including personality (Hoffman & Maier, 1961), training background (Pelz, 1956), leadership abilities (Ghiselli & Lodahl, 1958), and attitudes (Hoffman, Harburg, & Maier, 1962; Triandis, Hall, & Ewen, 1965; Willems & Clark, 1971). In addition, a meta-analysis of the evidence from twelve studies of problem-solving suggests that mixed-sex teams outperform same-sex teams (Wood, 1987).

Recently, strategic management researchers interested in improving the functioning of top management teams have also directed attention to linkages between team composition and performance of decision-making teams. Most of the relevant research has been guided by Hambrick and Mason's seminal article (1984) describing an "upper echelons" perspective. Prior to this article, the two views of leadership that predominated in the organizational literature were that leaders are largely irrelevant to an explanation of the organization's performance (the population-ecology argument), and that leadership is an individual activity carried out by the person at the apex of the organizational hierarchy (the traditional leadership perspective). By calling attention to the roles and activities of top management teams, Hambrick and Mason offer a third perspective on organizational leadership. Furthermore, they assert that the demographic composition of top management teams will partially determine team performance. In the special case of top management, team performance is reflected in organization-level indicators, such as competitive strategy and financial effectiveness.

A few published studies provide support for the general thesis that the composition of top management teams predicts the firm's strategic choices and performance. For example, a study of 199 top management teams in the banking industry found that levels of organizational innovation were correlated with team heterogeneity with respect to areas of job expertise (Bantel & Jackson, 1989). Several other studies of top management also support the general notion of a link between team composition and performance (Eisenhardt & Schoonhoven, 1990; Finkelstein & Hambrick, 1990; Michel & Hambrick, 1992; Murray, 1989; Singh & Harianto, 1989; Wiersema & Bantel, 1991), but the results of these studies are quite complex and not easily explained by available theories. In keeping with the assumption that studies of team diversity need to consider the embedding systems within which teams operate, a variety of organizational and environmental conditions appear to moderate associations between team composition and performance for top management (for a fuller discussion, see Jackson, 1992a).

Relations-Oriented Team Consequences. The process of carrying out a task can have an enduring impact on team relations. Membership stability (or instability) is one of the most important longer-term relations-oriented consequences. However, even for teams with stable membership, diversity may still produce important relations-oriented consequences. For example, a team will often adopt the social structures (norms and roles) established during performance on a prior task as the baseline when beginning a new task. Therefore, once established, norms and roles may persist indefinitely until changes in task requirements or team membership trigger modifications. Influence networks and friendship networks established during tasks are likely to persist as well.

Most of the existing research relevant to relations-oriented team consequences focuses on the link between team composition and membership stability. During the past decade, several studies have examined the relationship between team composition and team turnover rates. Many of these studies were stimulated by Pfeffer's discussion (1983) of organizational demography. Pfeffer speculates that the demographic distribution of employees may "do a better job at explaining variation in the dependent variables than measures of the presumed intervening constructs" (p. 351). These studies have not directly compared the relative predictive power of demographic diversity and the presumed intervening processes referred to by Pfeffer, but they do support the assertion that team turnover rates are predicted by demographic composition. In several studies, age or tenure heterogeneity have been shown to be correlated with turnover patterns (Jackson et al., 1991; McCain, O'Reilly, & Pfeffer, 1983; O'Reilly, Caldwell, & Barnett, 1989; Wagner, Pfeffer, & O'Reilly, 1984). In addition, heterogeneity in terms of college alma mater, curiculum studied, and industry experiences has been shown to predict turnover in top management teams (Jackson et. al, 1991).

When team composition is studied in laboratory settings, usually temporary teams are concocted for short-term projects, so that membership stability is not in fact a relevant issue. However, team cohesiveness and affective reactions to the team have been studied extensively. These are assumed to be indicative of the potential membership stability of these concocted groups. The pattern of results is generally consistent with the behavioral data from field studies: heterogeneity, in terms of readily detectable and underlying attributes, is associated both with lower cohesiveness and with more negative affective reactions to the team (Jackson, 1992b).

Evidence to support the conclusion that diversity has long-term consequences for friendship networks is plentiful as well. Employees with minority status, in terms of ethnicity or gender, often feel that they face special barriers to informal communication networks (Morrison & Von Glinow, 1990). Their reports are consistent with studies of communication patterns in work organizations, which indicate that demographic diversity is related to lower amounts of communication among co-workers. For example, a study of communication networks in five organizations has found that demographic homogeneity (on the dimensions of authority, education, sex, race, and organizational branch) consistently characterized communication chains, suggesting that diversity decreases communication overall (Lincoln & Miller, 1979). Other studies of communication patterns have shown that informal networks are segregated along demographic lines (Brass, 1984), that formal and informal meetings among peers and with immediate subordinates are lower in racially diverse groups (Hoffman, 1985), and that age and tenure similarities between co-workers predict levels of communication among project teams of engineers (Zenger & Lawrence, 1989). In keeping with these findings for teams and larger work units, similarity among friendship pairs (homophily) has been found for a variety of readily detectable and underlying attributes, including age, sex, race, education, prestige, social class, attitudes, and beliefs (Berscheid, 1985; Brass, 1984; Byrne, 1971; Cohen, 1977; Ibarra, 1992; McPherson & Smith-Lovin, 1987; Verbrugge, 1977; Zander & Havelin, 1960).

We have found no direct evidence linking diversity to influence networks (research on influence networks is generally scarce). However, it seems likely that diversity would affect influence patterns as well as friendship patterns. This notion is supported by research on attitude change and persuasion, which shows that people are more likely to be influenced by the opinions of demographically and ideologically similar others (McGuire, 1985). Conversely, influence attempts may be more likely to be directed toward others who are dissimilar. In the latter case, diverse teams would be characterized by relatively more, and relatively less effective, influence communications.

The empirical evidence clearly indicates that team composition is related to such longer-term team consequences as performance, membership stability, and friendship networks. Studies of team composition, when conducted in laboratory settings, have generally used groups of strangers brought together to work for a few minutes on a concocted (and often very simple) task that involves problem solving, creative idea generation, or judgmental choices of little importance to the team. By contrast, research conducted in the field has most often used natural groups working as teams on a variety of complex, job-related tasks over extended periods of time. Despite these dramatic differences, research in both settings supports the conclusion that team composition affects both task performance and interpersonal relations. Furthermore, these effects appear to be both complex and variable over the course of time (see Watson, Kumar, & Michaelsen, 1993).

At this time, no single theory explains the full set of established empirical relationships between aspects of diversity and longer-term consequences. Instead, a variety of theoretical explanations has been offered to account for these empirical findings, reflected in work on expectation states (Berger & Zelditch, 1985), composition of top management teams (Hambrick & Mason, 1984), organizational demography (Pfeffer, 1983), the attraction-selection-attrition model (Schneider, 1987), and group processes (Steiner, 1972). The framework presented in this chapter is consistent with these explanations but does not constitute a fully developed new theory that parsimoniously integrates all the available evidence. As a first step toward the eventual development of such a theory, however, our framework highlights the similarities across these many literatures while suggesting new directions for researchers working within established paradigms. Theoretical support for the proposed linkages is available from widely scattered sources. We turn now to a discussion of this evidence.

Explaining the Linkages

In our framework, the empirical linkages between team diversity and longer-term consequences are explained by two classes of intervening constructs, referred to as *mediating states and processes* and *short-term behavioral manifestations*. Behavioral manifestations can be observed directly. Mediating states and processes must be inferred. Mediating states and processes are also assumed to be more proximally determined by the readily detectable and underlying attributes represented by a team. In this section, we describe our classification system for the mediating states and processes (shown in the second column of Table 7.1) and then consider how these shape the short-term behavioral manifestations (shown in the third column of Table 7.1).

Mediating States and Processes

At the individual level of analysis, social, cognitive, and affective processes are considered the key mediators through which diversity influences behavior. From a psychological perspective, these are the most basic *processes* that serve as explanations for behavioral manifestations. By comparison, individual, interpersonal, and mediating *states* represent ambient conditions that affect how these processes unfold and, subsequently, are influenced by the resulting behaviors. Interpersonal mediating states are described by relational constructs that capture the structure of relationships between two entities, whereas team-level mediating states are described by compositional constructs that capture patterns that emerge when more than two entities are compared.

A full understanding of the dynamics of diversity requires a consideration both of situational structures associated with attribute distribution among team members and of psychological processes that explain why and how individuals respond to their situations. For example, in a team of professionals, suppose that the expertise-based status hierarchy reflects the formal credentials of team members. This hierarchy is likely to create performance expectations, which become the basis for a hierarchy of power and prestige (Berger, Conner, & Fisek, 1974; Berger, Fisek, Norman, & Zelditch, 1977) and may induce anxiety in a team member with no relevant formal credentials. This individual's anxiety may decrease her willingness to offer information during discussions. In turn, such behavior would be consistent with the performance expectations for low-status team members. Since this member is now viewed as having no valuable information or resources to offer, others seldom seek information from her, nor do they attempt to negotiate with her for the purpose of eventually forming a consolidated unit. At the team level, status differentials are reflected in sparse (versus dense) communication and influence networks, as well as in unequal (versus egalitarian) resource distribution and use (Ridgeway & Berger, 1986).

As this example and the general causal model portrayed in Figure 7.1 show, mediating states and processes and behavioral manifestations are inextricably intertwined, with each other and across the three levels of analysis. Continuous feedback and reciprocal causation keep the psychological and behavioral systems in flux as continuous adjustments occur. The discussion that follows, which is organized around task-related and relations-oriented phenomena, reflects this systemic interconnectedness.

Task-Related Mediating States and Processes

For individuals, task-related mediating *processes* include information processing and learning. Task-related mediating *states* include the task-based information that a person has at hand, the power to control tangible resources (including those within and external to the team), and the power to control human resources (team members, as well as others who are not on the team). Task-related interpersonal mediating states include differences regarding task-based cognitions, expertise-based status differentials, and differences in power over tangible and human resources. Task-based mediating constructs for teams as wholes include the overall shape of the expertise-based status hierarchy, the pattern of the task-based cognitions represented among team members, and the shapes of the distributions of power over tangible and human resources.

Cognitions. Task-based cognitions are especially relevant because decision making is an information-intensive activity. During decision making, the acquisition, representation, and processing of task information take center stage; working through cognitive-based differences is a central activity. Agreement or disagreement (and consensus or dissensus) can occur regarding the content of available information, the structure in which information is organized (often referred to as a cognitive map or model; see Cowan, 1986; Porac & Howard, 1990; Simon, 1987), information processing (including attention to and retrieval of information), and learning.

There is clear support for a relationship between diversity and creativity. The conclusion of the majority of studies in this area is that heterogeneous teams produce more innovative and unique solutions to problems (Jackson, 1992b). This effect is attributed to differences among team members in terms of the perspectives from which a problem is faced and in terms of experience in relevant situations (Haythorn, 1968; Hoffman, 1959; Hoffman & Maier, 1961; Pearce & Ravlin, 1987; Triandis, Hall, & Ewen, 1965).

Although supporting evidence is somewhat scarce (Walsh,

1988), it is widely assumed in the management literature that a person's task-based cognitions are associated with readily detectable task-related attributes. For example, the content of information one has available and one's cognitive maps and models are believed to be associated with organizational tenure and with the functional unit in which one is employed (Hambrick & Mason, 1984; Ginsberg, 1990). Task-related attributes also appear to influence information processing. For example, a person's accrued knowledge and expertise appear to guide what he or she attends to, encodes, and later retrieves (Simon, 1987). Consequently, a team of decision makers can be expected to experience disagreement throughout all phases of the decision process.

Accounts of complex decision making often treat both heterogeneity of perspectives and the resulting disagreements as valued resources that ensure the surfacing and discussion of conflicting opinions, a wide range of possible solutions, and full consideration of the possible consequences that might follow from each solution (Cosier, 1981; Janis, 1972; Schweiger, Sandberg, & Rechner, 1989; Schwenk, 1983). Such discussions can even serve as training forums for individual team members (Laughlin & Bitz, 1975; Nemeth, 1986). However, heterogeneity may become a liability when speed is important. Time pressures may encourage a fragmented team to adopt shortcuts, such as compromises and majority rule, to reach a quick resolution instead of persisting to a creative resolution that is acceptable to everyone. Reliance on compromise or majority rule may decrease team members' acceptance of and enthusiasm for the team's resolution, creating obstacles to decision implementation.

Most studies of team composition and creativity have been conducted in laboratory settings, using simple designs that presume a linear relationship between heterogeneity (on a single attribute) and creativity. The research conducted to date leaves open the possibility that composition influences the solutions that teams produce in more complex ways. For example, if team members are so heterogeneous that there is no basis for similarity, then they may be unable to work together; taking advantage of task-related heterogeneity may require team members to have some degree of similarity (see Lott & Lott, 1965). A similar notion is advanced by Hoffman (1959), who states that "a diversity of viewpoints must be accompanied by a tolerance for differences of opinion if the group is to exploit its potential creativity" (p. 114). As suggested below by the discussion of relations-oriented phenomena within decision-making teams, tolerance for task-based conflicts may be more common when team members are homogeneous in terms of some nontask attributes.

Status and Power. The texture of interactions observed within decision-making teams is surely not a function of task-based cognitions alone, although these receive the most attention in the decision-making literature. Observed behaviors also reflect differential expertise-based degrees of status, which can vary between equal status (zero differential) and extreme inequality (large differential), as well as power differentials, especially differential power over tangible and human resources. Surprisingly, there is little psychological or organizational research that empirically examines the consequences for decision-making teams of differences in expertise-based status or power over resources, yet few would argue that these are irrelevant to such behavioral manifestations as task-related communications, influence attempts, negotiations, exchanges, consolidations, and the resulting patterns of resource allocation and use. The lack of empirical research on this issue may indicate that most scholars assume that the consequences of expertise-based status and power over resources are straightforward and obvious (that is, rational). Such an assumption ignores the potentially important role of relations-oriented mediating states.

Relations-Oriented Mediating States and Processes

At the individual level, relations-oriented mediators include social cognitive processes (such as the operation of stereotypes and schema-based expectancies) and affective reactions (such as attraction, anxiety, fear, guilt, frustration, and discomfort). At the interpersonal level, relations-oriented mediating states include social familiarity (which can range from very low to very high), diffuse status differentials (which refer to status differences based on such attributes as age and sex, with little or no direct task relevance; see Berger, Cohen, & Zelditch, 1972), differences in social cognitions, and differences in affective responses (such as attraction and anxiety). Relations-oriented mediating states for teams include the stage of team socialization, the shape of the diffuse social-status hierarchy, patterns of social cognitions across team members, and patterns of affective responses found among team members.

Whereas some task-related mediating constructs are routinely called upon to explain behavior in decision-making groups, most relations-oriented mediating constructs receive less empirical attention. Nevertheless, many of the diversity training programs that are currently popular in organizations are based on the assumption that interaction difficulties between members of demographically defined groups (men and women, younger and older employees) are due to differences in relations-oriented underlying attributes, especially behavioral and cognitive styles, values, and beliefs.

Certainly, there is evidence that such differences exist. Differences in achievement scores for members of various cultural groups (Ackerman & Humphreys, 1991), which are reflected in the stereotypes held by the American work force (Fernandez, 1988), have been a topic of much concern and debate in this country. Gender and ethnic differences in nonverbal communication and interpersonal styles seem to be numerous (Cox, Lobel, & McLeod, 1991; Ferdman & Cortes, 1991; Hall, 1984; Triandis, 1993). Gender differences in leadership style (Eagly & Johnson, 1990) and influenceability (Eagly & Carli, 1981; Carli, 1989) exist. Cultural differences in values are increasingly well documented (Triandis, 1993), as are age and cohort differences in work attitudes and values (Elder, 1974, 1975; Rhodes, 1983; Thernstrom, 1973; "Work Attitudes," 1986). Moreover, the majors that students choose and their occupational choices are associated with personality characteristics (Costa, McCrae, & Holland, 1984; Holland, 1976). Such group differences probably account for some of the misunderstandings and conflicts that occur when people from different backgrounds interact.

But perhaps just as powerful as these actual differences are people's *perceptions* of group-based differences. For example, although the data from several million students indicate that differences in cognitive ability are negligible between males and females (Hyde, Fennema, & Lamon, 1990; Hyde & Linn, 1988), males are generally perceived as more intelligent than females (Wallston & O'Leary, 1981). Assessment-center ratings often yield stereotypic snapshots of men and women, although naturalistic studies find few differences (Eagly & Johnson, 1990). Similarly, although the evidence indicates that the deteriorating effects of age have little impact on intellectual capacity until the seventh decade of life (Labouvie-Vief, 1989), managers appear to denigrate employees who are older than the norm for particular jobs or positions (Lawrence, 1988).

In organizations, such stereotypes are important features of the social landscape, linking components of diversity to decision-making activities in an indirect manner. Readily detectable attributes are features of team members that trigger social cognitions (about the self and others) and affective responses. These in turn directly shape interpersonal relations and patterns of team interaction, thereby influencing the task-related information that is made available, attended to, and used in decision making.

Our taxonomy includes phenomena at three levels of analysis. Nevertheless, most of the relevant research has been conducted at the individual and interpersonal levels of analysis, and our discussion reflects their fact.

Cognitions. For team composition to influence the behavior of team members, differences between and among team members must be perceived and encoded. People more quickly notice and encode differences that are easily detectable (race, sex, age, attractiveness, style of dress, handicapped condition), attending less to differences that are subtle or less detectable (attitudes). Once noticed, differences are encoded automatically, and people are categorized on the basis of these differences (Stangor, Lynch, Duan, & Glass, 1992).

After a person has been categorized, subsequent information about the person is processed in relation to the relevant category, and interactions are shaped by it (Sherman, Judd, & Park, 1989). That is, cognitive structures influence social information processing, including what information is attended to, how quickly it is processed, and how it is organized and retained in memory. Cognitive structures also shape evaluations, judgments, and attributions made about others; consequently, they eventually influence interactions (Markus & Zajonc, 1985; Stephan, 1985).

Team composition (for example, heterogeneity) may elicit errors and biases associated with cognitive structures, such as schemas and stereotype-based expectancies. Because it makes social categories more salient (Turner, 1987), team composition activates the in-group and out-group schemas that provide people with naïve hypotheses about what members of different social groups are like and how they will act in specific situations; these tend to be biased in favor of in-group members (Ostrom & Sedikides, 1992; Stephan, 1985). Thus heterogeneity in terms of readily detectable attributes is likely to increase the prevalence of biases that occur when people relate to each other as members of in groups and out groups.

Affect. As already described, numerous studies show that members of homogeneous teams experience more positive affect than members of heterogeneous teams (Levine & Moreland, 1990; Lott & Lott, 1965; O'Reilly, Caldwell, & Barnett, 1989; Zander, 1979). One explanation for this finding is that attitude similarity is positively reinforcing and so serves as an unconditional stimulus that evokes a positive affective response (liking). Attitude dissimilarity, by contrast, evokes a negative affective response. In demographically heterogeneous teams there is presumably a higher probability of attitude dissimilarity among team members than in homogeneous teams.

Clearly, the attitude-similarity explanation for attraction to similar others, which was prevalent two decades ago, presumes that affect follows cognition. An alternative view, currently more prevalent, presumes that affect can precede cognition —

or, as argued by Zajonc (1980), preferences need no inferences. Affect may be directly triggered, along with unintended thoughts, when stereotypes that include affective components are spontaneously activated (see Fiske, 1982; Stangor, Sullivan, & Ford, 1991; Uleman & Bargh, 1989).

Affective responses may also result from conscious attempts to override automatic—but undesirable—impulses, as suggested by recent research on prejudice and compunction (feelings of guilt and self-criticism). Devine's model (1989) of automatic and controlled components of stereotyping and prejudice asserts that prejudicial thoughts or feelings are experienced even by people whose beliefs are not prejudiced. Stereotypes are automatically activated in the minds of all individuals in the presence of a member of a stereotyped group. To behave in nonprejudicial ways requires conscious and intentional inhibition of an activated stereotype. Even individuals who hold nonprejudiced beliefs may not be fully successful in trying to suppress prejudicial thoughts, feelings, and subtle behavioral signals. When one's beliefs do not match these automatic responses, the result is often a feeling of discomfort (Devine, Monteith, Zuwerink, & Elliot, 1991).

Devine's research suggests that members of heterogeneous teams may be more likely to experience negative affect than members of homogeneous teams. Because stereotypes about other team members are more likely to be activated automatically in heterogeneous teams, team members will have to consciously try to suppress them, and discomfort will be the result.

Research on social stigma sheds additional light on the role of affective responses. Such characteristics as race, physical attractiveness, and handicaps or disabilities have been linked to social stigma in organizations (for a review, see Stone, Stone, & Dipboye, 1992). Stigmatized individuals often experience a variety of negative feelings, including embarrassment, depression, fear, anxiety, and lowered self-esteem (Goffman, 1963). People who are not themselves stigmatized may be apprehensive or fearful about interacting with stigmatized others. Thus, to the extent that a team is heterogeneous in terms of any characteristics linked to stigma, its members can be expected to experience more negative affect.

Short-Term Behavioral Manifestations

Work-team diversity shapes the ways in which team members think and feel about interactions with other team members. These processes serve in turn as partial explanations for both task-related and relations-oriented behaviors.

Short-term behavioral manifestations are generic behavioral phenomena that are observable in work teams. Generally speaking, they include task- and relations-oriented communications, the management of tangible and human resources, and social influence. Through these behaviors, team members work to achieve their objectives and establish relationships, both within the team and with others in the external environment (see Ancona, 1987; Ancona & Caldwell, 1992; Ashforth & Humphrey, 1993; Bowen & Schneider, 1988; Gladstein, 1984; Lin, Dobbins, & Fahr, 1992; Maurer, Howe, & Lee, 1992).

In the broadest sense, the term *communications* refers to the management of task- and relations-oriented information. Communications involve producing, transmitting (sending), and interpreting (receiving) symbols (Roloff, 1987), through verbal as well as nonverbal channels, directly and indirectly, passively and proactively (see Miller & Jablin, 1991). Presumably, employees engage in work-related communications, which involve descriptive and evaluative task information, primarily for instrumental purposes. By contrast, friendship-based communications, which involve social information (that is, support), carry their own intrinsic value (Brass, 1984; Ibarra, 1990). Although communications often involve relatively benign exchanges, influence communications engaged in for the purpose of changing the attitudes, values, beliefs, and behaviors of others are particularly potent, which is why they are highlighted in our taxonomy. Through their communications, work teams manage information, tangible resources (equipment, tools, money), and human resources (skills, effort). Behavioral manifestations related to all of these activities can be conceptualized at the individual, interpersonal, and team levels of analysis.

   Individual Behavior. For individuals, short-term behavioral manifestations can be observed from two perspectives: individuals can be observed acting as agents who initiate action, and/or they can be observed as targets who receive and interpret the actions that others initiate. Our taxonomy includes constructs that reflect both perspectives. Thus, for individuals, task-related behaviors include seeking, offering, and/or receiving work-related information, tangible resources, or human resources; initiating influence attempts; and responding to influence attempts. Individuals' relations-oriented behaviors include seeking, offering, and/or receiving social information and support. Clearly, understanding the forces that shape individuals' influence-related behaviors is essential to understanding teams, for it is primarily through influence processes that a group of individuals becomes transformed into a team capable of coordinated action.

   In addition to recognizing that individuals both initiate actions toward others and respond to the actions of others, it is important to recognize that the others involved may or may not be members of the work team. The readily detectable and underlying attributes of team members, in combination with the composition of work teams and their embedding organizations, are important determinants of behaviors within a team. They can influence behaviors that link team members to the external environment. For example, the demographic composition of a work team can have important implications for managing one's identities and the interface between work and nonwork (Bell, 1990). It can also affect the extent to which other organizational members are sought out as sources of information and advice (Ibarra, 1992; Zenger & Lawrence, 1989).

   Interpersonal Behavior. When behavior is conceptualized as an individual-level phenomenon, it is often isolated from the interpersonal context in which it occurs. Moving to the interpersonal level of conceptualization requires viewing behavior as coordinated. Various types of coordinated action are possible, including exchanges, negotiations, and consolidation. These are treated as conceptually distinct from each other in our framework, although they may be difficult to untangle in natural settings.

A minimal amount of coordination is required in order for two entities to carry out an *exchange*. Indeed, when information and affect are transmitted through nonverbal channels, exchanges often occur even when they are not intended.

The give-and-take process of *negotiation,* which is the interpersonal analogue of influence attempts initiated and responded to by individuals, generally involves greater coordination than a mere exchange. As noted by Neale and Northcraft (1991), negotiation is "a joint interdependent process that entails coordinated action of parties with nonidentical preference structures [that] . . . results in the allocation of resources" (p. 148). Negotiations usually precede and often are an integral part of instrumental task-related exchanges.

Consolidation occurs when entities join to form coalitions — presumably, because they have reached a state of agreement. The construct of consolidation is seldom used by researchers who study group processes, however; instead, research and theory typically emphasize the opposite end of this behavioral dimension. That is, rather than focusing on consolidation as a behavioral manifestation of agreement, research often focuses on conflict, which is associated with disagreement. We have intentionally avoided use of the term *conflict* in our framework, given the ambiguity that surrounds this construct (see the entire May 1992 issue of *Journal of Organizational Behavior*). One source of this ambiguity is the general failure to distinguish between mediating states and processes (agreement and disagreement, power differentials) and behavioral manifestations associated with these states and processes (negotiation, consolidation).

Task-related exchanges, negotiations, and consolidations can all involve task-related information, tangible resources, and/or human resources (effort or skill). Relations-oriented exchanges and social consolidations (friendship units) involve social information and/or social support. The fact that relations-oriented negotiations are not included in our framework reflects the assumption that negotiations seldom precede expressive exchanges of social support and social information.

Team Behavior. Conceptualizing behavior at the level of the teams as a whole requires us to identify the patterns that characterize the total set of individual and interpersonal behaviors occurring within the team. For task-related and relations-oriented communications, behavioral manifestations can be described with the terminology of network analysis. Examples of useful measures for describing group communication patterns include heterogeneity, multiplexity, density, and stability (see Burt, 1982; Granovetter, 1973). Unfortunately, terminology and measurement conventions for describing patterns of behavior related to the allocation and use of human resources and tangible resources are less well developed, at least in the social sciences. It should be feasible to adapt network analysis to this purpose, however. Alternatively, measurement and tracking procedures used by researchers in operations management might be adapted. Thus, just as the measurement of team-level diversity is problematic, progress must be made regarding how to empirically assess team-level resource use and allocation before a full understanding of the dynamics of diversity can be achieved. With the major types of behavior that occur within work teams identified, it is now possible to explore how the mediating states and processes translate aspects of diversity into observable behaviors in work teams.

Behavioral Manifestations of Social Cognitions. Individuals are biased toward collecting expectancy-confirming information, and they evoke behavior that matches their expectancies (Jones et al., 1984; Snyder, Tanke, & Berscheid, 1977). For example, if team members hold the stereotype-based expectation that similar others are more likely to share their perspectives than are dissimilar others, then team members may selectively initiate and reciprocate self-disclosing interactions with those who are similar to them in age, gender, or ethnicity. Such disclosures in turn create understanding among similar team members and facilitate the creation of a shared perspective (that is, they facilitate consolidation). At the same time, because self-disclosures are made selectively to similar others, understanding is more difficult to establish between dissimilar others.

In heterogeneous teams, these processes are likely to create cliques of demographically similar teammates, with schisms separating these cliques. Because heterogeneous teams contain more out groups than do homogeneous teams, we can also expect in-group biases to have more influence on task-based and social interactions within heterogeneous teams. Thus several predictions can be made about team composition, in-group biases, and behavior, as follows: Members of heterogeneous teams will seek, offer, and receive information and resources (both tangible and human) from fewer team members than will members of homogeneous teams. When they do seek, offer, or receive information or resources, it will more likely be from in-group members than from out-group members. Similarly, interpersonal exchanges of information and resources will occur between fewer dyads in heterogeneous teams than in homogeneous teams, and when they do occur, they will more likely be between in-group members than between in-group members and out-group members. Given these dynamics, task-based and social consolidations probably occur at lower rates within heterogeneous teams, as compared to homogeneous teams.

Studies of communication networks in work organizations tend to support this view of how team composition affects behavior. For example, studies of communication patterns have shown that work-related communications between men and women are less frequent in units that are more diverse with respect to sex (South, Bonjean, Markham, & Corder, 1982), that formal and informal meetings among peers and with immediate subordinates are lower in racially diverse groups (Hoffman, 1985), and that age and tenure similarities between co-workers predict levels of communication among project teams of engineers (Zenger & Lawrence, 1989). The studies just cited all assess the amount of communication, not the nature of the communications, that occurred within work groups. Much of the research relevant to understanding the consequences of diversity for the nature of communications has been conducted to test hypotheses from expectation-states theory, which emphasizes the formation and consequences of status hierarchies (Berger, Cohen, & Zelditch, 1966, 1972).

Occupational attainment and income are indicators of status in our society. In the United States, sizable sex-, age-, and ethnicity-based differences in both income and occupational level are well documented, and decades of national opinion polls and psychological research on prejudice and discrimination show that subjective attitudes and status hierarchies mirror the economic and educational status indicators (Jaffe, 1987; Johnston & Packer, 1987; Katz & Taylor, 1988; Kraly & Hirschman, 1990; Markides, 1983; Bragger, 1985; *Chronicle of Higher Education*, 1992). Furthermore, there is some evidence that some members of ethnic minority groups internalize the majority group's view of their status (Jones, 1990; Rice, Ruiz, & Padilla, 1974).

Substantial evidence indicates that demographic cues trigger status assignments quickly, and that unfairly low (nontask) status assignments prove difficult to undo (Ridgeway, 1982), in part because the behavioral effects of initial status attributions are so pervasive. These and related findings have been established through empirical tests of the theory of status characteristics and expectation states (Berger, Cohen, & Zelditch, 1966, 1972). Although there is a debate within this literature regarding the processes that lead to status hierarchies, the fact that status is usually correlated with performance-irrelevant demographic characteristics is generally acknowledged (Ridgeway, 1987). Compared to those with lower status, higher-status persons display more assertive nonverbal behavior during communication, speak more often, criticize more, state more commands, and interrupt others more often. They have more opportunity to exert influence, attempt to exert influence more, and actually are more influential. Moreover, they are evaluated more positively and have higher self-esteem (Levine & Moreland, 1990). Some of these results have been found in children as well as in adults, suggesting that status cues are learned early in life (Cohen, 1982). Although studies of the effects of status differentials often involve observing dyadic communication patterns in laboratory settings, results of such studies appear to generalize to work teams. In a study of 224 R&D teams in twenty-nine large organizations, Cohen and Zhou (1991) found that, even after controlling for performance, higher status was attributed to males than to females.

Findings such as these suggest that participation in and input on task-related decision-making activities is likely to be unequal among members of teams characterized by greater status differentiation, with lower-status members participating less. Because demographics are the cues used in the initial assignment of status, differentiation occurs whenever demographic diversity is present. To the extent that status hierarchies do not match distributions of task-relevant expertise, unequal participation rates are likely to interfere with the team's performance because available resources will not be fully utilized. Teams may assign roles that are consistent with stereotypes, rather than with the actual underlying attributes of team members, and this tendency may lead to inappropriate assignment of roles and responsibilities.

Behavioral Manifestations of Affect. It is difficult to separate definitively behavioral consequences due to affect from those due to social cognition, and so it is likely that affect partially explains some of the behaviors we discussed in the section on social cognition. In addition, however, affect seems to have other interesting effects. Before we discuss these, two caveats are needed. First, most of the research on the relationship between affect and behavior focuses on positive affect, whereas the affective consequences of diversity tend to be negative. Moreover, positive and negative affect are considered to be independent dimensions (Watson & Tellegen, 1985), and so it cannot be assumed that the consequences of negative affect are the opposite of those of positive affect. Second, positive affect is typically induced in these studies by offering "small pleasures" (juice and cookies are available; the person "finds" a dime) to the participants in a study. For the sake of discussion, we will assume that the consequences of positive affect induced through these means are generalizable to situations in which positive affect is induced in other ways (for example, being with people one likes).

Among other consequences, positive affect promotes helping behavior and generosity, cooperation, and a problem-solving orientation during negotiations (for a review, see Isen & Baron, 1991). Helping (or prosocial) behaviors inherently involve the sharing and/or redistribution of resources, such as those referred to in our taxonomy, including information, tangible resources, and human resources (effort and time). Thus helping is likely to be beneficial in many types of work situations, as when it takes the form of mentoring (Kram, 1985) or generally offering assistance to colleagues. When positive affect occurs in the form of attraction to team members, it may be translated into greater motivation to contribute fully and perform well as a means of gaining approval and recognition (Festinger, Schachter, & Back, 1950). Conversely, anxiety may inhibit a person's participation in team activities (Allen, 1965; Asch, 1956).

For decision-making teams, studies of how affect influences negotiations are of particular interest. In these problem-solving situations, where flexible and creative thinking can lead to more effective resolutions than compromise can, positive affect is likely to be particularly beneficial for improving performance. For example, in a study of dispute resolution, negotiators who were induced to feel positive affect reached agreement more often, broke off from discussion less often, cooperated more, obtained better outcomes, and evaluated other negotiators more favorably by comparison to negotiators in a control condition (Carnevale & Isen, 1986). There was also some evidence that communication was more effective when positive affect was induced.

Descriptions of why and how the demographic diversity of groups can be expected to influence their internal processes and performance are often predicated on the assumption that demographic attributes are associated with a number of underlying characteristics, including abilities, behavioral styles, personalities, and attitudes and values. Many such associations do indeed exist, but they are often weak, and there are many holes in our knowledge.

The frequent assumption that demographically diverse work teams are also diverse in terms of underlying attributes (knowledge structures, behavioral styles) is supported only by logical extension of the findings for population-group differences. Generalizations based on population-level differences may not hold for decision-making teams within a particular organization, however, for all team members are likely to have passed through several screens designed to reduce variance in ability levels and perhaps also in behavioral styles, values, and attitudes (Schneider, 1987). Thus there is good reason to believe that the variation in the underlying attributes represented in demographically diverse work teams may actually be less than would be inferred on the basis of data showing correlations between demographics and underlying attributes in the general population. Clearly, the major conclusion to be drawn from the literature reviewed here is this: to understand and predict how diversity is likely to manifest itself in short-term behavior, attention must be paid both to readily detectable and to underlying attributes, including those that are task-related and those that are relations-oriented.

The same conclusion does not follow for perceived diversity, however. Here, the data indicate that perceptions of demographically based differences exaggerate true differences. Furthermore, the experiences of many organizations regarding affirmative action indicate that, regardless of actual practice, employees often do not believe that selection criteria are applied equally to all demographic groups. Consequently, it is likely that members of demographically diverse teams perceive greater diversity along the underlying dimensions than actually exists. These perceptions may be the more powerful determinants of behaviors.

Conclusion: Implications for Research and Practice

This chapter has offered an organizing framework for the study of diversity in work teams and described causal model that specifies relationships among the primary constructs in the framework. The framework's constructs are organized into four general categories, which correspond to their presumed roles in the general causal model. The general causal model, which subsumes the constructs within the framework, has several features: it acknowledges that work teams operate within broader organizational and societal contexts; it spans multiple levels of analysis (individual, interpersonal, team, and organizational); it reflects the basic assumption that all psychological and behavioral phenomena in work teams are jointly influenced by concerns about both tasks and social relationships; it differentiates between readily detectable and underlying aspects of diversity; it recognizes that the dynamics of diversity produce a set of longer-term consequences, for the team and the organization as a whole, that extend temporally beyond the completion of a task or even beyond the life of the team; and it is generally applicable to a broad range of different types of work teams.

Our model defines a number of paths through which diversity is hypothesized to exert its effects. As our review has shown, however, the amount of available evidence is sparse for some paths within the model. A systematic program of research is needed to fully explicate the relationships among constructs in the model. At the general level, research is needed to determine whether the mediating states and processes provide adequate explanations for the effects of diversity on short-term behavioral consequences. Such research should address primarily causal paths, depicted by the horizontal dimension of the model. In addition, although several studies have investigated the consequences of team composition for the outcomes of performance and membership stability, there is little research on the effects of team composition on other longer-term, task-related consequences, such as satisfaction with performance and learning. Future research should attempt to fill these gaps.

Research is also needed on the vertical aspects of the model and should focus on cross-level effects. For example, the composition of a team can be expected to influence the salience and potency of the cognitive and affective reactions of individual team members. The behaviors of individual team members also can be studied as determinants of both changes in team composition and patterns of information and resource allocation.

To improve our understanding of whether and how different dimensions of diversity affect team processes and outcomes differently, research designs are needed that simultaneously assess several dimensions of diversity. An implicit assumption of much of the early research on team composition was that different dimensions of diversity are associated with similar outcomes. For simplicity, we have adopted this assumption in some of our discussions in this chapter. However, the available evidence indicates that heterogeneity of personal attributes and heterogeneity of skills and abilities may have different consequences for teams (Jackson, 1992b). Future research might focus more specifically on identifying the effects of the full range of diversity dimensions, as well as multidimensional patterns of diversity. For example, it is not known how the readily detectable and underlying attributes, in combination, affect team processes and performance over the course of a team's life.

In developing our framework, we were guided primarily by the research literature, rather than by accounts in the popular media, where recently the dynamics of diversity have been discussed at length. Nevertheless, the framework presented here is intended not only as an aid to research but also as a resource for practitioners as they design, implement, and evaluate "managing diversity" initiatives. At the most general level, our discussion reinforces the importance of adopting a systems perspective when dealing with the issue of diversity. To manage diversity effectively requires understanding a multidimensional, multilevel, dynamic, and complex social system. As one consultant aptly puts it, "If you think 'managing diversity' is a *program*, you don't get it" (Miller, 1992, p. 27). Specifically, a deeper understanding of three issues will enable organizations to manage diversity more effectively: (1) the different types of diversity that can characterize work teams, (2) the dynamics of diverse teams, and (3) the consequences of diversity for individuals, teams, and the organization as a whole.

Types of Diversity

Many organizations use the term *diversity* to refer only to demographic differences among employees, with sex and ethnicity being the dimensions of greatest concern. As shown in our framework, however, diversity of many types characterizes teams in organizations, and differences along both readily detectable and underlying dimensions may produce consequences for the team. Increased awareness of the different dimensions of diversity should sensitize organizations to the many dynamics and outcomes associated with a team's total diversity. Consider a team of white males that is having difficulty coming to consensus on solutions to organizational problems. An organization that recognizes only sex and ethnicity as important dimensions of diversity may not consider diversity as a possible cause for the team's problems. However, recognition that diversity includes differences among team members in terms of job knowledge, behavioral styles, values, and beliefs, for example, opens up a new perspective for viewing this problem and makes it more likely that the organization will make an appropriate decision about whether and how to intervene, as well as about how to assess the total consequences of any intervention.

Dynamics of Diversity

Understanding the dynamics of diversity in work teams helps organizations manage the consequences of diversity by providing guidance in the choice and/or development of interventions. By using the framework to identify the processes and/or behaviors underlying the consequences of diversity, the organization can more accurately target interventions to the source of the problem(s). For example, the mediating states and processes outlined in the framework include affective responses, such as attraction and anxiety. When team members report high levels of anxiety associated with their participation in team activities, the framework enables the organization to consider diversity as a possible cause of the anxiety and to respond accordingly, with an intervention directed at managing anxiety *about diversity,* rather than just at managing anxiety.

Consequences of Diversity

The framework alerts practitioners to the wide range of team consequences that are potentially diversity-related processes and suggests how those consequences may be linked to diversity-related processes and behaviors. For example, when team membership is unstable, one can consider diversity as a possible cause. Then, using the framework as a guide, one can try to determine which diversity-related processes (stereotyping, anxiety) and/or behaviors (decreased exchange of information and resources) may be contributing to this instability. Identification of these processes and behaviors can then inform one's intervention strategy.

These hypothetical examples illustrate how the framework and model presented in this chapter can be used to systematically analyze whether and how the dynamics of diversity may account for some observed organizational phenomena. Clearly, however, our model is most appropriately used as a guide to generating hypotheses, rather than as a source of answers for effectively managing a diverse work force.

Furthermore, regardless of whether one's purpose in generating hypotheses is to guide research or inform practice, one's analysis will be incomplete unless unique organizational and societal conditions are taken into condition. Relevant organizational conditions may include the entire set of human resource management practices that impinge on a team, the composition of the organization(s) in which a team is embedded, historical context, organization culture(s), structures, and technologies. Relevant societal conditions may include the degree of ethnic and racial segregation that exists in housing and education, the general level of social unrest, ongoing debates about legislation that makes the conditions of a particular subgroup particularly salient or that is construed as targeted toward shaping relationships between particular groups, interventions (political, military, humanitarian) in countries considered "home" to a substantial portion of immigrants residing in the country, and so on. It is impossible to reflect here on the roles of all these organizational and societal conditions, but the imperative to manage diversity effectively makes it essential for these conditions to inform future diversity-based research and practice.

References

Ackerman, P. L., & Humphreys, L. G. (1991). Individual differences theory in industrial and organizational psychology. In M. D. Dunnette & L. M. Hough (Eds.), *Handbook of industrial and organizational psychology: Vol. 1* (pp. 223–282). Palo Alto, CA: Consulting Psychologists Press.

Adler, N., & Ghadar, F. (1991). Globalization and human resource management. In A. Rugman (Ed.), *Research in global strategic management: Vol. 1. A Canadian perspective* (pp. 179–205). Greenwich, CT: JAI Press.

Alderfer, C. P. (1992). Changing race relations embedded in organizations: Report on a long-term project with the XYZ Corporation. In S. E. Jackson and Associates (Eds.), *Diversity in the workplace: Human resources initiatives* (pp. 138–166). New York: Guilford Press.

Allen, V. L. (1965). Situational factors in conformity. In L. Berkowitz (Ed.), *Advances in experimental social psychology: Vol. 2* (pp. 133–175). San Diego, CA: Academic Press.

Ancona, D. G. (1987). Groups in organizations: Extending laboratory models. In C. Hendrick (Ed.), *Annual review of personality and social psychology: Group and intergroup processes* (pp. 207–231). Newbury Park, CA: Sage.

Ancona, D. G., & Caldwell, D. F. (1992). Bridging the boundary: External activity and performance in organizational teams. *Administrative Science Quarterly, 37,* 634–665.

Asch, S. E. (1956). Status of independence and conformity: A minority of one against a unanimous majority. *Psychological Monographs, 70* (9, Whole No. 416).

Ashforth, B. E., & Humphrey, R. H. (1993). Emotional labor in service roles: The influence of identity. *Academy of Management Review, 18,* 88–115.

Bantel, K. A., & Jackson, S. E. (1989). Top management and innovations in banking: Does the composition of the top team make a difference? *Strategic Management Journal, 10* (Special Issue), 107–124.

Baty, G., Evan, W., & Rothermel, T. (1971). Personnel flows as interorganizational relations. *Administrative Science Quarterly, 16,* 430–443.

Bell, E. L. (1990). The bicultural life experience of career-oriented black women. *Journal of Organizational Behavior, 11,* 459–477.

Berger, J., Cohen, B. P., & Zelditch, M., Jr. (1966). Status characteristics and expectation states. In J. Berger, M. Zelditch, Jr., & B. Anderson (Eds.), *Sociological theories in progress* (pp. 47–73). Boston: Houghton Mifflin.

Berger, J., Cohen, B. P., & Zelditch, M., Jr. (1972). Status characteristics and social interaction. *American Sociological Review, 37,* 241–255.

Berger, J., Conner, T. L., & Fisek, M. H. (Eds.). (1974). *Expectation states theory: A theoretical research program.* Cambridge, MA: Winthrop.

Berger, J., Fisek, M. H., Norman, R. Z., & Zelditch, M., Jr. (1977).

Status characteristics in social interaction: An expectation-states approach. New York: Elsevier Science.

Berger, J., & Zelditch, M., Jr. (Eds.). (1985). *Status, rewards, and influence.* San Francisco: Jossey-Bass.

Berscheid, E. (1985). Interpersonal attraction. In G. Lindsey & E. Aronson (Eds.), *The handbook of social psychology: Vol. 2* (pp. 413–484). New York: Random House.

Bolick, C., & Nestleroth, S. L. (1988). *Opportunity 2000: Creative affirmative action strategies for a changing workforce.* Washington, DC: U.S. Government Printing Office.

Bottger, P. C., & Yetton, P. W. (1988). An integration of process and decision-scheme explanations of group problem-solving performance. *Organizational Behavior and Human Decision Processes, 42,* 234–249.

Bowen, D. E., & Schneider, B. (1988). Services marketing and management: Implications for organizational behavior. In B. M. Staw & L. L. Cummings (Eds.), *Research in organizational behavior: Vol. 10* (pp. 43–80). Greenwich, CT: JAI Press.

Bragger, L. (1985). Older persons and the democratic process. In G. Lesnoff-Caravaglia (Ed.), *Values, ethics, and aging* (pp. 112–131). New York: Human Sciences Press.

Brass, D. J. (1984). Being in the right place: A structural analysis of individual influence in an organization. *Administrative Science Quarterly, 29,* 518–539.

Burt, R. S. (1982). *Toward a structural theory of action.* San Diego, CA: Academic Press.

Byrne, D. (1971). *The attraction paradigm.* San Diego, CA: Academic Press.

Carli, L. L. (1989). Gender differences in interaction style and influence. *Journal of Personality and Social Psychology, 56,* 565–576.

Carnevale, P. J., & Isen, A. M. (1986). The influence of positive affect and visual access on the discovery of integrative solutions in bilateral negotiation. *Organizational Behavior and Human Decision Processes, 37,* 1–13.

Chronicle of Higher Education (1992). The Chronicle of Higher Education Almanac. *Chronicle of Higher Education, 39,* 15.

Cohen, B. P., & Zhou, X. (1991). Status processes in enduring work groups. *American Sociological Review, 56,* 179–188.

Cohen, E. G. (1982). Expectation states and interracial interaction in school settings. *Annual Review of Sociology, 8,* 209–235.

Cohen, J. M. (1977). Sources of peer-group homogeneity. *Sociology of Education, 50,* 227–341.

Copeland, L. (1988). Valuing diversity: Part 1. Making the most of cultural differences in the workplace. *Personnel, 65,* 52–60.

Cosier, R. A. (1981). Dialectical inquiry in strategic planning: A case of premature acceptance? *Academy of Management Review, 6,* 643–648.

Costa, P. T., Jr., McCrae, R. R., & Holland, J. L. (1984). Personality and vocational interests in an adult sample. *Journal of Applied Psychology, 69,* 390–400.

Cowan, D. A. (1986). Developing a process model of problem recognition. *Academy of Management Review, 11,* 763–776.

Cox, T. H. (1993). *Cultural diversity in organizations.* San Francisco: Berrett-Koehler.

Cox, T. H., Lobel, S. A., & McLeod, P. L. (1991). Effects of ethnic group cultural differences on cooperative versus competitive behavior on a group task. *Academy of Management Journal, 34,* 827–847.

DeLuca, J. M., & McDowell, R. N. (1992). Managing diversity: A strategic "grass-roots" approach. In S. E. Jackson and Associates, *Diversity in the workplace: Human resources initiatives* (pp. 227–247). New York: Guilford Press.

Devine, P. G. (1989). Stereotypes and prejudice: Their automatic and controlled components. *Journal of Personality and Social Psychology, 56,* 5–18.

Devine, P. G., Monteith, M. J., Zuwerink, J. R., & Elliot, A. J. (1991). Prejudice with and without compunction. *Journal of Personality and Social Psychology, 60,* 817–830.

Dutton, J. E. (1988). Perspectives on strategic issue processing: Insights from a case study. In P. Shrivastava and R. Lamb (Eds.), *Advances in strategic management: Vol. 5* (pp. 223–244). Greenwich, CT: JAI Press.

Eagly, A. H., & Carli, L. L. (1981). Sex of researchers and sex-typed communications as determinants of sex differences in influenceability: A meta-analysis of social influence studies. *Psychological Bulletin, 90,* 1–20.

Eagly, A. H., & Johnson, B. T. (1990). Gender and leadership style: A meta-analysis. *Psychological Bulletin, 108,* 223–256.

Eisenhardt, K. M., & Schoonhoven, C. B. (1990). Organizational growth: Linking founding team, strategy, environment, and growth among U.S. semiconductor ventures, 1978–1988. *Administrative Science Quarterly, 35,* 504–529.

Elder, G. H., Jr. (1974). *Children of the great depression.* Chicago: University of Illinois Press.

Elder, G. H., Jr. (1975). Age differentiation and the life course. *Annual Review of Sociology, 1,* 165–190.

Ferdman, B. M. (1992). The dynamics of ethnic diversity in organizations: Toward integrative models. In K. Kelley (Ed.), *Issues, theory and research in industrial/organizational psychology* (pp. 339–384). New York: Elsevier Science.

Ferdman, B. M., & Cortes, A. C. (1991). Culture and identity among Hispanic managers in an Anglo business. In S. B. Knouse, P. Rosenfeld, & A. Culbertson (Eds.), *Hispanics in the workplace* (pp. 246–277). Newbury Park, CA: Sage.

Fernandez, J. P. (1988, July/August). New life for old stereotypes. *Across the Board,* pp. 24–29.

Festinger, L., Schachter, S., & Back, K. (1950). *Social pressures in informal groups: A study of human factors in housing.* New York: HarperCollins.

Filley, A. C., House, R. J., & Kerr, S. (1976). *Managerial process and organizational behavior.* Glenview, IL: Scott, Foresman.

Finkelstein, S., & Hambrick, D. C. (1990). Top-management-team tenure and organizational outcomes: The moderating role of managerial discretion. *Administration Science Quarterly, 35,* 484–503.

Fiske, S. T. (1982). Schema-triggered affect: Applications to social perception. In M. S. Clark & S. T. Fiske (Eds.), *Affect and cognition* (pp. 55–78). Hillsdale, NJ: Erlbaum.

Fugita, S. S., & O'Brien, D. J. (1991). *Japanese Americans: The persistence of community.* Seattle: University of Washington Press.

Fulkerson, J. R., & Schuler, R. S. (1992). Managing diversity: A strategic "grass-roots" approach. In S. E. Jackson & Associates, *Diversity in the workplace: Human resources initiatives* (pp. 248–277). New York: Guilford Press.

Ghiselli, E. E., & Lodahl, T. M. (1958). Patterns of managerial traits and group effectiveness. *Journal of Abnormal and Social Psychology, 57,* 61–66.

Ginsberg, A. (1990). Connecting diversification to performance: A sociocognitive approach. *Academy of Management Review, 15,* 514–535.

Gladstein, D. L. (1984). Groups in context: A model of task group effectiveness. *Administrative Science Quarterly, 29,* 499–517.

Goffman, E. (1963). *Stigma: Notes on the management of spoiled identity.* Englewood Cliffs, NJ: Prentice-Hall.

Granovetter, M. S. (1973). The strength of weak ties. *American Journal of Sociology, 78,* 1360–1380.

Hall, J. A. (1984). *Nonverbal sex differences: Communication accuracy and expressive style.* Baltimore: Johns Hopkins University Press.

Hambrick, D. C., & Mason, P. A. (1984). Upper echelons: The organization as a reflection of its top managers. *Academy of Management Review, 9*(2), 193–206.

Haythorn, W. W. (1968). The composition of groups: A review of the literature. *Acta Psychologica, 28,* 97–128.

Hoffman, E. (1985). The effect of race-ratio composition on the frequency of organizational communication. *Social Psychology Quarterly, 48,* 17–26.

Hoffman, L. R. (1959). Homogeneity and member personality and its effect on group problem solving. *Journal of Abnormal Social Psychology, 58,* 27–32.

Hoffman, L. R. (1979). Applying experimental research on group problem solving to organizations. *Journal of Applied Behavioral Science, 15,* 375–391.

Hoffman, L. R., Harburg, E., & Maier, N.R.F. (1962). Differences and disagreement as factors in creative group problem solving. *Journal of Abnormal and Social Psychology, 64,* 206–214.

Hoffman, L. R., & Maier, N.R.F. (1961). Quality and acceptance of problem solutions by members of homogeneous and heterogeneous groups. *Journal of Abnormal and Social Psychology, 62,* 401–407.

Hofstede, G. (1991). *Cultures and organizations.* New York: McGraw-Hill.

Holland, J. L. (1976). Vocational preferences. In M. D. Dunnette (Ed.), *Handbook of industrial and organizational psychology* (pp. 521–570). Skokie, IL: Rand McNally.

Hyde, J. S., Fennema, E., & Lamon, S. J. (1990). Gender differences in mathematics performance: A meta-analysis. *Psychological Bulletin, 107,* 139–155.

Hyde, J. S., & Linn, M. C. (1988). Gender differences in verbal ability: A meta-analysis. *Psychological Bulletin, 104,* 53–69.

Ibarra, H. (1990, August). *Differences in men and women's access to informal networks at work: An intergroup perspective.* Paper presented at the meeting of the Academy of Management, San Francisco.

Ibarra, H. (1992). Homophily and differential returns: Sex differences in network structure and access in an advertising firm. *Administrative Science Quarterly, 37,* 422–447.

Ibarra, H. (1993). Personal networks of women and minorities in management: A conceptual framework. *Academy of Management Review, 18,* 57–87.

Isen, A. M., & Baron, R. A. (1991). Positive affect as a factor in organizational behavior. In L. L. Cummings and B. M. Staw (Eds.), *Research in organizational behavior: Vol. 13* (pp. 1–53). Greenwich, CT: JAI Press.

Jacklin, C. N. (1989). Female and male: Issues of gender. *American Psychologist, 44,* 127–133.

Jackson, S. E. (1992a). Consequences of group composition for the interpersonal dynamics of strategic issue processing. In P. Shrivastava,

A. Huff, & J. Dutton (Eds.), *Advances in Strategic Management: Vol. 89* (pp. 345-382). Greenwich, CT: JAI Press.

Jackson, S. E. (1992b). Team composition in organizational settings: Issues in managing a diverse work force. In S. Worchel, W. Wood, & J. Simpson (Eds.), *Group process and productivity*. Newbury Park, CA: Sage.

Jackson, S. E., & Alvarez, E. B. (1992). Working through diversity as a strategic imperative. In S. E. Jackson and Associates (Eds.), *Diversity in the workplace: Human resources initiatives* (pp. 13-35). New York: Guilford Press.

Jackson, S. E., Brett, J. F., Sessa, V. I., Cooper, D. M., Julia, J. A., & Peyronnin, K. (1991). Some differences make a difference: Individual dissimilarity and group heterogeneity as correlates of recruitment, promotions, and turnover. *Journal of Applied Psychology, 76,* 675-689.

Jackson, S. E., Stone, V. K., & Alvarez, E. B. (1993). Socialization amidst diversity: Impact of demographics on work team oldtimers and newcomers. In L. L. Cummings and B. M. Staw (Eds.), *Research in organizational behavior: Vol. 15* (pp. 45-110). Greenwich, CT: JAI.

Jaffe, M. P. (1987). Workforce 2000: Forecast of occupational change. In the technical appendix to W. B. Johnston & A. E. Packer, *Workforce 2000: Work and workers for the 21st century* (p. 23). Washington, DC: U.S. Department of Labor.

Janis, I. L. (1972). *Groupthink: Psychological studies of policy fiascoes* (2nd ed.). Boston: Houghton Mifflin.

Janis, I. L. (1989). *Crucial decisions: Leadership in policy-making and management*. New York: Free Press.

Johnston, W. B., & Packer, A. E. (1987). *Workforce 2000: Work and workers for the 21st century*. Washington, DC: U.S. Department of Labor.

Jones, E. E. (1990). *Interpersonal perception*. New York: Freeman.

Jones, E. E., Farina, A., Hastorf, A. H., Markus, H., Miller, D. T., Scott, D., & de Sales-French (1984). *Social stigma: The psychology of marked relationships*. New York: Freeman.

Kanter, R. M. (1977). *Men and women of the corporation*. New York: Basic Books.

Kanter, R. M. (1989). *When giants learn to dance*. New York: Simon & Schuster.

Kanter, R. M. (1991, May-June). Transcending business boundaries: 12,000 world managers view change. *Harvard Business Review,* pp. 151-164.

Katz, P. A., & Taylor, D. A. (1988). *Eliminating racism: Profiles in controversy*. New York: Plenum Press.

Kerr, N. (1992). Group decision making at a multialternative task: Extremity, interaction distance, pluralities, and issue importance. *Organizational Behavior and Human Decision Processes, 52,* 64–95.

Kraly, E. P., & Hirschman, C. (1990). Racial and ethnic inequality among children in the United States—1940 and 1950. *Social Forces, 69,* 33–51.

Kram, K. E. (1985). *Mentoring at work: Developmental relationships in organizational life.* Glenview, IL: Scott, Foresman.

Labouvie-Vief, G. (1989). Intelligence and cognition. In J. E. Birren and K. W. Schaie (Eds.), *Handbook of the psychology of aging* (pp. 500–530) (2nd ed.). New York: Van Nostrand Reinhold.

Laughlin, P. R., & Bitz, D. S. (1975). Individual versus dyadic performance on a disjunctive task as a function of initial ability level. *Journal of Personality and Social Psychology, 31,* 487–496.

Lawrence, B. S. (1988). New wrinkles in a theory of age: Demography, norms, and performance ratings. *Academy of Management Journal, 31,* 309–337.

Lawrence, B. S. (1991). *The black box of organizational demography.* Unpublished manuscript. University of California, Los Angeles.

Levine, J. M., & Moreland, R. L. (1990). Progress in small-group research. *Annual Review of Psychology, 41,* 585–634.

Lin, T., Dobbins, G. H., & Fahr, J. (1992). A field study of race and age similarity effects on interview ratings in conventional and situational interviews. *Journal of Applied Psychology, 77,* 363–371.

Lincoln, J. R., & Miller, J. (1979). Work and friendship ties in organizations: A comparative analysis of relational networks. *Administrative Science Quarterly, 24,* 181–199.

Lindblom, C. E. (1959). The science of "muddling through." *Public Administration Review, 19,* 79–88.

Lott, A. J., & Lott, B. E. (1965). Group cohesiveness and interpersonal attraction: A review of relationships with antecedent and consequent variables. *Psychological Bulletin, 64,* 259–302.

McCain, B. E., O'Reilly, C., & Pfeffer, J. (1983). The effects of departmental demography on turnover: The case of a university. *Academy of Management Journal, 26,* 626–641.

Maccoby, E. E., & Jacklin, C. N. (1974). *The psychology of sex differences.* Stanford, CA: Stanford University Press.

McGrath, J. E. (1984). *Groups: Interaction and performance.* Englewood Cliffs, NJ: Prentice-Hall.

McGuire, W. J. (1985). Attitudes and attitude change. In G. Lindzey and E. Aronson (Eds.), *Handbook of social psychology: Vol. 2* (pp. 233–346). New York: Random House.

McPherson, J. M., & Smith-Lovin, L. (1987). Homophily in voluntary organizations: Status distance and the composition of face-to-face groups. *American Sociological Review, 52,* 370–379.

Markides, K. S. (1983). Minority aging. In M. W. Riley, B. B. Hess, & K. Bond (Eds.), *Aging in society: Selected reviews of recent research* (pp. 207–231). Hillsdale, NJ: Erlbaum.

Markus, H., & Zajonc, R. B. (1985). The cognitive perspective in social psychology. In G. Lindzey and E. Aronson (Eds.), *Handbook of social psychology: Vol. 2.* (pp. 137–178). New York: Random House.

Maurer, S. D., Howe, V., & Lee, T. W. (1992). Organizational recruiting as marketing management: An interdisciplinary study of engineering graduates. *Personnel Psychology, 45,* 807–834.

Michel, J. G., & Hambrick, D. C. (1992). Diversification posture and top management team characteristics. *Academy of Management Journal, 35,* 9–37.

Miller, F. (1992). Discussant commentary. Leadership Diversity Conference: *Beyond awareness into action.* Center for Creative Leadership, Greensboro, NC.

Miller, V. D., & Jablin, F. M. (1991). Information seeking during organizational entry: Influence, tactics, and a model of the process. *Academy of Management Review, 16*(1); 92–120.

Morrison, A. M., & Von Glinow, M. A. (1990). Women and minorities in management. *American Psychologist, 45*(2), 200–208.

Murray, A. I. (1989). Top management group heterogeneity and firm performance. *Strategic Management Journal, 10,* 125–141.

Mydans, S. (1991, June 30). For these Americans, ties to Mexico remain. *New York Times,* p. L12.

Neale, M. A., & Northcraft, G. B. (1991). Experts, amateurs, and refrigerators: Comparing expert and amateur negotiators in a novel task. *Organizational Behavior and Human Decision Processes, 38,* 305–317.

Nemeth, C. J. (1986). Differential contributions of majority and minority influence. *Psychological Review, 91,* 23–32.

Nkomo, S. M. (1992). The emperor has no clothes: Rewriting "race in organizations." *Academy of Management Review, 17,* 487–513.

O'Reilly, C. A., III, Caldwell, D. F., & Barnett, W. P. (1989). Work group demography, social integration, and turnover. *Administrative Science Quarterly, 34,* 21–37.

Ostrom, T. M., & Sedikides, C. Out-group homogeneity effects in natural and minimal groups. *Psychological Bulletin, 112,* 536–552.

Pearce, J. A., & Ravlin, E. C. (1987). The design and activation of self-regulating work groups. *Human Relations, 40*(11), 751–782.

Pelz, D. C. (1956). Some social factors related to performance in a research organization. *Administrative Science Quarterly, 1,* 310–325.

Pfeffer, J. (1983). Organizational demography. *Research in Organizational Behavior, 5,* 299–357.

Pfeffer, J., & Leblebici, H. (1973). Executive recruitment and the development of interfirm organizations. *Administrative Science Quarterly, 18,* 449–461.

Porac, J. F., & Howard, H. (1990). Taxonomic mental models in competitor definition. *Academy of Management Review, 2,* 224–240.

Race in the workplace (1991, July 8). *Business Week,* pp. 50–63.

Rhodes, S. R. (1983). Age-related differences in work attitudes and behavior. A review and conceptual analysis. *Psychological Bulletin, 93,* 328–367.

Rice, A. S., Ruiz, R. A., & Padilla, A. M. (1974). Person perception, self-identity, and ethnic group preference in Anglo, black, and Chicano preschool and third-grade children. *Dissertation Abstracts International, 33,* 3404–3405.

Ridgeway, C. L. (1982). Status in groups: The importance of motivation. *American Sociological Review, 47,* 76–88.

Ridgeway, C. L. (1987). Nonverbal behavior, dominance, and the basis of status in task groups. *American Sociological Review, 52,* 683–694.

Ridgeway, C. L., & Berger, J. (1986). Expectations, legitimation, and dominance behavior in task groups. *American Sociological Review, 51,* 603–617.

Roloff, M. E. (1987). *Interpersonal communication: The social exchange approach.* Newbury Park, CA: Sage.

Rousseau, D. M. (1985). Issues of level in organizational research: Multilevel and cross-level perspectives. In L. L. Cummings and B. M. Staw (Eds.), *Research in organizational behavior: Vol. 7* (pp. 1–37). Greenwich, CT: JAI Press.

Schneider, B. (1987). The people make the place. *Personnel Psychology, 40,* 437–453.

Schweiger, D. M., Sandberg, W. R., & Rechner, P. L. (1989). Experiential effects of dialectical inquiry, devil's advocacy, and consensus approaches to strategic decision making. *Academy of Management Journal, 32,* 722–745.

Schwenk, C. R. (1983). Laboratory research on ill-structured decision aids: The case of dialectical inquiry. *Decision Sciences, 14,* 140–144.

Selbert, R. (1987). Women at work. *Future Scan, 554,* 1–3.

Sessa, V. (1992). Managing diversity at the Xerox Corporation: Balanced workforce goals and caucus groups. In S. E. Jackson & Associates

(Ed.), *Diversity in the workplace: Human resources initiatives* (pp. 37–64). New York: Guilford Press.

Shaw, M. E. (1981). *Group dynamics: The psychology of small-group behavior.* New York: McGraw-Hill.

Sherman, S. J., Judd, C. M., & Park, B. (1989). Social cognition. *Annual Review of Psychology, 40,* 281–326.

Simon, H. A. (1987, February). Making management decisions: The role of intuition and emotion. *Academy of Management Executive,* 57–64.

Singh, H., & Harianto, F. (1989). Top management tenure, corporate ownership structure, and the magnitude of golden parachutes. *Strategic Management Journal, 10,* 143–156.

Snyder, M., Tanke, E. D., & Berscheid, E. (1977). Social perception and interpersonal behavior: On the self-fulfilling nature of social stereotypes. *Journal of Personality and Social Psychology, 36,* 1202–1212.

Solomon, C. M. (1989). The corporate response to work force diversity. *Personnel Journal, 34,* 43–52.

South, S. J., Bonjean, C. M., Markham, W. T., & Corder, J. (1982). Social structure and intergroup interaction: Men and women of the federal bureaucracy. *American Sociological Review, 47,* 587–599.

Stangor, C., Lynch, L., Duan, C., & Glass, B. (1992). Categorization of individuals on the basis of multiple social features. *Journal of Personality and Social Psychology, 62*(2), 207–218.

Stangor, C., Sullivan, L. A., & Ford, T. E. (1991). Affective and cognitive determinants of prejudice. *Social Cognition, 9,* 359–380.

Steiner, I. D. (1972). *Group process and productivity.* San Diego, CA: Academic Press.

Stephan, W. G. (1985). Intergroup relations. In G. Lindzey and E. Aronson (Eds.), *Handbook of social psychology: Vol. 2* (pp. 599–658). New York: Random House.

Stone, E. F., Stone, D. L., & Dipboye, R. L. (1992). Stigmas in organizations: Race, handicaps, and physical unattractiveness. In K. Kelley (Ed.), *Issues, Theory, and Research in Industrial/Organizational Psychology* (pp. 42–70). New York: Elsevier Science.

Sundstrom, E., De Meuse, K. P., & Futrell, D. (1990). Work teams: Applications and effectiveness. *American Psychologist, 45,* 120–133.

Thernstrom, S. (1973). *The other Bostonians: Poverty and progress in the American metropolis, 1880–1970.* Cambridge, MA: Harvard University Press.

Thomas, D. A. (1990). The impact of race on managers' experiences of developmental relationships (mentoring and sponsorship): An intraorganizational study. *Journal of Organizational Behavior, 11,* 479–492.

Tichy, N. M., & Sherman, S. (1993). *Control your destiny or someone else will.* New York: Bantam Books.

Triandis, H. C. (1993). Theoretical and methodological approaches in the study of collectivism and individualism. In U. Kim, H. C. Triandis, & G. Yoon (Eds.), *Individualism and collectivism: Theoretical and methodological issues.* Newbury Park, CA: Sage.

Triandis, H. C., Hall, E. R., & Ewen, R. B. (1965). Member heterogeneity and dyadic creativity. *Human Relations, 18,* 33–55.

Tsui, A. S., Egan, T. D., & O'Reilly, C. A., III, (1992). Being different: Relational demography and organizational attachment. *Administrative Science Quarterly, 37,* 549–579.

Tsui, A. S., & O'Reilly, C.A., III (1989). Beyond simple demographic effects: The importance of relational demography in superior-subordinate dyads. *Academy of Management Journal, 32,* 402–423.

Turner, J. C. (1987). *Rediscovering the social group: A self-categorization theory.* Oxford, England: Basil Blackwell.

Uleman, J. S., & Bargh, J. A. (Eds.). (1989). *Unintended thought.* New York: Guilford Press.

Verbrugge, L. M. (1977). The structure of adult friendship choices. *Social Forces, 56,* 576–597.

Von Glinow, M. A., & Mohrman, S. (1990). *Managing complexity in high-technology organizations.* New York: Oxford University Press.

Wagner, W. G., Pfeffer, J., & O'Reilly, C. A., III. (1984). Organizational demography and turnover in top-management groups. *Administrative Science Quarterly, 29,* 74–92.

Walker, B. A., & Hanson, W. C. (1992). Valuing differences at Digital Equipment Corporation. In S. E. Jackson & Associates (Eds.), *Diversity in the workplace: Human resources initiatives* (pp. 119–137). New York: Guilford Press.

Wallston, B. S., & O'Leary, V. E. (1981). Sex and gender make a difference: Differential perception of women and men. *Review of Personality and Social Psychology, 2,* 9.

Walsh, J. P. (1988). Selectivity and selective perception: An investigation of managers, belief structures, and information processing. *Academy of Management Journal, 31,* 873–896.

Watson, D., & Tellegen, A. (1985). Toward a consensual structure of mood. *Psychological Bulletin, 98,* 219–235.

Watson, W. E., Kumar, K., & Michaelsen, L. K. (1993). Cultural diversity's impact on interaction process and performance: Comparing homogeneous and diverse task groups. *Academy of Management Journal, 36,* 590–602.

Wiersema, M. F., & Bantel, K. A. (1991). Top management team demography and corporate strategic change. *Academy of Management Journal, 35,* 91–121.

Willems, E. P., & Clark, R. D., III. (1971). Shift toward risk and heterogeneity of groups. *Journal of Experimental and Social Psychology, 7,* 302–312.

Wood, W. (1987). Meta-analytic review of sex differences in group performance. *Psychological Bulletin, 102,* 53–71.

Work Attitudes: Study reveals generation gap (1986, October 2). *Bulletin to Management,* p. 326.

Zajonc, R. B. (1980). Feeling and thinking: Preferences need no inferences. *American Psychologist, 35,* 151–175.

Zander, A. (1979). The psychology of group processes. *American Review of Psychology, 30,* 417–451.

Zander, A., & Havelin, A. (1960). Social comparison and interpersonal attraction. *Human Relations, 13,* 21–32.

Zenger, T. R., & Lawrence, B. S. (1989). Organizational demography: The differential effects of age and tenure distribution on technical communications. *Academy of Management Journal, 32*(2), 353–376.

8

TEAMWORK STRESS: IMPLICATIONS FOR TEAM DECISION MAKING

Ben B. Morgan, Jr., Clint A. Bowers

As stress researchers recognize, a voluminous literature has accumulated during the past several decades concerning the effects of stress on human performance. In general, the results of research in this area provide a rather substantial basis for understanding the relationship between stress and performance in individuals (see Goldberger & Breznitz, 1982, and Appley & Trumbull, 1986, for reviews of the research and discussions of this relationship; see Boff & Lincoln, 1988, for a consolidation of findings in several stress areas). Unfortunately, however, there has not been an equivalent improvement in our understanding of the effects of stress on team performance.

Several reviews of the literature indicate that our understanding of team structure, operation, performance, and training is rather inadequate (e.g., Dyer, 1984; Modrick, 1986; Salas, Dickinson, Converse, & Tannenbaum, 1992), and that there have been relatively few investigations of the effects of stress on teams and team performance (e.g., Boff & Lincoln, 1988). Furthermore, the state of the art for investigating team performance and the factors that affect it have been severely criticized on methodological grounds (Dyer, 1984; Modrick, 1986; Morgan, Lassiter, & Salas, 1989). Methodological difficulties notwithstanding, there is a clear and urgent need for a greater understanding of team performance, the stressors that effect it, and the interventions that might increase the efficiency and effectiveness of team performance under stress.

This need is particularly evident with regard to the effects of stress on teams' *decision-making performance*. A review of the existing knowledge base regarding team decision making reveals only a few theoretical papers, and even fewer empirical investigations of the factors that influence decision-making performance. The dearth of research in this area is becoming particularly critical because of the fact that, in both the military sector and the civilian sector, many of today's jobs are dependent on the ability of groups of individuals to work together as a team, to cope with the demands and stresses of complex occupational environments, and to make quick and effective team decisions. For example, when one considers the nature of the tasks performed and the stresses encountered by aircraft crews, combat information-center personnel, air-traffic controllers, nuclear power plant operators, and people in other occupations that demand teamwork, it is easy to understand how errors in communication and coordination can produce disastrous consequences in these settings. In the case of air crews, it has been reported that the majority of accidents can be attributed to human error and to the inadequate allocation of crew resources (Cooper, White, & Lauber, 1980), both of which may be indicative of faulty teamwork (Prince, Chidester, Cannon-Bowers, & Bowers, 1992). The extent to which stress contributes to these kinds of failures in team decision-making performance is not well understood. Additional research is clearly needed in this area.

In view of the critical nature of the effects of stress on team decision making and the dearth of research, several military and civilian agencies have recently initiated research programs to investigate team decision-making performance. As a result of this activity, a more substantial scientific literature will soon emerge in this area (the development of this literature is reflected by the fact that the American Psychological Association added the word *team* to the subject list of its *Psychological Abstracts* in 1987). However, it is important for researchers to understand the critical need for investigations of basic team decision-making performance and the degree to which such performance might be affected by a number of stress-related variables found in naturalistic settings. In order to provide a foundation and guide for such research, this chapter reviews the literature concerning the effects of stress on team decision-making performance, offers a conceptualization of the nature and effects of stresses that affect team decision-making processes, and provides hypotheses concerning how these effects might be reduced in operational settings.

The Nature of Stress

The effect of stress on human performance has been an area of scientific interest for many years, and many researchers have studied the effects of many different stressors. As a result, several different theoretical perspectives have developed, each with its own particular emphasis, of the various aspects of the overall construct regarding stress (see Goldberger & Breznitz, 1982, and Singer & Davidson, 1986, for reviews). Thus stress has been defined and treated in a variety of ways. Table 8.1 summarizes the definitions of seven different aspects, or dimensions, or types of stress, as emphasized by different researchers.

As indicated in the table, *psychological stress* has been defined as "a response state [whose] induction depends on the mediation of some appraising, perceiving, or interpreting mechanism" (Appley & Trumbull, 1967, p. 9; see also Lazarus, 1974; Lazarus & Folkman, 1984). This definition emphasizes the importance of the individual's perception and assessment of a situation as the critical element in the development of a stress response. Research from this theoretical perspective tends to focus on the measurement of psychological changes, usually in the form of subjective data, as the primary index of stress. Similarly, *cognitive stress* has been defined as "those cognitive events, processes, or operations that exceed a subjective individualized level of average processing capacity" (Hamilton, 1982, p. 109). This definition

Table 8.1. Definitions of Various Types of Stress.

Type	Definition
Psychological	"A response state and . . . its induction [which] depends on the mediation of some appraising, perceiving, or interpreting mechanism" (Appley & Trumbull, 1967, p. 9)
Cognitive	The effects caused by "those cognitive events, processes, or operations that exceed a subjective individualized level of average processing capacity" (Hamilton, 1982, p. 109)
Environmental	Responses to "the aversive effects of an unfavorable physical environment, [responses] to the effects of crowding, noise, social and economic deprivations, frustrations experienced while commuting to and from work, or [responses] to the effects of large-scale housing in a previously quiet rural area" (Hamilton, 1979, p. 6)
Occupational	"Social psychological characteristics of work that are detrimental to [the] employee's health" (Beehr, 1987, p. 74)
Organizational	"The general, patterned, unconscious mobilization of the individual's energy when confronted with any organizational or work demand" (Quick & Quick, 1984, p. 9)
Physiological	"The state manifested by a specific syndrome which consists of all the nonspecifically-induced changes within a biologic system" (Selye, 1956)
Social	"Psychosocial stress reflect[ing] the subject's inability to forestall or diminish perception, recall, anticipation, or imagination of disvalued circumstances, those that in reality or fantasy signify a great and/or increased distance from desirable (valued) experiential states" (Kaplan, 1983, p. 196)

emphasizes the mental processes required by task demands, and the individual's capacity for executing those processes effectively. Researchers who adopt this perspective usually measure stress in terms of physiological changes or performance decrements under conditions where processing capacities are exceeded. To draw a final example from Table 8.1, *organizational stress* has been defined as "the general, patterned, unconscious mobilization of the individual's energy when confronted with any organizational demand or work" (Quick & Quick, 1984, p. 9; see also Ivancevich & Donnelly, 1975). This definition emphasizes the individual's mobilization of energy resources in response to work requirements. Other researchers have developed perspectives that deal with individual responses to the effects of physiological stress (Frankenhaeuser, 1982; Selye, 1956), environmental stress (Boff & Lincoln, 1988; Kaminoff & Prohansky, 1982), social stress (Pearlin, 1982), and occupational stress (Caplan, Cobb, French, Van Harrison, & Pinneau, 1975; Hurrell, Murphy, Sauter, & Cooper, 1980).

The purpose of this discussion is to illustrate the fact that several types of stress have been identified and to note that these stresses have been defined in ways that permit the development of theoretical perspectives and measurement approaches that are appropriate to the purposes of researchers in the respective areas. In an analogous fashion, the remainder of this chapter defines a "new" type of stress — *teamwork stress* — and provides a theoretical perspective for investigating the effects of such stress. It is hoped that this discussion will lead to the development of measurement approaches and experimental paradigms for investigating the effects of stress on team decision making in organizations.

The foregoing discussion also illustrates the fact that prior investigators have defined stress almost exclusively in terms of its effects on individuals. Each of the definitions in Table 8.1 emphasizes the response of individuals. As others have stated, "stress is regarded as an *intraorganismic* concept" (Haythorn & Altman, 1967, p. 363; emphasis in original). Very few stressors have been investigated in terms of their effects on teams. However, given the importance of developing a greater understanding of team decision making, it should be instructive to focus attention on stresses that have a direct impact on the decision-making processes of teams. As indicated previously, this chapter seeks to highlight those stressors, describe the nature of their effects on team decision-making processes, and provide a framework from which to investigate the effects of stress on teams. Thus, without ignoring or denying the effects of stress on individuals (indeed, we hope to build on that knowledge), the following discussion focuses on the team-level effects of stress, thereby treating stress as an *intrateam* concept.

Teamwork Stress

For the purposes of this discussion, a *team* is defined as "a distinguishable set of two or more individuals who interact interdependently and adaptively to achieve specified, shared, and valued objectives" (Morgan, Glickman, Woodard, Blaiwes, & Salas, 1986, p. 3). Similarly, *teamwork* is defined as the "actions, processes, and behaviors which contribute to a team's ability to achieve specific, shared, and valued objectives" (Glickman et al., 1987). Effective teamwork has been further defined in terms of behaviors that contribute to "error identification and resolution, coordinated information exchange, and intermember reinforcement" (Oser, McCallum, Salas, & Morgan, 1989). Drawing from these prior definitions, teamwork stress is considered to consist of those stimuli or conditions that (1) directly affect the team members' ability to interact interdependently or (2) alter the team's interactive capacity for obtaining its desired objectives. These are seen as stressors that have a direct influence on the processes of team interaction and coordination. They would often make it more difficult for team members to work together in order to identify and resolve errors. They might stimulate (or inhibit) the coordination of information exchange and team actions, and they could act to reduce intermember reinforcement and motivation.

The effects of teamwork stress should be measured primarily in terms of changes in teamwork behaviors (e.g., changes in communication patterns, coordination behaviors, etc.) and/or performance in teams that are required to "interact interdependently" in the performance of assigned tasks. These changes might normally be evidenced as decrements in the quality and quantity of teamwork behaviors. However, there is evidence to suggest that this type of stress can result in an increase in the amount of communication (e.g., Drabek & Haas, 1969) or a change in the overall pattern (e.g., Oser, McCallum, Salas, & Morgan, 1989) of teamwork behaviors. Thus, as with other types of stress, it is recognized that under certain conditions teamwork stress can serve to stimulate or energize relevant behaviors, whereas under other conditions (unspecifiable at the current time) the stressors will certainly inhibit or reduce the occurrence of adaptive teamwork behaviors. In assessing the effects of teamwork stress, therefore, researchers should be careful to measure changes from the baseline of relevant behaviors.

Teamwork stress can emerge from external conditions, as part of the task requirements or work environment (e.g., work load, time pressure), or from conditions within the team, as part of the team's interaction processes (e.g., role conflict). It should be noted that teamwork stress might arise from the same stimuli as those discussed with regard to the types of stress listed in Table 8.1. However, teamwork stress differs with respect to the focus of its impact and the nature of its effects on teams. Specifically, our identification of this additional "type" of stress is intended to highlight the fact that, in addition to its impact on individuals, teamwork stress also has an impact on the processes required for effective team coordination and cooperation.

Thus the key factor in identifying teamwork stress is a change in team interaction processes and performance. While this definition pertains to teams from a variety of settings, this chapter focuses particularly on the performance of teams where differentiated members (differentiated in terms of authority, perspective, tenure, or expertise) combine resources to make and implement decisions in high-stakes naturalistic environments characterized by ambiguity, high workloads, time constraints, and system embeddedness (see Orasanu, 1990).

Potential Teamwork Stressors

In reviewing the literature regarding stress and human performance, one is struck by the sheer number of stimuli that have been considered as stressors. However, because the majority of these stimuli have been investigated only at the individual level, it is extremely difficult to draw implications concerning their potential impact on teams. The literature is only slightly more instructive in that only a few studies of the effects on teams of a few specific stressors have been reported. Nevertheless, this section seeks to review the existing research in terms of the effects on team performance of specific conditions that appear to meet the definitional criteria of teamwork stress, as discussed above. Thus this section identifies several factors that have been shown to influence teamwork processes and describes how these team-work stressors can change the ways in which team members work together. This discussion is not intended as an exhaustive compilation of teamwork stressors. Rather, we will review the variables that appear to satisfy the criteria for teamwork stressors and that have a sufficient research literature to suggest their effects. The selected stressors, their definitions, and the hypothesized effects on team decision making are presented in Table 8.2.

Team Training Load. Several elements of training may influence the processes and productivity of teams. One factor that has received considerable attention in the training development literature is the assimilation of new members (Ketchum & Trist, 1992). Empirically, one series of experiments has specifically investigated the effects of removing a trained member of the team and replacing that individual with another, separately trained or untrained, individual. Early studies of this type indicated little effect of this manipulation (Horrocks & Goyer, 1959; Horrocks, Heerman, & Krug, 1961). However, later studies suggested that the effects of these replacements on team performance were dependent on the competence of the replacement (new) crew member (Naylor & Briggs, 1965). These results also indicated that the negative effects of inserting less skilled replacements were greater than the positive effects of adding more highly skilled members.

Researchers at Old Dominion University investigated the systematic replacement of increasing numbers of team members in an established (trained) team (Morgan, Coates, Kirby, & Alluisi, 1984). They required five-person teams to perform a "synthetic job," which involved performing a variety of individual- and team-performance functions. Data from several one-week trials were combined so as to provide estimates of the performance effects of systematically increasing the percentage (in 10 percent increments) of untrained team members assigned to a fully trained team. Results indicated that performance

Table 8.2. Teamwork Stressors: Definitions and Hypothesized Effects.

Stressor	Definition	Hypothesized Effect on Team Decision Making
Team training load	The replacement of trained team members with untrained individuals	Increased team training load should result in inferior decision-making performance.
Team workload	"The relationship between the finite cognitive capacities of a team and the demands placed on the team" (Bowers, Braun, & Morgan, 1992)	Increased team workload might alter communication patterns among team members, resulting in poorer performance.
Team size	The number of members who comprise a team	Large teams may limit the amount of information shared among members in order to make decisions.
Team composition	Concerns the degree to which team members are similar to one another (i.e., in interests and abilities, type of information available regarding task, etc.)	Homogeneity is likely to result in conformity and accelerated decision making.
Team structure	Has to do with whether members are equally ranked (horizontal) or inequally ranked (hierarchical)	Structures other than partial overlap are at risk for degraded performance.
Team cohesion	The mutual attraction among members of a group and the resulting desire to remain in the group (Eddy, 1985)	Lack of cohesion is likely to result in poor decision-making performance.
Goal structure	The ultimate performance standard on which the team must be evaluated (i.e., individual versus group goal setting; adapted from Matsui, Kakuyama, & Onglatco, 1987)	Individual goals might lead to decreased performance.

decrements were directly related to the degree of team training load. In other words, teams with higher percentages of untrained team members demonstrated increased decrements in performance. It is interesting to note that this pattern of results occurred with regard to both individual- and team-level measures of performance.

Thus it appears that increasing the percentage of less skilled (untrained) individuals reduces not only the average performance of individuals but also the ability of team members to interact effectively in producing team solutions to problems. Although the team task used in this experiment imposed a relatively low decision-making load on the team, relatively low levels of training load (20 percent to 30 percent) produced rather substantial reductions in team performance. Therefore, it is concluded that team training load (the replacement of trained team members with untrained individuals) imposes teamwork stress on teams with interdependent members.

This finding suggests that performance-relevant training or experience should also reduce the effects of teamwork stress. While this notion has not been tested directly, there is some evidence to suggest that training might effectively enhance team decision-making performance. For example, Diehl (1990) reports the results of a program evaluation of aeronautical decision-making interventions. He reviews six empirical studies designed to test the effects of a variety of decision-making interventions. The results indicate that all paradigms were effective in reducing errors in trained subjects as compared to controls (results ranged from 8 percent to 46 percent error reduction). However, the particular behaviors or processes that result in this performance improvement are not clear from Diehl's report.

It should be noted that training may not have universally beneficial effects on team performance. Helmreich and Wilhelm (1989) describe a "boomerang effect" in a cockpit management training program. This training was designed to improve crew members' attitudes concerning the effectiveness of cockpit resource management behaviors. However, the authors note a paradoxical effect of this training, such that attitudes actually became less favorable after training. Whether these negative effects influence crew performance is unknown. However, the study highlights the point that training is no guarantee of improved performance.

In summary, the studies described above illustrate that various aspects of team training may increase or decrease the level of teamwork stress. In other words, team training factors may have an impact on team decision-making performance: directly, by enhancing the team's technical skills, or indirectly, by altering the processes of team interaction. Although further empirical work is needed to understand the effects of team training factors more completely, it would certainly be expected that specific team skill training should serve as a useful intervention for enhancing team decision-making performance. However, future studies of the effects of team training variables should always include assessments of the effects of these variables on teamwork processes as well as on performance outcomes.

Team Workload. The effect of workload on individual performance has been investigated rather extensively (see Gopher & Donchin, 1986, for a review). Although the results have been somewhat mixed, a considerable amount of research indicates that increased workload tends to degrade performance (Biers, Polzella, & McInerney, 1988; Damos & Lintern, 1981; Vidulich & Pandit, 1986). However, the impact of workload on the performance of teams has received considerably less attention from researchers. In fact, team workload has only recently been defined as "the relationship between the finite cognitive capacities of a team and the demands placed on the team" (Bowers, Braun, & Morgan, 1992). Nevertheless, the existing literature indicates that team workload should be considered as an important contribution to teamwork stress. Several studies show that simply participating in a team can impose its own resource demands, above and beyond those necessary to complete an assigned task. For example, Naylor and Briggs (1965) demonstrate that the performance of operators in a simulated air-intercept task was superior when the subjects worked independently of one another. Decrements in performance were observed when operators were placed in an organizational structure that encouraged interaction among the operators. This finding has been replicated in several studies (Briggs & Naylor, 1965; Johnston, 1966; Williges, Johnston, & Briggs, 1966), including a commercial air-traffic control simulation (Kidd, 1961). In explaining these performance decrements, it has been suggested that the coordination component of teamwork imposes workload above and beyond that of task demands. Kidd (1961) concludes that "intrinsic to team performance is the requirement of coordination. This requirement is superimposed on the normal demands of the task itself and leads to a proportionate reduction of exclusively task-directed behavior" (p. 199). However, the extent to which this additional component of workload affects team decision making has not yet been investigated.

It should also be noted that the effects of participating in a team are not necessarily negative. It appears that, in some situations, the benefits of teamwork compensate for or even exceed the costs of coordinating with team members. This phenomenon is demonstrated by Johnston and Briggs (1968). In their study, pairs of subjects served as air-traffic controllers in a simulated approach task. Subjects were required to alternate in directing aircraft approaches under two different conditions of task load. The subjects were also assigned to either a compensatory condition (i.e., a subject could coordinate with his partner to compensate for an early or late approach) or a noncompensatory condition. Under conditions of high task load, performance in the compensatory condition was found to be superior to that demonstrated by subjects in the noncompensatory condition. Furthermore, the disruptive effect of communication between team members was observed only in the noncompensatory condition.

A study by Morrisette, Hornseth, and Shellar (1975) demonstrates similar benefits to team performance. In this experiment, the monitoring performance of two-man teams was compared with that of individuals. In this study, the performance of teams was found to be superior to that of individuals, especially when teams were organized to maximize redundancy. However, communication was not directly assessed. Therefore, it is not possible to know whether this beneficial effect of teamwork superseded the demands of coordination or whether the assigned task simply required little communication for successful performance.

The results of a study by Bieth (1987) also indicate that team participation serves to decrease the subjective workload of team members. This study compared the perceived workload imposed by a complex cognitive task performed by individuals and teams. After task completion, workload ratings were solicited with the NASA bipolar method (Hart & Staveland, 1988). Team members were also asked to estimate the overall team workload imposed by the task. Individuals assigned to the team condition estimated their personal workload to be approximately 20 percent lower than subjects assigned to the individual condition. Furthermore, workload ratings appeared to decrease as communication increased. No significant differences in performance were found between the individual and team conditions. Thus the decreased workload ratings cannot simply be attributed to decreased team productivity.

The available data support the idea that team workload may be an important teamwork stressor. However, the nature and degree of impact on team decision making is not clearly suggested by this research. Recently reported data by Kleinman and his associates (Kohn, Kleinman, & Serfaty, 1987; Kleinman & Serfaty, 1989) may assist in broadening the understanding of this issue. These investigators required teams of three subjects to perform a dynamic resource allocation task, presented via the computer. The task was designed so that teams were required to make decisions regarding the appropriate allocation and utilization of a pool of common resources in order to engage a series of simulated targets. Objective team workload was manipulated by altering the target arrival rate. The dependent variables in this study included not only team performance but also frequency of computer-mediated communication behaviors (such as requests for resource transfers). The results of this study indicate that as workload increased from low to medium, subjects increased the frequency of task-related communication, or "explicit coordination." However, as workload increased from medium to high, the rate of communication decreased drastically, so that most resource transfers were unsolicited. This pattern is described by Kleinman and Serfaty (1989) as "implicit coordination." This research effectively demonstrates how team processes are altered in response to an external stimulus. Thus, in this instance, workload would be considered as a teamwork stressor (because interaction processes were altered by workload), even in the absence of subjective or physiological stress responses among the individuals who comprised the teams.

Although the results reported by Kleinman and his associates represent an important finding in team decision-making research, they must be interpreted with some caution. The degree to which they can be replicated in other tasks or generalized to the naturalistic environment has not yet been established. Research with team tasks that involve nonreplenishable resources or non–computer mediated communication may yield somewhat different results. This concern is supported by the results of an earlier study by Drabek and Haas (1969), who manipulated workload within a "realistic simulation" of a police dispatch task. Experienced police dispatch teams performed a task in which they were required to respond to simulated situations reported via telephone calls. The results of this study indicate that as workload increased, communication within the team also increased. However, the lack of performance measurement within this task makes it difficult to determine whether decision-making accuracy or efficiency suffered as a function of the increased communication.

The apparent contradiction between the results of these two studies is not intended as a criticism of the research. Rather, it serves to highlight a fundamental concern in team-performance research — namely, the extreme difficulty of determining the extent to which results obtained with one type of team task will be generalized to other teams performing other types of tasks. Thus teams making decisions regarding resource allocations may in fact "implicitly coordinate" in response to increased workload, while teams given more complex demands may coordinate explicitly. Furthermore, differences in team processes may be attributable to variations in experience, interdependence, competence, other independent variables, or interactions among several variables. These conceptual complexities are relevant not just to workload but also to all of the teamwork stressors discussed here.

In summary, team workload appears to be a promising area for further team decision-making research. So far, it seems that workload is most likely to affect team performance by altering communication patterns among team members. However, future research may identify other disruptions in team process resulting from workload.

Team Size, Composition, and Structure. At first glance, it may seem odd to include such variables as team size and team structure in a review of stressors. They most likely do not generate the physiological changes or subjective reports that traditionally have indicated the presence of stress. Yet, given the emphasis on performance implied by the definition of teamwork stress, this may be an appropriate and important area for future study. Several variables within the domain of team composition and staffing have been identified as potentially important influences on team behavior (see Bass, 1982, and Morgan & Lassiter, 1992, for reviews). This review will focus on three of these variables—team size, team composition, and team structure—as potential teamwork stressors.

Many reports converge to suggest that the size of a team can determine the quality and quantity of interactions within the team. Early reports suggested that the amount of information processed, as well as the skill level obtained, increased in a linear manner with the size of the team (Cattell, 1953). However, increases in team size have not produced consistently beneficial effects. Bass (1982) reports that as team size increases, coordination between team members becomes increasingly difficult. This effect has been demonstrated empirically by Morgan and his colleagues (Morgan, Coates, & Rebbin, 1970), who found that team performance actually improved when one team member was missing from five-person teams. This result was interpreted to mean that "coordination among four crewmembers should have been easier than among five" (p. 18). There is also evidence to suggest that both the frequency and the content of communications may be affected by increased team size. As size increases, individual team members tend to communicate less frequently (Gerard, Wilhelmy, & Conolley, 1968; Indik, 1965).

Furthermore, individuals may alter their statements to conform to the perceived beliefs of the overall team (Gerard, Wilhelmy, & Conolley, 1968; Rosenberg, 1961).

The effects described above suggest several important implications in terms of team size and team decision-making performance. The reduced frequency of communication observed in larger teams may also limit the amount of information utilized in arriving at a decision. Moreover, the conformity effect observed in larger teams may result in a team's making decisions without complete or even accurate information. There is a need for continued empirical research to assess these effects directly.

Team composition may also directly affect the nature and frequency of interaction within a team. The results of several studies indicate that teams with members who are alike in interests and abilities are at less risk for conflict than are heterogeneous teams (Bass, 1965; Hoffman, 1959). Moreover, homogeneity appears to facilitate interaction among team members (Bass, 1982). Homogeneity has also been found to increase cooperation in teams required to complete complex physical tasks (Lodahl & Porter, 1961). Nevertheless, it has been shown that heterogeneity among members may actually enhance problem solving within teams. For example, heterogeneous groups seem less willing to accept incorrect responses from fellow team members without questioning them, according to Goldman, Dietz, and McGlynn (1968); in fact, the more homogeneous teams performed worse than individuals in these researchers' experiment. In another study (Hoffman & Maier, 1961), teams who were heterogeneous in terms of team members' personality profiles produced better responses on a team problem-solving task.

Finally, Adelman and his colleagues (Adelman, Zirk, Lehrer, Moffett, & Hall, 1986) investigated the impact of "cognitive model similarity" on teams performing a low-fidelity air-defense task. Three-person teams completed an exercise which demanded the dynamic allocation of resources to defend against simulated enemy aircraft. In the "similar cognitive model" condition, subjects were given identical instructions and "intelligence" predictions about the direction of the attacks. In the "dissimilar" condition, subjects received conflicting predictive information. The results of this study indicate that although teams from the two conditions demonstrated different teamwork behaviors in the execution of the task, the overall effectiveness score was not significantly different between the two groups of teams.

It should be noted that the existing research pertaining to team composition has been conducted only in laboratory situations utilizing somewhat contrived decision-making tasks. The extent to which these results can be generalized to naturalistic situations, where members have a more personal stake in the results of the team's performance, needs to be assessed directly.

Variables related to team structure may also influence the process and eventual outcome of team decision making. For this reason, self-managed work teams—teams that can alter their structure according to task demands—have become very popular in industry. For the purposes of this chapter, we will focus the review of the empirical literature on one condition that has recently attracted attention in the decision-making literature: horizontally structured (single-level, equally ranked) versus hierarchically structured teams. Hierarchical team decision making involves the processes by which team members with varying degrees of information, rank, authority, and responsibility coordinate their activities to arrive at a conclusion that maximizes benefit to the team. It is easy to imagine that hierarchical teams would display a different configuration of behaviors from those of rankless teams in completing a decision-making task. Subordinate team members might be inhibited from questioning information coming from superiors, even if they believed that this information was incorrect. In fact, because team members might have access to qualitatively different data bases, decision making might be at risk of becoming a "diffuse" process in which decision events would be less likely to be well coordinated among team members (cf. Connolly, 1977).

To date, there has been relatively little empirical research regarding the effects of hierarchical structure on team decision making. Studies in the business and management literature have emphasized such factors as leadership style (Vroom & Yetton, 1973) and democratic process (Sims & Hand, 1975) within differing organizations. However, this literature provides little information about the effects of team organization on team decision-making processes or outcomes. More recently, human-factors scientists have described results that may be more helpful in this regard. For example, Kleinman and Serfaty (1989) describe an experiment in which they varied the degree of overlap of responsibility in a two-person, distributed decision-making task. In the low-overlap condition, subjects had completely separate responsibilities (i.e., one subject could prosecute only air targets, and the other only sea targets). The experimenter also included partial-overlap and total-overlap conditions. Each overlap condition was then crossed with three levels of workload (which was manipulated via both tempo and difficulty). The results of this study indicate that under low and medium workload conditions, increasing team members' overlap was positively related to team performance. However, during the high workload condition, partial overlap resulted in significantly better performance. Thus this study provides an example of how distributed responsibility — one facet of hierarchical team decision making — affects team decision-making performance. However, it is unclear how the addition of rank among team members would further affect this relationship, or whether this pattern could be generalized to other stressors.

Team Cohesion. A fairly large literature suggests that high levels of cohesion are associated with positive outcomes for a variety of teams and groups. *Cohesion* has been defined as the mutual attraction among members of a group and the resulting desire to remain in the group (Eddy, 1985). Overall, highly cohesive teams have been shown to set goals more easily (Festinger, Schachter, & Back, 1950) and to be more likely to achieve those goals (Seashore, 1954). However, these results have been obtained mostly through somewhat contrived laboratory tasks. Whether these trends can be generalized to naturalistic decision-making teams is somewhat less clear.

Much of the literature pertaining to cohesion and team decision making is found in the business game literature (see Wolfe & Box, 1988, for a review). Early research in this area indicated little relationship between team cohesion and decision-making performance (McKinney & Dill, 1966; Norris & Niebuhr, 1980). However, these studies have been criticized because of their correlational nature and because the teams received relatively few incentives for high levels of performance on tasks. A recent study investigated the effects of team cohesion under higher levels of motivation (Wolfe & Box, 1988). These researchers required thirty-six teams to play a complex business game that entailed a significant demand for decision making. Motivation was imposed by making the team's performance equal to 40 percent of the grade received in a college business course. Results of this study indicate significant correlation between team cohesiveness and performance. Thus it is suggested that the strength of the relationship between cohesion and performance can be moderated by the degree of motivation among team members. However, further research is needed to determine the degree to which the two are related in naturalistic settings.

Goal Structure. Several studies have indicated that the goal structure of a team affects the team's performance. A substantial body of research indicates that individual goal setting is an effective tool for improving performance (Lee, 1989; Locke & Latham, 1985; Wood, Mento, & Locke, 1987). However, the contribution of goals to team performance has received somewhat less attention. The central question in this regard is whether individual goals have a similarly beneficial effect on team performance or whether team goals are a more effective way of eliciting desired levels of performance. This question has been investigated empirically in an experiment by Matsui and his colleagues (Matsui, Kakuyama, & Onglatco, 1987). In their study, undergraduate subjects were assigned to one of two goal conditions, individual or dyad, to complete a counting task. Subjects in the individual goal condition were told that they would win a prize if their performance was ranked among the top six scores. Subjects in the team goal condition were offered a prize if their summed scores were ranked among the top six team scores. Subjects in the individual condition were asked to specify a performance goal, and subjects in the group condition were asked to establish both individual and group goals. The results of the study indicate that subjects in the group condition demonstrated higher performance and goal acceptance than did subjects in the individual condition, despite the fact that there was no significant difference in individual goals. The authors argue that the difference is a function of the increased difficulty imposed by the group goal. Although the study demonstrates the effects of goal structure on group performance, it can be argued that these results may not be generalizable to all team performances, since the team task did not require interdependent performance. Thus Mitchell and Silver (1990) performed a similar experiment to determine the effect of goal structure on performance in a more interdependent task.

Subjects in their study were assigned to one of four goal conditions: no goal, individual goal, group goal, or individual and group goal. The subjects were then given goals appropriate to the condition and were required to complete a tower-building task. The results of the study indicate that subjects in the individual goal condition performed more poorly than subjects in any of the other groups. Subjects in the individual goal condition also reported less perceived cooperation among team members. There was no significant difference in performance or perceived cooperation among the remaining three groups.

Thus a limited body of experimental evidence suggests that certain goal structures (e.g., individual goal only) may seem to produce teamwork stress. However, it should be noted that these studies have not utilized a decision-making task. From the literature on individual performance, one might expect goal structure to have a less salient effect on decision-making tasks. For example, a meta-analysis of the individual literature by Wood and his colleagues (Wood, Mento, & Locke, 1987) indicates a relatively strong effect of goal on performance of easy tasks (such as reaction-time tasks) but much milder effects on more difficult tasks (e.g., business game simulations). Therefore, further experimental research is required in order to understand more fully the effects of goal structure on team decision making.

Teamwork Stress and Team Decision Making

Inasmuch as there is no generally accepted model of team decision making, we will summarize the foregoing discussion by
drawing conclusions concerning the impact of teamwork stress
on the four components of team decision making described by
Orasanu (1990). These components are situation assessment,
metacognition, shared mental models, and resource management. According to this conceptualization, team decision making begins with *situation assessment,* which refers to the detection
and interpretation of cues in order to recognize the existence of
a problem. *Metacognition* involves developing the definition of the
problem and creating a strategy to solve it. This component also
includes directing an information search, should adequate information be unavailable. This process leads to the development
of *shared mental models,* or the ability of team members to develop
a common understanding of the problem and a strategy for solving it. This includes an agreement about each member's role in
the team and expectations about behavior. Finally, team decision making requires *resource management,* or the efficient utilization of the team's skills and abilities in the execution of the task.

Teamwork stress may affect each of these components of
team decision making. For example, the process of situation assessment demands not only vigilance on the part of team members (an individual function) but also communication of perceived
situations to the rest of the team. Thus conditions that reduce
team members' willingness or ability to communicate would
produce teamwork stress likely to affect team decision making.
On the basis of the existing literature, therefore, it is hypothesized that decreased team cohesion, team heterogeneity, and work
load may all be important stressors in terms of their effects on
a team's ability to assess problem situations. Composition variables may also influence the speed with which a team is able to
reach agreement on the existence or nature of critical signals.

In the case of metacognition, the team (or some subset
of the team) must define the problem and develop a plan of action. Again, communication is an important factor in this process, and conditions that impede communication may produce

salient teamwork stress. It is during this component of team decision making that stressors related to the organization or role structure of the team are likely to influence the decision-making process. It is hypothesized that hierarchically structured teams are at risk for problems in this phase of team decision making because subordinate members may be unwilling to contribute information. Similarly, teamwork stress associated with conformity may also affect decision-making performance by reducing the willingness of team members to suggest alternative viewpoints.

The development of shared mental models depends on the ability of team members to understand the decision-making situation, effectively communicate this understanding to other team members, and develop a unified approach to reaching a final team decision. Intuitively, we can say that homogeneous teams should possess some advantage in this phase, particularly if team members are similar with respect to training experience and development of cognitive schemata. However, the current research does not provide effective guidance concerning which variables are the most salient ones in this regard. It is also likely that shared mental models will develop less quickly in hierarchical organizations because all team members are not likely to be involved in the metacognition phase. Admittedly, this is a construct that does not lend itself to empirical study. However, the paradigm described by Kleinman and Serfaty (1989) provides a tool for the study of shared mental models and the factors that may facilitate their development. The implicit coordination behaviors resulting from the paradigm are hypothesized to indicate the presence of shared mental models among team members.

Finally, resource allocation requires team members to be familiar with one another's abilities, so that resources can be allocated in the best possible manner for the completion of the task. Therefore, one might hypothesize that teams with greater experience would be better at this phase of decision making (as supported by Morgan, Coates, Kirby, & Alluisi, 1984). Furthermore, because this is a process required throughout the decision-making cycle, it may tend to suffer as team workload is increased.

Conclusion

The large literature regarding the effects of stress on human performance has nearly overlooked the effects on team processes and performance. By invoking the concept of teamwork stress, this chapter has sought to highlight the importance of investigating these effects and has attempted to suggest some likely effects on the basis of the existing research. There remains, however, a need for a substantial amount of empirical research on the effects of stress on team performance and team processes before an adequate understanding of these effects will be possible. It is hoped that this discussion will stimulate and guide such research.

References

Adelman, L., Zirk, D. A., Lehrer, P. E., Moffett, R. J., & Hall, R. (1986). Distributed tactical decision making. Conceptual framework and empirical results. *IEEE Transactions on Systems, Man, and Cybernetics, 16*(6), 794–805.

Appley, M. H., & Trumbull, R. (Eds.). (1967). *Psychological stress.* New York: Meredith.

Appley, M. H., & Trumbull, R. (1986). Dynamics of stress and its control. In M. H. Appley & R. Trumbull (Eds.), *Dynamics of stress* (pp. 309–327). New York: Plenum Press.

Bass, B. M. (1965). When planning for others. *Journal of Applied Behavioral Science, 6,* 151–171.

Bass, B. M. (1982). Individual capability, team performance, and team productivity. In E. A. Fleishman & M. D. Dunnette (Eds.), *Human performance and productivity: Human capability assessment* (pp. 179–232). Hillsdale, NJ: Erlbaum.

Beehr, T. A. (1987). The themes of social-psychological stress in work organizations: From roles to goals. In A. W. Riley & S. J. Zaccaro (Eds.), *Occupational stress and organizational effectiveness* (pp. 71–101). New York: Praeger.

Biers, D. W., Polzella, D. J., & McInerney, P. (1988). *A physical measure of subjective workload.* Paper presented at the annual meeting of the Human Factors Society, Santa Monica, CA.

Bieth, B. H. (1987). *Subjective workload under individual and team performance conditions.* Paper presented at the annual meeting of the Human Factors Society, Santa Monica, CA.

Boff, K. R., & Lincoln, J. E. (1988). *Engineering data compendium: Human perception and performance.* Wright-Patterson Air Force Base, OH: Harry G. Armstrong Medical Research Laboratory.

Bowers, C. A., Braun, C. C., & Morgan, B. B., Jr. (1992, September). *Workload and team performance.* Presentation at the University of South Florida Workshop on Team Performance Measurement, Tampa.

Briggs, G. E., & Naylor, J. C. (1965). Team versus individual training, training-task fidelity, and task-organization effects on transfer performance by three-man teams. *Journal of Applied Psychology, 49,* 387–392.

Caplan, R. D., Cobb, S., French, J.R.P., Van Harrison, R., & Pinneau, S. R. (1975). *Job demands and worker health* (NIOSH Research Report). Washington, DC: National Institute of Occupational Safety and Health.

Cattell, R. B. (1953). On the theory of group learning. *Journal of Applied Psychology, 37,* 27–52.

Connolly, T. (1977). Information processing and decision making in organizations. In B. M. Staw & G. R. Salancik (Eds.), *New directions in organizational behavior.* Chicago: St. Clair Press.

Cooper, G. E., White, M. D., & Lauber, J. K. (Eds.). (1980). *Resource management on the flightdeck: Proceedings of a NASA/industry workshop* (NASA Technical Report No. CP-2120). Moffett Field, CA: National Aeronautics and Space Administration–Ames Research Center.

Damos, D. L., & Lintern, G. (1981). A comparison of single- and dual-task measures to predict sim ilator performance of beginning student pilots. *Ergonomics, 24*(9), 673–684.

Diehl, A. (1990). *The effectiveness of aeronautical decision-making training.* Paper presented at the annual meeting of the Human Factors Society, Santa Monica, CA.

Drabek, T. E., & Haas, J. E. (1969). Laboratory simulation of organizational stress. *American Sociological Review, 34,* 223–238.

Dyer, J. (1984). Team research and training: A state-of-the-art review. In F. A. Muckler (Ed.), *Human factors review: 1984* (pp. 285–323). Santa Monica, CA: Human Factors Society.

Eddy, W. B. (1985). *The manager and the working group.* New York: Praeger.

Festinger, L., Schachter, S., & Back, K. (1950). *Social pressures in informal groups: A study of human factors in housing.* New York: HarperCollins.

Frankenhaeuser, M. (1982). Challenge-control interaction as reflected in sympathetic-adrenal and pituitary-adrenal activity: Comparison between the sexes. *Scandinavian Journal of Psychology* (Suppl. 1), 158–164.

Gerard, H. B., Wilhelmy, R. A., & Conolley, E. S. (1968). Conformity and group size. *Journal of Personality and Social Psychology, 8*(1), 79–82.

Glickman, A. S., Zimmer, S., Montero, R. C., Guerette, P. J., Campbell, W. J., Morgan, B. B., Jr., & Salas, E. (1987). *The evolution of teamwork skills: An empirical assessment with implications for training* (NTSC Technical Report No. 87–016). Orlando, FL: Naval Training Systems Center.

Goldberger, L., & Breznitz, S. (Eds.). (1982). *Handbook of stress: Theoretical and clinical aspects.* New York: Free Press.

Goldman, M., Dietz, D. M., & McGlynn, A. (1968). Comparison of individual and group performance related to heterogeneous-wrong responses, size, and patterns of interaction. *Psychological Reports, 23*(2), 459–465.

Gopher, D., & Donchin, E. (1986). Workload: An examination of the concept. In K. R. Boff, L. Kaufmann, & J. P. Thomas (Eds.), *Handbook of perception and human performance: Vol. 2. Cognitive processes and performance* (pp. 41-1–42-49). New York: Wiley-Interscience.

Hamilton, V. (1979). Human stress and cognition: Problems of definition, analysis, and integration. In V. Hamilton & D. M. Warburton (Eds.), *Human stress and cognition* (pp. 3–8). New York: Wiley.

Hamilton, V. (1982). Cognition and stress: An information model. In L. Goldberger & S. Breznitz (Eds.), *Handbook of stress: Theoretical and clinical aspects* (pp. 105–120). New York: Free Press.

Hart, S. G., & Staveland, L. E. (1988). Development of NASA-TLX: Results of empirical and theoretical research. In P. A. Hancock & N. Meshkati (Eds.), *Human mental workload* (pp. 139–183). New York: Elsevier Science.

Haythorn, W. W., & Altman, I. (1967). Personality factors in isolated environments. In M. H. Appley & R. Trumbull (Eds.), *Psychological stress* (pp. 363–399). New York: Meredith.

Helmreich, R. L., & Wilhelm, J. A. (1989). When training boomerangs: Negative outcomes associated with cockpit resource management programs. In R. S. Jensen (Ed.), *Proceedings of the fifth symposium on aviation psychology* (pp. 692–697). Columbus: Ohio State University Press.

Hoffman, L. R. (1959). Group problem solving. In L. Berkowitz (Ed.), *Advances in experimental social psychology: Vol. 2* (pp. 99–132). San Diego, CA: Academic Press, 1965.

Hoffman, L. R., & Maier, N.R.F. (1961). Quality and acceptance of problem solutions by members of homogeneous and heterogeneous groups. *Journal of Abnormal and Social Psychology, 62,* 401–407.

Horrocks, J. E., & Goyer, R. (1959). *Human factors analysis of team training* (NTDC Technical Report No. 198-3). Orlando, FL: Naval Training Device Center.

Horrocks, J. E., Heerman, E., & Krug, R. E. (1961). *Team training III: An approach to optimum methods and procedures* (NTDC Technical Report No. 198-3). Orlando, FL: Naval Training Device Center.

Hurrell, J. J., Murphy, L. R., Sauter, S. L., & Cooper, C. L. (Eds.) (1980). *Occupational stress: Issues and developments in research.* New York: Taylor & Francis.

Indik, B. P. (1965). Organization size and member participation: Some empirical tests of alternative explanations. *Human Relations, 18*(4), 339–350.

Ivancevich, J. M., & Donnelly, J. H., Jr. (1975). Relation of organizational structure to job satisfaction, anxiety-stress, and performance. *Administrative Science Quarterly, 20,* 272–280.

Johnston, W. A. (1966). Transfer of team skills as a function of type of training. *Journal of Applied Psychology, 50,* 102–108.

Johnston, W. A., & Briggs, G. E. (1968). Team performance as a function of team arrangement and work load. *Journal of Applied Psychology, 52*(2), 89–94.

Kaminoff, R. D., & Prohansky, H. M. (1982). Stress as a consequence of the urban physical environment. In L. Goldberger & S. Breznitz (Eds.), *Handbook of stress: Theoretical and clinical aspects* (pp. 380–409). New York: Free Press.

Kaplan, H. B. (1983). Psychological distress in sociological context: Toward a theory of psychosocial stress. In H. B. Kaplan (Ed.), *Psychosocial stress: Trends in theory and research* (pp. 195–264). San Diego, CA: Academic Press.

Ketchum, L., & Trist, E. (1992). New-paradigm training in a paradigm shift. In *All teams are not created equal* (pp. 249–280). Newbury Park, CA: Sage.

Kidd, J. S. (1961). A comparison of one-, two-, and three-man work units under various conditions of workload. *Journal of Applied Psychology, 45,* 195–200.

Kleinman, D. L., & Serfaty, D. (1989, April). *Team performance assessment in distributed decision making.* Paper presented at the Simulation and Training Research Symposium on Interactive Networked Simulation for Training, University of Central Florida, Orlando.

Kohn, C., Kleinman, D. L., & Serfaty, D. (1987). Distributed resource allocation in a team. Paper presented at the JDL Symposium on Command-and-Control Research, Washington, DC.

Lazarus, R. S. (1974). Cognitive and coping processes in emotion. In B. Wiener (Ed.), *Cognitive views of human motivation* (pp. 21–32). San Diego, CA: Academic Press.

Lazarus, R. S., & Folkman, S. (1984). *Stress appraisal and coping*. New York: Springer.

Lee, C. (1989). The relationship between goal setting, self-efficacy, and female field-hockey team performance. *International Journal of Sport Psychology, 20*(2), 147-161.

Locke, E. A., & Latham, G. P. (1985). The application of goal setting to sports. *Journal of Sport Psychology, 7*(3), 205-222.

Lodahl, T. M., & Porter, L. W. (1961). Psychometric score patterns, social characteristics, and productivity of small industrial work groups. *Journal of Applied Psychology, 45*, 73-79.

McKinney, J. L., & Dill, W. R. (1966). Influences on learning in simulation games. *American Behavioral Scientist, 10*(2), 28-32.

Matsui, N., Kakuyama, T., & Onglatco, M. U. (1987). Effects of goals and feedback on performance in groups. *Journal of Applied Psychology, 72*(3), 416-425.

Mitchell, T. R., & Silver, W. S. (1990). Individual and group goals when workers are interdependent: Effects on task strategies and performance. *Journal of Applied Psychology, 75*(2), 185-193.

Modrick, J. A. (1986). Team performance and training. In J. Zeidner (Ed.), *Human productivity enhancement: Vol. 1. Training and human factors in systems design* (pp. 130-166). New York: Praeger.

Morgan, B. B., Jr., Coates, G. D., Kirby, R. H., & Alluisi, E. A. (1984). Individual and team performances as functions of the team-training load. *Human Factors, 26*, 127-142.

Morgan, B. B., Jr., Coates, G. D., & Rebbin, T. J. (1970). *The effects of Phlebotomus fever on sustained performance and muscular output* (Tech. Rep. No. ITR-70-14). Louisville, KY: University of Louisville, Performance Research Laboratory.

Morgan, B. B., Jr., Glickman, A. S., Woodard, E. A., Blaiwes, A., & Salas, E. (1986). *Measurement of team behaviors in a Navy environment* (NTSC Technical Report No. 86-014). Orlando, FL: Naval Training Systems Center.

Morgan, B. B., Jr., & Lassiter, D. (1992). Team composition and staffing. In R. W. Swezey and E. Salas (Eds.), *Teams: Their training and performance* (pp. 75-100). Norwood, NJ: Ablex.

Morgan, B. B., Jr., Lassiter, D., & Salas, E. (1989, April). *Networked simulation applications for team training and performance research*. Paper presented at the Simulation and Training Research Symposium on Interactive Networked Simulation for Training, University of Central Florida, Orlando.

Morrisette, J. O., Hornseth, J. P., & Shellar, K. (1975). Team organization and monitoring performance. *Human Factors, 17*(3), 296–300.

Naylor, J. C., & Briggs, G. E. (1965). Team training effectiveness under various conditions. *Journal of Applied Psychology, 49*, 223–229.

Norris, D., & Niebuhr, R. E. (1980). Group variables and gaming success. *Simulation and Games, 11*(3), 301–312.

Orasanu, J. M. (1990, July). *Shared mental models and crew decision making.* Paper presented at the annual conference of the Cognitive Science Society, Massachusetts Institute of Technology, Cambridge.

Oser, R. L., McCallum, G. A., Salas, E., & Morgan, B. B., Jr. (1989). *Toward a definition of teamwork: An analysis of critical team behaviors* (NTSC Technical Report No. 89-018). Orlando, FL: Naval Training Systems Center.

Pearlin, L. I. (1982). The social contexts of stress. In L. Goldberger & S. Breznitz (Eds.), *Handbook of stress: Theoretical and clinical aspects* (pp. 367–379). New York: Free Press.

Prince, C., Chidester, T. R., Cannon-Bowers, J., & Bowers, C. (1992). Aircrew coordination: Achieving teamwork in the cockpit. In R. W. Swezey & E. Salas (Eds.), *Teams: Their training and performance* (pp. 329–353). Norwood, NJ: Ablex.

Quick, J. C., & Quick, J. D. (1984). *Organizational stress and preventive management.* New York: McGraw-Hill.

Rosenberg, L. (1961). Group size, prior experience, and conformity. *Journal of Abnormal and Social Psychology, 63*(2), 436–447.

Salas, E., Dickinson, T., Converse, S. A., & Tannenbaum, S. I. (1992). Toward an understanding of team performance and training. In R. W. Swezey & E. Salas (Eds.), *Teams: Their training and performance* (pp. 3–29). Norwood, NJ: Ablex.

Seashore, S. S. (1954). *Group cohesiveness in the industrial work group.* Ann Arbor: University of Michigan, Institute for Social Research.

Selye, H. (1956). *The stress of life.* New York: McGraw-Hill.

Sims, H. P., & Hand, H. H. (1975). Performance trade-off in management games. *Simulation and Games, 6*(1), 61–72.

Singer, J. E., & Davidson, L. M. (1986). Specificity and stress research. In M. H. Appley and R. Trumbull (Eds.), *Dynamics of stress* (pp. 47–61). New York: Plenum Press.

Vidulich, M. A., & Pandit, P. (1986). *Training and subjective workload in a category search task.* Paper presented at the annual meeting of the Human Factors Society, Dayton, OH.

Vroom, V. A., & Yetton, P. W. (1973). *Leadership and decision making*. Pittsburgh, PA: University of Pittsburgh Press.

Williges, R. C., Johnston, W. A., & Briggs, G. E. (1966). Role of verbal communication in teamwork. *Journal of Applied Psychology, 50,* 473–478.

Wolfe, J., & Box, T. M. (1988). Team cohesion effects on business game performance. *Simulation and Games, 19*(1), 82–98.

Wood, R. E., Mento, A. J., & Locke, E. A. (1987). Task complexity as a moderator of goal effects: A meta-analysis. *Journal of Applied Psychology, 72*(3), 416–425.

9

STAFFING FOR EFFECTIVE
GROUP DECISION MAKING:
KEY ISSUES IN MATCHING
PEOPLE AND TEAMS

Richard Klimoski, Robert G. Jones

As previous chapters have made clear, decision-making teams are confronted with an enormous variety of tasks, opportunities, and threats with which they must effectively deal. Jackson (1991) has shown that group composition can have an important impact on the processes and outcomes involved. What is probably not so clear is how groups come to be composed the way they are. How do mixtures of individual skills, personal tendencies, and roles come together? What do we need to know about this process in order to enhance team effectiveness? These questions will be addressed in this chapter.

It will become quite obvious that much more needs to be known about how the staffing process influences team effectiveness. Because of the lack of evidence concerning this process, we will examine staffing issues with an inductive approach. First, we will describe five examples of decision-making teams in terms of the tasks they perform and the demands placed on members. What we will be searching for are key issues affecting staffing processes in the five teams. Next, we will consider the traditional approach to staffing and will describe models of individual

291

and group effectiveness (Ackerman & Humphreys, 1990; Hackman, 1987; Guzzo, 1986). The team model and the five teams will be used to illustrate how traditional and innovative approaches to staffing could be used to address special problems inherent in staffing teams. We will try to answer this question: What might be special about the team staffing process?

Five Working Decision-Making Teams

The Command-and-Control Team

Perhaps the best-defined type of group staffing challenge comes from the command-and-control team. Such a team is engaged in a highly coordinated, usually prescribed response to environmental events. Some research has shown how the individual, well-defined skills and abilities of group members affect the effectiveness of this type of team (see Ginnett, 1990; Tziner & Eden, 1985). For example, Tziner and Eden show that a tank crew should be composed of people with uniformly high ability. These researchers have found that the high abilities of one or two crew members would not make up for the low ability of a third member. In order for the crew to perform adequately, all members would need to be able to perform well the functions of their specific positions.

Given the nature of task performance in this type of group, these results are not surprising. Specifically, the functions of each job are highly specialized and interdependent. Decisions are made in real time and often meet with immediate consequences. Functional specialization in making these decisions means that team members' roles are usually well defined and that their training is extensive. Effective team leaders, for example, integrate and feed back performance information as it occurs (Komaki, Zlotnick, & Jensen, 1986; Komaki, Desselles, & Bowman, 1989). Interdependence means that if one person cannot accomplish his or her duties in the time available, then the entire team suffers the consequences.

The Production Team

Relatively less systematic research has been done concerning the ways in which team characteristics may influence the effec tiveness of production teams. Added complexity of the task parameters of this type of team may also make staffing issues more complex. For example, with the type of autonomous production team now appearing on the U.S. work scene (for instance, at the Saturn & NUMMI auto plants), this complexity becomes especially clear. The functional responsibilities of each worker are extremely broad. (In fact, Brown, 1987, reports that there are only three job descriptions for all production-team jobs at NUMMI; rather than being highly specialized, team members are trained to perform many jobs, and team leaders are trained to perform all the duties of the team.) This implies a type of interdependence different from that of the command-and-control team. Along with sequential, reciprocal, and pooled interdependence (Thompson, 1967), workers rely on each other to fulfill myriad functions, rather than only one. This creates a capacity to shift workers quickly to perform particular tasks, which may allow for greater flexibility in such work teams, but it also creates greater complexity in team coordination. Thus cross-functional generalization and flexible interdependence create a need for coordination.

Characteristics of decision making in high-involvement production teams also underscore the complexity of staffing for such teams. First, decisions in this type of work team may be both strategic and tactical. That is, work-group members may decide how to structure their jobs over time, but many of the day-to-day decisions are made in real time, as in the command-and-control team. Moreover, the consequences of these decisions may be either immediate or long-term ones. Awaiting long-term outcomes creates a degree of ambiguity that some workers find stressful. Furthermore, team leaders' functions are more complex, especially since the leaders often share both information-analysis and primary decision-making duties in such groups. Overall, these elements show how role sharing creates complexity for those making staffing decisions.

The Customer-Service Team

Despite the growing prominence of this form of team in the U.S. economy, research on it has only recently been done. The

individual functions of the members of a service team are related
to the demands of clients, but the function of the team as a source
of support may also be particularly important for this type of
team.

Saavedra, Cohen, and Denison (1990) differentiate performance in such teams according to variables with direct implications for staffing. Case studies of well- and poorly performing teams (in beer sales and delivery, and in the airline industry)
were used to identify variables thought to have affected performance. The variables identified were quite different for the two
types of teams. For beer salespeople, group composition appears
to have been key to performance. Specifically, the homogeneous
team (in terms of levels of knowledge and skills, interpersonal
styles, and age) performed better than the less homogeneous
team. By contrast, all members of two teams of flight attendants
were hired on the basis of similar standing with regard to enthusiasm, managerial talent, service, and desire to learn and
grow. Whether these attributes were adequately measured in
the staffing process is an important issue, but the authors imply that these were not the sources of performance difference
in the teams. What does appear to have been important to these
teams is early experiences of success. (As will be seen, both early
experiences and hiring methods are part of the staffing system.)

One important issue for staffing the customer-service team
is whether there are important functions that all team members
must be able to fulfill. The homogeneity of the team of high-
performing sales people supports the idea that roles are shared
by all members, both with regard to their customers and with
regard to each other. Other supporting evidence comes from
a study of grocery store clerks (Rafaeli, 1989), which demonstrates that service may actually suffer when other people are
present. Specifically, Rafaeli shows that a server's expression
of positive emotion to a client was less likely when other workers or clients were present. It is not clear why such an inhibitory
response should occur, but Rafaeli suggests that self-awareness
may be important in explaining such behavior in service settings. Regardless, the more general question for staffing in such
situations is this one: What kinds of people inhibit positive emotional responses in the presence of others?

A closer look at the types of decisions made by customer-service teams also helps integrate the findings of these studies. Customer-service workers need to make decisions about how to respond to the needs of the people they are serving. Unlike the situation in production or command-and-control teams, where stimuli are provided by machines or standardized interactions, the stimuli for service teams are the perceptions that members have of other people. Accurate perception of clients' needs, choices of optimum (or even adequate) responses, and execution of these responses can be difficult. As if these parts of the task were not daunting enough, feedback about decisions takes many forms, requires accurate assessment of problem sources, and may occur immediately or months later. Overall, the decision-making tasks in service teams, and the possible problems inherent in such teams, make staffing a challenge.

A further feature of service teams that poses a challenge to staffing is frequent use of the "handoff" approach to responsibility for meeting clients' or customers' needs. For instance, one individual (a customer-service representative) may be the point of initial contact with the organization. This individual may be able to respond to the customer immediately and resolve the inquiry or provide the service requested. It is more likely, however, that he or she will gather information on the customer's needs or concerns and then go on to involve one or more other employees. The quality of the information gathered at the point of contact, the level of rapport developed, and the promises or commitments made or implied will certainly affect the nature of the dynamics between the customer and those other company personnel. Similarly, the ultimate satisfaction of the customer will depend on the performance of all these agents relative to the expectations that have been created. To the extent that the customer or client relationship is expected to endure over time, the behavior and performance of the team will affect future contacts with the organization. If the company is large enough, the initial representative may or may not be involved again, which creates still another "handoff" event.

The distinction made by Hasenfeld and English (1974) between people-processing and people-transforming service teams has important implications for staffing. People processing requires staff (bank tellers, traditional hospital-care workers) to provide service on the basis of specific criteria. People transforming requires staff (family therapists, mental hospital workers) to attempt to change basic attributes of people according to general, value-defined objectives. People processing does not necessarily require the active involvement of the persons being served; people transforming does. There are at least two implications here for team decision making. First, in people transforming, there is a need for the active participation of the client. This means that the person being served is accomplishing some of the team's functions: the client is, in effect, a partial employee (Mills & Morris, 1986), and the ability of the service team to include the client as an extra member is important. Second, as Katz and Kahn (1978) have pointed out, transforming requires a larger and more flexible role for staff members, given the breadth of definition of organizational goals and therefore of performance effectiveness. Thus people-transforming teams require flexible, broadly skilled people capable of including outsiders in the transformation process.

The Professional (Technical) Decision-Making Team

This type of team arguably includes a larger variety of functions, structures, and processes than the teams just described. Actually, this category encompasses a variety of work teams, ranging from permanent product or venture teams to more ad hoc cross-functional and problem-solving teams (Sundstrom, De Meuse, & Futrell, 1990). As such, the decision-making tasks assigned to such teams vary widely. Group composition is usually heterogeneous, however, and the number of different organizational levels (vertical differentiation) and job areas (horizontal differentiation) will be greater than in other groups (O'Reilly & Roberts, 1977). In fact, David, Pearce, and Randolph (1989) have shown that this degree of differentiation interacts with decision-making variables to influence performance in such groups. Among other things, these researchers have examined relationships between group composition and decision variables and aggregated individual performance of forty-two groups of managers in banking organizations. Their results show that horizontal differentiation improved the performance of teams facing unpredictable tasks, whereas vertical integration improved the performance of teams facing difficult-to-analyze problems. These results suggest that group composition does need to be considered in staffing for different decision-making tasks.

Since the gamut of strategic, tactical, analytical, and creative decisions is faced by such teams, staffing for this category of work groups presents important questions. For example, it is not clear from the David, Pearce, and Randolph study (1989) whether more is better when it comes to considering horizontal differentiation for an unpredictable task. Instead, it may be that the right mix of knowledge, skills, and abilities (KSAs) is only more likely if there is a larger pool of team members to draw from, but numbers alone are not enough to ensure success. (Questions related to the exact skill mixes required, and to perceived group-efficacy influences on performance, will be considered later.)

In a classic paper, Patchen (1974) points out that the level of motivation or type of orientation of the various team members involved in organizational decisions will also make a difference in group process and results. Patchen found that individuals who had more direct stakes in the outcomes of group deliberations were more influential and might be considered champions of particular points of view: they not only gathered and presented more information in team meetings but were also perceived as more influential (and were even deferred to) for this reason.

Another important feature of professional teams concerns the representational role dynamics that are in operation (Adams, 1976); that is, individuals on these teams speak not only for themselves but usually also for some constituency. Thus a team put together to introduce a new product may include specialists from distribution, marketing, sales, and production. Discussions and decisions would certainly affect the individuals on the team, but they would also hold implications for the people in the departments or divisions represented. The need to report back and justify the team's decision, and often to "sell" the decision, has profound effects on team process (see Klimoski & Ash, 1974; Dutton & Ashford, 1993).

The Executive Team

Perhaps a special case of the professional decision-making team is the executive team. In order to maintain organizational objectives, executive teams are required to respond in a strategic fashion to poorly defined problems presented by environmental forces. Feedback about the outcomes of these decisions is usually not available for months or even years. Staffing for this type of team requires consideration of the long-range plans of the organization, rather than the type of short-range, specific goals we have been considering with respect to other teams. To complicate matters (as with the autonomous teams at Saturn; see Newstrom, Lengnick-Hall, & Rubenfeld, 1987), these groups make their own staffing choices to a great extent. They are also self-propagating, with junior members often owing loyalty to senior members. Moreover, they usually expect to remain intact for extended periods. These characteristics may entirely reframe the staffing process, since the usual external forces (for example, human resource team management functions) have less opportunity to monitor team membership decisions. As will be seen, the traditional conceptions of individual-based staffing probably have less applicability to executive teams than to any other kind.

There is a large and growing literature, stimulated by the work of Hambrick, on the dynamics of executive teams. Many of these studies emphasize managerial background characteristics (Hambrick & Mason, 1984). For example, Szilagyi and Schweiger (1984) argue that particular factors, such as level of knowledge (both industry- and company-specific) and a manager's social-integration skills (his or her internal and external personal contacts and networks) and administrative skills, will be relevant to both the development and the execution of corporate strategy. Similarly, Nutt (1986), relying on the Myers-Briggs typology, reports on individual differences in top executives' preferences for strategic information. Eisenhardt (1989) and Frederickson and Mitchell (1984) report reliable individual differences in managers' preferences with respect to making speedy decisions (often with limited information).

Work on the composition of strategic teams also exists. To illustrate, Baysinger and Hoskinsson (1990) derive predictions, based on the literature, regarding effects of the mix of managers, inside directors, and outside directors of boards on strategic and financial-control policies that these same boards employ. When boards are made up primarily of outside directors, objective financial-performance criteria are more likely to be used than more subjective factors in assessing top management. Zenger and Lawrence (1989) report that age and tenure distributions within teams also affect the amount and patterning of communications that take place.

Our five examples of teams derive both from consulting practice and from what can be found in the basic and applied literatures. We do not wish to argue that our set represents a typology of a taxonomy. Following the approach of Sundstrom, De Meuse, and Futrell (1990), we have reviewed these examples in order to provide a basis for the contrasts we wish to call attention to later, when it comes to examining issues of team staffing. At the minimum, our set of examples serves to highlight the fact that a differentiated view must be maintained in considerations of team staffing. All teams do not present the same problems. More optimistically, we also feel that readers may find our simple classification more useful than what is currently available.

The Traditional Staffing Model

Position Requirements

Staffing is a process of defining position requirements and then recruiting, assessing, and selecting people to fill these needs (Schneider & Schmitt, 1976). Staffing for individual effectiveness usually proceeds along the following lines. A job analysis is completed, in which important requirements (KSAs) are identified.

This is usually done by gathering information about the target job from job incumbents and supervisors. Next, measures are developed for detecting applicants' abilities with respect to the requirements. This part of the staffing process is conducted largely within the boundaries of the organization, often by human resource professionals.

Recruiting

Recruiting involves identifying and attracting applicants, from both inside and outside the organization, for specific openings. Recruiting activities require attention to a number of questions: whether to focus on current employees as the potential pool of applicants; whether, when, and where to post notices of job openings; what search activities to invest in; how much expense and effort to invest in the search process; how to induce the right kind of person to apply for a position; and how to gain acceptance from the desired applicant once an offer has been made (Breaugh, 1992). Most writers in the recruiting area recognize the fact that truly capable people are hard to find and even harder to persuade to change employers (since they are often valued in their current jobs). One issue thought to have an important impact is the recruiting source (Kirnan, Farley, & Geisinger, 1989; Conard & Ashworth, 1986) and the resulting person-organization fit (Chatman, 1989). There is inconsistent evidence concerning this staffing step (Rynes & Boudreau, 1986), but findings support the hypothesis that referrals by organization members provide better applicants (Conard & Ashworth, 1986), probably because of prescreening by knowledgeable people who make such referrals (Kirnan, Farley, & Geisinger, 1989). Thus fit between organization and applicant is thought to be enhanced by the use of referral systems.

Assessment and Selection

Probably the most extensively studied staffing steps are assessment and selection. Here, measures chosen or developed during job analysis are applied to applicants. These selection devices are intended to identify the people most able to perform the job in question. Because they are based directly on the quality of job-analysis sources and methods, they are limited by the adequacy (comprehensiveness, contamination) of these sources and methods (Jones, 1992). Assessment for selection purposes will also be affected by the number and nature of the instruments or techniques used (tests, interviews, simulations), the levels of validity that exist for these instruments or techniques, and the number of people to be assessed. For example, selecting the right individual to fill an executive position may involve the preliminary screening of hundreds of individuals by means of interviews, tests, and references.

Other staffing issues relevant to selection involve such things as assumptions about the size of the talent pool and the criteria to use in making a final choice (for example, whether to use a compensatory or an additive approach in the integration of information on candidates). Yet another critical aspect of selection practices concerns who is to be involved in selection decisions. Currently, it is most common for the manager who will be supervising the new employee to make the selection decisions (usually with the assistance of a human resources specialist). It is possible for a committee to make the decision, however. It is also recognized that current organizational members who will be affected by the performance of the new hire have a valid point of view. There are some advantages to use these people in the selection process, but there is also some evidence that doing so may have unintended effects on fit. For example, Klimoski and Strickland (1977) and Klimoski and Brickner (1987) have argued that staff in assessment centers may score people as much on the characteristics they see as fitting profiles of who will get along and succeed in the company as on the required KSAs.

Heuristic Models of Effectiveness

To adequately address team staffing issues, it is necessary to consider the process through which staffing choices may influence performance outcomes. We will therefore need some understanding of both individual effectiveness and team effectiveness.

Individual Effectiveness

We do not have a complete theory of individual effectiveness, but most writers acknowledge the importance of three factors: individual capacities, motivation, and role expectations (Ackerman & Humphreys, 1990). *Individual capacities* are any innate or learned KSAs necessary to performing a given task. *Motivation* refers to the effort that must be exerted in accomplishing the task. *Role expectations* are related to performance according to how clearly and unambiguously they are understood by applicants or role incumbents. It is abundantly clear that performance outcomes will depend on the extent to which these determinants of individual effectiveness are accounted for in staffing programs.

An individual's capacity to perform effectively on a team will be related to such things as the pattern of his or her specific aptitudes, general abilities (especially verbal intelligence), and individual and task-specific team abilities. Capacity is also rooted in training and experience. The motivation level brought to the team task will usually be a function of the individual's needs, interests, and values as well as of the extent to which performance of the individual or team task can satisfy those needs, resonate with those interests, and reinforce personal values. Role expectations are also affected by experience and training, but they may be influenced by such things as popular culture, organizational communication, and the beliefs and opinions of others. All this is to say that when it comes to staffing for individual performance, whether in a team context or not, we are usually talking about selecting individuals who display the appropriate mix of abilities, needs, and values (personality) and expectations.

Team Effectiveness

A widely used and modified model of the processes leading to effectiveness of group performance has been formulated by Hackman (1987). Schmitt and Klimoski (1991) and others (Ancona, 1990; Guzzo, 1986) have adapted this model in ways related to issues presented here. A version of Hackman's model is presented in Figure 9.1.

Figure 9.1. A Model of Group Effectiveness.

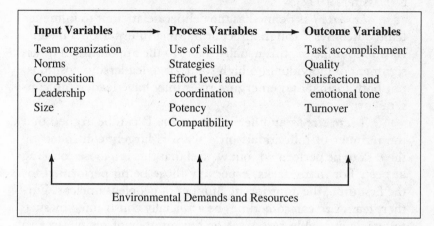

Input Variables ⟶ Process Variables ⟶ Outcome Variables

Input Variables	Process Variables	Outcome Variables
Team organization	Use of skills	Task accomplishment
Norms	Strategies	Quality
Composition	Effort level and	Satisfaction and
Leadership	coordination	emotional tone
Size	Potency	Turnover
	Compatibility	

Environmental Demands and Resources

Source: Adapted from Hackman, 1987.

Inputs. Many of the issues related to input variables have been implicitly referred to in our descriptions of the five team forms. Nevertheless, brief definitions follow.

Team organization refers to the division of labor and authority among group members. This can be created by team mandate, by the task to be performed, or by tradition. We maintain that little can be done through staffing practices per se to influence this, but it cannot be ignored when staffing decisions are to be made.

Group *norms* are the informal rules of conduct that groups develop to regulate their members. These may be related both to work and to personal interactions. In some respects, normative properties reflect not only the values of team members but also a work group's history.

Group *composition* refers to the mixture of KSAs and other characteristics of group members. Thus general and task-related abilities, values, and needs of the various team members become collectively important. Moreover, when it comes to team performance, other sets of individual-difference variables are relevant to composition as an input factor. These include such demographic attributes as gender, race, and age, as well as team-leadership preferences and team-leadership abilities (Morgan & Lassiter, 1992).

Leadership is defined as the deliberate attempt to influence team outcomes through direct or indirect interpersonal means. As an input factor, this usually refers to the appointment or assignment of individuals to high status or to leadership positions, but both formal and emerging roles may have leadership consequences.

Team *size* as another input factor. It can be argued that the number of individuals on a team is largely controlled by the task to be performed, but we feel that this is a loose coupling at best. For many tasks, especially those being performed for the first time, the appropriate number of people is unclear. Further, team size can sometimes be artificially constrained by such things as available resources or the number of people free to participate. Moreover, team size is often at the discretion of the leader or manager, whose personal beliefs and preferences may predominate over logical requirements.

Processes. Process variables with direct importance to staffing decisions include effort, skill utilization, and strategies. We are not dealing only with levels of effort or use of skills per se; also important are teamwork and team interactions, as well as timing and *patterns* in the use of these factors. Even if all team members are exerting their "personal best," there is no guarantee of success if there is no coordination or group strategy.

Processes also include interpersonal dynamics and are typically reflected in the base and level of interpersonal compatibility that exists or develops among team members (Morgan & Lassiter, 1992). To the extent that hostility or distrust exists, it seems unlikely that high levels of concerted effort or effective sharing of information will take place, at least not without process costs (more time, more of the leader's effort, more incentives). High compatibility, however, carries the potential of easy communication and smooth interaction (Bass, 1982).

When it comes to levels of compatibility among group members, it does seem clear that staffing decisions will have an effect. In general, team members who are similar in attitudes, values, and preferences are likely to get along well together. Morgan and Lassiter (1992) conclude that it is best to staff teams with homogeneous personalities if what is wanted is compatibility. There will be occasions, however, when a task calls for particular abilities, and here a heterogeneous group may be more advantageous. Such a group may still be compatible if the people brought together have common needs and values, despite their differences in ability. We would also argue that compatibility will exist if the team is staffed with the right number and mix of individuals to ensure the team's success. This argument is predicated on a repeated finding: experiences of success usually promote positive moods in those involved in making success possible (Berg, 1978; Clark & Isen, 1982; George & Brief, 1992). In this scenario, success breeds success.

Because this model is primarily of heuristic value, there has been little systematic effort to examine the dynamics of the specific intervening variables described. As for staffing questions, it is not clear how effort and skill utilization will be affected by different patterns of composition. This is undoubtedly a complex question. However, Schmitt and Klimoski (1991) and others (O'Reilly & Roberts, 1977; Jones & White, 1985; Guzzo, 1986; Bottger & Yetton, 1988; Ancona, 1990) offer suggestions for explicating intervening influences.

To illustrate, Schmitt and Klimoski (1991) use Bales's interaction-process analysis as a link between team inputs and team outcomes. This empirically derived system uses socioemotional and task-oriented dimensions to describe group interactions. Positive (joking, laughing) and negative (antagonistic, tension-producing, rejecting) socioemotional activities are related to agreement, tension reduction, and cohesion. Task behaviors (giving and asking for information) are related to communication, evaluation, and control. These activities are thought to enhance or deter the optimal use of group resources.

This approach and related approaches to intervening-process description (Jones & White, 1985; O'Reilly & Roberts, 1977) focus on the internal decision-making variables that intervene between inputs and outcomes. Other authors have suggested that processes related to external forces are also important to effectiveness (Friedlander, 1987; Ancona, 1990; Thomas & McDaniel, 1990). Ancona (1990) suggests three strategies, related to dealing with external pressures, that are also influenced by composition. *Informing* is characterized by a concern for internal group processes, to the exclusion of environmental issues. *Parading* is essentially the advertising of group activities to important constituents, without necessarily involving attention to these constituents' needs. Probing involves immediate and primary concern for the actual needs of constituents. If these activities clearly have skill components, then they are linked to individual members, particularly to team leaders, and, in turn, will be influenced by staffing practices.

One other variable, related both to external demands and to internal capacities, has been suggested by Guzzo (1986) and by Guzzo, Yost, Campbell, and Shea (1993). This is *potency,* or members' perceptions of the team's adequacy in meeting its contextual demands. Members' perceptions of the types and levels of expertise on the team presumably have an influence on their performance expectations and, ultimately, on outcomes.

Outcomes. Performance and other outcome variables, such as commitment and adaptation, are of particular concern to many organization members and researchers. The links between the staffing-process variables and individual and organizational effectiveness have received no research attention. For the sake of argument, however, it will be assumed that important links do exist in this domain. For example, Ancona (1990) has suggested that the probing strategy leads to high performance on new teams facing novel situations. If probing requires teams composed of scientifically oriented members, then organizations will be well advised to employ such staff members under novel conditions.

As the framework in Figure 9.1 shows, *task accomplishment* can be meaningfully separated from *quality* of outcomes, especially for service teams. As anyone who has had contact with service personnel will testify, "going through the motions" is not enough to produce a satisfied customer. The ability of members of service teams to provide a supportive, pleasant atmosphere can have a direct influence on return business and, ultimately, on incremental organizational effectiveness. In fact, to the extent that the team's *emotional tone* influences this element of quality, it belongs in the process-variable category.

Along with the intervening influence of emotional tone, team staffing should account for members' *satisfaction, commitment,* and so on, for other reasons as well. Since satisfaction and commitment are related to *turnover,* they have important influences on the stability of team membership. For example, O'Reilly, Caldwell, and Barnett (1989) have shown that group composition (operationalized as distribution of age and tenure) can influence both social integration of groups (including members' interactions) and, ultimately, the decision to remain in the organization. Thus staffing decision makers, as their practices affect composition, would affect both social integration and turnover.

What Is Different About Team Staffing?

Team staffing requires consideration of the conditions that enhance both individual and team performance. The individual performance-effectiveness model describes some of these conditions. However, as the team-effectiveness model and the five examples of teams suggest, the approaches that improve individual effectiveness are not always sufficient to enhance team performance. In this section, we will describe ways in which staffing processes can affect team effectiveness. We will discuss, in turn, several ways in which issues of team effectiveness should alter each of the staffing steps.

Establishing the Team Size

As noted earlier, the number of people needed on a team is affected by several factors, especially by the nature of the job or task to be performed. In some contexts, however, establishing the appropriate number is a challenge. Too few people will result in undue stress on team members; too many will produce a condition of "overmanning." The latter condition not only is a waste of resources but also has predictable effects on levels of individual effort (Latane & Nida, 1981; Penner & Craiger, 1992). Cummings (1978) emphasizes the related difficulty of determining at times the real boundaries of autonomous production-work groups (who is in and who is out), since the systems nature of most production processes creates interdependency among many sets of workers.

Defining the Job of the Team Member

Traditional staffing emphasizes the KSAs associated with the job that is to be performed by an incumbent. When it comes to teams, a person's "job" may be quite ambiguous (as in the case of a strategic team) or quite variable (as in the new style of production team). Moreover, at higher levels of the organization, incumbents themselves are likely to define the jobs (or roles) that they typically perform. There is the case, as well, of the group that determines what its task will be(come) and therefore determines what its individual members may be doing; many task forces operate in this way.

Individual KSAs: Expanded Definition

As we have seen, staffing involves defining position needs and then finding and choosing people to meet those needs. Initial identification of job requirements is no less essential to team effectiveness than to individual effectiveness. In particular, we agree with Hackman and Morris (1975), who argue that choices regarding team staffing (composition) should be made on the basis of a description of team members' task requirements. It is also clear, however, that choosing team members on the basis of individual-task KSAs alone is not enough to ensure optimal effectiveness. Except perhaps in the case of a command-and-control team, there is a need for an expanded definition of job requirements.

Successful performance of various team tasks depends not only on the KSAs required for individual task performance but also on those characteristics of individual team members that facilitate team functioning. Along with traditional job skills and interests, the preferences, personalities, and interaction styles of individuals as team members will also require attention (see George, 1990; Jackson, 1991; Nathan, Ledford, Bowen, & Cummings, 1993; Parker, 1990). For example, Hackman and Morris (1975) suggest that team members need to be able to readily accommodate their ways of performing tasks to a continuous learning process. Thus the team is both a vehicle and a context for learning and adaptation. In settings characterized by continuous change, team learning requires risk taking and tolerance for stress (Hackman & Morris, 1975). Both innovative production teams and professional decision-making teams require such flexibility. Here, consideration should be given to learning ability, tolerance for stress, and risk-taking propensities, as well as to the existing KSAs of team members. Indeed, there is some research to support the idea that staffing for stress reduction can influence group decision-making performance (Callaway, Marriott, & Esser, 1985).

Other characteristics of high-involvement production teams, identified in our example, also highlight the need for an expanded definition of job requirements. Because of the broad, cross-functional human resource capacity and the concomitant flexible interdependence of these teams, there is a particular need for individual initiative. In fact, Nathan, Ledford, Bowen, and Cummings (1993) tested this expectation by comparing scores from personality inventories related to initiative with performance in an extensive preemployment testing program ($n = 287$). Correlations indicated a weak but significant relationship between personality and assessed individual performance. Similarly, Flynn, McCombs, and Elloy (1990) report in a case study that assessed willingness to accept responsibility is related to turnover. Whether such a relationship holds with regard to team performance remains to be seen.

Regardless, the basic argument here—that interdependence creates special job requirements—highlights the potential importance of considering the type of interdependence of teams. Fortunately, interdependence has received research attention with respect to team performance. For example, O'Brien and Owens (1969) have shown how elements of a group's task structure can influence performance. Like Tziner and Eden (1985), these authors show that, for a coordinated (serially interdependent) task, individual group members' skills strongly influence task performance. Traditional assembly lines and command-and-control teams require this type of coordination. In collaborative tasks, however, where team interaction is less restricted, O'Brien and Owens (1969) have found that performance is unrelated to individual members' skills. Bottger and Yetton, (1987, 1988) have shown that the expertise of group members may have an impact on performance of a relatively collaborative task. Interaction-process variables did moderate this relationship (Bottger & Yetton, 1988). Other studies (Hill, 1982; Sniezek & Henry, 1989, 1990; Watson, Michaelsen, & Sharp, 1991) have shown that group performance is usually better than individual members' performance on collaborative tasks. Libby, Trotman, and Zimmer (1987) have integrated these findings, to some extent, by showing that recognition of group members' expertise by other group members influences performance. (We will discuss this point further in the next section.)

A second justification for a new definition of KSAs is related to the external demands placed on the group. It comes as no surprise that the team environment influences the group's decision tasks, and these task characteristics should in turn drive worker requirements. External circumstances can directly affect staffing choices as well, however. Consider service teams, for example. Here, both the enacted and the real environment influences team functioning in an interactive manner. To meet clients' changing needs effectively, service teams are continuously defining the functions of their members. This role definition is itself an important team task. Like other team members involved with changing conditions, service-team members must be able to probe and adjust to environmental needs through adaptable role definition. Thus team members should be selected on the basis of their ability to adapt their team's tasks to environmental demands.

A third aspect of defining requirements differently is related to sources of job-relevant information. The KSAs identified through typical sources (incumbents, supervisors) will not be adequate for meeting team as well as individual requirements. Team job requirements may be related to norms peculiar to the specific team. In a typical job analysis, the aim is to identify the *broad* KSAs related to behaviorally defined tasks. Therefore, the peculiarities of *small* portions of an incumbent sample are likely to be completely missed or, at the very least, filtered out by the aggregation of KSA ratings across the larger incumbent sample. Thus the typical job-analysis process may discard or fail to identify specifically important team inputs, such as work-group norms. It may also be true that incumbents and supervisors are not actually aware of the requirements that make for team effectiveness. Unless the search for these is prompted by the analyst, important interaction skills or normative expectations may be overlooked or taken for granted.

Establishing Team-Level KSAs

The need to consider probable interactions between group- and individual-level factors (George, 1990; Markham, 1988) means that consideration of the individual level alone is insufficient for measuring, predicting, and controlling team performance. This notion can be framed as an issue of establishing the best "mix" of personnel for effective team performance.

Staffing for the right mix of individuals in a team implies attention to worker requirements on at least three dimensions: ability, values/personality, and politics. The ability-mix question revolves around the identification of *team* task requirements for individual tasks and identification of general and specific task performance. At times, this results in requirements for particular individuals that may complement the abilities that others will bring to the task. Alternatively, it may be that we would argue for similarity in ability profiles. Apart from type of skills, *mix* here can also refer to the levels of ability that are needed. For some tasks (conjunctive), team performance is influenced by the ability of the least capable person. Thus VanZelst (1952) found that members of a construction team, allowed to select one another for production work, would tend to choose one another on the basis of perceived ability. Groups that were homogeneous and low in average ability were created (and, predictably, performed at low levels), but the output of homogeneous, high-ability groups more than made up for this. The work force as a whole performed better under the new arrangement.

Creating the right mix can also mean controlling for those factors that account for interpersonal compatibility. Thus establishing team requirements, in this case, would involve the issue of just what personality, style, or values congruence would be necessary. In fact, it may be that ability differences among team members would be tolerated if *all* members subscribed to the same key set of values or assumptions. Alternatively, compatibility may rely partly on members' recognition of each other's special KSAs (Libby, Trotman, & Zimmer, 1987). Ability differences within professional or technical teams, for example, may need to be recognized and valued by team members before effective processes can take place.

Team task requirements may also be conceived of as being political in nature. The term *political* is being used here in a neutral way, to refer to considerations of worker requirements that have little to do with ability or interpersonal compatibility but that are based on themes of due process (fairness) and team output or acceptance. To be specific, a given mix of team members may be preferred because it represents a desired profile of subgroups (hourly employees, racial minorities) or administrative units (sales, manufacturing) that should be involved in the task or decision if perceptions of procedural justice are to be ensured. Employee disciplinary committees or appeals committees have this requirement. Alternatively, team mix may be based on the need to have those key players involved who will be asked to implement team decision. Team members need to be selected less on the basis of their potential to make a technically correct decision than on their future role in making things happen once a decision is reached.

Recruiting

It seems unlikely that staffing programs can rely on an applicant's ability to recognize expertise. Nevertheless, information given about the team during the recruiting process could include clear statements about existing members' areas of expertise. Recruiting by the team members themselves should also increase chances of recognition. If members are asked to search for potential team members with particular expertise, that kind of recognition could be instituted into the staffing process. This should influence team effectiveness through coordinated use of these skills (Jackson et al., 1993). This practice should also affect team members' perceptions of efficacy.

Team members' confidence—what Guzzo (1986) calls *potency*—is largely a result of actual ongoing interactions with environments (Hackman, 1990). Ancona (1990) and (Hackman, 1990) have suggested that the initial effectiveness of a team's response to the demands of organizational and external environments will have important implications for later performance. This may occur through the agency of self-efficacy of the group members, which can be influenced by feedback from the team environment (Wood & Bandura, 1989); that is, feedback from early efforts leads to shared perceptions of team efficacy. Staffing a group in these conditions means recruiting people from enough different functions and levels to meet decision-making needs. Identifying the functional and hierarchical mix appropriate to environmental demands is, of course, a further element of enhanced analysis of worker requirements.

Perceptions on the part of team members concerning the adequacy of the team's resources for meeting contingencies, in addition to actual efficacy, may be what actually influences team performance (see Mullen, 1991; Penner & Craiger, 1992). Whether mix affects these perceptions through actual performance feedback or through prior perceptions, however, the result is better performance. The important question for team staffing is whether the actual mix of members must be manipulated or whether convincing team members of the appropriateness of their congregate KSAs will suffice to affect the team's responses to environmental demands. If actual group composition is the answer, then staffing for appropriate composition should be sufficient. If perceptions are part of the answer, then recruiting practices may have to be different.

Identification of task requirements is largely reactive to contextual influences, but recruiting practices also can be used to make teams context-resistant. For example, if the members of a successful team are allowed to have a meaningful influence on recruitment of new members, then the establishment of group efficacy through contextual interaction may be less necessary, for several plausible reasons. Along with recognition of the expertise of new members, awareness of team expertise on the part of incoming members may also be more likely. The affective tone of the group may also be communicated through social cues during recruiting. And if, as part of recruitment, new team members are given initial efficacy-building information or experience, then efficacy establishment through actual contextual experiences could be more successful. In each of these cases, recruiting variables are used to control for potential contextual influences.

Recruiting for team effectiveness is complicated by the fact that, in most settings, team members come and go, sometimes by design; there may be an organizational norm of rotation. Alternatively, individuals may have specified terms of office (or tours of duty). Frequently, however, changes in membership are driven by personal considerations or economic opportunities. Depending on such things as a company's compensation policies and external employment conditions, turnover patterns may produce new openings on a regular basis. This means that the skill mix in a team can be quite variable from time to time. In recruiting replacements, then, one issue to be resolved is the extent to which one anticipates or predicts the kinds of replacements that will be needed in the future. (More about this will be said in the context of selection.)

Certainly, in the recruiting of new team members, it often makes sense to create or take advantage of an internal labor market. Thus current employees in other departments or functions are viewed as the prime source of talent. A case study on a total quality management program, reported by Schuler and Harris (1991), describes the successful use of this philosophy. The company has a policy of internal job posting and job rotation. If an employee moves or advances in the company and the new position does not work out, he or she is allowed to return to the former position. If an employee with a good record leaves the company to pursue an opportunity, and if he or she then desires to return (for whatever reason), this too is encouraged. The same company promotes the involvement of existing employees in the recruiting of new people. In addition to using them as a source of referrals, team members have a chance to interact with applicants in a meaningful way before any decisions are made. For instance, applicants who appear suitable for production work are "hired" for a day to work alongside current employees, without any commitment on the part of either party. What this does is provide both the applicant and current employees a chance to get to know one another. The employees can then help recruit those finalists who appear to fit best into the culture. They are also asked to provide input for the hiring manager. (Incidentally, such recommendations for a capable and compatible new hire, if followed, are likely to increase feelings of team potency.) Needless to say, this procedure also helps the applicant confirm that the company is the right place for him or her to work.

For some teams (executive and professional), existing team leadership will determine recruiting practices. If the leader is an individual, he or she will set the terms and conditions of who will be assigned, perhaps even making a unilateral decision about the specific individuals who will be involved or invited to participate. Recruiting may also be driven by team charter (when different functions must be represented) or by group norms (when group members vote on how it is done).

Key aspects of recruiting have been noted by Jackson et al. (1993) in their study of team-composition effects at senior levels of the banking industry. Using archival data, the researchers were able to conclude that teams were more homogeneous with regard to age, education, and experience than would be expected by chance. Furthermore, relatively higher homogeneity was associated with higher turnover, for all types of reasons. More to the point, however, team homogeneity was also related to the recruitment of new members from within the company; that is, such teams operated as if they assumed an internal labor market. Jackson (1992) speculates that homogeneous teams are more risk-averse than heterogeneous teams: because more information is available on internal recruits, they may represent a more certain outcome.

Occasionally, recruiting for effective teamwork involves finding appropriate ways *not* to use certain individuals while still maintaining their commitment. This is particularly true when participation has great symbolic or instrumental value. Thus, in staffing committees, task forces or cabinets, the responsible manager must determine just how public to be about the opportunity and must be careful about the use of particular referral agents. Too wide-ranging and public a search would produce disaffection among those considered and rejected.

In summary, recruiting will have an important influence on the individual-team fit. In fact, we would expect that this is part of the reason why recruitment through referrals is particularly effective. Again, we would expect to enhance balance and fit by allowing committed group members to do some or all of their own recruiting. Using internal labor markets could have much the same effect, enhancing performance on service teams. This practice is not without risks, however. In many circumstances, member recruiting may promote homogeneity, which can be a liability.

Assessment and Selection

Idiographic Selection Methods

As we have seen, traditional staffing includes development of generally applicable assessment procedures and decision rules. Even supposing that the identification of job requirements took team issues into account and that recruiting was adequate, developing and implementing selection tools for assessing potential team members would still require a different approach. Specifically, "fit" variables have important implications for the selection procedure used. The "subtle criterion contamination" described by Klimoski and Brickner (1987), with reference to assessment centers, might actually be desirable in some team contexts. That is, by capturing idiosyncrasies of teams along with more general work requirements in their ratings, assessors or other decision makers would increase the likelihood that the applicants selected would both perform well individually and enhance team effectiveness.

Team Life Cycles

As we have implied, a new team needs to establish its own efficacy in order to survive (Hackman, 1990; Ancona, 1990). More generally, the stage in a team's life has important implications both for worker requirements and for who should be a member (Hellrigel, Slocum, & Woodman, 1983; Mintzberg, 1973; Gabarro, 1987; Katz, 1982). Once efficacy perceptions are established, both by group members themselves and by influential outsiders, the task of replacement staffing takes on other complexities. The traditional staffing model may have been devised for teams with established ways of doing things; even so, the traditional model has rarely taken life-cycle issues into account.

For a team nearing the end of its life (by failure or design), other issues need to be addressed. For example, which vital functions must be retained, and which can be phased out? What managerial skills will ease the difficulty of disbanding the team? When should a staffing shakeup be used to resuscitate a salvageable team? Clearly, the assessment and selection procedures to be followed for a team that is just forming and for one that is in crisis must be different. Not only would the KSAs change, but the pool of feasible candidates and the potential for members' involvement would also vary. To be specific, a turnaround situation usually favors selection of an outsider. For a team on a (planned) path to dissolution, staffing may be particularly difficult in light of the specialized skills needed and the very small number of candidates who make themselves known.

One general way to deal with the changing needs of groups is to build context and life-cycle controls into the system for assessment and selection. We have seen in service teams particularly that there are both stable and changing sets of task requirements. Ideally, assessment devices would have high integrity with regard to stable team requirements and be highly modifiable, to accommodate change. Although periodic task-requirement analysis could provide some of each quality, perhaps a more effective and efficient means would be to design assessment procedures that include employees as observers, information gatherers, and evaluators. If these people are selected on the basis of their expertise in identifying contextual, life-cycle, and internal team and organizational needs, then assessment teams can be formed to meet changing needs in the staffing of particular teams. Such an arrangement could take the form of an assessment center or a panel of interviewers and would include members of the targeted teams.

A particular challenge of selection concerns the current state of science and practice when it comes to the assessment of the key traits or attributes felt to be associated with team effectiveness. Such things as team orientation (preference for teamwork), responsibility, task focus, and commitment to continous improvement are hard to define and measure. Similarly, there is a need for instruments that a manager can use to pick people for team assignments so as to ensure synergy and interpersonal compatibility. There is some evidence that personality and values measurement for purposes of selection is feasible and improving (Barrick & Mount, 1991; Klimoski, 1992), and there are examples of assessment in these nontraditional areas being applied to team staffing. For instance, Nathan, Ledford, Bowen, and Cummings (1993) and Hauenstein (1992) report on the use of assessment centers in selecting candidates for high-involvement work environments. McKenna and McHenry (1992) have found that subscales of the California Personality Inventory can be used to classify team members, and that similarities and differences in profiles among team members can predict team productivity. Hallam and Campbell (1992) report that, under the right circumstances, a questionnaire built around a theory of team effectiveness can be useful (see also Driskell, Hogan, & Salas, 1987). These success stories notwithstanding, much remains to be done when it comes to measuring the key traits or qualities needed for team members' success and for team effectiveness with instruments that are practical and construct-valid.

In many cases, staffing for team effectiveness involves using assessment data to identify individuals who are thought to be of the right type (that is, intellectually and dispositionally suited to team membership, given the team's mission and task environment). Thus we are interested in predicting or anticipating how the individual under consideration will typically behave in a group context. In some settings, however, as in a command-and-control team, we also want to be able to assess candidates with regard to their behavior and performance during infrequent but critical periods (such as under attack conditions). To put it differently, we want to predict some aspects of maximum performance (Driskell & Salas, 1991; Roberts, 1990). Herein lies an additional challenge for selection specialists. At present, we have only the most rudimentary technologies for assessing personnel with regard to their probable behavior and performance under stress and demanding conditions, especially for situations where we are not recruiting experienced individuals. Here, we must often make do with inferences from arguably relevant past episodes in a person's life, or from simulations with low ecological validity.

An additional problem stems from the fact that staffing decisions generally come under increased scrutiny from agencies and interest groups (both inside and outside the organization), to ensure that the decisions are fair to protected subgroups in American society. Team staffing decisions are no exception. This implies that, beyond merely following any model for member assignments that is thought to ensure individual and team effectiveness, the manager or human resources specialist must give appropriate consideration to issues of diversity.

Team Management

So far, we have argued that our thinking about assessment and selection needs to change so as to accommodate requirements for team staffing. An additional consideration is related to selecting individuals as team leaders. For example, basing their work on the ideas of Shaw (1976), Klimoski, Friedman, and Weldon (1980) have shown how specific managerial roles affect group functioning. In the Klimoski, Friedman, and Weldon study (1980), the amount of information held and the formal powers of team leaders in an assessment center were manipulated. The results showed that the leader's influence was greatest when he or she was well informed and held formal powers. Team members' reactions were also affected; considerable disaffection was felt when a leader had a formal vote but was regarded as having little knowledge about the decision to be made. Katz (1982) also implicates the role of the team leader in the decrement of effectiveness over time.

These and other authors (such as Hallam & Campbell, 1992) suggest the need to consider team leaders' roles with regard to team decision making and outcomes. Other work on managerial roles in teams provides additional clues for team staffing. Komaki, Zlotnick, and Jensen (1986) and Komaki, Desselles, and Bowman emphasize the importance of a leader's propensity for monitoring team members' performance and communicating of consequences. Mintzberg (1973) has pointed out that the roles required of managers throughout an organization change as the stages in the organization's life cycle change (this is a reprise of the issue of staffing for changing jobs, except that it is phrased entirely in terms of roles rather than KSAs). Cummings (1978) argues that for truly empowered teams, managers must assume support functions (such as member development and boundary maintenance). Other potentially important managerial roles include reality testing and devil's advocacy in decision making and promoting vertical organizational communities (Ancona & Caldwell, 1992).

Assuming that some of these various roles played by the managers of a team also change as the team's life cycle changes, there is a need to account for these roles in some way. A common thread is the maintenance of flexible responsiveness to environmental events. This can be seen in all five of our team examples. In all cases, at least one part of team management is to facilitate team responses to changing environmental demands. Whether management is by direct individual control or through recognition of expertise in a flexibly interdependent fashion, the optimal use of resources is accomplished through this responsiveness role.

This means that we should be staffing either for individual managers' flexibility or for team leadership. As we have seen, empowerment of team members to create feelings of competence is probably desirable (see Eden, 1990), especially for high-involvement and professional teams. In these circumstances, staffing professionals are faced with a difficult balancing act. On the one hand, ensuring that the team effectively manages its early responses to environmental demands requires considerable control over staffing decisions by personnel specialists. On the other hand, empowering the team and building in flexible responses on an ongoing basis may require allowing the team to do its own staffing and management. One way to deal with this would be to provide all information about the trade-offs to members and then allow them to decide what to do.

More generally, because of evidence that the essential functions of managerial roles are related to contextual, life-cycle, and other changing task requirements, using the built-in flexibility of human assessment systems (perhaps augmented by expert-system support) could enhance team management. Assessment centers should again prove useful here. Not only do they tap managers' job schemas directly (see Jones, 1992), they also incorporate changing needs on the basis of organizational and team realities.

Conclusion

There is more to staffing a team than simply choosing potentially successful individual members. Consideration should be given to the issues we have discussed here, in order to staff adequately for team effectiveness. Individual KSAs are important, but so are other team-relevant individual characteristics, team structures, changing task demands, policies, contexts, life cycles, and management needs, all of which influence team performance. Furthermore, in team staffing-needs analysis, consideration must be given to interactions between individual and team variables that will affect performance.

Even assuming that our arguments are reasonable, however, we are not in a good position to follow them. All of this means that some novel methods are required at each step of the process. The fact is that developmental work of both a theoretical and applied nature is critically needed before this will be possible. Table 9.1 recapitulates some of the issues that we have raised. It can also be used to guide future efforts, but it is meant only to be illustrative and to highlight the potential benefits of keeping a differentiated view of the "teams" that exist in modern organizations.

Table 9.1. Team Staffing Issues.

Team Type	Job Requirements	Recruitment	Assessment/Selection
Command-and-control	Identifying team KSAs	Fitting new consumers into established teams	Assessing maximum performance
Production	Identifying nontraditional individual KSAs	Establishing right mix of talents	Determining roles of team members
Customer service	Identifying team boundaries	Creating team potency	Developing valid measures
Professional/technical	Establishing mission boundaries	Establishing right mix (talent and potential)	Assessment of hidden agendas
Executive	Determining who specifies KSAs	Establishing right mix (values, experience, and contacts)	Determining who selects

For command-and-control teams, when it comes to worker requirements, it is critical that team-level knowledge, procedures, capacities, and other attributes be established. In this regard, some of the work reported by Swezey and Salas (1992) could be used as a starting point. Recruiting becomes especially problematic whenever there is a need to replace a team member from a well-trained and integrated team. To what extent can a newcomer be successfully recruited, one who will fit into a group with a rich tradition? Or should the team be reconstituted and a whole new set of members recruited? Given current assessment technology, we feel that it is especially difficult to identify those individuals who would make effective team members when the team is under stress or pressure.

The staffing of production teams has its own set of challenges. To illustrate, the practitioner seeking to hire for this context must resolve just what nontraditional KSAs are important. Concepts like learning orientation, tolerance for ambiguity, and preference for teamwork have been proposed, but there are many others to choose from. A special version of this concern is related to just how much emphasis the job analyst should place on the attributes needed for immediate team success versus those that would be relevant to long-term team viability. Similarly, guidance from recruiting research and practice is needed to establish the right mix of talents for effective production-team functioning. This is particularly problematic, since each team will present a special case. The role of team members in the recruiting process seems uncontroversial, but getting them involved in actual selection decisions presents many issues to be resolved.

Customer-service teams exist in many configurations. One could accept management's definitions of just who is part of a given team, but more sophisticated analytical approaches are needed to truly establish the groupings necessary and sufficient for predictable customer satisfaction. This is especially the case when the delivery of products or services requires extensive customer involvement, or when it calls for a continuous relationship. There are usually many internal players involved, and they need to be identified and linked up, both administratively and phenomologically (see Mullen, 1991, for insights into the latter point).

Service teams need to exhibit a sense of potency in order to reassure customers or clients of their capacity to meet high expectations, but just how to create potency for a service team is not clear. For instance, in Spink's study (1990) of the collective efficacy of sports teams, the best predictor was level of group cohesion or member integration, but Spink postulates that such factors as individual members' feelings of efficacy and the teams' past performance also have a role. It also seems likely that careful management of process and symbols at the time of recruiting may be relevant. Such things as thoroughness of the recruiting search, announcement of the finalists, and how the preferred applicant is introduced and treated may all enhance the collective perception of "great things happening" to the team and make members feel good about their prospects, but this notion remains to be tested. Moreover, there is no shortage of ideas regarding the KSAs needed for effective service, but we do lack reliable and valid measures for selection purposes.

Quality circles, new-product development teams, task forces, and committees are all specific cases of professional/technical teams. When it comes to identifying job requirements, they all share the potential problem of having to operate under vague mission boundaries. In fact, many of these groups come into existence with the mandate, in part, to define problem areas and issues that eventually would imply boundaries. If we are not entirely sure what we are to do, how do we know that we are bringing the right people together? It is often hard to tell, and this has implications for recruiting. In particular, which individuals should be assigned to a team, in order for it to have real credibility and clout within the organization? What mix will ensure that the team's work or work products will be accepted as valid, or there is a high probability of its recommendations' being implemented (Nutt, 1983)?

Nevertheless, assessment of potential team members needs to go beyond a focus on their technical knowledge or experience. In fact, the staffing of professional/technical teams often involves a process that we would call *deselection* — the elimination of individuals who, although otherwise qualified, are thought to be undesirable, usually because of personal style, or because they are likely to bring too many personal needs or hidden agendas into the group's deliberations. This may be a common problem, but there is little guidance in the literature for dealing with the social and political aspects of the situation while still preserving the ideal of selection based on competence or merit (see Farrell & Petersen, 1982; Welsh & Slusher, 1986).

Executive teams present different issues. Traditionally,

they are created, staffed, and managed by senior managers, but the expertise may lie elsewhere when it comes to the design and staffing of truly effective executive teams. How can knowledge derived from organizational research be shared with leaders and effectively integrated into their views on the capabilities they should be seeking as they staff their teams? This issue is still to be resolved. Similarly, the right mix of talents to be recruited at a given time in the organization's history is frequently uncertain. Once again, there is no shortage of suggestions in the literature (Alexander, 1979; Thomas & McDaniel, 1990; Stumph, Zand, & Freedman, 1979; Szilagyi & Schweiger, 1984), but there is not much in the way of research evidence for whose ideas are correct.

When it comes to selection for executive teams, the superordinate manager has traditionally had a major role. However, some organizations regularly use outside consultants and search firms to prescreen and recommend candidates for executive positions (and, therefore, elite decision-making teams). But there do exist fairly developed techniques and management practices that have implications for the selection of individuals for executive teams. We need to know how these can best be integrated into a practical and effective selection system.

It should be obvious that theoretical and applied work on the staffing of teams must be linked to new methods for data analysis because team processes and outcomes are affected by so many things (individual team members' attributes, team leaders' attributes, team-level attributes, processes, context variables). Therefore, data from multiple sources and levels of aggregation must be obtained and integrated before we can truly understand the role and impact of alternative staffing practices. In this regard, the work of Dansereau, Alutto, and Yammarino (1984), Markham (1988), and Glick (1985) may be useful. For example, Dansereau, Alutto, and Yammarino emphasize within-and-between analysis (WABA) as an analytical technique that can be used to simultaneously assess individual- and team-level effects. With this approach, data on the effects of key variables on both individual and team performance can be examined even for interactions between the two levels that do not appear to have clear theoretical underpinnings. We would also expect greater use of quasi-experimental approaches to have important benefits for team staffing theory and practice (VanZelst, 1952), particularly in light of the importance of the various context effects that we have argued for throughout this chapter.

References

Ackerman, P. L., & Humphreys, L. G. (1990). Individual differences theory in industrial and organizational psychology. In M. D. Donnette & L. M. Hough (Eds.), *Handbook of industrial and organizational psychology: Vol. 1* (pp. 223–282). Palo Alto, CA: Consulting Psychologists Press.

Adams, J. S. (1976). The structure and dynamics of behavior in organizations: Boundary roles. In M. D. Dunnette (Ed.). *Handbook of industrial and organizational psychology* (pp. 1175–1200). Skokie, IL: Rand McNally.

Alexander, E. A. (1979). The design of alternatives in organizational contexts. *Administrative Science Quarterly, 24,* 382–404.

Ancona, D. G. (1990). Outward bound: Strategies for team survival in an organization. *Academy of Management Journal, 33*(2), 334–365.

Ancona, D. G., & Caldwell, D. F. (1992). Bridging the boundary: External activity and performance in organizational teams. *Administrative Science Quarterly, 37,* 634–665.

Barrick, M. R., & Mount, M. K. (1991). The big five personality dimensions and job performance: A meta-analysis. *Personnel Psychology, 44,* 1–26.

Bass, B. M. (1982). Individual capability, team performance, and team productivity. In E. A. Fleishman and M. D. Dunnette (Eds.), *Human performance and productivity: Human capability assessment* (pp. 285–302). Hillsdale, NJ. Erlbaum.

Baysinger, B., & Hoskinsson, R. E. (1990). The composition of boards of directors and strategic control: Effects on corporate strategy. *Academy of Management Review, 15*(1), 72–87.

Berg, B. (1978). Helping behavior on the gridiron: It helps if you are winning. *Psychology Reports, 42,* 531–534.

Bottger, P. C., & Yetton, P. W. (1987). Improving group performance by training in individual problem solving. *Journal of Applied Psychology, 72,* 651–657.

Bottger, P. C., & Yetton, P. W. (1988). An integration of process and decision-scheme explanations of group problem-solving performance. *Organizational Behavior and Human Decision Processes, 12,* 234–249.

Breaugh, J. (1992). Recruitment: Science and practice. Boston: PWS-Kent.

Brown, S. J. (1987). The Japanese approach to labor relations: Can it work in America? *Personnel, 64*(4), 20–29.

Callaway, M. R., Marriott, R. G., & Esser, J. K. (1985). Effects of dominance on group decision making: Toward a stress-reduction explanation of groupthink. *Journal of Personality and Social Psychology, 49*(4), 949–952.

Chatman, J. A. (1989). Improving interactional organizational research: A model of person-organization fit. *Academy of Management Review, 14*(3), 333–349.

Clark, M. S., & Isen, A. M. (1982). Toward understanding the relationship between feeling states and social behavior. In A. Hartorf and A. M. Isen (Eds.), *Cognitive social psychology* (pp. 89–111). New York: Elsevier Science.

Conard, M., & Ashworth, S. D. (1986). *Recruiting-source effectiveness: A meta-analysis and reexamination of two rival hypotheses.* Paper presented at the meeting of the Society for Industrial and Organizational Psychology, Chicago.

Cummings, T. (1978). Self-regulating work groups: A sociotechnical synthesis. *Academy of Management Review, 3*(3), 625–634.

Dansereau, F., Alutto, J. A., & Yammarino, F. J. (1984). *Theory testing in organizational behavior: The variant approach.* Englewood Cliffs, NY: Prentice-Hall.

David, F. R., Pearce, J. A., II, & Randolph, W. A. (1989). Linking technology and structure to enhance group performance. *Journal of Applied Psychology, 74*(2), 233–241.

Driskell, J. E., Hogan, R., & Salas, E. (1987). Personality and group performance. In C. Hendrick (Ed.), *Personality and Social Psychology* (pp. 91–112). Newbury Park, CA: Sage.

Driskell, J. D., & Salas, E. (1991). Group decision making under stress. *Journal of Applied Psychology, 76*(3), 473–478.

Dutton, J., & Ashford, S. (1993). Selling issues to top management. *Academy of Management Review, 18*(3), 397–428.

Eden, D. (1990). Pygamalion without interpersonal contrast effects: Whole groups gain from raising manager expectations. *Journal of Applied Psychology, 75*(4), 394–398.

Eisenhardt, K. M. (1989). Making fast strategic decisions in high-velocity environments. *Academy of Management Journal, 32*(3), 543–576.

Farrell, D., & Petersen, J. C. (1982). Patterns of political behavior in organizations. *Academy of Management Review, 7*(3), 403–412.

Flynn, R., McCombs, T., & Elloy, D. (1990). Staffing the self-managing work team. *Leadership and Organizational Development Journal, 11*(1), 26–31.

Frederickson, J., & Mitchell, T. (1984). Strategic decision processes: Comprehensiveness and performance in an industry with an unstable environment. *Academy of Management Journal, 27,* 399–423.

Friedlander, F. (1987). The ecology of work groups. In J. W. Lorsch (Ed.), *Handbook of organizational behavior* (pp. 301–314). Englewood Cliffs, NJ: Prentice-Hall.

Gabarro, J. J. (1987). The development of working relationships. In J. W. Lorsch (Ed.), *Handbook of organizational behavior* (pp. 172–189). Englewood Cliffs, NJ: Prentice-Hall.

George, J. M. (1990). Personality, affect, and behavior in groups. *Journal of Applied Psychology, 75*(2), 107–116.

George, J. M., & Brief, A. P. (1992). Feeling good–doing good: A conceptual analysis of the mind at work — organizational spontaneity relationships. *Psychological Bulletin, 12,* 310–329.

Ginnett, R. C. (1990). Airline cockpit crews. In J. R. Hackman (Ed.), *Groups that work (and those that don't): Creating conditions for effective teamwork* (pp. 427–448). San Francisco: Jossey-Bass.

Glick, W. H. (1985). Conceptualizing and measuring organizational and psychological climates: Pitfalls in multilevel research. *Academy of Management Review, 10,* 601–616.

Guzzo, R. A. (1986). Group decision making and group effectiveness in organizations. In P. Goodman (Ed.), *Designing effective work groups* (pp. 34–71). San Francisco: Jossey-Bass.

Guzzo, R. A., Yost, P. R., Campbell, R. J., & Shea, G. P. (1993). Potency in groups: Articulating a construct. *British Journal of Social Psychology, 32,* 87–106.

Hackman, J. R. (1987). The design of work teams. In J. W. Lorsch (Ed.), *Handbook of organizational behavior* (pp. 315–342). Englewood Cliffs, NJ: Prentice-Hall.

Hackman, J. R. (Ed.). (1990). *Groups that work (and those that don't): Creating conditions for effective teamwork.* San Francisco: Jossey Bass.

Hackman, J. R., & Morris, C. G. (1975). Group tasks, group interaction process, and group performance effectiveness: A review and proposed integration. *Advances in Experimental Social Psychology, 8,* 45–99.

Hallam, G. L., & Campbell, D. (1992, May). *Selecting people for teams? Start with a theory of team effectiveness.* Paper presented at the annual meeting of the Society for Industrial and Organizational Psychology, Montreal.

Hambrick, D. C., & Mason, P. A. (1984). Upper echelons: The organization as a reflection of its top managers. *Academy of Management Review, 9*(2), 193–206.

Hasenfeld, Y., & English, R. A. (1974). *Human service organizations.* Ann Arbor: University of Michigan Press.

Hauenstein, P. C. (1992, May). *Selecting candidates for high-involvement work environments.* Paper presented at the annual meeting of the Society for Industrial and Organizational Psychology, Montreal.

Hellrigel, D., Slocum, J. W., & Woodman, R. W. (1983). *Organizational behavior* (3rd ed.). St. Paul, MN: West.

Hill, G. W. (1982). Group versus individual performance: Are $n + 1$ heads better than one? *Psychological Bulletin, 91,* 517–539.

Jackson, S. E. (1991). Consequences of group composition for the interpersonal dynamics of strategic issue processing. In P. Shrivastava, A. Huff, & J. Dutton (Eds.), *Advances in strategic management: Volume 8* (pp. 345–382). Greenwich, CT: JAI Press.

Jackson, S. E. (1992). Team composition in organizational settings: Issues in managing an increasingly diverse work force. In S. Worchel, W. Wood, and J. Simpson (Eds.), *Group process and productivity* (pp. 138–173). Newbury Park, CA: Sage.

Jackson, S. E., Brett, J. F., Sessa, V. I., Cooper, D. M., Julia, J. A., & Peyronnin, K. (1993). Some differences make a difference: Individual dissimilarity and group hetergeneity as correlates of recruitment, promotions, and turnover. *Journal of Applied Psychology, 76,* 675–689.

Jones, R. E., & White, C. S. (1985). Relationships among personality, conflict-resolution styles, and task effectiveness. *Group and Organization Studies, 10*(2), 152–167.

Jones, R. G. (1992). Construct validation of assessment center final dimension ratings: Definition and measurement issues. *Human Resource Management Review, 2*(3), 195–220.

Katz, D., & Kahn, R. L. (1978). *The social psychology of organizations* (2nd ed.). New York: Wiley.

Katz, R. (1982). The effects of group longevity on project communication and performance. *Administrative Science Quarterly, 27,* 81–104.

Kirnan, J. P., Farley, J. A., & Geisinger, K. F. (1989). The relationship between recruiting source, applicant quality, and hire performance: An analysis by sex, ethnicity, and age. *Personnel Psychology, 42,* 293–308.

Klimoski, R. J. (1992). Predictor constraints and their measurement. In N. Schmitt & W. Borman, & Associates, *Personnel selection in organizations.* San Francisco: Jossey-Bass.

Klimoski, R. J. & Ash, R. (1974). Accountability and negotiation behavior. *Organizational Behavior and Human Performance, 11,* 409–425.

Klimoski, R. J., & Brickner, M. (1987). Why do assessment centers work? The puzzle of assessment center validity. *Personnel Psychology, 40*, 243–260.

Klimoski, R. J., Friedman, B. A., & Weldon, E. (1980). Leader influence in the assessment of performance. *Personnel Psychology, 33*, 389–401.

Klimoski, R. J., & Strickland, W. J. (1977). Assessment centers: Valid or merely prescient? *Personnel Psychology, 30*, 353–361.

Komaki, J. L., Desselles, M. L., & Bowman, E. D. (1989). Definitely not a breeze: Extending an operant model of effective supervision to teams. *Journal of Applied Psychology, 74*(3), 522–529.

Komaki, J. L., Zlotnick, S., & Jensen, M. (1986). Development of an operant-based taxonomy and observational index of supervisory behavior. *Journal of Applied Psychology, 71*, 260–269.

Latane, B., & Nida, S. (1981). Ten years of research on group size and helping. *Psychological Bulletin, 89*, 308–324.

Libby, R., Trotman, K. T., & Zimmer, I. (1987). Member variation, recognition of expertise and group performance. *Journal of Applied Psychology, 72*, 81–87.

McKenna, D. D., & McHenry, J. J. (1992, May). *The chemistry of personality compounds: Effects on team productivity.* Paper presented at the annual meeting of the Society for Industrial and Organizational Psychology, Montreal.

Markham, S. E. (1988). Pay-for-performance dilemma revisited: Empirical example of the importance of group effects. *Journal of Applied Psychology, 73*(2), 172–180.

Mills, P., & Morris, J. (1986). Clients as "partial" employees of service organizations: Role development in client participation. *Academy of Management Review, 11*, 726–735.

Mintzberg, H. (1973). *The nature of managerial work.* New York: Harper-Collins.

Morgan, B. B., Jr., & Lassiter, D. (1992). Team composition and staffing. In R. Swezey & E. Salas (Eds.), *Teams: Their training and performance.* Norwood, NJ: Ablex.

Mullen, B. (1991). Group compensation, salience and cognitive representations: The phenomenon of being in a group. *Journal of Experimental Social Psychology, 27*, 1–27.

Nathan, B. R., Ledford, G. E., Bowen, D. E., & Cummings, T. G. (1993). *Predicting person-organization fit in high-involvement organizations: A personality-test validation study.* Manuscript submitted for publication.

Newstrom, J., Lengnick-Hall, M., & Rubenfeld, S. (1987). How employees can choose their own bosses. *Personnel Journal, 66*(12), 121–126.

Nutt, P. C. (1983). Implementation approaches for project planning. *Academy of Management Review, 8*(4), 600–611.

Nutt, P. C. (1986). Decision style and strategic decisions of top executives. *Technological Forecasting and Social Change, 30,* 39–62.

O'Brien, G. E., & Owens, A. G. (1969). Effects of organizational structure on correlations between member attitudes and group productivity. *Journal of Applied Psychology, 53*(6), 525–530.

O'Reilly, C. A., III, Caldwell, D. F., & Barnett, W. P. (1989). Work group demography, social integration and turnover. *Administrative Science Quarterly, 34,* 21–37.

O'Reilly, C. A., III, & Roberts, K. (1977). Task group structure, communication, and effectiveness in three organizations. *Journal of Applied Psychology, 62,* 674–681.

Parker, G. M. (1990). *Team players and teamwork: The new competitive business strategy.* San Francisco: Jossey-Bass.

Patchen, M. (1974). The locus and basis of influence on organizational decisions. *Organizational Behavior and Human Performance, 11,* 195–221.

Penner, L. A., & Craiger, J. P. (1992). The market link: The performance of individual team members. In R. Swezey & E. Salas (Eds.), *Teams: Their training and performance* (pp. 130–141). Norwood, NJ: Ablex.

Rafaeli, A. (1989). When clerks meet customers: A test of variables related to emotional expressions on the job. *Journal of Applied Psychology, 74*(3), 385–393.

Roberts, K. H. (1990). Some characteristics of high-reliability organizations. *Organizational Science, 1,* 1–17.

Rynes, S. L., & Boudreau, J. W. (1986). College recruiting in large organizations: Practice, evaluation, and research implications. *Personnel Psychology, 39,* 729–757.

Saavedra, R., Cohen, S. G., & Denison, D. R. (1990). Customer service teams: Selling products and services. In J. R. Hackman (Ed.), *Groups that work (and those that don't): Creating conditions for effective teamwork* (pp. 359–406). San Francisco: Jossey-Bass.

Schmitt, N., & Klimoski, R. J. (1991). *Research Methods in Human Resources Management.* Cincinnati, OH: South-Western.

Schneider, B., & Schmitt, N. (1976). *Staffing organizations* (2nd ed.). Glenview, IL: Scott, Foresman.

Schuler, R. S., & Harris, D. L. (1991). Deeming quality improvement: Implications for human resources management as illustrated in a small company. *Human Resource Planning, 14*(3), 191–207.

Shaw, M. R. (1976). *Group dynamics: The psychology of small-group behavior.* New York: McGraw-Hill.

Sniezek, J. A., & Henry, R. A. (1989). Accuracy and confidence in group judgment. *Organizational Behavior and Human Decision Processes, 43*, 1–28.

Sniezek, J. A., & Henry, R. A. (1990). Revision, weighting, and commitment in consensus group judgment. *Organizational Behavior and Human Decision Processes, 45*, 66–84.

Spink, K. S. (1990). Collective efficacy in the sport setting. *International Journal of Sport Psychology, 21*, 380–395.

Stumph, S. A., Zand, D. E., & Freedman, R. D. (1979). Designing groups for judgmental decisions. *Academy of Management Review, 4*(4), 589–600.

Sundstrom, E., De Meuse, K. P., & Futrell, D. (1990). Work teams: Applications and effectiveness. *American Psychologist, 45*, 120–133.

Swezey, R. W., & Salas, E. (1992). *Teams: Their training and performance.* Norwood, NJ: Ablex.

Szilagyi, A. D., Jr., & Schweiger, D. M. (1984). Matching managers to strategies: A review and suggested framework. *Academy of Management Review, 9*(4), 626–637.

Thomas, J. B., & McDaniel, R. R., Jr. (1990). Interpreting strategic issues: Effects of strategy and the information-processing structure of top management teams. *Academy of Management Journal, 33*(2), 286–306.

Thompson, J. D. (1967). *Organizations in action.* New York: McGraw-Hill.

Tziner, A., & Eden, D. (1985). Effects of crew composition on crew performance: Does the whole equal the sum of its parts? *Journal of Applied Psychology, 70*, 85–93.

VanZelst, R. H. (1952). Sociometrically selected work teams increase production. *Personnel Psychology, 47*, 299–301.

Watson, W., Michaelsen, L., & Sharp, W. (1991). Member competence, group interaction, and group decision making: A longitudinal study. *Journal of Applied Psychology, 76*(6), 803–809.

Welsh, M. A., & Slusher, E. A. (1986). Organizational design as a context for political activity. *Administrative Science Quarterly, 31*, 389–402.

Wood, R. E., & Bandura, A. (1989). Social cognitive theory of organizational management. *Academy of Management Review, 14*, 361–384.

Zenger, T. R., & Lawrence, B. S. (1989). Organizational demography: The differential effects of age and tenure distributions on technical communication. *Academy of Management Journal, 32*(2), 353–376.

10

DEFINING COMPETENCIES AND ESTABLISHING TEAM TRAINING REQUIREMENTS

Janis A. Cannon-Bowers, Scott I. Tannenbaum,
Eduardo Salas, Catherine E. Volpe

When it comes to training teams, little exists to guide human resource practitioners who must design training systems. In fact, empirically based prescriptions, guidelines, and specifications are virtually nonexistent for team training (Swezey & Salas, 1992). Nevertheless, recent efforts indicate that a systematic approach to establishing the parameters of team training is possible. In this chapter, we present a conceptual framework for describing team competencies that is based on past research and theorizing on team performance. The purpose of this framework is to guide specification of the competencies required for various types of teams in the workplace. We hope that this framework and associated propositions regarding training requirements and strategies will generate future research and theorizing so that empirically based principles of team training can be defined further.

First, we present a general discussion of the team-performance area, in order to provide a context in which to introduce ideas about team competencies. A conceptual framework follows, which specifies the nature of the competencies required for effective performance in various types of teams. Next, selected past work is reviewed, to delineate the particular team competencies (expressed as knowledge, skills, and attitudes) associated with categories in the framework. Finally, we describe the implications of the framework for establishing the training requirements for a particular team (with attention to organizational and task constraints) and for selecting appropriate training strategies.

Teams and Team Competencies

In general, theorizing about team performance and training has not yielded generalizable principles with practical utility, partly because of the complexity of the team area—in particular, because of the number of variables and constructs that must be considered in the study of teams in the natural environment (Salas, Dickinson, Converse, & Tannenbaum, 1992). In fact, teams in the work environment are required to perform diverse types of tasks and to operate under a variety of task and environmental conditions. This means that such constructs as team performance and team training can be understood only in light of the contexts in which they occur. These notions are summarized in Figure 10.1, which indicates that a number of factors influence team performance. The model in Figure 10.1 was proposed originally as a means of conceptualizing team performance and training (for more detail on the model and its development, see Tannenbaum, Beard, & Salas, 1992). We have modified it to emphasize the role of team competencies in team training and performance. According to the model, organizational and situational characteristics have an impact on several aspects of the functioning of teams and team performance. Thus it is difficult to think about teams without considering the contexts within which they operate. Further, the model suggests that task and work characteristics determine which individual task competencies and team competencies are required for successful team performance. Possession of these competencies is hypothesized to be a prerequisite of effective team performance. Overall, then, the model suggests that having the appropriate competencies

Figure 10.1. Model of Team Effectiveness.

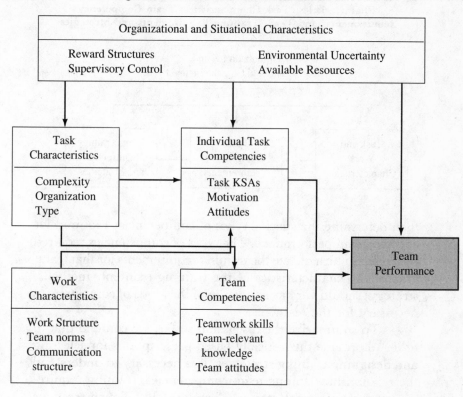

Source: Adapted from Tannenbaum, Beard, & Salas, 1992.

to fit the environment, task, and work situation will determine whether a team performs effectively.

Of primary importance to the current discussion is the notion that determining the team's competency requirements is crucial to establishing the training requirements (and hence the appropriate training strategy) for a team. Figure 10.2 depicts this relationship by extracting key concepts from the performance model (see Figure 10.1) and linking them specifically to training requirements and strategies. The path from left to right in Figure 10.2 shows that characteristics of the situation and the organization affect task and work characteristics. These factors

Figure 10.2. Relationships Among Organizational and Situational Characteristics, Task Characteristics, Team Competency Requirements, and Team Training Requirements and Strategies.

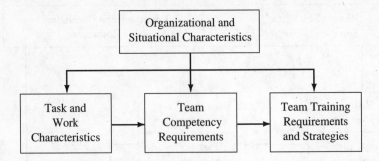

then determine the specific types of competencies required for effective team performance. The types of competencies required by a team in turn dictate the training requirements for that team; that is, the characteristics of the training (content, methods, strategy) should vary as a function of the kinds of competencies necessary for the team.

To summarize the discussion so far, we contend that in order to provide theoretically based prescriptions for selecting and designing training strategies, it is necessary to understand the relationships among team competencies, training requirements, and training strategies. Therefore, the following sections expand and refine our notion of team competencies and present a framework in which team competencies can be conceptualized.

A Conceptual Framework for Specifying Team Competencies

Before pursuing the topic of team competencies, we must clarify what we mean by the term *team competency*. To begin with, team competencies can be thought of as being separate and distinct from individual competencies (see Figure 10.1). Essentially, team competencies can be thought of as (1) the requisite *knowledge*, principles, and concepts underlying the team's effective task performance; (2) the repertoire of required *skills* and behaviors necessary to perform the team task effectively; and (3) the appropriate *attitudes* on the part of team members (about themselves and the team) that foster effective team performance.

Obviously, this approach is similar to the knowledge, skills, and abilities (KSA) approach typically applied to individual training specification (see Goldstein, 1986) except that in the present case our definition of these terms is somewhat different. Specifically, we define *knowledge* similarly to Goldstein (1986), but our definition of *skill* is broadened to include both the psychomotor and cognitive competencies required to perform the job (essentially, we combine what Goldstein refers to as *skill* and *ability*). Moreover, in keeping with Dick and Carey (1990), we are concerned with attitudes as necessary competencies, since it has been shown that job-related attitudes can have an impact on performance. Furthermore, the matter of specifying the required knowledge, skills, and attitudes for effective team performance is somewhat more complicated than specifying the knowledge, skills, and attitudes for individual performance (see Salas, Dickinson, Converse, & Tannenbaum, 1992). This is because teams possess competencies that transcend the individual team members, providing a collective influence on performance.

To go on with the discussion, we believe that there are different kinds of team competencies. Specifically, Figure 10.3 presents several related categories of team competencies that are important to an understanding of team performance. These categories depend on (1) whether the competency is specific to a particular team and (2) whether the competency is specific to a particular task. They are described below in more detail.

As stated, the first delineation of the team competencies shown in Figure 10.3 involves whether a competency is *team-specific* or *team-generic*. Team-generic competencies are held by individual team members and can influence team performance regardless of the particular teammates involved; they are "generic," or transportable to other teams. Examples of these include communication skills, interpersonal skills, leadership skills, and attitudes toward teamwork. What these competencies have in common is that they can have a direct impact on the performance

Figure 10.3. Nature of Team Competencies.

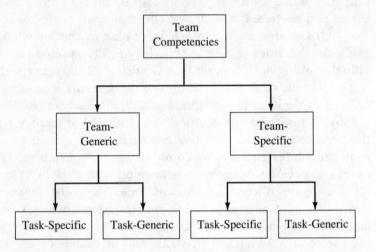

of any team with whom the individual works. By contrast, the second class of team competencies has meaning only with respect to specific team members. Examples of team-specific competencies include knowledge of teammates' characteristics, specific compensation strategies, and team cohesion (all of which depend on the particular team members involved). As another example of this distinction, it is appropriate to think of an attitude, such as collective orientation (an individual's general propensity to work on a team; see Driskell & Salas, 1992), as not necessarily specific to a particular team, whereas collective efficacy (belief in the team's competence; see Riggs, 1989) depends on the particular team members involved. The team competencies shown in Figure 10.3 may also be either specific or generic with respect to the *task*. That is, some team competencies involve the execution of teamwork behaviors in a specific task and/or context (the task's interaction requirements), whereas other team competencies are more generic with respect to a particular task (interpersonal skills, planning skills). The essential difference between these types of competencies rests on the degree to which they can be transported to other tasks. For example, general planning skills may be of use in several team tasks (they are transportable); knowledge of the specific role responsibilities in a particular team task may be applicable only to that task.

      Combining these factors yields four related categories of team competencies, as shown in Figure 10.4. The first of these categories describes competencies that are specific to both the task and team. These are labeled *context-driven competencies* because they are dependent both on the nature of the task involved and on the particular team members involved. The second category of team competencies is labeled *team-contingent*. This category refers to competencies that are specific to a particular team but are generic with respect to the task (they can apply to a variety of tasks). Conversely, *task-contingent competencies* are specific to a particular task but can apply to a variety of teams (with varying membership). The final category of competencies is labeled *transportable competencies* because they are not specific to any particular task or team.

Delineation of Team Competencies

The framework presented in Figure 10.4 provides several general categories of team competencies and suggests that the situational and task characteristics impinging on a team will determine the

Figure 10.4. Types of Team Competencies.

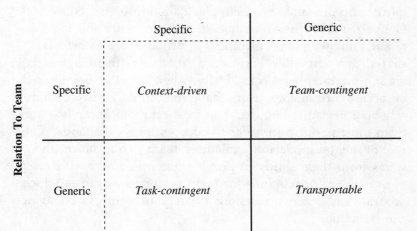

type of competencies it requires. A next step in using this frame-work to guide the specification of training requirements and strategies is to delineate the specific team competencies that fall into each category. To do this, we shall present a selected review of past research, defining the various knowledge, skills, and attitudes that have been hypothesized to be associated with effective team performance. We will then show how the framework in Figure 10.4 can be used to categorize the various types of team knowledge, skills, and attitudes, so that they can be associated more directly with training requirements and strategies.

Knowledge Competencies for Teams

Several past efforts have provided insights into the knowledge requirements of teams. Team knowledge requirements include accurate, shared mental models; an understanding of the nature of teamwork and teamwork skills; knowledge of overall team goals, objectives, and missions; knowledge about boundary spanning; knowledge about fellow team members' roles and responsibilities; and cue-strategy associations (the association of cues in the environment to appropriate coordination strategies). Each of these knowledge competencies is described in more detail in the following sections.

Recently, several researchers have employed the concept of mental models in an effort to understand the knowledge requirements of teams. For example, Cannon-Bowers, Salas, and Converse (1993) maintain that effective teams are able to adapt to and anticipate other member's information needs because of shared or compatible knowledge structures (mental models) among the members. Specifically, when novel or unexpected events are encountered, teams that cannot strategize overtly must rely on preexisting knowledge and expectations about how the team must perform in order to cope with task demands. The role of mental models in explaining team performance, then, stems from their ability to provide team members with a set of organized expectations for team performance, from which accurate and timely predictions about team members' behavior can be made.

This hypothesis suggests that team members must hold knowledge structures about the task and the team that are compatible with those held by fellow team members. According to Rouse, Cannon-Bowers, and Salas (1992), team knowledge consists of several types of knowledge (declarative knowledge, procedural knowledge, and explanations), which can move from the specific and concrete to the general and abstract. Declarative team knowledge includes knowledge about the roles of team members, relationships among team members, and temporal patterns of team performance. Procedural team knowledge includes knowledge about how team members perform their functions, how team members perform together, and the overall mechanisms of team performance (how the task is accomplished). Explanatory team knowledge includes knowledge about why and how various team members are needed and about why the team performs its functions as it does in support of task accomplishment.

In a related formulation, Cannon-Bowers, Salas, and Converse (1993) maintain that team knowledge consists of mental models of the team's equipment, task, and team interactions—that is, models of how members' roles interact, how the various team roles are related to one another, which information sources are important, and the appropriate communication channels and patterns of information flow. Such knowledge forms the basis of team members' expectations in a task situation. By definition, holding task and team-interaction models that are compatible with those of one's teammates requires knowledge that is specific to a particular team and task. For example, team members must have knowledge about the specific team itself—about each of the other team members and the role he or she plays. This includes knowledge about the skills, abilities, preferences, experiences, and tendencies of specific teammates, along with knowledge about the roles they play on the team. This type of team-level knowledge affects (or should affect) a team member's selection of coordination strategies. For example, when working with a particularly competent teammate, a team member may be more willing to delegate responsibility to balance task load than when the teammate is perceived to be incompetent.

Baker, Salas, Cannon-Bowers, and Spector (1992) contend

that a specific type of team knowledge, called *interpositional knowledge,* is crucial to effective team functioning. These authors define a construct labeled *interpositional uncertainty,* which refers to the extent to which team members hold accurate knowledge about the role responsibilities of other members (a component of shared mental models, as defined by Cannon-Bowers, Salas, & Converse, 1993). It is hypothesized that high interpositional uncertainty among team members is associated with ineffective or degraded performance (Baker, Salas, Cannon-Bowers, & Spector, 1992). Preliminary evidence to support this contention was found with a simulated air-combat task.

Other categories of team-relevant knowledge required for effective teamwork are associated with an understanding of the nature of teamwork for accomplishing task goals. In this regard, team members must know about the teamwork skills that are required for successful team performance. In addition, team members must have knowledge of overall team goals and objectives, the team's mission, and other team-level constructs, such as norms and resources. Team members must also have knowledge of the boundary-spanning role (Sundstrom, De Meuse, & Futrell, 1990) that individual members play, as well as of the team's relationship to the larger organization.

Lanzetta and Roby (1960) propose that several general team functions contribute to effective performance. Two of these are consistent with our conceptualization of the team's knowledge competencies. First, *orientation* refers to the process by which the team becomes aware of the factors impinging on the task environment, and of where the team stands on these. This is similar to what was noted above: namely, that team members must have knowledge of the overall goals, mission, norms, and resources of the team. Second, *mapping* is the process by which the group learns the action-outcome contingencies that exist under various task conditions.

The concept of mapping requires further discussion because it is crucial to team performance. In fact, we maintain that cue-strategy associations are of paramount importance to team performance. In order to be effective, team members must recognize the task and environmental cues that trigger specific strategy changes. In other words, team members must learn to recognize when particular interaction processes are appropriate and how they must be implemented. In some ways, appropriate strategy formation is the cornerstone of teamwork because it assumes that team members can determine when teamwork behavior is required, and what type. The development of appropriate cue-strategy associations is highly task-specific, as well as team-specific in the sense that behavior will change as a function of the particular team members who are present.

To summarize, past research suggests several categories of team knowledge that are hypothesized to be important for effective team performance. This knowledge forms the basis of team functioning by providing an understanding of global teamwork concepts (understanding of teamwork skills) and specific aspects of team performance (knowledge of team goals). In addition, requisite team knowledge lays the groundwork for development of the necessary teamwork skills.

Skill Competencies in Teams

In recent years, there has been a trend toward defining teamwork behaviorally, as a set of teamwork skills (Glickman et al., 1987; Prince & Salas, 1993; McIntyre & Salas, this volume). This trend has been most pronounced in research concerning military teams, but the results have implications for other types of teams where interdependence and coordination are required. Unfortunately, the literature in this area is often confused and contradictory. In fact, it is safe to conclude that the literature is plagued by inconsistency, both in the labels and in the definitions of teamwork skills used in past work. Specifically, researchers have often used different labels to refer to the same skills, or similar labels to refer to different skills. Moreover, the definitions of skills (and subskills) employed in the literature have often been ignored by subsequent researchers, so that each new effort appears to define a new set of skills.

In an attempt to impose some order on this state of affairs, we conducted an extensive review of the literature, both empirical and theoretical. Table 10.1 presents a summary of the

Table 10.1. Teamwork Skill Dimensions.

Skill Dimension	Definition	Subskills/Alternative Labels
Adaptability[a]	The process by which a team is able to use information gathered from the task environment to adjust strategies through the use of compensatory behavior and reallocation of intrateam resources	Flexibility Capacity for closure Development of innovations Mutual adjustment Compensatory behavior Backing-up behavior Provide/ask for assistance Fail stop Dynamic reallocation of functions
Shared situational awareness[b]	The process by which team members develop compatible models of the team's internal and external environment; includes skill in arriving at a common understanding of the situation and applying appropriate task strategies	Situational awareness Orientation Team awareness Development of integrated model of environment Development of system awareness Shared problem-model development
Performance monitoring and feedback[c]	The ability of team members to give, seek, and receive task-clarifying feedback; includes the ability to accurately monitor the performance of teammates, provide constructive feedback regarding errors, and offer advice for improving performance	Intramember feedback Performance feedback Planning review Feedback/reinforcement Acceptance of/giving suggestions, criticism Mutual performance monitoring Monitoring and cross-checking Systems monitoring Performance monitoring Error identification/correction Intrateam monitoring Strategy development Procedure maintenance

Category	Description	Components
Leadership/team management[d]	The ability to direct and coordinate the activities of other team members, assess team performance, assign tasks, motivate team members, plan and organize, and establish a positive atmosphere	Task structuring Delegation and assignment Task assignment Resource distribution Resource management Performance direction Establishment of priorities Mission analysis Motivation of others Leadership control Goal setting Drive to completion Goal orientation
Interpersonal relations[e]	The ability to optimize the quality of team members' interactions through resolution of dissent, utilization of cooperative behaviors, or use of motivational reinforcing statements	Conflict resolution Cooperation (interpersonal) Assertiveness Morale building (behavioral reinforcement) Boundary spanning
Coordination[f]	The process by which team resources, activities, and responses are organized to ensure that tasks are integrated, synchronized, and completed within established temporal constraints	Task organization Coordination of task sequence Integration Task interaction Technical coordination Response coordination Timing and activity pacing
Communication[g]	The process by which information is clearly and accurately exchanged between two or more team members in the prescribed manner and with proper terminology; the ability to clarify or acknowledge the receipt of information	Information exchange Closed-loop communication Information sharing Procedural talk Volunteering/requesting information Consulting with others Effective influence Open exchange of relevant interpretations Evaluative interchange

Table 10.1. Teamwork Skill Dimensions, Cont'd.

Skill Dimension	Definition	Subskills/Alternative Labels
Decision making[h]	The ability to gather and integrate information, use sound judgment, identify alternatives, select the best solution, and evaluate the consequences (in team context, emphasizes skill in pooling information and resources in support of a response choice)	Problem assessment Problem solving Emergence of solutions Probabilistic structure Hypothesis formulation Information processing Information evaluation Planning Plan development Use of information Metacognitive behavior Implementation (jurisdiction)

Sources: [a] Alexander & Cooperband, 1965; Johnston & Briggs, 1968; McCallum, Oser, Morgan, & Salas, 1989; McIntyre & Salas, this volume; Streufert & Nogami, 1992.
[b] Alexander & Cooperband, 1965; Briggs & Johnston, 1967; Franz, Prince, Cannon-Bowers, & Salas, 1990; Lanzetta & Roby, 1960; Nieva, Fleishman, & Reick, 1978; Orlady & Foushee, 1987.
[c] Alexander & Cooperband, 1965; Briggs & Johnston, 1967; Cooper, Shiflett, Korotkin, & Fleishman, 1984; Gaddy & Wachtel, 1992; Glickman et al., 1987; McCallum, Oser, Morgan, & Salas, 1989; McIntyre & Salas, this volume; Morgan, Glickman, Woodard, Blaiwes, & Salas, 1986; Orlady & Foushee, 1987; Oser, McCallum, Salas, & Morgan, 1989; Swezey & Salas, 1992.
[d] Bales, 1950; Federman & Siegel, 1965; Franz, McCallum, Lewis, Prince, & Salas, 1990; Franz, Prince, Cannon-Bowers, & Salas, 1990; Nieva, Fleishman, & Reick, 1978; Orasanu, 1990; Orlady & Foushee, 1987; Prince, Chidester, Cannon-Bowers, & Bowers, 1992; Shiflett, Eisner, Price, & Schemmer, 1982; Siegel & Federman, 1973.
[e] Franz, McCallum, Lewis, Prince, & Salas, 1990; Franz, Prince, Cannon-Bowers, & Salas, 1990; Gaddy & Wachtel, 1992; Jordan, Jensen, & Terebinski, 1963; McCallum, Oser, Morgan, & Salas, 1989; Orlady & Foushee, 1987; Oser, McCallum, Salas, & Morgan, 1989; Prince, Chidester, Cannon-Bowers, & Bowers, 1992; Tannenbaum, Beard, & Salas, 1992.
[f] Kleinman & Serfaty, 1989; Nieva, Fleishman, & Reick, 1978; Orlady & Foushee, 1987; Shiflett, Eisner, Price, & Schemmer, 1982; Siskel & Flexman, 1962.
[g] Federman & Siegel, 1965; Franz, McCallum, Lewis, Prince, & Salas, 1990; Franz, Prince, Cannon-Bowers, & Salas, 1990; Gaddy & Wachtel, 1992; McCallum, Oser, Morgan, & Salas, 1989; McIntyre & Salas, this volume; Orasanu, 1990; Orlady & Foushee, 1987; Oser, Prince, & Morgan, 1990; Siegel & Federman, 1973; Streufert & Nogami, 1992.
[h] Alexander & Cooperband, 1965; Federman & Siegel, 1965; Franz, McCallum, Lewis, Prince, & Salas, 1990; Franz, Prince, Cannon-Bowers, & Salas, 1990; Lanzetta & Roby, 1960; Orasanu, 1990; Orlady & Foushee, 1987; Prince, Chidester, Cannon-Bowers, & Bowers, 1992; Siegel & Federman, 1973; Streufert & Nogami, 1992.

skill labels, definitions, subskills, and alternative labels presented by various researchers. In deriving this table, we first generated an initial list of over 130 skill labels found in the literature to describe the skills required for teamwork. This list was sorted into major skill dimensions, with associated subskills, by two independent raters. Where appropriate, similar skills (based on definitions provided by authors) were grouped together, and a common definition of the skill dimension (column 2) was extracted. This sorting process also led to the generation of a list of major subskills associated with each skill dimension, and to a list of alternative labels that have been used to refer to the same subskills (these are listed under each subskill). The notes to Table 10.1 give the sources from which skill labels and definitions were extracted.

Our conclusion is that a core set of skill dimensions common to all (or most) investigations can be generated. These are adaptability, shared situational awareness, performance monitoring and feedback, leadership/team management, interpersonal skills, coordination skills, communication skills, and decision-making skills. It should be noted that we are not presenting this table as a means of suggesting that the skills shown in it comprise a new definition of teamwork; rather, we present this table as a means of synthesizing a great deal of rather disjointed, often conflicting, and certainly confusing literature about teams. The following sections review the research used to derive the skills shown in Table 10.1.

To begin with, Morgan, Glickman, Woodard, Blaiwes, and Salas (1986) employed a critical-incidents technique with instructors in a U.S. Navy training program to generate examples of effective and ineffective behaviors for the following skill dimensions: communication, adaptability, cooperation, acceptance of suggestions or criticism, giving suggestions or criticism, team spirit and morale, and coordination. Results of a field study indicate that the effective teams exhibited proportionately more effective behaviors and fewer ineffective behaviors in each of these skill areas, as compared to the ineffective teams.

Similarly, Oser, McCallum, Salas, and Morgan (1989) analyzed the specific behaviors exhibited by effective and ineffective

U.S. Navy command-and-control teams. They conclude that teamwork can be defined behaviorally to include identification and resolution of errors, coordinated information exchange, and team reinforcement. Oser, McCallum, Salas, and Morgan (1992) conducted a subsequent analysis with a different type of U.S. Navy team and found that intermember assistance (prompting and directing other members), intrateam reinforcement (praising other members, thanking another member for correcting an error), and intrateam monitoring (acknowledging and correcting each other's errors) were all associated with effective team performance, as rated by experts.

McIntyre and Salas (this volume) have summarized the results of several investigations of teamwork, including those reported above. Based on lessons learned about the nature of teamwork, as presented by these authors, the following implications for specifying teamwork skills can be generated: performance monitoring, feedback, closed-loop communication, and backing-up behaviors.

Working with cockpit crews, Franz, Prince, Cannon-Bowers, and Salas (1990) conducted a needs analysis of air-crew coordination skills, using structured interviews and a behavioral rating form. The researchers generated thirty-seven behavioral statements related to effective teamwork in the cockpit. These were augmented via interviews with job experts (pilots), leading to a total fifty-five behavioral statements. A sample of 134 job experts then rated behaviors on the basis of criticality, difficulty, frequency, and importance to train. Results indicate that the job experts rated teamwork behaviors as critical to their jobs, frequently occurring, and important to train. These researchers also conclude that the teamwork behaviors can be classified into seven skill dimensions: mission analysis (which includes planning and strategizing), assertiveness, adaptability/flexibility, situational awareness, decision making, leadership, and communication. Preliminary support for the efficacy of these skill dimensions was found by Franz, McCallum, Lewis, Prince, and Salas (1990).

Also in the area of aviation training, Prince, Chidester, Cannon-Bowers, and Bowers (1992) indicate that commercial aviation programs have sought to train a host of related team-work skills in order to enhance cockpit crews' performance. Unfortunately, there has been a lack of standardized definitions for skill dimensions among programs, so that similar skill labels can refer to different behaviors across programs. Overall, commonly trained skill dimensions appear to include planning, situation awareness, leadership, communication, assertiveness, problem solving, and feedback.

Other researchers have offered definitions of teamwork that can be used to infer the required team skills. For example, Siskel and Flexman (1962) define *coordination* as the ability of team members to work together, anticipate each other's needs, inspire confidence, and communicate in an efficient manner. Alexander and Cooperband (1965) maintain that *cooperation* can be defined as a skill whereby team members possess information regarding the strengths and weaknesses of one another, offer help only when other team members need it, pace their activities to fit the needs of the team, and behave in an unambiguous manner so that their actions are not misinterpreted. (It should be noted that this definition incorporates both knowledge and skill competencies, as defined here.)

In other work, Lanzetta and Roby (1960) define a team skill labeled *jurisdiction,* which is the process by which the team chooses its responses and implements decisions during task performance. Bass (1982) suggests that group effectiveness is determined by behaviors that involve goal setting, information sharing, and intermember consultation. Bass also hypothesizes that interaction processes are a crucial aspect of team functioning. Bass contends, in this regard, that the content of interaction (goal setting, information sharing, consulting with others), as well as patterns of interaction (number of communications, length of time spent talking, time to make a decision) and outcomes of interaction (task versus interpersonal focus, turnover, flexibility of the group), modify how individual performance contributes to performance of the team. With respect to the current discussion, we can hypothesize that interaction processes describe an important set of skills required for successful team performance. These appear to be most closely related to what Bass calls the *pattern of interaction*—how teams communicate and arrive at decisions.

Several researchers have also hypothesized that interpersonal skills are required for effective teamwork. Empirical tests of this contention have yielded mixed results. For example, Johnston and Briggs (1968) have found that errors were less frequent on teams where members were allowed to correct and provide feedback to one another.

A number of propositions regarding effective teamwork skills can be inferred from a review by Briggs and Johnston (1967) describing the results of several studies with U.S. Navy teams. On the basis of findings from these and other studies, the following teamwork skills can be delineated: load balancing, compensatory behavior, adaptability, and flexibility. An early study by Chapman, Kennedy, Newell, and Biel (1959) also provides support for the notion that flexibility is a desirable teamwork skill. These researchers show that teams are better able to handle increased task loads if allowed to use flexible work structures in an air-defense task.

Other researchers have been concerned specifically with communication skills as a requirement for effective teamwork. For example, Oser, Prince, and Morgan (1990) have found that cockpit crews in nonroutine (emergency) conditions are more likely to offer commands, suggestions, statements of intent, and replies than in routine situations. Also working with cockpit crews, Foushee (1982) reports a tendency for ineffective crews to communicate less in a study conducted with a full-mission simulator. Communication content differences were also associated with crew effectiveness. Other work (described above) conducted with U.S. Navy teams suggests that effective teamwork includes the ability to communicate effectively (Morgan, Glickman, Woodard, Blaiwes, & Salas, 1986).

Orasanu (1990) and Orasanu and Salas (1993) argue that teams must dynamically form shared models of the situation and appropriate strategies for coping with task demands (called *shared problem models*). We distinguish this concept from shared mental models in that shared mental models are preexisting knowledge structures developed over time and generalized to a variety of situations. These mental models exist in individual team members and provide the *knowledge* foundation necessary for successful team performance. Development of shared problem models, by contrast, involves a *skill* that team members develop, which enables them to apply task and team knowledge to the formation of compatible responses in a task situation.

In a related formulation, Kleinman and Serfaty (1989) suggest that teams can develop implicit coordination skills in order to cope with high workloads. Specifically, team members in a simulated command-and-control task were able to maintain performance under high workload conditions, even though overt communication decreased. The authors reason that the team members were exercising mutual mental models of the task (discussed above), so that the need for overt coordination of activity was reduced. Kleinman and Serfaty label this an *implicit coordination strategy* (decreasing communication but maintaining performance). Therefore, skill in employing implicit coordination strategies involves a team member's recognizing when and how to rely on assumptions regarding task performance and when to use more explicit (communication) strategies.

Another team-level competency involves skill in dynamically reallocating functions (also called *load balancing* by some researchers; see Briggs & Johnston, 1967). Dynamic reallocation of functions is a process whereby a team can shift the workload among its members to achieve balance during high-workload, time-pressured, or emergency situations. It is also a skill that requires more than one team member in that the appropriate reallocation of any function depends on the functional responsibilities and workloads of other members at any particular time.

Other team-level skills that have been hypothesized in past research are related to the required mechanisms of interaction in teams. In this regard, Nieva, Fleishman, and Reick (1978) have developed a taxonomy of the interactive functions hypothesized to enable a team to perform effectively, above and beyond the performance of individual members. According to these researchers, four categories of interactive functions allow a team to achieve its objectives: orientation, organization, adaptation, and motivation. *Orientation* refers to the processes by which information relevant to task accomplishment is generated and disseminated to team members (as such, it is most appropriately categorized as a knowledge competency, under the current formulation). *Organization* is the process by which team members coordinate their tasks, pace their activities, balance the work load among themselves, and assign task priorities. *Adaptation* refers to the processes that enable teams to accomplish their tasks via compensatory adjustment and timing, mutual performance monitoring, and error adjustment. *Motivation* refers to those team processes in which team objectives are defined and the team is energized to achieve the objectives, through norm development, conflict resolution, and reinforcement (we include this as a team attitude, discussed further in a later section).

To summarize, it is obvious that a considerable amount of theorizing and research has been devoted to the delineation of teamwork *skills*. In fact, there is quite a bit more of this type of research than there is about required team *knowledge* and/or *attitudes*.

Attitude Competencies in Teams

So far, we have concentrated on the cognitive and behavioral skills necessary for team performance, but we must also address the affective or attitudinal factors critical to team functioning. Numerous researchers have studied attitudes in terms of individual performance and training objectives (Gagné, 1985; Dick & Carey, 1990; Noe, 1986; Tannenbaum & Yukl, 1992). Nevertheless, their impact on team functioning and effectiveness has been largely ignored. The few investigations that do exist suggest that attitudes are strongly associated with team performance, however (Ruffell-Smith, 1979; Helmreich, Foushee, Benson, & Russini, 1986).

For the purpose of this discussion, we define *attitude* in keeping with Dick and Carey (1990): as *an internal state that influences an individual's choices or decisions to act in a certain way under particular circumstances*. We focus our discussion on those attitudes that are unique to the team context—that is, those that have been shown to have a direct bearing on the team's interaction processes and on the ability of an individual to flourish in a team context. These include attitudes toward teamwork, the team concept, a collective orientation, collective efficacy, cohesion, mutual trust, and shared vision. The following sections describe these constructs in more detail.

Several studies have shown that an individual's attitudes toward teamwork can have a significant impact on performance. For example, a study by Cooper, White, and Lauber (1980) analyzes the causes of aircraft accidents and isolates a number of attitudes related to effective and ineffective crew performance. Similarly, the study conducted by Helmreich, Foushee, Benson, and Russini (1986) found that attitudes can be used to separate effective from ineffective cockpit managers. Further, work with the Cockpit Management Attitudes Questionnaire (Gregorich, Helmreich, & Wilhelm, 1990) suggests that beliefs about the importance of teamwork skills — coordination and communication, command responsibility, and the ability to recognize stressor effects — may significantly affect crew processes and performance outcomes, although direct causal links have yet to be established; further research into this relationship is needed.

Another important attitude for team members to possess is that of a well-developed team concept, or belief in placing the team's goals above and beyond those of its individual members. This belief, referred to as a *collective orientation,* can be defined as an attraction to the team as a means of task accomplishment (Driskell & Salas, 1992). It involves the capacity to take others' behavior into account during group interaction, as well as the belief that a team approach is superior to an individual one.

Several theorists have shown a relationship between collective orientation and cooperative behavior in groups (Deutsch, 1960; Meeker, 1983; Rubin & Brown, 1975), but very little is known about how attitudes toward collectivity affect the team's task performance. An exception is a study by Davis (1969) in which performance on a problem-solving task was predicted by the collective orientation of the group members.

Further evidence in support of the positive effect of collective orientation on team performance was provided recently by Driskell and Salas (1992). Results of a study with two-person teams (classified beforehand as either egocentric or collectively oriented) indicate that the egocentric teams performed no better than their members did as individuals. By contrast, collectively oriented teams performed significantly better than the individual members that comprised them. Driskell and Salas argue that these findings show that the collectively oriented teams outperformed their egocentric counterparts because their members took advantage of the benefits offered by teamwork.

Another attitude that has been hypothesized to be important in a team context is collective efficacy, which refers the ability of the team to perform effectively as a unit, given some set of specific task demands (Bandura, 1986). It can be defined specifically as an individual team member's assessment of his or her team's collective ability to perform the task at hand (Riggs, 1989). This concept is similar to that of potency (Guzzo, 1986). The notion of collective efficacy is amplified by Shamir (1990) to include other attitudinal components, such as the individual's perception of the collective success of the group, judgments regarding team leadership, the team's power base, its cohesiveness, and its structure.

With respect to performance, collective efficacy is hypothesized to have a facilitating affect (Shamir, 1990; Bandura, 1986; Guzzo, 1986). Moreover, there is general agreement that the mechanism by which collective efficacy affects performance is motivational (team members with high efficacy will be more motivated to perform well). Despite the fact that a relationship between collective efficacy and team performance has been theorized by several researchers (Bandura, 1986; Guzzo, 1986; Travillian, Baker, & Cannon-Bowers, 1992), little empirical research has been conducted to support these claims. These and the few other studies that do exist, however, support the contention that increased collective efficacy improves task performance (Forward & Zander, 1968; Shea & Guzzo; 1987). These findings suggest that members' confidence in the task-specific ability of the team is a contributing factor to the team's actual performance — that is, for team members to be motivated to perform the necessary teamwork behaviors (depending on and assisting their teammates), they must be confident that the team can master the task objectives.

Another team-level attitude of interest here is cohesion. Cohesion, or team morale, has long been considered one of the most critical aspects of team functioning (Mayo, 1933). A basic assumption held by most researchers is that the higher the team's cohesiveness, the more effective the team will be in performing a task (Martens & Peterson, 1971). The most widely accepted definition of *cohesion* is provided by Festinger, Schachter, and Back (1950) who conceptualized it as the "total field of forces which act on members to remain in the group" (p. 164). Unfortunately, since the time it was proposed, this definition has led to numerous conceptualizations and operationalizations of the construct in subsequent research. For example, some studies have operationalized cohesion as a socially oriented attitude toward developing and maintaining interpersonal relationships within the team. Others have defined it as a task-oriented belief about achieving the group's goals through commitment to the team approach (Rainey & Schweickert, 1988). As a consequence, many conflicting and inconsistent results have been obtained from past work. For example, some researchers have found positive associations between cohesion and team functioning (Greene & Schriesheim, 1980; Hare, 1962; Hemphill & Sechrest, 1952; Straub, 1975). Others have obtained negative results (Roby, 1953; Stogdill, 1972; Weick & Penner, 1969). Still others have found nonsignificant results (Lodahl & Porter, 1961; Terborg, Castore, & DeNinno, 1976; Tziner & Vardi, 1982).

It is difficult to draw definitive conclusions in this area, but it appears that when the team is well trained, has confidence in its abilities, and is goal-oriented, the effects of cohesion will only serve to strengthen team effectiveness. It should be noted, however, that the instrumentality of cohesion is for the most part a function of the social norms prevalent in the team; that is, a cohesive team is likely to perform effectively only if its members are committed to the organization within which the team functions (Tziner & Vardi, 1983). When this is not the case, a cohesive team can set internal norms that are counterproductive to performance (Stogdill, 1972; Tziner, 1982).

A number of other job-related attitudes can be hypothesized to affect team performance. For example, Nieva, Fleishman, and Reick's concept of motivation (1978) suggests that teams must be energized to achieve valued objectives through norm development, conflict resolution, and reinforcement. In addition, such variables as mutual trust and shared vision can be expected to affect team performance. *Mutual trust* can be defined as an attitude held by team members regarding the aura or mood of the team's internal environment. It connotes an atmosphere where the opinions of team members are allowed to emerge, where members are respected by their co-workers, and where innovative proactive behavior is rewarded (Rehder & Smith, 1986; Vaziri, Lee, & Krieger, 1988). Rehder and Smith point out that mutual trust can be created through the implementation of a collaborative, problem-solving approach to team management. The importance of mutual trust is further supported by Vaziri, Lee, and Krieger, who describe how fostering mutual trust and a sense of openness in management and decision-making processes can lead to a more harmonious and productive team environment.

Shared vision refers to a commonly held attitude regarding the direction, goals, and mission of an organization or team. Niehoff, Enz, and Grover (1990) have explored this concept in depth and examined the relationship between management actions that foster a shared vision and the degree of commitment, job satisfaction, and role ambiguity present in employees. The results indicate that managers' actions to inspire shared vision were related to the outcomes of interest. Although these outcomes were not directly related to performance, it can be proposed that a shared vision of mission and goals will affect performance quality. In fact, a study by Tjosvold and Tsao (1989) examines this hypothesized relationship at the organizational level. The results indicate that a shared vision contributes to effective collaboration, commitment, and productivity.

To summarize, a number of attitudes have been hypothesized to affect team performance. Putting them together with the skill and knowledge competencies already delineated, we can now formulate a comprehensive picture of the competencies required for effective team performance.

Proposed Competencies for Effective Team Performance

Table 10.2 summarizes what has been presented so far. Specifically, this table conceptualizes each team competency (knowledge, skills, attitudes) as falling into context-driven, team-contingent, task-contingent, or transportable categories. It should be noted that all these competencies may be important and may contribute to team effectiveness, but their relative importance and the feasibility of developing them will be influenced by the nature of the task and the environment in which the team operates. What follows is a brief discussion of the conditions in which competencies in each of the four categories are most important, and of the specific competencies associated with each category.

Context-Driven Team Competencies

When a task is highly demanding, it requires a team that is able to quickly adjust its strategy in response to task demands. In such a case, team members will benefit from competencies that are specific to both the task and the team. As noted, this category of situation is labeled *context-driven,* to refer to the fact that the nature of the required teamwork competencies is driven by the particular task and team involved. Teams that have fairly stable membership and perform a single or small number of tasks are more likely to require the competencies in this category. Examples of teams that would benefit from context-driven competencies include surgery and other medical teams, combat teams, sports teams, and air crews.

Knowledge Competencies

On the basis of theorizing about shared mental models, we hypothesize that several team-specific, task-specific knowledge requirements exist for teams in this category. Specifically, team members must have accurate knowledge about one another (the task-related competence, preferences, tendencies, strengths, and weaknesses of teammates) as a basis for formulating specific expectations for teammates' performance. In addition, team members must have knowledge about the specific role responsibilities

Table 10.2. Proposed Competencies for Teams.

Nature of Team Competency	Description of Team Competency	Knowledge	Skills	Attitudes
Context-driven	Team-specific; task-specific	Cue-strategy associations Task-specific teammate characteristics Team-specific role responsibilities Shared task models Team mission, objectives, norms, resources	Task organization Mutual performance monitoring Shared problem-model development Flexibility Compensatory behavior Information exchange Dynamic reallocation of functions Mission analysis Task structuring Task interaction Motivation of others	Team orientation (morale) Collective efficacy Shared vision
Team-contingent	Team-specific; task-generic	Teammate characteristics Team mission, objectives, norms, resources Relationship to larger organization	Conflict resolution Motivation of others Information exchange Intrateam feedback Compensatory behavior Assertiveness Planning Flexibility Morale building Cooperation	Team cohesion Interpersonal relations Mutual trust

Task-contingent	Team-generic; task-specific	Task-specific role responsibilities Task sequencing Team role-interaction patterns Procedures for task accomplishment Accurate task models Accurate problem models Boundary-spanning role Cue-strategy associations	Task structuring Mission analysis Mutual performance monitoring Compensatory behavior Information exchange Intrateam feedback Assertiveness Flexibility Planning Task interaction Situational awareness	Task-specific teamwork attitudes
Transportable	Team-generic; task-generic	Teamwork skills	Morale building Conflict resolution Information exchange Task motivation Cooperation Consulting with others Assertiveness	Collective orientation Belief in importance of teamwork

in the team (which may change as a function of the particular team members present). Further, team members must have common task models (must interpret task information and demands in a similar manner) and understand the task-specific information flow required for effective performance. Team members must also have accurate knowledge regarding cue-strategy associations (that is, how and when to change coordination strategies). Finally, a team in this category must have a common understanding of the team goal and mission, team norms, and team resources. All these competencies have in common that they are meaningful only for dealing with a specific team and task. When either of these changes, the knowledge must be adjusted or augmented to incorporate new team members and/or different task demands.

Skill Competencies

Several team-specific, task-specific skills enable teams to optimize performance in demanding situations (see Table 10.2). For example, team members must have skill in task organization (that is, in sequencing and integrating task inputs according to team and task demands). Team members must also possess skill in dynamically reallocating functions (or balancing workloads) according to both task demands and the ability of teammates (a teammate's level of competence will determine when and how reallocation of functions can and should occur). Teams must also develop shared problem models. This skill requires being able to recognize and integrate task contingencies and then form, adjust, and act on models of the problem that are compatible with those held by teammates. Finally, team members must be flexible — able to adapt their strategies according to the particular task demands at hand — and must be skilled in exchanging information efficiently, analyzing the task or mission accurately, monitoring each other's performance, interacting constructively, and maintaining task motivation.

It should be noted here that knowledge and skill competencies are closely related. Specifically, the existence of accurate task and team models enables team members to execute crucial skills. For example, at the knowledge level, members must hold accurate models of their teammates' characteristics, so that expectations for performance are formed. At the skill level, this knowledge allows team members to adjust task strategies so that they are optimal with respect to their teammates' expected performance.

Attitude Competencies

In keeping with the nature of the competencies in this category, we hypothesize that certain team attitudes are meaningful only in the context of a particular task and team. For example, the development of collective efficacy can be hypothesized to be both team- and task-dependent, since it rests on beliefs about the competence of a particular team performing a particular task. In addition, we hypothesize that team orientation is specific to the team members involved and is affected by the task and the task situation.

Team-Contingent Competencies

In some cases, the team will require competencies that are specific to that team but not to a particular task. Such a situation involves a team whose members are consistent and who must work together across a variety of tasks. Self-managing work teams, management teams, quality circles, and teams that comprise functional departments are all examples of teams that fall into this category.

Knowledge Competencies

Relying again on the theory of shared mental models, we hypothesize that team members must share all the knowledge specified for context-driven team competencies that is specific to the team, but not to the task. This includes knowledge about teammate characteristics (general abilities, preferences, tendencies, strengths, weaknesses), and team norms, resources, mission, and objectives. All of this shared knowledge contributes to the members' ability to come to a shared assessment of a problem quickly and to coordinate, with little or no need to communicate verbally. It helps ensure that the team members' resources are being applied to the accomplishment of a common goal. In addition, team members must have an understanding of how the team fits into the larger organization, so that they are aware of how they must interact with other organizational units, of what is expected of them, and of how they fit into the accomplishment of the larger organizational goals.

Skill Competencies

Team competencies associated with this category include several of the skills or subskills summarized in Table 10.1. In particular, we hypothesize that teams in this category require skill in interpersonal relations and leadership/team management (including conflict resolution, assertiveness, maintaining task motivation, morale building, and cooperation). Other important skills in this category involve information exchange, intrateam feedback, compensatory behavior, flexibility, and planning. All these skills are hypothesized to affect team performance, but they are not necessarily limited to a particular task; that is, a team member can be trained in transportable information-exchange skills (how to speak clearly, concisely, and in an unambiguous manner) that can improve his or her ability to communicate across a variety of team tasks. Moreover, we contend that team members in this category will benefit from training that improves their ability to work together as a team, even when the particular task functions vary.

Attitude Competencies

A number of attitudes can be listed in this category. For example, team cohesion can develop among members who work together to perform several different tasks. Similarly, interpersonal relations and mutual trust fall into this category, since they are dependent on particular team membership; that is, these competencies are dependent on the particular team members involved but are not necessarily specific to a particular task. For example, a team of individuals who work together consistently can develop sound interpersonal relations that cut across particular tasks.

Task-Contingent Competencies

In situations where team members perform a specific team task but do not work with a consistent set of teammates (because of organizational policy or rapid turnover), they must possess team competencies that are specific to the task but not dependent on particular teammates. Examples of teams that fall into this category include some firefighting teams, air crews, medical teams, and others for which the task remains constant but team membership does not.

Knowledge Competencies

Borrowing again from the theory of shared mental models, we hypothesize that teams in this category must possess accurate models of the task and problem, and an understanding of task-specific role responsibilities (independent of the particular people who may occupy these roles), requirements for task sequencing, team role-interaction patterns, and mechanisms and procedures for task accomplishment. These types of knowledge provide team members with a basis for generating predictions of how the task will unfold and expectations for how they should perform. A final type of knowledge involves understanding the boundary-spanning role and its impact on team functioning.

Skill Competencies

Many task-specific skills are not dependent on or specific to a particular team. These include skills in leadership or team management (task structuring, mission analysis), feedback and performance monitoring (mutual performance monitoring and intra-team feedback), and coordination (task interaction). In addition, several other skills (assertiveness, planning, situational awareness) are hypothesized to be important for teams that must perform when the task but not the team remains constant. In fact, the difference between the competencies in this category and those specified in the team-contingent category is that we are referring here to skills that involve particular task-related behaviors. For example, team members may possess transportable information-exchange skills that have no particular task referents. By contrast, team members may possess information-exchange skills that are more task-specific (for example, knowing that the receipt of certain messages should be verified, given their criticality to the task, regardless of the particular team members involved).

Attitude Competencies

On the basis of research conducted with air crews, we hypothesize that task-specific attitudes toward teamwork are important to team performance. These can be defined as the attitudes that the team members have toward working as a team. For example, if a member of a team in research and development does not believe that there is any advantage to working on a team to develop a proposal, then he or she probably will not act in a manner that encourages participation from teammates.

Transportable Team Competencies

Transportable team and task competencies are required when team members work on a variety of tasks and with a variety of teams. Examples of teams in this category include task forces, process-action teams, and project teams. Organizations may also want employees to have transportable team competencies as a first step in establishing a team culture or philosophy. In these circumstances, an organization may want to train employees in the team competencies that are applicable to a variety of team situations, regardless of the particular task or team. More specific training (specific to the task or team) is often desirable, but it may not be possible or feasible (as when turnover is rapid). In such cases, training in transportable team competencies may be a viable option. Furthermore, there may be value in training these as task- or team-specific.

Knowledge Competencies

In this category, we hypothesize that team members must possess an understanding of the teamwork skills necessary for effective team performance. This provides the conceptual underpinnings required to execute crucial teamwork skills (that is, team members have knowledge that enables them to perform the necessary skills).

Skill Competencies

We hypothesize that several transportable team skills can affect team performance. These include interpersonal skills (morale building, conflict resolution, cooperation), communication skills (information exchange, consulting with others), and task motivation. All these skills are important to team functioning but are not specific to a task or a team. For example, employees can be trained in general conflict-resolution skills that are applicable to a wide range of team endeavors.

Attitude Competencies

Individuals who work in teams can also be hypothesized to require several team-related attitudes that are not specific to a particular team or task. For example, team members should possess a collective (versus egocentric) orientation and should appreciate the importance of teamwork for success. These attitudes may contribute to the performance of a team member across situations and teams.

Team Competencies and Team Training

Up to this point, we have made the case that team competencies can be conceptualized as having team- and task-specific or generic components. Using these concepts to begin specifying training requirements, we now offer sixteen propositions regarding the nature of the team training required for developing particular competencies in teams and regarding the strategies that are likely to be successful. The propositions fall into two related categories: those that involve the manner in which environmental (task and situational) characteristics influence the nature of the team's competency requirements, and those that link the categories of team competencies to training requirements and strategies. After each proposition, we provide an explanation of our reasoning, based on the framework and associated ideas set forth in this chapter. It should be noted that these propositions are offered only as food for thought; we realize that many of them require further attention and systematic study.

Propositions Linking Situational or Task Characteristics to Team Competencies

PROPOSITION 1: *High interdependency in a team task requires team members to possess context-driven competencies.*

Greater interdependency in teams requires a greater reliance on teammates. Team members must shift their strategies in a coordinated manner, one that also permits teammates to execute their functions effectively. Theory about shared mental models suggests members of such teams must be able to anticipate the behavior of specific teammates through familiarization with task-specific teammate characteristics (as in anticipating when a teammate will require particular information). When task interdependence is relatively low, transportable teamwork competencies are probably sufficient, depending on the nature of other task or environmental factors.

PROPOSITION 2: *Teams that operate in an environment that is fairly stable require task-specific but not necessarily team-specific competencies.*

When a task is stable, it requires less behavioral discretion on the part of team members. This relaxes the necessity for team members to be familiar with particular teammates, because their responses will be defined by the task and can be expressed more easily as standard operating procedures. Therefore, in such situations, team members must have competencies that are specific to the task for optimal performance. Low stability in task requirements would suggest that team members be familiar with one another, so as to be able to predict the behavior and requirements of teammates (team-specific competencies would be required).

PROPOSITION 3: *In teams where turnover is rapid, task-specific competencies are required and team-specific competencies are less crucial.*

It may not be fruitful to establish team-specific competencies for teams whose membership changes rapidly. Task-specific competencies — understanding the roles and role significance of different positions on the team, regardless of who occupies them — are crucial in such instances. When turnover is low, developing team-specific competencies is more logical. Task-specific competencies may also be appropriate for teams with low turnover; this will depend on other task and environmental factors.

PROPOSITION 4: *Team members who hold membership in multiple teams require, at the minimum, transportable team competencies.*

An employee who moves from one team to another would benefit from competencies that enable him or her to be an effective team member. In such a case, training transportable team competencies should improve performance across tasks and teams. More specific team or task competencies may also be required, however, as determined by the nature of the team situations in which the employee participates.

PROPOSITION 5: *When team members interact together across a variety of tasks, team-specific competencies are required; task-specific competencies may be less feasible (or necessary) to develop in such cases.*

In cases where team members perform together across a variety of tasks, effectiveness will be enhanced when the members are familiar with each other. Familiarity fosters coordination and helps team members anticipate each other's behavior. When a team performs a single task, or only a few tasks, it may be fruitful to develop task-specific competencies as well.

Propositions Linking Team Competencies to Training Requirements and Strategies

PROPOSITION 6: *Teams that require team-specific competencies, whether they fall into the team-contingent or context-driven categories, will benefit from training as intact teams.*

Team-specific competencies are required when team members require an understanding of their teammates' characteristics (often to facilitate changes in task strategy). In order to develop these, team members must be given experience with their teammates so that they can learn about one another, and develop the necessary skills and attitudes.

PROPOSITION 7: *Teams that require task-specific competencies, whether they fall into the task-contingent or context-driven categories, should be allowed to practice in the actual task environment (or in one as close as possible).*

To optimize performance in a team that carries out a consistent task, team members will benefit from training that allows them to experience the actual task environment. This enables them to learn crucial task contingencies, develop accurate task models, and learn how to adjust task strategies in response to specific task demands.

PROPOSITION 8: *Training for teams that require team-specific competencies, in either the context-driven or team-contingent categories, should incorporate feedback that leads to shared or common expectations for task performance.*

Several lines of research suggest that members of an effective team share knowledge about the task and the team. Such knowledge can be developed during team training via feedback and discussion among team members. In particular, encouraging team members to explain why they behave as they do in accomplishing the task should help teammates gain the necessary knowledge.

PROPOSITION 9: *When transportable competencies are required, some training can be focused at the individual level.*

Many of the kinds of knowledge, skills, and attitudes necessary to teamwork can be demonstrated and trained at the individual level (assertiveness, accurate task models, importance of teamwork). Other competencies may require training in a group or team setting (interpersonal skills, task sequencing, collective orientation), even though the teammates in training may not be the same as in the operational environment.

PROPOSITION 10: *Task simulation may be an effective training strategy for teams that require task-specific competencies requiring actual practice. Further, task simulation can be an effective means of imparting team-contingent competencies if the operational team members are allowed to practice together (and only under these conditions).*

When team members require exposure to the actual task, it is sometimes difficult to provide direct task experience (as when issues of safety or cost arise). Therefore, simulation of the task environment may be effective in these cases. Task simulation can be achieved in a variety of ways, from sophisticated flight simulators that replicate the cockpit to simpler personal computer–based games or tasks.

PROPOSITION 11: *Cross-training may be effective for teams that require exposure to the task (that is, task-specific competencies, whether they fall into the context-driven or task-contingent categories).*

When team members must understand the roles and responsibilities of other team positions, cross-training can help develop this knowledge by exposing team members to other positions. In particular, cross-training can provide team members with accurate expectations for the task by showing them what other positions require. Cross-training may include job rotation or simply letting team members train in each other's roles for some period of time.

PROPOSITION 12: *Positional knowledge training may be useful for teams with task-specific competency requirements, either context-driven or task-contingent.*

Knowledge about the roles and responsibilities of teammates is required when team members are performing a specific task together. Such training, which may be as simple as providing team members with information about their teammates' roles, gives team members an understanding of how their jobs fits into the overall team task.

PROPOSITION 13: *Training to impart context-driven competencies should include guided practice that exposes the actual team members to the variety of situations they may confront on the job. When the actual team cannot be trained intact, guided practice may be useful as a means of training task-specific (but not team-specific) competencies.*

Research suggests that unguided practice may not lead to effective performance (Frederiksen & White, 1989). However, guided practice — allowing the team to practice while being monitored and given feedback by instructors — may be an effective training strategy for context-driven competencies. This is particularly true if the guided practice is designed to lead the team through a series of situations they are likely to confront on the job.

PROPOSITION 14: *Lecture-based training may be appropriate for transportable competencies but should be considered only as a first step for other types of competencies, since these require experience with the actual task or team.*

Training for context-driven or task-contingent competencies requires experience with the task. As an initial means of imparting knowledge, however, lectures are probably useful for all categories of competencies. For transportable competencies, lecture-based training may even suffice.

PROPOSITION 15: *Role playing may be used effectively to train team-contingent competencies when it involves the actual (operational) team.*

By interacting with one another in role-playing situations, team members can learn each other's knowledge, skills, abilities, and preferences. This information increases the probability that team members will develop accurate expectations for their own performance and the performance of teammates. When the intact team is not available, role playing may be useful for developing task-contingent competencies if trainees are allowed to use role playing in situations they are likely to confront in the actual task.

PROPOSITION 16: *Passive demonstrations of the task may be an effective means of training task-contingent competencies.*

In attempting to build a procedural knowledge base in trainees, it may be useful to demonstrate task processes, to show where and how inputs are made by various team positions. This may be accomplished with flow diagrams or computer animation. Passive demonstrations may be an effective way to train team members on sequencing task inputs and accomplishing task procedures, for example.

Implications for Training Design

We hope that the ideas put forth in this chapter can be used to stimulate thinking about how to train various types of teams. Echoing the line of reasoning presented thus far, we contend that the specification of training requirements should rest on an analysis of the nature of the competencies required by the team (that is, it must be established whether a team requires context-driven, team-contingent, task-contingent, or transportable team competencies). In fact, the competencies shown in Table 10.2 can be used to guide a traditional needs analysis (Wexley & Latham, 1981). For example, a person analysis could be tailored to look for the competencies listed in Table 10.2; a task analysis could be conducted to establish the kinds of competencies required for task success. Once the competency requirements for a team are established, the next step in specifying appropriate training strategies is to link competency requirements to specific training characteristics. We have taken a first step in this direction with our sixteen propositions, summarized in Table 10.3. The far-left column of the table delineates some of the factors that we hypothesize as moderating the nature of team competencies. This is not an exhaustive list but serves to highlight some of the important variables. The third and fourth columns summarize our ideas about relationships among team competencies, requirements, and training strategies. The table is best considered as a first step toward theoretically based guidelines for thinking about and designing training for various types of teams in industry.

Conclusion

In this chapter, we have attempted to bridge the gap between several areas of theorizing and investigation in the area of team training. The conceptual framework offered here is designed to make explicit the various team competencies that must be trained in order to achieve effective team performance. We used it as a basis of structuring a brief review of the literature and establishing the specific competencies required for various types of teams. We then elaborated on the nature of team competencies and linked these to task and situational factors. Finally, we attempted to match competency requirements with recommended training methods.

From the standpoint of research, we have offered sixteen propositions about the nature of team competencies and how

Table 10.3. Summary of Propositions for Training Design.

Task/ Environmental Factor	Level	Nature of Required Competencies	Training Strategies
Task interdependence	High	Context-driven	Task simulation (intact team) Cross-training Guided task practice (intact team) Role playing (intact team)
	Low	Transportable	Lecture Passive demonstration
Task/ environmental stability	High	Task-contingent	Task simulation Cross-training Guided task practice Role playing Passive demonstration
	Low	Team-contingent	Task simulation (intact team) Guided task practice (intact team) Role playing (intact team)
Team member turnover	High	Task-contingent	Task simulation Cross-training Guided task practice Role playing Passive demonstration
	Low	Team-contingent	Task simulation (intact team) Guided task practice (intact team) Role playing (intact team)
Membership in multiple teams	High	Transportable	Lecture Passive demonstration
	Low	Team-contingent	Task simulation (intact team) Guided task practice (intact team) Role playing (intact team)
Variety of tasks performed by team	High	Team-contingent	Task simulation (intact team) Guided task practice (intact team) Role playing (intact team)
	Low	Task-contingent	Task simulation Cross-training Guided task practice Role playing Passive demonstration

these can best be trained. These propositions are easily stated as testable hypotheses or research questions. From a more practical standpoint, we have provided a structure in which guidance for practitioners can be couched and have attempted to pull together state-of-the-art knowledge regarding how best to train various types of teams. We hope that both communities will be stimulated by our thinking, so that our understanding of this crucial area can continue to evolve.

References

Alexander, L. T., & Cooperband, A. S. (1965). *System training and research in team behavior.* Santa Monica, CA: System Development Corporation.

Baker, C. V., Salas, E., Cannon-Bowers, J. A., & Spector, P. (1992, April). *The effects of interpositional uncertainty and workload on team coordination skills and task performance.* Paper presented at the annual meeting of the Society for Industrial and Organizational Psychology, Montreal.

Bales, R. F. (1950). *Interaction process analysis: A method for the study of small groups.* Reading, MA: Addison-Wesley.

Bandura, A. (1986). *Social foundations of thought and action.* Englewood Cliffs, NJ: Prentice-Hall.

Bass, B. M. (1982). Individual capability, team performance, and team productivity. In E. A. Fleishman & M. D. Dunnette (Eds.), *Human performance and capability: Human capability assessment.* Hillsdale, NJ: Erlbaum.

Briggs, G. E., & Johnston, W. A. (1967). *Team training* (NTDC Technical Report No. 1327-4). Orlando, FL: Naval Training Device Center.

Cannon-Bowers, J. A., Salas, E., & Converse, S. A. (1993). Shared mental models in expert team decision making. In N. J. Castellan, Jr. (Ed.), *Current issues in individual and group decision making* (pp. 221–246). Hillsdale, NJ: Erlbaum.

Chapman, R. L., Kennedy, J. L., Newell, A., & Biel, W. C. (1959). The system research laboratory's air defense experiments. *Management Science, 5,* 250–269.

Cooper, G. E., White, M. D., & Lauber, J. K. (Eds.). (1980). *Resource management on the flightdeck: Proceedings of a NASA industry workshop.* (NASA Technical Report No. CP-2120.) Moffett Field, CA: National Aeronautics and Space Administration–Ames Research Center.

Cooper, M., Shiflett, S., Korotkin, A., & Fleishman, E. (1984). *Command-and-control teams: Techniques for assessing team performance.* Washington, DC: Advanced Research Resources Organization.

Davis, J. H. (1969). *Group performance.* Reading, MA: Addison-Wesley.

Deutsch, M. (1960). The effect of motivational orientation on trust and suspicion. *Human Relations, 13,* 123-140.

Dick, W., & Carey, L. (1990). *The systematic design of instruction* (3rd ed.). Glenview, IL: Scott, Foresman.

Driskell, J. E., & Salas, E. (1992). Collective behavior and team performance. *Human Factors, 34,* 277-288.

Federman, P., & Siegel, A. (1965). *Communications as a measurable index of team behavior* (NTDC Report No. 1537-1). Orlando, FL: Naval Training Device Center.

Festinger, L., Schachter, S., & Back, K. (1950). *Social pressures in informal groups: A study of human factors in housing.* New York: HarperCollins.

Forward, J., & Zander, A. (1968). Choice of unattainable group goals and effects on performance. *Organizational Behavior and Human Performance, 6,* 184-189.

Foushee, H. C. (1982). The role of communications, sociopsychological, and personality factors in the maintenance of crew coordination. *Aviation, Space, and Environmental Medicine, 53,* 1062-1066.

Franz, T. M., McCallum, G. A., Lewis, M. D., Prince, C., & Salas, E. (1990, April). Pilot briefings and aircrew coordination evaluation: Empirical results. *Proceedings of the 12th symposium on psychology in the Department of Defense* (pp. 92-96). Springfield, VA: National Technical Information Services.

Franz, T. M., Prince, C., Cannon-Bowers, J. A., & Salas, E. (1990, April). The identification of aircrew coordination skills. *Proceedings of the 12th symposium on psychology in the Department of Defense* (pp. 97-101). Springfield, VA: National Technical Information Services.

Frederiksen, J., & White, B. (1989). An approach to training based upon principled task decomposition. *Acta Psychologica, 71,* 89-146.

Gaddy, C. D., & Wachtel, J. A. (1992). Team skills training in nuclear power plant operations. In R. W. Swezey & E. Salas (Eds.), *Teams: Their training and performance* (pp. 379-396). Norwood, NJ: ABLEX.

Gagné, R. M. (1985). *The conditions of learning* (4th ed.). Troy, MO: Holt, Rinehart & Winston.

Glickman, A. S., Zimmer, S., Montero, R. C., Guerette, P. J., Campbell, W. J., Morgan, B. B., Jr., & Salas, E. (1987). *The evolution of teamwork skills: An empirical assessment with implications for training.* (NTSC Technical Report No. 87-016). Orlando, FL: Naval Training Systems Center.

Goldstein, I. L. (1986). *Training in organizations: Needs assessment, development, and evaluation.* Pacific Grove, CA: Brooks/Cole.

Greene, C. N., & Schriesheim, C. A. (1980). Leader-group interactions: A longitudinal field investigation. *Journal of Applied Psychology, 65,* 50–59.

Gregorich, S. E., Helmreich, R. L., & Wilhelm, J. A. (1990). The structure of cockpit management attitudes. *Journal of Applied Psychology, 75,* 682–690.

Guzzo, R. A. (1986). Group decision making and group effectiveness in organizations. In P. Goodman (Ed.), *Designing effective work groups* (pp. 34–71). San Francisco: Jossey-Bass.

Hare, A. P. (1962). *Handbook of small-group research.* New York: Free Press.

Helmreich, R. L., Foushee, H. C., Benson, R., & Russini, R. (1986). Cockpit management attitudes: Exploring the attitude-performance linkage. *Aviation, Space, and Environmental Medicine, 57,* 1198–1200.

Hemphill, J. K., & Sechrest, L. (1952). A comparison of three criteria of air crew effectiveness in combat over Korea. *American Psychologist, 7,* 391.

Johnston, W. A., & Briggs, G. E. (1968). Team performance as a function of team arrangement and work load. *Journal of Applied Psychology, 52,* 89–94.

Jordan, N., Jensen, B., & Terebinski, S. (1963). The development of cooperation among three-man crews in a simulated man-machine information processing system. *Journal of Social Psychology, 59,* 175–184.

Kleinman, D. L., & Serfaty, D. (1989, April). *Team performance assessment in distributed decision making.* Paper presented at the Simulation and Training Research Symposium on Interactive Networked Simulation for Training, University of Central Florida, Orlando.

Lanzetta, J. T., & Roby, T. B. (1960). The relationship between certain group-process variables and group problem-solving efficiency. *Journal of Social Psychology, 52,* 135–148.

Lodahl, T. M., & Porter, L. W. (1961). Psychometric score patterns, social characteristics, and productivity of small industrial work groups. *Journal of Applied Psychology, 45,* 73–79.

McCallum, G. A., Oser, R., Morgan, B. B., Jr., & Salas, E. (1989, August). *An investigation of the behavioral components of teamwork.* Paper presented at the annual meeting of the American Psychological Association, New Orleans.

Martens, R., & Peterson, J. (1971). Group cohesiveness as a determinant of success and member satisfaction in team performance. *International Review of Sport Sociology, 6,* 49–61.

Mayo, E. (1933). *The human problems of an industrial civilization.* New York: Macmillan.

Meeker, B. F. (1983). Cooperative orientation, trust, and reciprocity. *Human Relations, 37,* 225–243.

Morgan, B. B., Jr., Glickman, A. S., Woodard, E. A., Blaiwes, A., & Salas, E. (1986). *Measurement of team behaviors in a Navy environment.* (NTSC Technical Report No. 86-014). Orlando, FL: Naval Training Systems Center.

Niehoff, B. P., Enz, C. A., & Grover, R. A. (1990). The impact of top-management actions on employee attitudes and perceptions. *Group and Organization Studies, 15,* 337–352.

Nieva, V. F., Fleishman, E. A., & Reick, A. (1978). *Team dimensions: Their identity, their measurement, and their relationships* (Contract No. DAH 19-78-C-0001). Washington, DC: Advanced Research Resources Organization.

Noe, R. (1986). Trainees' attributes and attitudes: Neglected influences on training effectiveness. *Academy of Management Review, 11,* 736–749.

Orasanu, J. (1990, October). *Shared mental models and crew performance.* Paper presented at the annual meeting of the Human Factors Society, Orlando, Florida.

Orasanu, J., & Salas, E. (1993). Team decision making in complex environments. In G. Klein, J. Orasanu, R. Calderwood, and C. E. Zsambok (Eds.), *Decision making in action: Models and methods* (pp. 327–345). Norwood, NJ: ABLEX.

Orlady, H., & Foushee, C. (Eds.). (1987). *Cockpit resource management training: Proceedings of a NASA/MAC workshop* (NASA Technical Report No. CP-2455). Moffett Field, CA: National Aeronautics and Space Administration–Ames Research Center.

Oser, R. L., McCallum, G. A., Salas, E., & Morgan, B. B., Jr. (1989). *Toward a definition of teamwork: An analysis of critical team behaviors* (NTSC Technical Report No. 89-004). Orlando, FL: Naval Training Systems Center.

Oser, R. L., McCallum, G. A., Salas, E., & Morgan, B. B., Jr. (1992). *Toward a definition of teamwork: Behavioral elements of successful teams* (NTSC Technical Report No. 89-018). Orlando, FL: Naval Training Systems Center.

Oser, R. L., Prince, C., & Morgan, B. B., Jr. (1990, October). *Differences in aircrew communication content as a function of flight requirement: Implications for operational aircrew training.* Paper presented at the annual meeting of the Human Factors Society, Orlando, FL.

Prince, C., Cannon-Bowers, J. A., Salas, E., Owens, J. M., & Morgan, B. B., Jr. (1989). *Aircrew coordination training: Requirements and challenges.* Unpublished manuscript.

Prince, C., Chidester, T. R., Cannon-Bowers, J., & Bowers, C. (1992). Aircrew coordination: Achieving teamwork in the cockpit. In R. W. Swezey & E. Salas (Eds.), *Teams: Their training and performance* (pp. 329–353). Norwood, NJ: ALBEX.

Prince, C., & Salas, E. (1993). Training and research for teamwork in the military aircrew. In E. Wiener, B. Kanki, & R. Helmreich (Eds.), *Cockpit resource management* (pp. 337–366). San Diego, CA: Academic Press.

Rainey, D. W., & Schweickert, G. J. (1988). An exploratory study of team cohesion before and after a spring trip. *Sport Psychologist, 2,* 314–317.

Rehder, R. R., & Smith, M. M. (1986). *Kaizen* and the art of labor relations. *Personnel Journal, 65,* 82–93.

Riggs, M. L. (1989). *The development of self-efficacy and outcome scales for general applications.* Paper presented at the annual meeting of the Society of Industrial and Organizational Psychology, Boston.

Roby, T. B. (1953). *Problems of rational group assembly exemplified in the medium bomber crew* (Technical Report No. 53-18). San Antonio, TX: Lackland Air Force Base, Human Resources Research Center.

Rouse, W. B., Cannon-Bowers, J. A., & Salas, E. (1992). The role of mental models in team performance in complex systems. *IEEE Transactions on Systems, Man, and Cybernetics, 22,* 1296–1308.

Rubin, J., & Brown, B. (1975). *The social psychology of bargaining and negotiation.* San Diego, CA: Academic Press.

Ruffell-Smith, H. P. (1979). *A simulator study of the interaction of pilot workload with errors* (NASA Technical Report No. TM-78482). Moffett Field, CA: National Aeronautics and Space Administration–Ames Research Center.

Salas, E., Dickinson, T., Converse, S. A., & Tannenbaum, S. I. (1992). Toward an understanding of team performance and training. In R. W. Swezey & E. Salas (Eds.), *Teams: Their training and performance* (pp. 3–29). Norwood, NJ: ABLEX.

Shamir, B. (1990). Calculations, values, and identities: The sources of collectivistic work motivation. *Human Relations, 43,* 313–332.

Shea, G. P., & Guzzo, R. A. (1987). Group effectiveness: What really matters? *Sloan Management Review, 3,* 25–31.

Shiflett, S. C., Eisner, E. J., Price, S. J., & Schemmer, F. M. (1982). *The definition and measurement of team functions.* Bethesda, MD: Advanced Research Resources Organization.

Siegel, A. J., & Federman, P. J. (1973). Communications content training as an ingredient in effective team performance. *Ergonomics, 4,* 403–416.

Siskel, M., & Flexman, R. (1962). *Study of the effectiveness of a flight simulator for training complex aircrew skills.* Unpublished data, Bell Aeronautics Company.

Stogdill, R. M. (1972). Group productivity, drive, and cohesiveness. *Organizational Behavior and Human Performance, 8,* 26–43.

Straub, W. F. (1975). Team cohesiveness in athletics. *International Journal of Sport Psychology, 6,* 125–133.

Streufert, S., & Nogami, G. (1992). Cognitive complexity in team decision making. In R. W. Swezey & E. Salas (Eds.), *Teams: Their training and performance* (pp. 127–151). Norwood, NJ: ABLEX.

Sundstrom, E., De Meuse, K. P., & Futrell, D. (1990). Work teams: Applications and effectiveness. *American Psychologist, 45,* 120–133.

Swezey, R. W., & Salas, E. (1992). Guidelines for use in team-training development. In R. W. Swezey & E. Salas (Eds.), *Teams: Their training and performance* (pp. 219–245). Norwood, NJ: ABLEX.

Tannenbaum, S. I., Beard, R. L., & Salas, E. (1992). Team building and its influence on team effectiveness: An examination of conceptual and empirical developments. In K. Kelley (Ed.), *Issues, theory, and research in industrial/organizational psychology* (pp. 117–153). New York: Elsevier Science.

Tannenbaum, S. I., & Yukl, G. (1991). Training and development in work organizations. *Annual Review of Psychology, 43,* 399–441.

Terborg, J. R., Castore, C., & DeNinno, J. A. (1976). A longitudinal investigation of the impact of group composition on group performance and cohesion. *Journal of Personality and Social Psychology, 34,* 782–790.

Tjosvold, D., & Tsao, Y. (1989, April). Productive organizational collaboration: The role of values and cooperative goals. *Journal of Organizational Behavior, 10,* 189–195.

Travillian, K., Baker, C. V., & Cannon-Bowers, J. A. (1992, March). *Correlates of self and collective efficacy with team functioning.* Paper presented at the annual meeting of the Southeastern Psychological Association, Knoxville, TN.

Tziner, A. (1982). Differential effects of group cohesiveness types: A clarifying overview. *Social Behavior and Personality, 10,* 227–239.

Tziner, A., & Vardi, Y. (1982). Effects of command style and group cohesiveness on the performance effectiveness of self-selected tank crews. *Journal of Applied Psychology, 67,* 769–775.

Tziner, A., & Vardi, Y. (1983). Ability as a moderator between cohesiveness and tank crews' performance. *Journal of Occupational Behavior, 4,* 137–143.

Vaziri, M. T., Lee, J. W., & Krieger, J. L. (1988). Onda Moku: The true pioneer of management through respect for humanity. *Leadership and Organization Development Journal, 9,* 3–7.

Weick, K. E., & Penner, D. D. (1969). Discrepant membership as an occasion for effective cooperation. *Sociometry, 32,* 413–424.

Wexley, K., & Latham, G. (1981). *Developing and training human resources in organizations.* Glenview, IL: Scott, Foresman.

11

CONCLUSION:
COMMON THEMES
AMONGST THE DIVERSITY

Richard A. Guzzo

What is the state of research and theory on team decision making and team performance as represented in the foregoing chapters? To some extent, it may seem that we are still feeling the elephant: different researchers grasp and examine different parts of the elephant, each examination yielding a distinctive account of the nature of the beast. But teams working in organizations are not pachyderms and, unlike the proverbial blind men, we describe teams neither in simple terms nor with data from only one sense. Indeed, the chapters of this book communicate substantial understanding of teams making decisions at work.

We know a lot. We have gained that knowledge by using diverse methods of research (experiments, observations, simulations), by studying a wide variety of teams and organizations, by studying phenomena relevant to entities other than just groups (stress, information processing), and by studying individuals. This book's chapters reflect that diversity.

It would seem, too, that the preceding chapters indicate that we are poised to learn a lot more about teams, their decision making, and their effectiveness in organizations. What we know so far opens many doors for further investigation. And, although applications are not its primary focus, this book has much to say about applying our current and future knowledge to the improvement of team effectiveness.

Common Themes

This chapter describes some themes common to the preceding chapters. A focus on effectiveness in organizational decision-making teams is what binds all the chapters together; other themes tie together some but not all chapters. The latter themes are the ones this chapter examines, first for their implications for future research and, second, for their implications for practice.

From Individual to Group

Several chapters in this book seek to understand team decision making and effectiveness by starting with the accumulated wisdom of research literatures that concern individual behavior. Some chapters have little choice. For example, Chapter Eight's examination of stress and team performance is strongly rooted in previous research on individual performance and stress because that literature is extensive. It would seem impossible to consider matters of stress and team performance without recourse to what is known about individuals. But as the authors make clear, the literature on individual stress and performance is not simply transportable to the domain of team stress. Many other factors come into play in considering teams within organizations.

      The authors of Chapter Five could have analyzed team decision making with little reference to individually rooted literature but chose instead to make a direct extrapolation to teams from the methods and findings of a particular stream of individual-based decision research: cue utilization and judgment. Like the line of research on which they draw, the authors are centrally concerned with describing the process by which information ("cues") gets transformed into decisions in teams. But they go beyond traditional, individually centered thinking by introducing several structural parameters that reflect certain "facts of life" of teams in organizations: the fact that information in teams is differentially distributed among members, the fact that members occupy different places in an organization's hierarchy, and the fact that a team's final decision is perhaps best understood as the ultimate product of a series of decisions made by members as information is acquired. Given these parameters, the authors offer both conceptual and data-collection paradigms for understanding team's decision effectiveness in organizations.

Chapter Ten shows how effectiveness at the team level is a function of the competencies held by the team's individual members. The authors' interest is in specifying important competencies that can be developed through formal training, experiences, and other techniques. The test of their analysis, of course, is whether or not interventions at one level of analysis result in performance changes at another level. Does individual-level training and development result in team-level improvements in performance? The easy answer is yes, and there is prior research to support it. But the authors go far beyond the easy answer, organizing our thinking about the nature of team-relevant individual competencies (for example, different types of knowledge) and sources of the demand for those competencies (for example, requirements of the task).

These chapters illustrate well both the problems and the potential of analyzing such phenomena as decision making and performance at more than one level of analysis. As Chapter One discussed, this book is predicated on the assumption that team decision making and performance are too complicated to be understood from only one level of analysis. Nevertheless, questions can always be raised about the transportability of concepts and explanations from one level to another. Do relationships between stress and performance at the individual level hold true at the group level? Are the cognitive processes of cue utilization found in individuals deciding alone the same processes as those found when they decide in teams? At times, explanations and concepts (for example, competencies) relevant to one level of analysis are but heuristics for another. In other instances, a close verisimilitude exists between concepts and explanations at one level and those at another. The usefulness and transportability of explanations from one level of analysis to another may often be issue-specific. Consequently, researchers who study teams by starting from different levels of analysis need to be very deliberate in their reasoning and extrapolations. Movement from the individual to the team level of analysis is apparent in several other chapters as well, including Chapter Two, which gives explicit attention to level of analysis in team-effectiveness research.

Relational Aspects of Teams

Connections between the individual and group levels of analysis are also evident in those chapters that deal with team composition. Chapter Nine, for example, elevates many traditional concerns of staffing (e.g., specification of position requirements, sources of recruiting new members), usually thought of in terms of individuals and their jobs, to the team level. The authors recognize, however, that the universe of things to be accounted for expands when the question is one of staffing for team effectiveness. For example, the list of knowledge, skills, and abilities for effectiveness in teams is longer than that for individual effectiveness in jobs that are not embedded in teams. Part of the reason is the *relational* nature of teams — that is, rather than being considered individual attributes in isolation, those attributes must be considered vis-a-vis the attributes of other team members in order to maximize effectiveness. Chapter Nine's discussion of the differing requirements of leaders in team-based organizations partly illustrates this, as does the discussion of establishing the best mix of team-level knowledge, skills, and abilities.

Chapter Seven is based almost entirely on the importance of relational properties within groups. The authors' concern is diversity, with the nature of the individual *compared to* that of others in the same team. Thus the gender or culture of one member by comparison with other members is the key issue, not gender or culture alone. As the chapter shows, the relational properties of team composition can affect individuals, dyads within teams, and the team as a whole. Chapter Five also stresses relational issues in part, with its concern for *relative* expertise in groups.

Understanding the effects of various relational configurations in teams is a difficult matter. One reason is that large numbers of combinations and permutations of members' characteristics can be investigated in relation to one another. Seemingly simple questions — "Does being an ethnicity-based minority in a group at work have the same consequences as being a gender-based minority?" — become complicated when we consider the many possible combinations of ethnicities and the many permutations of gender minorities in larger groups. Nevertheless, several of this book's chapters make considerable headway, increasing our understanding of the impact of selected relational issues on the effectiveness of teams in organizations, teams in which decision making is a key component of the work. Future research on team effectiveness as a consequence of relational aspects of team dynamics is needed. To judge by what can be seen in the preceding chapters, such research is likely to be of much value.

New Emphases in Group Process

All the chapters, although to differing degrees, speak to the connection between group process and group performance. *Group process* is defined broadly here and includes all manner of intermember communication, leadership acts within a team, flows of information within a group, chaining of member' actions in the service of a group product, attitudes and beliefs that arise from group interaction, and so on. Certain chapters, however, more deeply address aspects of group process and their consequences. Chapter Three, for example, is centrally concerned with how computers affect the process by which groups do their work. As the authors point out, computers affect how information is used, how members communicate, and the rules or structures by which teams execute their work. These are very different dimensions of process, and the authors seek to understand the flow of effects of computer-assisted group work "in context" (that is, under various operating conditions, with varying group member inputs). They also direct our attention to an understanding of computer-assisted group process over extended periods of time.

Chapter Four also examines a selected aspect of group process: the process that underlies the successful resolution of crises and other episodes of decision making and team performance. Using a long-standing distinction between cooperation and conflict, the author marshals evidence for the effectiveness of that style of group interaction labeled *constructive controversy*. Cooperation and conflict, of course, are phenomena relevant not only to groups — consider, for example, individuals or departments within an organization — and the author's discussion of the origins and management of cooperation and conflict in groups makes it clear that the larger social context in which groups exist is a critical consideration. An easy illustration of this point is the role of the reward system in an organization. It is a source of either cooperation or conflict, depending on what gets rewarded. The author's analysis of group process is also performed at a rather abstract level. Rather than being concerned with highly discrete behaviors that occur in groups, his concern is with a more generalized tone or character of members' interactions.

Another rather global aspect of group process is the degree of interdependence among group members as they carry out their work. The more a task demands integrated and coordinated actions by members, the greater the task interdependence. Task interdependence in groups is an idea that has been in the literature for a long time. In this book, however, we see some novel uses of that concept. Chapter Nine addresses the implications of interdependence for team staffing. The authors assert that interdependence creates special job requirements, which must be accounted for in any optimal staffing process for teams. Chapter Ten states that high interdependence requires context-specific competencies that can be acquired through training. These two chapters extend our thinking about the implications of task interdependence for creating and maintaining effectiveness in organizational teams.

Measurement: Process and Performance

Another recent development, well represented in this volume, is the advances in measurement of group process and performance. Chapter Six describes the application of several formal analytical tools (for example, Petri nets, artificial neural networks) to the depiction of group interaction. These tools do not create new things to study; rather, they solve some of the old problems in group research concerning how best to represent complex, sequential interaction. In this sense, they cast the familiar in new ways, which can result in novel insights into and explanations of a group's performance effectiveness.

Whereas Chapter Six presents methods of analyzing team interaction that are in principle immediately applicable to teams performing in many task domains, Chapter Two presents methods of measuring performance process that are derived from the study of tactical decision-making teams in military settings. The authors give examples of behaviors in teams that are critical to performance, and they categorize those behaviors in ways that make them relevant to teams in settings other than the military. For example, one of the essential teamwork behaviors is reported to be *performance monitoring* — that is, effective teams, in this analysis, are those in which members are aware of and attend to the actions of fellow team members. Such awareness permits members to cover for each other as necessary and to offer each other insights and advice for improving performance. It is easy to imagine how performance monitoring can contribute to success in sales teams, service teams, executive teams, and many other kinds of teams. In fact, the line of research represented in Chapter Two offers several new concepts and measurement techniques for use in research on teams' performance effectiveness.

As already noted, Chapter Five presents both a conceptual paradigm and a research paradigm. The two are intertwined. On the conceptual paradigm, the emphasis on cue utilization is tied to methods of research that permit the measurement of relations between cues and decisions in teams. Hence, a simulation technology has been created that places each team member in a unique role (both as "information source" and as "information user"), permits experimental manipulation of cues to team members, and enables researchers to relate cue manipulation and cue use to decisions. This approach makes for very direct relations between concepts and their measures.

Teams over Time

Several chapters share an explicit concern with understanding team decision making and effectiveness over time. Chapter Nine considers how staffing procedures can be adapted to the life cycles of teams (for example, staffing start-up versus established teams). Chapter Two reports visible changes in teamwork over time, where time spent *as a team* (and not just cumulative individual experience) is the critical factor in the successful evolution of team functioning. The criticality of time to the work of computer-assisted teams is also pointed out by the authors of Chapter Three. Computer-mediated communication allows individuals to work as a team without meeting in "real time," since messages (that is, interactions among members) can be stored and delivered as convenient, rather than in face-to-face meetings or conference calls. Many findings from the relevant literature are catalogued in Chapter Three, but it is also evident that much of the existing research does not adequately account for performance over the spans of time in which teams perform in organizations. In almost all the other chapters, performance over time is important to (if implicit in) the consideration of team decision making and effectiveness in organizations.

There is no single conclusion to be drawn about the role of time and time-related changes to deam decision making and effectiveness. The commonality seems to reside more in the appreciation of time and change in teams than in the identification of specific temporal qualities or dynamics. However, the increasing appreciation of temporality is gratifying, given its long-standing neglect.

Teams in Context

Several chapters in this volume place considerable emphasis on *context* as an important influence on team decision making and effectiveness. The general context of interest for this book is the organization in which a team works, military and otherwise. A team's organizational context may have many relevant features, of course, and not all possible contextual influences come under this volume's microscope. It is apparent, however, that research and theory are no longer wedded to the traditional view of individual attributes and group interaction as the primary determinants of team effectiveness. Instead, the role of the organizational context as a prime cause of effectiveness is being elevated and made salient.

To illustrate, Chapter Three cites the importance of several contextual features in its analysis of effective computer-assisted group performance. These features include the technological, task, and temporal contexts of teams. The "operating conditions" under which teams perform are thought both to have a direct effect on performance and to moderate the impact of computer-based technology on teams. Chapter Four cites contextual influences on cooperation and conflict in groups. An emphasis on organizational goals that promote cooperation between departments, for example, is found to be associated with team effectiveness, and rewarding teams for their collective (rather than individual) accomplishments is argued to promote cooperation within teams. Chapter Eight analyzes the stress-performance connection in teams and cites several contextual features as sources of stress. For example, time pressures and the work load placed on a team by its organization appear to affect stress and performance. The chapter also reviews evidence indicating that a team's interaction process does indeed change in response to such contextual pressures, and that the subjective experience of a stressor may be changed merely by its occurring in a team (as indicated, for example, by the finding that individuals working on a complex cognitive task in a team reported their personal work loads to be 20 percent lower than those of individuals working alone). Chapter Ten attaches considerable importance to organizational and situational characteristics as determinants of the specific competencies required for effective team performance, and as determinants of the types of training strategies that will be most successful for raising team effectiveness in varying circumstances. These chapters (and others) are quite consistent with the widening awareness of the impact of contextual influences on team effectiveness at work. They offer several testable research ideas about the impact of a team's context on its effectiveness when decision making is central to work.

Themes and Their Implications

Six themes that run through the varied perspectives and issues addressed in these chapters have just been identified. The existence of each of these themes has implications for one or more of the following: (1) theorizing about and explaining team decision making and effectiveness, (2) conducting team research, and (3) intervening to improve team effectiveness. These implications are briefly considered in this section.

A theme common to several chapters concerns the reliance on more than one level of analysis in the research and theory on teams. It is becoming clear that the use of multiple levels of analysis (for example, individual, group, organizational) constitutes a necessary condition for full explanations of team decision making and effectiveness in organizations. Yet it also seems clear that any one program of research tends to limit itself to only one or two levels of analysis. There may be many reasons for this. Research paradigms (for example, laboratory experiments) favored by certain investigators may not be applied to obtaining data at multiple levels of analysis. Likewise, the job of extrapolating research findings and concepts from one level to another is often filled with uncertainty. Whatever the reason, the tendency of investigators to restrict their focus to one or two levels of analysis is not necessarily a problem. In fact, it would be unwise to demand that team investigators and theorists deal with all relevant levels of analysis. That would be a prescription for research paralysis. More realistically, we can ask researchers to be conscious of locating their own levels of analysis in relation to other, alternative levels, and we can ask researchers to recognize explicitly other levels than the one(s) they adopt by discussing this issue in their research reports and papers. Such explicit consideration of varying levels of analysis would, I believe, contribute to the increased integration of research literatures on team effectiveness and create a stronger potential for synergy among those literatures. We can also ask researchers to be sensitive to potential problems as they export ideas from one level of analysis to another. Some concepts, such as cue utilization, may travel well; others may not.

A second theme residing in several chapters concerns the importance of the relational aspects of groups. Chapters that address the proper *mix* of competencies or knowledge in a group are concerned with relations among members' attributes (as is any discussion of members' diversity). Relational issues are not just a theoretical concern. They speak to the practical matter of how a team should be staffed and developed for effectiveness. Staffing and developing are two key responsibilities of the human resource function in organizations. The success with which they are executed in the service of team effectiveness may depend heavily on a clear understanding of the relational properties of team composition.

A third theme is the renewed stress on selected aspects of a group's interaction process as a key determinant of effectiveness. The importance of interaction process to the ultimate task effectiveness of a group has usually been assumed. The debates traditionally have been about which aspects of process to pay attention to in explaining differences in team effectiveness. Two old interaction-process issues, cooperation and task interdependence, have been revived in interesting, practice-oriented ways in the preceding chapters. The degree of task interdependence in team members' interactions has been identified as important to both the staffing and the training of teams for effectiveness. Cooperation has been tied to conditions and practices outside the group. Thus the reconsideration of these interaction-process issues has resulted in new practical insights for improving team performance in organizations. We also see in several chapters a reinvigorated interest in identifying discrete, concrete behaviors that embody teamwork. Data-collection methods for measuring and representing these behaviors have also been discussed.

A fourth theme, that of innovations in the measurement of interaction process and performance, is related to the renewed interest in group interaction process. This fourth theme's implications mainly concern the conduct of team research, and more than one chapter discusses its own implications for future research and measurement. Certain chapters, for example, discuss methods for measuring and representing those behaviors considered to be indicative of teamwork. Other chapters discuss alternative strategies for quantitatively or pictorially representing the flow of activities or information through teams. One must not overlook the possible practical and conceptual ramifications of new research and measurement techniques. As pointed out in Chapter Six, new ways of depicting group interaction process can easily become new ways of providing feedback to teams and diagnosing their performance problems. Thus advances in methods and measures in team research can have instant applied value. Moreover, since theory and method never are (or never should be) decoupled, innovations in the methods of studying teams may spark new theories and explanations of team effectiveness.

Two other themes run through subsets of chapters: teams over time, and contextual influences. The appearance of these two themes has implications for theory, research, and practice. The increased attention to temporal aspects of team effectiveness is an addition to the prevailing theorizing, since most of that theorizing pays little explicit attention to time. However, as several chapters have made clear, we are a long way from sophisticated, comprehensive accounts of temporal dynamics in teams and their effect on decision making and team performance. The increased emphasis on context as a conceptual matter is largely an issue of how we allocate our explanatory eggs: Do we put them all in the interaction-process basket, say, or do we spread them among process, members' attributes, and organizational contexts as we seek to create valid explanations of why some teams perform more effectively than others? The emphases on time and context carry with them some rather straightforward implications for tactics of research—namely, they suggest that studies of team decision making and effectiveness should be concerned with teams that are performing for prolonged intervals in real organizational contexts. The emphasis on context as a cause of team effectiveness also has clear significance for practice. Accordingly, team effectiveness can be expected to increase when we set the right conditions for maximum team effectiveness. Such conditions may include organizational staffing and reward practices, the technology of computer-assisted group work, goal structures in organizations, decision-support systems, and the management of team stressors. The implications may be clear, but it is unfortunate that relatively little research to date has shown increases in team performance to follow changes in organizational context. The practical implications of temporal dynamics in groups are less clear than those of context. As for time, it is plausible that the success of different ways of managing teams, or of intervening to raise their effectiveness, will depend on where a team is in its evolution or history, although there is relatively little evidence to support this plausible idea.

Themes and Diversity

There is no unity of theory or method among investigators of decision making and team effectiveness in organizations. Differences outweigh similarities, and this diversity is a reality that must be accepted at present. In fact, it should be embraced because it has many positive qualities.

This state of affairs resembles what Guzzo and Shea (1992) found in their review of decades of literature on group performance. They found this literature to be driven by several competing schools of thought. Each school of thought emphasizes different explanatory variables (such as group interaction process, task demands, or group maturation), and each school of thought is characterized by considerable internal variation, rather than by strict uniformity of perspective. Although this book has narrowed the scope of concern to effective task performance by teams in organizations whose work requires them to make decisions, the properties noted by Guzzo and Shea still apply.

Rather than interpret the lack of unity in perspectives as incoherence and confusion, I shall suggest here that it indicates high-energy research and inquiry. Programs of research are dissimilar for many reasons, and one reason concerns the terribly complex nature of the phenomena being studied: teams, decision making, effectiveness, and organizations. These targets of study sometimes move. Teams and organizations change with new technologies, new cultural emphases, and other factors. Another reason for the diversity of research perspectives has to do with the varied starting points of research and inquiry, as evidenced by the differing levels of analysis adopted and by the varied existing literatures that provide the foundation for team-oriented research. The diversity of research perspectives also exists because in recent years many researchers have been drawn into the study of teams, researchers whose initial interests did not center on teams. These include researchers on individual differences, training, judgment, and conflict, among other topics. The truly interdisciplinary nature of current research necessarily brings with it contrast and divergence, which I believe can accelerate the field's progress. Finally, it is a significant strength that this varied but high-energy body of research yields many practical ways of enhancing team effectiveness in organizations. Although the application of research knowledge to improving effectiveness is not the central concern of this book, several chapters have made their implications for practice clear. We have at our fingertips many research-supported tactics that we can use to actively manage teams for effectiveness. The greater the diversity of research perspectives brought to bear on team effectiveness, the more numerous the available tactics.

Reference

Guzzo, R. A., & Shea, G. P. (1992). Group performance and intergroup relations in organizations. In M. A. Dunnette & L. M. Hough (Eds.), *Handbook of industrial and organizational psychology.* Palo Alto, CA: Consulting Psychologists Press.

NAME INDEX

A

Ackerman, P. L., 233, 249–250, 292, 302, 326
Adamopolus, J., 120–121, 143, 146
Adams, J. S., 297, 326
Adelman, L., 59, 64, 277–278, 284
Adler, N., 207, 250
Aldag, R. J., 106, 107
Alderfer, C. P., 211, 250
Alexander, E. A., 325, 326
Alexander, L. T., 346n, 349, 374
Allen, V. L., 244, 250
Alluisi, E. A., 269, 283, 288
Alper, S., 94, 107
Altman, I., 266, 286
Alutto, J. A., 140, 142, 145, 325, 327
Alvarez, E. B., 214, 220, 255
Ancona, D. G., 237, 250, 302, 305, 306, 313, 317, 320, 326
Andrews, I. R., 93, 107
Appley, M. H., 262, 264, 265, 284
Argote, L., 119, 120, 144
Argyris, C., 30, 43

Arunachalam, V., 59, 64
Asch, S. E., 244, 250
Ash, R., 298, 329
Ashford, S., 298, 327
Ashforth, B. E., 237, 250
Ashworth, S. D., 300, 327

B

Back, K., 244, 253, 279, 285, 355, 375
Baker, C. V., 341–342, 354, 374, 379
Bales, R. F., 305, 346n, 374
Bandura, A., 313, 332, 354, 374
Bantel, K. A., 224, 225, 250, 261
Bargh, J. A., 236, 260
Barker, J., 93, 107
Barnett, W. P., 226, 235, 257, 307, 331
Baron, R. A., 244, 254
Barrick, M. R., 318, 326
Bass, B. M., 276, 277, 284, 304, 326, 349–350, 374
Bastianutti, L. M., 59, 65–66

SUBJECT INDEX

A

Adaptability, as skill, 344, 347, 348, 350, 352
Affect: and behavior, 243–244; and diversity, 235–237
Airplane safety: and cooperation theory, 83–86; and team decision making, 114, 122
Alphatech, 163, 201
American Psychological Association, 263–264
Antisubmarine Warfare (ASW) team, performance of, 17–18, 20
Arizona, University of, studies at, 73
Artificial intelligence (AI): and artificial neural network, 194–200; concept of, 179–180; conclusion on, 201; and expert systems, 181; and fuzzy set theory, 185–194; and production rules, 180–185
Artificial neural networks (ANNs): applications of, 199–200; architecture of, 195–196; and artificial intelligence, 194–200; characteris-

tics of, 197–198; and learning, 197; in team research, 198–199
Assessment and selection, for staffing, 300–301, 316–321, 322
Attitudes: competencies in, 352–356, 358–365; concept of, 352; in teamwork, 27–29

B

Behavior: and affect, 243–244; back-up, 26–27; and diversity, 237–244; production rules for, 183–184; and social cognitions, 240–243
Boomerang effect, in training, 271–272
Brunswik lens model, of team decision making, 116, 125–127, 128–129, 133

C

California, diversity in, 206
California Personality Inventory, 318

407

Carnegie-Mellon University, studies
at, 73
Change, in teams, 31–32
Chaos theory, and nonlinear relationships, 161
China, cooperation in, 105
Coalition formation: and consolidation, 239; in team decision making, 119–120
Cockpit Management Attitudes
Questionnaire, 353
Cognitions: relations-oriented,
234–235; social, and behavior,
240–243; task-based, 230–232
Cohesion: attitude of, 355; stress
from, 270, 279–280; in teamwork, 30
Collective efficacy, attitude of,
354–355
Collective orientation, as attitude,
353–354
Communication: closed-loop, in
teamwork, 25–26; computer
mediation of, 48–78; concept of,
237; networks for, 241–242; as
skill, 345, 347, 348, 349, 350;
structuring of, 51, 53–54,
131–132
Compatibility: and knowledge, 340;
and team processes, 304–305,
312, 315, 318
Competencies: aspects of, 333–380;
in attitudes, 352–356, 358–365;
background on, 333–334; concept
of, 336–337; conceptual framework for, 336–339; conclusion
on, 372–374; context-driven, 357,
358, 360–361, 366, 370, 389;
delineated, 339–356; and group
process, 386; in knowledge,
340–343, 357–365; nature of,
337–339; proposed, 357–359; in
skills, 343–352, 358–365; in
staffing, 302; task-contingent,
359, 363–364, 366–368, 369–370,
371; team-contingent, 358,
361–363, 366–367, 369, 371; of
team members, 38–39; and team
performance, 334–336, 383; and
training, 365–371; transportable,
359, 364–365, 367, 369, 370–371

Competition: and goals, 88; negative
dynamics in, 91; research needed
on, 103–104. *See also* Cooperation
and constructive controversy
Computer-assisted groups: aspects
of, 46–78; background on, 46–47;
bibliography on, 64–72; conclusion on, 76–78; and context, 389;
features of, 47–57; findings on,
61–63; literature review on,
57–73; methodologies in studies
of, 58–73; model for, 55–57; processes for, 385–386; quadrants of
task circumplex for, 52–54; research needed on, 77–78; summary on, 73–76; and team life
cycle, 388
Consensus, in team decision making, 119
Consequences, longer-term, 221–227
Consolidation, and coalition forming, 239
Constructive controversy. *See*
Cooperation and constructive
controversy
Context, organizational: and competencies, 357, 358, 360–361,
366, 370, 389; for diversity,
210–211, 249; implications of,
392–393; nature of, 5–6, 388–390
Continuous learning, for team effectiveness, 309
Cooperation and constructive controversy: and airplane safety,
83–86; antecedents of, 104;
aspects of, 79–112; concept of,
89–90; conclusion on, 105–107;
and context, 389; in crises,
86–92; cross-cultural studies of,
105; and customer service,
94–96; developing teamwork for,
97–103; experiments on, 92–93;
and goals, 88, 89, 98–100, 104;
and group process, 386; implications of, 391; interactions in,
91–92; and organizational innovation, 96–97; research needed
on, 103–105; research on, 92–97;
as skill, 347, 349; in teamwork,
100–101
Coordination: effects of, 182–183;

M

Management, team: as skill, 345, 348, 349; staffing for, 319-321; and team performance, 9-45

Mapping, and knowledge, 342-343

Measurement: advances in, 387-388; implications of, 391-392; and team performance, 9-45, 152-153

Mediating states and processes: for diversity, 228-229; research needed on, 246; relations-oriented, 232-237; task-related, 230-232

Mental models, shared, and team-work stress, 282, 283

Metacognition, and teamwork stress, 282-283

Metasoftware, 163, 203

Minnesota, University of, studies at, 73

Modeling and simulating: advantages of, 158-160; and artificial intelligence, 179-200; aspects of, 149-203; assumptions in, 160-161; conclusion on, 200-201; isomorphic and paramorphic, 156-157; as methods, 157; Petri nets for, 161-179; problems with, 13; role of uncertainty in, 184-185; of shopping, 164-167; of team performance, 153-161; as training strategy, 369; variables in, 159-160

Models: for computer-assisted groups, 55-57; for distributed decision making, 129-135; for diversity, 209-210; for effectiveness, 335; in leadership, 34, 35; mental, shared, 282, 283; for staffing, 301-307; for team decision making, 124-140

Monitoring. See Feedback and performance monitoring

Motivation: as attitude, 356; and cohesion, 280; and skills, 352; in staffing, 302

MYCIN, evaluation of, 181

Myers-Briggs typology, 298

N

National Aeronautics and Space Administration (NASA), 122, 274

Naval Gunfire-Support (NGFS) team, performance of, 15-17, 20

Negotiation: and affect, 244; and coordination, 239

Netherlands, cooperation in, 105

New York, diversity in, 206

NUMMI, autonomous teams at, 293

O

Old Dominion University, stress studied at, 269

Organizations: diverse forms of, 207-208, 249; team interface with, 211, 214-215. See also Context, organizational

Orientation: collective, 353-354; and competencies, 342, 351-352

Outcomes, for team effectiveness, 306-307

Overall Team Performance Form, 20, 21

P

Perceptronics, 163, 203

Performance. See Team performance

Performance appraisal: cooperative, 97; and fuzzy logic, 187-189

Performance monitoring. See Feedback and performance monitoring

Petri nets: and alternative representations, 173-175; aspects of, 161-179; components of, 163-164; conclusion on, 200-201; as dynamic representation, 168, 170; elaborated, 175-178; example of, 164-167; highlights of, 163; issues of, 161-163; structure of, 164; in team research, 178-179

Power, task-related, 232

Problem solving, team decision making for, 138, 139

Production rules: and artificial intel-